P9-CKD-735

AN AMERICAN BOOK COMPANY MODERN LANGUAGE PUBLICATION

CONVERSATIONAL GERMAN ONE

LOTHAR KAHN
Central Connecticut State College

DONALD D. HOOK
Trinity College

VAN NOSTRAND REINHOLD COMPANY
New York Cincinnati Toronto London Melbourne

44460

TAPES
accompanying
Conversational German One

Number of Reels: 21 (seven-inch, full-track)
Speed: 3¾ IPS
Running Time: 22 hours (approximate)

Materials Recorded:

    All *Unterhaltungen,* first at normal speed, then by phrases with pauses for student repetition.

    All *Kombinationen* in four-phased sequences: cue—pause—correct response—pause.

    All *Sagen und Fragen* exercises in four-phased sequences.

    All pronunciation drills in the Phonology section and in Lessons 1–5, with pauses for student repetition.

    All *Aufsätze* at normal speed for listening comprehension.

    All *Übungen* designed for audio-lingual practice in four-phased sequences: cue—pause—correct response—pause.

Van Nostrand Reinhold Company Regional Offices:
Cincinnati   New York   Chicago   Millbrae   Dallas

Van Nostrand Reinhold Company Foreign Offices:
London   Toronto   Melbourne

PF
3112
.K25

Copyright © 1970 by Litton Educational Publishing Inc.

Library of Congress Catalog Number 74-96821

All rights reserved. No part of this work covered by the copyright hereon may be reproduced or used in any form or by any means—graphic, electronic, or mechanical, including photocopying, recording, taping, or information storage and retrieval systems—without written permission of the publisher. Manufactured in the United States of America.

Published by Van Nostrand Reinhold Company
450 West 33rd Street, New York, New York 10001

Published simultaneously in Canada by
D. Van Nostrand Company (Canada), Ltd.

10 9 8 7 6 5 4 3 2 1

PREFACE

Conversational German One is a basic text for beginning courses in German. Presenting a balanced program for the major language skills, the text is accompanied by a student workbook and a comprehensive tape program. An Instructor's Manual is also available.

While our book is aimed at multiple-skill learning, we have predicated our initial approach on the assumption that it is more important to speak German—and pronounce correctly—than to talk about it. To this end, a preliminary chapter introduces the student to the sounds of German through short dialogs, exercises and everyday expressions, and we provide continuing pronunciation practice in the first five lessons. Thus, instructors who favor a "prereading" approach at the beginning, will find the introductory material appropriate.

Each of the twenty lessons consists of a carefully programmed sequence for the acquisition of skill in comprehension, speaking, reading, and writing:

    I. *Unterhaltung:* A conversation featuring the basic structural elements taught in the lesson, along with useful vocabulary. An English version of the dialog in reduced type is provided at the bottom of the page.

    II. *Kombinationen:* Syntactical and lexical variations and recombinations of the key utterances of the conversation.

    III. *Sagen und Fragen:* Cue-response sequences for further reinforcement and control of structural and lexical elements.

    IV. *Aufsatz:* A composition related in theme to the lesson conversation and introducing cultural material. A series of questions about the *Aufsatz* provides a check on student comprehension and affords opportunity for oral practice.

    V. *Wortschatz:* An alphabetical summary of the lesson vocabulary for review and reference.

    VI. *Erklärungen und Übungen:* Descriptive explanations of structural points, with examples. Exercises, most of which are designed for audio-lingual practice, directly follow each major grammatical segment. The headings of grammatical topics are provided in the margins for maximum clarity.

Four Reviews, one after every fifth lesson, provide additional and cumulative practice and dialog exercises. As a further aid in reviewing, the German-English end vocabulary identifies the lesson in which a word is first used. Appendices include complete listings of regular and irregular verbs as well as Fraktur versions of the *Aufsätze*.

In an average three-hour course, each of the first five lessons may be covered in four class meetings, and the remaining ones at the rate of a lesson a week for a full-year program in which provision is made for separate supplementary reading material. We assume that additional laboratory sessions will be scheduled. The book may also be completed in an intensive one-semester or two-quarter course.

We express our deep appreciation to Mr. Gerhard Strasser, who read portions of the manuscript with meticulous care and whose suggestions proved invaluable.

Information about the tapes accompanying *Conversational German One* appears on the copyright page of this book.

CONTENTS

CONTENTS

1. Genitive Case. 2. Prepositions with the Genitive. 3. Adverbial Use of the Genitive. 4. **Da-** and **wo-**Compounds. 5. Declension of the Interrogatives **wer** and **was.** 6. **Kennen-Wissen-Können.**

1. Separable Prefixes. 2. Reflexive Pronouns. 3. Present Tense of **werden** (*to become*).

1. Regular and Irregular Verbs. 2. Simple Past of Regular Verbs. 3. Compound Past of Regular Verbs.

1. Simple Past of Irregular Verbs. 2. Compound Past of Irregular Verbs. 3. Principal Parts. 4. Verbs with Additional Irregularities. 5. Mixed Verbs. 6. **Aber** and **sondern.**

1. **Der-**Words. 2. **Der-**Words as Pronouns. 3. Plurals of Nouns. 4. Future Tense. 5. **Hin** and **her.**

1. **Ein-**Words. 2. Plural of Nouns, continued.

CONTENTS

CONTENTS

Introduction to Pronunciation

A. DAILY EXPRESSIONS

Through the phrases below you will be introduced to common German sounds. Listen carefully as your instructor pronounces them or as you hear them on the tape. Then repeat them after your instructor or the speaker.

Note that many of the expressions are idiomatic and that the English meanings do not necessarily represent basic meanings of the German words. Memorize these expressions after learning to pronounce them, bearing in mind their English equivalents:

1. Guten Morgen. Wie geht es Ihnen, Herr Bachmann?
2. Danke, gut. Und Ihnen?
3. Es geht mir auch gut.
4. Auf Wiedersehen.

5. Guten Abend. Wie heißen Sie, bitte?
6. Ich heiße Meier.
7. Sind Sie Fritz Meier?
8. Nein, mein Name ist Peter.
9. Sie sind Musiker, nicht wahr?
10. Nein, ich bin Lehrer.
11. Ach, Verzeihung!

12. Guten Tag. Wo kommen Sie denn her?
13. Ich komme aus den Vereinigten Staaten von Amerika.
14. Aus welcher Stadt kommen Sie?

1. Good morning. How are you, Mr. Bachmann?
2. Fine, thank you. And you?
3. I'm fine too.
4. Good-by.

5. Good evening. What is your name, please?
6. My name is Meier.
7. Are you Fritz Meier?
8. No, my name is Peter.
9. You are a musician, aren't you?
10. No, I am a teacher.
11. Oh, I beg your pardon.

12. Hello. Tell me, where do you come from?
13. I come from the United States of America.
14. What city do you come from?

1

15. Ich komme aus Chicago.

16. Ach, guten Tag, Herr Doktor! Darf ich bekannt machen? Herr Engelmann, Herr Doktor Löwenstein.

17. Sehr angenehm.

18. Haben Sie Geschwister, Fräulein Krieger?

19. Ja, ich habe zwei Brüder und drei Schwestern.

20. Sind sie alle verheiratet?

21. Nein, mein älterer Bruder ist noch ledig.

22. Womit kann ich dienen?

23. Ich möchte diese Packung Zigaretten, bitte.

24. Sonst noch etwas?

25. Eine Schachtel Streichhölzer. Wieviel kostet das?

26. Das macht zwei Mark fünf zusammen.

27. Wo ist ein Telefon, bitte?

28. Gleich links um die Ecke ist eine Zelle.

29. Übrigens—haben Sie Feuer?

30. Wie bitte? Was haben Sie gesagt?

31. Darf ich um Feuer bitten?

32. Ja, natürlich. Und darf ich um eine Zigarette bitten?

33. Aber bitte schön.

15. I come from Chicago.

16. Oh, hello, doctor! Mr. Engelmann, I'd like you to meet Dr. Löwenstein.

17. How do you do.

18. Do you have any brothers and sisters, Miss Krieger?

19. Yes, I have two brothers and three sisters.

20. Are they all married?

21. No, my older brother is still single.

22. What can I do for you?

23. I'd like this pack of cigarettes, please.

24. Anything else?

25. A box of matches. How much does that cost?

26. That makes DM 2.05 all together.

27. Where is a telephone, please?

28. Just around the corner to the left is a booth.

29. By the way, do you have a light?

30. Excuse me. What did you say?

31. May I ask for a light?

32. Yes, of course. And may I ask for a cigarette?

33. Why, certainly.

34. Guten Tag, Frau Röhl. Was möchten Sie heute essen?
35. Rinderbraten mit gekochten Kartoffeln, bitte.
36. Wünschen Sie auch Salat?
37. Ja, bringen Sie mir bitte einen grünen Salat mit Essig und Öl!
38. Und was möchten Sie trinken? Wein?
39. Nichts, danke. Nur Kaffee nach dem Essen.

34. Hello, Mrs. Röhl. What would you like to eat today?
35. Pot roast and boiled potatoes, please.
36. Would you like a salad, too?
37. Yes, please, bring me a green salad with oil and vinegar.
38. And what would you like to drink? Wine?
39. Nothing, thank you. Just coffee after the meal.

B. USEFUL CLASSROOM EXPRESSIONS

Listen carefully to the instructor or tape, then repeat and memorize:

1. Schlagen Sie bitte die Bücher auf!
2. Öffnen Sie Ihr Buch auf Seite drei!
3. Lesen Sie auf deutsch!
4. Übersetzen Sie, bitte!
5. Stehen Sie bitte auf!
6. Gehen Sie an die Tafel!
7. Schreiben Sie Übung A an die Tafel!
8. Setzen Sie sich!
9. Hören Sie gut zu!
10. Wiederholen Sie!
11. Noch einmal, bitte!
12. (Wiederholen Sie) alle zusammen!

1. Open your books, please.
2. Open your book to page three.
3. Read in German.
4. Translate, please.
5. Stand (get) up, please.
6. Go to the blackboard.
7. Write Exercise A on the board.
8. Sit down.
9. Listen carefully.
10. Repeat.
11. Once again, please.
12. (Repeat) all together.

13. Spreche ich zu schnell?
14. Ja, sprechen Sie bitte langsamer!
15. Ich verstehe Sie sehr schlecht.
16. Verstehen Sie mich jetzt besser?
17. Sprechen Sie lauter, bitte!
18. Spreche ich jetzt laut genug?
19. Noch ein bißchen lauter, bitte.
20. Sie haben eine Frage, Fräulein Weber?
21. Ja, wie heißt „Beispiel" auf englisch?
22. Es heißt „example".
23. Wer ist jetzt an der Reihe?
24. Was bedeutet diese Frage?
25. Auf englisch?
26. Für morgen Aufgabe zwei.

13. Am I speaking too fast?
14. Yes, please speak more slowly.
15. I have a lot of trouble understanding you.
16. Do you understand better now?
17. Speak louder, please.
18. Am I speaking loud enough now?
19. Still a little louder, please.
20. You have a question, Miss Weber?
21. Yes, what does "Beispiel" mean in English?
22. It means "example."
23. Whose turn is it now?
24. What does this question mean?
25. In English?
26. For tomorrow Lesson 2.

C. THE ALPHABET

Learn to say the German alphabet. You will often need to spell your name and certain place names. Also study the phonemic symbols below. They will be used in the pronunciation exercises.

Repeat after your instructor or the speaker:

/a:/[1]	a	/ef/	f
/be:/	b	/ge:/	g
/tse:/	c	/ha:/	h
/de:/	d	/i:/	i
/e:/	e	/yot/	j

1. Two dots following a sound indicate length.

4

/ka:/	k	/es/	s
/el/	l	/te:/	t
/em/	m	/u:/	u
/en/	n	/faw/	v
/o:/	o	/ve:/	w
/pe:/	p	/iks/	x
/ku:/	q	/üpsilon/	y
/er/	r	/tset/	z

D. VOWELS

German distinguishes five vowel phonemes, /a/, /e/, /i/, /o/, and /u/, each of which may occur as close and long or open and short. English does not distinguish between long and short, but between tense and lax sounds. Be careful, therefore, not to produce an offglide or "drawl" when pronouncing a long sound in German.

Listen to your instructor or the speaker and compare the difference in the English and German vowels in each of the pairs below:

gate — **geht**
knee — **nie**
toot — **tut**

German sounds more clipped than English. Not only are the short sounds very short, but whenever a vowel or diphthong begins a syllable, a glottal catch precedes. Listen carefully to your instructor or the speaker:

ein alter Ochs
die Vereinigten Staaten
in Ihrem Amt
über euch

Now practice the following (Observe the various ways of spelling a particular sound):

Phoneme   Spelling
Short a /a/   a

Repeat after your instructor or the speaker:

1.	/takt/	**Takt**	*measure*
2.	/pak/	**Pack**	*packet*
3.	/ban/	**Bann**	*ban*
4.	/kam/	**Kamm**	*comb*
5.	/zat/	**satt**	*satiated*

5

Phoneme	Spelling
Long a[1] /a:/	a, ah, aa

Repeat after your instructor or the speaker:

1.	/ta:t/	**Tat**	*deed*
2.	/ka:n/	**Kahn**	*skiff*
3.	/ba:n/	**Bahn**	*roadway*
4.	/pla:n/	**Plan**	*plan*
5.	/za:l/	**Saal**	*hall*

Repeat the pairs after your instructor or the speaker:

/a/ vs. /a:/

1.	**schlaff**	*limp*	—	**Schlaf**	*sleep*
2.	**wann**	*when*	—	**Wahn**	*delusion*
3.	**Stall**	*stable*	—	**Stahl**	*steel*
4.	**Stadt**	*city*	—	**Staat**	*state*
5.	**Lamm**	*lamb*	—	**lahm**	*lame*

Phoneme	Spelling
Short e /e/	e, ä

Repeat after your instructor or the speaker:

1.	/fest/	**fest**	*firm*
2.	/vekst/	**wächst**	*grows*
3.	/den/	**denn**	*for*
4.	/bet/	**Bett**	*bed*
5.	/lest/	**läßt**	*lets*

Phoneme	Spelling
Long e[2] /e:/	e, eh, ee

Repeat after your instructor or the speaker:

1.	/ge:t/	**geht**	*goes*
2.	/fe:kt/	**fegt**	*sweeps*
3.	/ve:r/	**Wehr**	*defense*
4.	/me:r/	**Meer**	*ocean*
5.	/le:st/	**lest**	*read*

1. A vowel is usually long when followed by a single consonant, an **h**, or a doubling of the vowel.
2. Long e is also indicated by a following consonant plus -**t**.

Repeat the pairs after your instructor or the speaker:

/e/ vs. /e:/[1]

1.	**Bett**	*bed*	— **Beet**	*flower bed*
2.	**stellen**	*to put*	— **stehlen**	*to steal*
3.	**denn**	*for*	— **den**	*the (accusative)*
4.	**wenn**	*whenever*	— **wen**	*whom*
5.	**Herr**	*gentleman*	— **Heer**	*army*

The phoneme /ə/, spelled **e**, never receives primary stress.[2] Listen as your instructor or the speaker pronounces the following:

stellen	/štelən/	*to put*
Dame	/da:mə/	*lady*
Gebet	/gəbe:t/	*prayer*

Phoneme	Spelling
Short i /i/	i

Repeat after your instructor or the speaker:

1.	/tiš/	**Tisch**	*table*
2.	/bis/	**Biß**	*bite*
3.	/vits/	**Witz**	*joke*
4.	/gəvis/	**gewiß**	*certainly*
5.	/mit/	**mit**	*with*

Phoneme	Spelling
Long i /i:/	i, ie, ih

Repeat after your instructor or the speaker:

1.	/mi:r/	**mir**	*to me*
2.	/i:n/	**ihn**	*him*
3.	/bri:f/	**Brief**	*letter*
4.	/gli:t/	**Glied**	*limb*
5.	/ti:f/	**tief**	*deep*

1. There is also an open and long sound /ɛ:/, spelled ä and äh, which occasionally contrasts with /e:/ and /e/:
   lädst /lɛ:tst/ (*you*) *load* vs. **letzt** /letst/ *last*
   währen /vɛ:rən/ *to last* vs. **wehren** /ve:rən/ *to defend*
2. This phoneme is known as *schwa*. In English it occurs initially and finally in the word *amoeba* and medially in such words as *cut, but.*

Repeat the pairs after your instructor or the speaker:

/i/ vs. /iː/

1.	**in**	*in*	— **ihn**	*him*
2.	**bitten**	*to ask*	— **bieten**	*to offer*
3.	**still**	*quiet*	— **Stil**	*style*
4.	**sich**	*himself*	— **siech**	*sickly*
5.	**List**	*cunning*	— **liest**	*reads*

Phoneme	Spelling
Short o /o/	o

Repeat after your instructor or the speaker:

1.	/fon/	**von**	*from*
2.	/volf/	**Wolf**	*wolf*
3.	/op/	**ob**	*whether*
4.	/vonə/	**Wonne**	*ecstasy*
5.	/doktor/	**Doktor**	*doctor*

Phoneme	Spelling
Long o /oː/	o, oh, oo

Repeat after your instructor or the speaker:

1.	/toːn/	**Ton**	*tone*
2.	/loːs/	**los**	*loose*
3.	/voːl/	**wohl**	*well*
4.	/oːdər/	**oder**	*or*
5.	/toːt/	**Tod**	*death*

Repeat the pairs after your instructor or the speaker:

/o/ vs. /oː/

1.	**offen**	*open*	— **Ofen**	*oven*
2.	**floß**	*flowed*	— **Floß**	*raft*
3.	**Bonne**	*governess*	— **Bohne**	*bean*
4.	**sollen**	*to be supposed to*	— **sohlen**	*to sole*
5.	**Roggen**	*rye*	— **Rogen**	*roe*

Phoneme	Spelling
Short u /u/	u

Repeat after your instructor or the speaker:

1.	/klup/	**Klub**	*club*

2.	/vustə/	**wußte**	*knew*
3.	/zumən/	**summen**	*to hum*
4.	/grunt/	**Grund**	*reason*
5.	/kaput/	**kaputt**	*broken*

Phoneme	Spelling
Long u /u:/	u, uh

Repeat after your instructor or the speaker:

1.	/gu:t/	**gut**	*good*
2.	/vu:t/	**Wut**	*rage*
3.	/kultu:r/	**Kultur**	*culture*
4.	/ku:/	**Kuh**	*cow*
5.	/štu:l/	**Stuhl**	*chair*

Repeat the pairs after your instructor or the speaker:

/u/ vs. /u:/

1.	**Bucht**	*bay*	—	**bucht**	*books (verb)*
2.	**Sucht**	*mania*	—	**sucht**	*seeks*
3.	**muß**	*has to*	—	**Mus**	*puree*
4.	**Rum**	*rum*	—	**Ruhm**	*fame*
5.	**Flucht**	*escape*	—	**flucht**	*curses*

In addition to the full vowels described and practiced above, there are two modified vowels /ö/ and /ü/, both of which occur as close and long or open and short. These will be described and practiced in Lesson 1.

E. DIPHTHONGS

Diphthongs consist of a vowel and a semivowel.

Diphthong	Spelling
/aw/	au

Repeat after your instructor or the speaker:

1.	/bawm/	**Baum**	*tree*
2.	/brawn/	**braun**	*brown*
3.	/lawt/	**Laut**	*sound*
4.	/zawm/	**Saum**	*hem*
5.	/hawt/	**Haut**	*skin*

9

Diphthong	Spelling
/ay/	ei, ai, ay

Repeat after your instructor or the speaker:

1.	/vayn/	**Wein**	*wine*
2.	/may/	**Mai**	*May*
3.	/bayərn/	**Bayern**	*Bavaria*
4.	/ayt/	**Eid**	*oath*
5.	/aynst/	**einst**	*once*

Diphthong	Spelling
/oy/	eu, äu

Repeat after your instructor or the speaker:

1.	/loytə/	**Leute**	*people*
2.	/boymə/	**Bäume**	*trees*
3.	/toyšən/	**täuschen**	*to deceive*
4.	/oyro:pa/	**Europa**	*Europe*
5.	/froydə/	**Freude**	*joy*

F. CONSONANTS

We have described and practiced German vowels at some length because of the wide range of vowel variation and the differences from English in German vowel sound patterns.

There are 20 consonant phonemes in German. Many of them are pronounced like or almost like English.

Repeat the following after your instructor or the speaker:

Pho-neme	Spelling	Examples			
/b/	b	1.	/bakən/	**backen**	*to bake*
		2.	/ebə/	**Ebbe**	*low tide*
		3.	/li:bə/	**Liebe**	*love*
/d/	d	1.	/du:/	**du**	*thou, you*
		2.	/mildə/	**milde**	*mild*
		3.	/diŋ/	**Ding**	*thing*
/g/	g	1.	/za:gən/	**sagen**	*to say*
		2.	/ge:bən/	**geben**	*to give*
		3.	/ma:gər/	**mager**	*thin*

/p/	p, -b	1.	/pinzəl/	**Pinsel**	*paintbrush*
		2.	/lapən/	**Lappen**	*rag*
		3.	/liːp/	**lieb**	*dear*
/t/	t, -d	1.	/taːt/	**Tat**	*deed*
		2.	/treːtən/	**treten**	*to step*
		3.	/hant/	**Hand**	*hand*
/k/	k, ck, -g (except after i); c, ch (before back vowels and following consonant; x (ks)	1.	/katsə/	**Katze**	*cat*
		2.	/tikən/	**ticken**	*to tick*
		3.	/taːk/	**Tag**	*day*
		4.	/kafeː/	**Café**	*café*
		5.	/koːr/	**Chor**	*choir*
		6.	/zeks/	**sechs**	*six*
/v/	w, v	1.	/vasər/	**Wasser**	*water*
		2.	/novembər/	**November**	*November*
/z/	s	1.	/zayn/	**sein**	*to be*
		2.	/beːzən/	**Besen**	*broom*
		3.	/zoːlə/	**Sohle**	*sole*
/ž/	j, g	1.	/žurnalist/	**Journalist**	*journalist*
		2.	/režiː/	**Regie**	*stage management*
		3.	/ruːž/	**Rouge**	*rouge*
/f/	f, v, ph	1.	/findən/	**finden**	*to find*
		2.	/faːtər/	**Vater**	*father*
		3.	/filozoːf/	**Philosoph**	*philosopher*
/s/	s, ss, ß[1]	1.	/es/	**es**	*it*
		2.	/pasən/	**passen**	*to suit*
		3.	/fuːs/	**Fuß**	*foot*
/š/	sch, s[2]	1.	/šuː/	**Schuh**	*shoe*
		2.	/špuːlə/	**Spule**	*spool*
		3.	/štat/	**statt**	*instead of*
/h/	h	1.	/huːt/	**Hut**	*hat*
		2.	/heft/	**Heft**	*notebook*
		3.	/hart/	**hart**	*hard*

1. **ß** is a lower-case letter only and occurs after a long vowel or diphthong, before a consonant, and in final position: **schließen, heißen, mußt, muß.**
2. Occurs before **p** and **t** in syllable-initial position.

/m/	m	1.	/amt/	**Amt**	*office*
		2.	/mayn/	**mein**	*my*
		3.	/im/	**im**	*in the*
/n/	n	1.	/nus/	**Nuß**	*nut*
		2.	/brenən/	**brennen**	*to burn*
		3.	/in/	**in**	*in*
/ŋ/	ng	1.	/fiŋər/	**Finger**[1]	*finger*
		2.	/kliŋən/	**klingen**[1]	*to sound*
		3.	/haŋ/	**Hang**[1]	*slope*

Other consonant sounds peculiar to German and unusual clusters will be described and practiced in the first few lessons.

INTRODUCTORY VOCABULARY

You have practiced the words listed below in context in this chapter. Commit them more firmly to memory now. They will form a helpful nucleus for the study of the first few lessons.

German words have no stress symbols. Most German words are stressed on the first or root syllable. To help you with exceptions, we use a dot (ạ) to indicate stress on a short vowel and a dash (ā) to indicate stress on a long vowel or a diphthong:

der **Abend**	evening	**etwas**	something
aber	but, however	die **Frage**	question
alle	all	die **Frau**	woman, Mrs.
alle zu-	all together	das **Fräulein**	young woman,
sạmmen			Miss
auch	also	**gehen**	to go
die **Aufgabe**	lesson	**gut**	good
aus	from	**haben**	to have
besser	better	**heißen**	to be called
bitte	please	der **Herr**	gentleman, Mr.
bitte schön	please; you're	**heute**	today
	welcome, of	**heute**	this morning
	course	**morgen**	
bringen	to bring	**ja**	yes
der **Bruder**	brother	**jetzt**	now
danke	thanks	der **Kaffee**	coffee
das	that, this	**kommen**	to come
der **Doktor**	doctor	**kosten**	to cost
die **Ecke**	corner	der **Lehrer**	teacher
englisch	English	**machen**	to make, do
auf eng-	in English	die **Mark**	mark (*currency*)
lisch		**mit**	with
essen	to eat	der **Morgen**	morning

1. Note that in this word there is no g sound.

der	Name	name		sehr	very
	natürlich	naturally, of course		sprechen	to speak
			der	Staat	state
	nein	no	die	Stadt	city
	nicht	not	der	Tag	day
	nicht wahr?	isn't it, won't they, etc.		trinken	to drink
				und	and
	noch	still, yet		übrigens	by the way
	noch einmal	again, once again, once more		verstehen	to understand
				was	what
				wie	how, as
	nur	only, just		wo	where
	sagen	to say		wünschen	to want
die	Schwester	sister		zu	to, too

Hamburg, Hafenszene an der Elbe
HENLE FROM MONKMEYER

I. UNTERHALTUNG

DIE ANKUNFT

Kurt Klein: Guten Tag. Ich bin Kurt Klein aus Amerika.

Frau Kolb: So, Sie sind Herr Klein. Sie sprechen aber fabelhaft Deutsch.

Kurt Klein: Ich spreche schon lange Deutsch. Meine Eltern sind in Deutschland geboren.

Frau Kolb: Das ist sehr interessant. Wo wohnen Sie jetzt?

Kurt Klein: Wir wohnen jetzt im Staate Wisconsin. Die Stadt heißt Milwaukee. Viele Deutsche wohnen dort.

Frau Kolb: Ist das Ihr Koffer da drüben? Bringen Sie ihn doch in Ihr Zimmer!

Kurt Klein: Wo ist denn das Zimmer? Ist es oben oder unten?

Frau Kolb: Hier unten, links um die Ecke.

Kurt Klein: Haben Sie Post für mich?

Frau Kolb: Ja, hier ist ein Brief aus Amerika. Er ist für Sie.

Kurt Klein: Vielen Dank. Bis später, Frau Kolb.

Frau Kolb: Auf Wiedersehen, Herr Klein.

THE ARRIVAL

Kurt Klein: Hello, I'm Kurt Klein from America.

Mrs. Kolb: So you're Mr. Klein. My, you speak marvelous German.

Kurt Klein: I've been speaking German for a long time. My parents were born in Germany.

Mrs. Kolb: That's very interesting. Where do you live now?

Kurt Klein: We now live in the state of Wisconsin. The city is called Milwaukee. Many Germans live there.

Mrs. Kolb: Is that your suitcase over there? Why don't you take it to your room?

Kurt Klein: But where is my room? Is it upstairs or downstairs?

Mrs. Kolb: Down here, around the corner to the left.

Kurt Klein: Do you have any mail for me?

Mrs. Kolb: Yes, here's a letter from America. It's for you.

Kurt Klein: Thank you. I'll see you later, Mrs. Kolb.

Mrs. Kolb: See you later, Mr. Klein.

LESSON 1

II. KOMBINATIONEN

Sagen Sie auf deutsch:

a. 1. Hello, Mr. Klein. 2. Hello, Mrs. Kolb. 3. Hello, Mr. Kolb.
4. Hello, Miss (Fräulein) Kolb.

b. 1. So, you are Mr. Klein. —Yes, I'm Mr. Klein. 2. So, you are
Mrs. Kolb. —Yes, I'm Mrs. Kolb. 3. So, you are Mr. Kolb.
—Yes, I'm Mr. Kolb. 4. So you're Miss Kolb. —Yes, I'm Miss
Kolb.

c. 1. My, you speak marvelous German. 2. My, you speak marvelous English. 3. I have been speaking German for a long
time. 4. I've been speaking English for a long time.

d. 1. My parents were born in America. 2. My parents were
born in the state of Wisconsin. 3. My parents were born in
Milwaukee. 4. We now live in Milwaukee. 5. Many Germans live there.

e. 1. Where is the room? —Is it upstairs? 2. Or is it downstairs? 3. It's around the corner to the left. 4. It's over
there.

f. 1. Do you have any mail for me? 2. Yes, here is a letter from
America. 3. Here is a letter from Wisconsin. 4. Here is a
letter for you, Mr. Klein. 5. Here is a letter for you, Mrs.
Kolb.

g. 1. See you later, Kurt. 2. See you later, Mrs. Kolb. 3. Good-
by, Miss Kolb.

III. SAGEN UND FRAGEN

a. *Sie sind Kurt Klein. Sie sagen:*

1. Sie sind aus Amerika. 2. Sie sprechen schon lange
Deutsch. 3. Ihre (*your*) Eltern sind in Deutschland geboren.
4. Sie wohnen jetzt im Staate Wisconsin. 5. Viele Deutsche
wohnen in Milwaukee. 6. Der Koffer ist da drüben. 7. Das
Zimmer ist unten, links um die Ecke. 8. Frau Kolb hat Post
für Sie. 9. Auf Wiedersehen, Frau Kolb.

b. *Sie sind Frau Kolb. Sie fragen Kurt:*

1. ob (*whether*) er (*he*) Kurt Klein ist.[1] 2. ob er aus Amerika
ist. 3. wo er jetzt wohnt. 4. ob das Kurts Koffer ist. 5. ob
der Koffer da drüben ist.

1. In this part of the Sagen und Fragen exercise, we use indirect questions, in which the verb always stands last. Example: Fragen Sie,
ob er in Milwaukee wohnt! Ask him *whether he lives in Milwaukee.*

IV. PRONUNCIATION PRACTICE

Modified Vowels The following sounds do not exist in English:

Phoneme	Spelling
/ü/, /ü:/	ü, üh

The umlaut **u** sounds are pronounced high and far forward with the lips rounded and protruded. Round the lips for:

look	and try to pronounce	lick	>	**Lücke**	*gap*
took		tick	>	**Tücke**	*prank*
coon		keen	>	**kühn**	*bold*
room		ream	>	**rühmen**	*to praise*

Short ü *Repeat after your instructor or the speaker:*

1. /hülə/   **Hülle**   *husk*
2. /dürftə/   **dürfte**   *might*
3. /vürdə/   **Würde**   *dignity*
4. /nütsən/   **nützen**   *to be of use*
5. /glük/   **Glück**   *luck*

Long ü *Repeat after your instructor or the speaker:*

1. /fü:sə/   **Füße**   *feet*
2. /frü:/   **früh**   *early*
3. /ü:bəl/   **Übel**   *evil*
4. /šü:lər/   **Schüler**   *pupil*
5. /kü:l/   **kühl**   *cool*

Repeat the pairs after your instructor or the speaker:

/ü/ vs. /ü:/

1.	**Dünne**	*slenderness*	— **Düne**	*dune*
2.	**Hütte**	*hut*	— **Hüte**	*hats*
3.	**wüßte**	*knew (subjunctive)*	— **Wüste**	*desert*
4.	**flügge**	*fledged*	— **Flüge**	*flights*
5.	**füllen**	*to fill*	— **fühlen**	*to feel*

Two other modified vowels not found in English are:

Phoneme	Spelling
/ö/, /ö:/	ö, öh

The umlaut **o** sounds are pronounced in the front of the mouth with protruded lips, but are somewhat lower than **ü**. Round the lips for:

goats	and try to pronounce	gets	>	**Götz**	*(a name)*
phone		feign	>	**Föhn**	*(a south wind)*
tote		tate	>	**töten**	*to kill*

17

Short ö

Repeat after your instructor or the speaker:

1.	/mördər/	**Mörder**	*murderer*
2.	/höltsərn/	**hölzern**	*wooden*
3.	/fölkər/	**Völker**	*peoples*
4.	/öfnən/	**öffnen**	*to open*
5.	/hölə/	**Hölle**	*hell*

Long ö

Repeat after your instructor or the speaker:

1.	/lö:və/	**Löwe**	*lion*
2.	/bö:mən/	**Böhmen**	*Bohemia*
3.	/tsö:gərn/	**zögern**	*to hesitate*
4.	/švö:rən/	**schwören**	*to swear*
5.	/grö:sə/	**Größe**	*size*

Repeat the pairs after your instructor or the speaker:

/ö/ vs. /ö:/

1.	**Blöcke**	*blocks*	—	**blöke**	*bleat (imperative)*
2.	**flösse**	*flowed (subjunctive)*	—	**Flöße**	*rafts*
3.	**Hölle**	*hell*	—	**Höhle**	*cave*
4.	**sönne**	*thought (subjunctive, archaic)*	—	**Söhne**	*sons*
5.	**schösse**	*shot (subjunctive)*	—	**Schöße**	*laps*

V. AUFSATZ

DER STUDENT KURT KLEIN

Der Student Kurt Klein wohnt in der Stadt Milwaukee. Die Stadt Milwaukee liegt im[1] Staate Wisconsin. Kurts Vater wohnt schon viele Jahre in Milwaukee. Die Mutter kommt aus New York. Sie wohnt[2] erst zwanzig (20) Jahre in Wisconsin. Kurt ist neunzehn
5 (19) Jahre alt. Er ist groß und stark für sein Alter.

Kurt stammt aus[3] einer deutschen Familie. Er spricht Deutsch, aber er möchte[4] es besser lernen. „Darf ich in Deutschland studieren?" fragt er seine Eltern. „Selbstverständlich", antwortet Herr Klein.

10 Kurt kauft eine Fahrkarte nach Deutschland. Er reist nach New York; von da fährt er mit dem Dampfer[5] nach Hamburg. In Ham-

1. in the. 2. has been living. 3. comes from. 4. would like.
5. steamship.

18

burg nimmt er den Zug nach Köln. Er bleibt nur ein Jahr in Köln. Das Studium ist sehr teuer.

Kurt ist jetzt in Köln. Er sucht ein Taxi und gibt dem Chauffeur[6]
15 eine Adresse. „Bitte fahren Sie mich[7] zu dieser Adresse", sagt Kurt. Das Haus gehört Frau Kolb. Frau Kolb öffnet die Tür. Kurt trägt seinen Koffer ins[8] Haus.

Frau Kolb ist nett und freundlich. Sie zeigt Kurt das Zimmer. Es ist sauber und schön. Die Miete[9] ist billig. „Bis später," sagt er.
20 „Auf Wiedersehen", antwortet Frau Kolb.

Beantworten Sie die folgenden Fragen:

1. Wo wohnt der Student Kurt Klein?   2. Wie viele Jahre wohnt Kurts Vater in Milwaukee?   3. Wie alt ist Kurt?   4. Was fragt Kurt seine Eltern?   5. Was kauft Kurt?   6. Wie fährt er nach Hamburg?   7. Was sucht er in Köln?   8. Was gibt er dem Chauffeur?   9. Wem gehört das Haus?   10. Wer öffnet die Tür? 11. Was trägt Kurt ins Haus?   12. Wie ist Frau Kolb?   13. Was zeigt sie Kurt?   14. Wie ist das Zimmer?   15. Wie ist die Miete?

6. driver.   7. me.   8. into the.   9. rent.

VI. WORTSCHATZ

die **Adresse**	address	**deutsch**	German
alt	old		(*adjective*)
das **Alter**	age	**auf**	
(das) **Amerika**	America	**deutsch**	in German
an	on	(das) **Deutsch**	German (*noun*)
antworten	to answer	**Deutschland**	Germany
auf	on, at	**doch**	*emphatic particle*
billig	cheap	**dort**	there
bis	until	**dürfen (darf)**	to be permitted,
bleiben	to remain		may
der **Brief**	letter	die **Eltern**	parents
da	there	**erst**	only (*with ex-*
da drüben	over there		*pressions of*
der **Dank**	thanks, gratitude		*time*)
vielen	many thanks	**fabelhaft**	marvelous
Dank		**fahren**	to go (*by vehicle*)
denn	*particle used in*	**(fährt)**	
	questions to	die **Fahrkarte**	ticket
	indicate a	die **Familie**	family
	genuine inter-	**fragen**	to ask
	est in the	**freundlich**	friendly
	answer	**für**	for

19

geben	to give	so	so
gehören	to belong to	spät	late
groß	big, tall	später	later
das Haus	house	stark	strong
hier	here	stehen	to stand
in	in	der Student	student
interessant	interesting	studieren	to study
das Jahr	year	das Studium	studies, study
kaufen	to buy	suchen	to look for, seek
das Kind	child	das Taxi	taxi
der Koffer	suitcase	teuer	expensive
das Land	country, land	tragen (trägt)	to carry; to wear
lange	a long time	die Tür	door
lernen	to learn	unten	downstairs
links	left, to the left	der Vater	father
die Mutter	mother	viele	many
nach	to	von	of, from
nehmen	to take	vor	in front of
(nimmt)		warum	why?
nett	nice	wem	to whom?
oben	upstairs	wen	whom?
öffnen	to open	wer	who?
die Post	mail	wie	how? as
reisen	to travel	wie viele	how many?
sauber	clean	wohnen	to live, reside
schon	already	das Zimmer	room
schön	pretty	der Zug	train
sein (bin, ist, sind)	to be		

VII. ERKLÄRUNGEN UND ÜBUNGEN

1. Articles and Gender

Each noun in German has a characteristic gender which is indicated either by an ending or a determiner. Determiners include the definite and indefinite articles.

The assignment of gender is largely a grammatical matter. More often than not there is no sex connection between an inanimate object and its gender.

a. Definite Article

Masculine	Feminine	Neuter
der Vater *key sound:* /r/	**die Mutter** *key sound:* /i:/	**das Kind** *key sound:* /s/
der Koffer	**die Fahrkarte**	**das Haus**
der Staat	**die Stadt**	**das Land**

Nouns denoting male beings are usually masculine (**der Vater, der Bruder**), female beings usually feminine (**die Mutter, die Tochter**).

Since inanimate objects may be masculine, feminine, or neuter, be sure to learn the definite article with every noun. Consider that gender is an inherent part of each word and learn to associate the key sound of each gender with its noun.

b. Indefinite Article

Masculine	Feminine	Neuter
ein Vater	**eine Mutter**	**ein Kind**
no key sound	*key sound:* /ə/	*no key sound*
ein Koffer	**eine Fahrkarte**	**ein Haus**
ein Staat	**eine Stadt**	**ein Land**

The indefinite article is **ein** for masculine and for neuter nouns, **eine** for feminine nouns.

PRACTICE

A. *Answer the following questions affirmatively:*

> *Example:* Wohnt der Student in Milwaukee?
> Ja, der Student wohnt in Milwaukee.

1. Wohnt der Vater in Milwaukee? 2. Kommt die Mutter aus New York? 3. Ist der Student stark für sein Alter? 4. Ist die Stadt Milwaukee groß? 5. Ist der Staat Wisconsin auch groß? 6. Ist das Zimmer hier schön? 7. Ist das Zimmer auch sauber? 8. Ist die Miete billig? 9. Ist das Studium teuer? 10. Gehört das Haus Frau Kolb? 11. Gehört der Koffer Kurt? 12. Ist die Post für Kurt? 13. Ist der Brief auch für Kurt?

B. *Answer the following questions with the indicated phrases:*

> *Example:* Wo ist die Stadt Milwaukee? (*in Wisconsin*)
> Die Stadt Milwaukee ist in Wisconsin.

1. Wo ist der Staat Wisconsin? (in Amerika) 2. Wo ist eine Universität (*university*) in Wisconsin? (in Madison) 3. Wo ist eine Universität in Deutschland? (in Köln) 4. Wo ist die Stadt Köln? (am Rhein) 5. Wo ist der Dampfer? (in Bremerhaven) 6. Wo ist das Haus von Frau Kolb? (links um die Ecke) 7. Wo ist das Zimmer für Kurt? (oben) 8. Wo ist die Post für Kurt? (unten) 9. Wo ist ein Brief für Frau Kolb? (auch unten) 10. Wo ist ein Taxi? (vor dem Haus)

C. *Replace the subject of each sentence with the indicated noun:*

> *Example:* Ein Lehrer steht an der Ecke. (*Student*)
> Ein Student steht an der Ecke.

1. Ein Taxi steht vor dem Haus. (Koffer) 2. Ein Student spricht

21

mit dem Chauffeur. (Frau) 3. Eine Postkarte für Kurt ist hier. (Brief) 4. Eine Frau Kolb wohnt hier. (Fräulein) 5. Ein Student ist im Zimmer. (Herr)

D. *Say in German:*

1. a father
   a mother
   a house
   a family

2. This is the father.
   This is the mother.
   This is the address.

3. a room
   a year
   a state
   a ticket

4. This is a ticket
   This is a corner.
   This is a letter.

2. Case

The case of a noun or pronoun indicates its function in the sentence.

a. Nominative

Der Koffer ist da drüben. (noun subject)
The suitcase is over there.

Er kauft eine Fahrkarte. (pronoun subject)
He's buying a ticket.

Kurt ist **Student.**[1] (predicate noun)
Kurt is a student.

Auf Wiedersehen, **Herr Klein.** (direct address)
Good-by, Mr. Klein.

The nominative is the case of the subject, the predicate noun, and direct address.

b. Replacing Nouns with Pronouns

er replaces nouns with **der** or **ein** (*masculine*)

sie replaces nouns with **die** or **eine** (*feminine*)

es replaces nouns with **das** or **ein** (*neuter*)

sie replaces nouns with **die** (*plural, all genders*)

Das ist **der Vater.**
That's the father.

Er ist freundlich.
He's friendly.

Das ist **der Koffer.**
That's the suitcase.

Er ist groß.
It's large.

Eine Fahrkarte ist teuer.
A ticket is expensive.

Sie ist teuer.
It's expensive.

1. With unmodified nouns of occupation and nationality the indefinite article is not used.

Hier ist Kurts **Zimmer**.	**Es** ist sauber.
Here is Kurt's room.	*It's clean.*
Wo sind Kurts **Eltern?**	**Sie** sind in Amerika.
Where are Kurt's parents?	*They are in America.*

A pronoun in place of a noun varies with the gender of the noun.

PRACTICE

A. *Answer the following questions using subject pronouns and the expressions indicated:*

> *Example:* Wie ist Frau Kolb? (*nett*)
> Sie ist nett.

1. Wo wohnt Kurt? (in Amerika) 2. Wo wohnen Kurts Eltern? (in Milwaukee) 3. Wie ist Kurt für sein Alter? (groß und stark) 4. Wie ist das Studium in Köln? (billig) 5. Wem gehört das Haus? (Frau Kolb) 6. Wo ist das Zimmer? (unten) 7. Wo ist die Tür? (links um die Ecke) 8. Wie ist das Haus? (sehr sauber)

B. *Answer affirmatively, using a subject pronoun:*

> *Example:* Ist der Student hier?
> Ja, er ist hier.

1. Ist Frau Kolb nett? 2. Ist Herr Kolb freundlich? 3. Ist Kurt jetzt in Köln? 4. Ist das Studium teuer? 5. Spricht der Lehrer gut Englisch? 6. Ist das Taxi hier? 7. Trägt Kurt den Koffer ins Haus? 8. Ist der Koffer im Zimmer? 9. Sind Kurts Eltern in Deutschland geboren? 10. Bleibt Kurt lange in Deutschland?

3. Present Tense of Regular Verbs

In the **Wortschatz** we usually give the infinitive form of the verb: sagen (*to say*)

The present stem is formed by dropping **-en** from the infinitive: **sag-**

To this stem are then added the personal endings of the present indicative:

ich	sag**e**	*I am saying, I say*
du	sag**st**	*you are saying, you say*
er, sie, es	sag**t**	*he, she, it is saying, he, she, it says*
wir	sag**en**	*we are saying, we say*
ihr	sag**t**	*you are saying, you say*
sie	sag**en**	*they are saying, they say*
Sie	sag**en** (*conventional form*)	*you are saying, you say*

23

Infinitive: **antworten** (*to answer*)

Present stem: **antwort-**

ich	antworte	*I am answering, I answer*
du	antwortest	*you are answering, you answer*
er, sie, es	antwortet	*he, she, it is answering, he, she, it answers*
wir	antworten	*we are answering, we answer*
ihr	antwortet	*you are answering, you answer*
sie	antworten	*they are answering, they answer*
Sie	antworten	*you are answering, you answer*

Verbs whose present stem ends in **d, t,** or a single **m** or **n** usually retain **e** in the 2nd person singular and plural and 3rd person singular except when **m** or **n** is preceded by **r, l,** or **h**: du antwort**est**; er antwort**et**; du find**est** (*find*), er find**et**; du atm**est** (*breathe*), er atm**et**; du öffn**est**, er öffn**et**; *but* du lernst, er lernt.

PRACTICE

A. Conjugate in the present tense:

1. fragen; 2. kommen; 3. suchen; 4. arbeiten; 5. öffnen

*B. Change the verb to the **er** and **wir** forms:*

> *Example:* Ich studiere in München.
> Er studiert in München.
> Wir studieren in München.

1. Ich wohne in München. 2. Ich komme aus New York. 3. Ich reise nach Deutschland. 4. Ich suche eine Adresse. 5. Ich bleibe ein Jahr hier. 6. Ich sage „Guten Tag".

*C. Change the verb to the **ich** and **ihr** forms:*

> *Example:* Sie lernen Englisch.
> Ich lerne Englisch.
> Ihr lernt Englisch.

1. Sie kaufen eine Fahrkarte. 2. Sie fahren nach München. 3. Sie öffnen die Tür. 4. Sie gehen ins Zimmer. 5. Sie antworten auf deutsch. 6. Sie sagen „Auf Wiedersehen".

D. Say in German:

1. I am asking. 2. I am studying. 3. I buy. 4. I am looking for a house. 5. He opens. 6. He answers. 7. He is going. 8. He is studying. 9. She is staying. 10. She is buying. 11. She

lives. 12. She is asking. 13. They are coming from New York. 14. They are learning German. 15. They are looking for the address. 16. They are studying at the university.

E. *Answer the following questions affirmatively:*

    Example: Fahren Sie nach Köln?
               Ja, ich fahre nach Köln.

1. Sprechen Sie Deutsch? 2. Gehen Sie zur (*to the*) Universität? 3. Studieren Sie hier? 4. Stammen Sie aus Amerika? 5. Reisen Sie nach Europa? 6. Fahren sie mit dem Zug? 7. Öffnen Sie das Haus? 8. Wohnen Sie in Köln?

4. Irregular Present-Tense Forms

fahren		sprechen	
ich	fahre	ich	spreche
du	fährst	du	sprichst
er, sie, es	fährt	er, sie, es	spricht
wir	fahren	wir	sprechen
ihr	fahrt	ihr	sprecht
sie	fahren	sie	sprechen
Sie	fahren	Sie	sprechen

A few irregularities occur in present-tense forms. Some verbs change their stem vowel in the **du** form and in the **er, sie, es** forms from **a** to **ä** or from **e** to **ie** (or **i**). All the plural forms of all German verbs except **sein** are regular.

Other verbs with similar vowel change:

ich trage, du trägst, er trägt
ich sehe, du siehst, er sieht (**sehen** *to see*)

Note the additional irregularity in **nehmen**:

ich nehme, du nimmst, er nimmt

PRACTICE

Give the correct present-tense verb forms:

1. du (kommen, sprechen, studieren, fahren, geben, suchen) 2. er (wohnen, sprechen, sagen, kaufen, suchen, tragen) 3. sie (*singular*) (sagen, suchen, geben, nehmen, sehen, fahren)

5. Present Tense of <u>sein</u> (*to be*)

ich	**bin**	*I am*
du	**bist**	*you are*
er, sie, es	**ist**	*he, she, it is*

LAREDO JUNIOR COLLEGE
LAREDO, TEXAS

wir	sind	*we are*
ihr	seid	*you are*
sie	sind	*they are*
Sie	sind	*you are*

PRACTICE

A. *Change the sentence by using the subjects indicated:*

Example: Er ist jetzt in Köln. (*ich*)
Ich bin jetzt in Köln.

1. Er ist Student. (ich)   2. Ich bin in Amerika. (wir)   3. Frau Kolb ist nett. (Herr Kolb)   4. Du bist in Deutschland. (ich)   5. Er ist auf der Universität. (wir)   6. Ihr seid auf dem Dampfer. (ich)   7. Sie ist in dem Zug. (ich)   8. Ich bin in Köln. (er)

B. *Say in German:*

1. I'm Kurt Klein.   2. I'm nineteen years old.   3. I'm tall. 4. My parents are in America.   5. I'm now in Cologne.   6. So, you're Mrs. Kolb?   7. The suitcase is over there.   8. The room is here.   9. The house is clean.   10. We are at the university. 11. Many Germans are at the university.   12. They are very nice. 13. Are you upstairs, Mrs. Kolb?   14. No, I'm downstairs. 15. Children, are you in the house?

6. du, ihr, Sie

Du bist groß für dein Alter, Kurt. (*one child*)
You are tall for your age, Kurt.

Kinder, **ihr geht** jetzt ins Haus. (*several children*)
Children, you are now going into the house.

Herr Klein, **Sie sprechen** fabelhaft Deutsch. (*an adult or stranger*)
You speak marvelous German, Mr. Klein.

There are three German equivalents for the pronoun *you* in direct address:

a. Use **du** as a familiar form of address when speaking with a relative, close friend, child, or animal.

b. Use **ihr** as a familiar form of address when speaking to more than one relative, friend, child, or animal.

c. Use **Sie** (*always capitalized*) as the conventional form of address, both singular and plural.

FINAL PRACTICE   *Say first, then write in German:*

1. I live in Connecticut, but Kurt lives in Milwaukee.   2. He is now in Cologne.   3. He is studying at the university.   4. He is

looking for Mrs. Kolb's house.   5. He is talking to Mrs. Kolb. 6. She is very friendly.   7. Miss Kolb is also very nice.   8. Mrs. Kolb is saying, "So, you are Mr. Klein."   9. She also says, "You speak marvelous German."   10. Miss Kolb says, "The room is downstairs."   11. She shows Kurt the room.   12. Kurt is carrying the suitcase into the house.   13. Kurt is looking for a cab. 14. The cab is over there.   15. Kurt is speaking German.   16. Kurt asks Mrs. Kolb, "Do you have any mail for me?"   17. Here is a letter from America.   18. It is for Kurt.   19. He says, "Thank you and good-by."

Der Kölner Dom
HENLE FROM MONKMEYER

I. UNTERHALTUNG

KURT FÄHRT IN DIE STADT

Frau Kolb:	Was tun Sie denn heute morgen, Herr Klein?
Kurt:	Heute morgen fahre ich in die Stadt. Ich besuche den Dom, die Bibliothek und das Opernhaus.
Frau Kolb:	Sie kennen doch die Stadt nicht. Haben Sie wenigstens einen Stadtplan?
Kurt:	Leider nicht. Ich brauche wirklich einen Plan. Haben Sie einen?
Frau Kolb:	Ich habe einen Stadtplan, aber er ist ziemlich alt. Sie können ihn aber doch gebrauchen. Hier ist er. Nehmen Sie ihn!
Kurt:	Das ist wirklich nett von Ihnen. Recht vielen Dank. Wo ist der Dom, Frau Kolb? Ist er weit von hier?
Frau Kolb:	Aber gar nicht. Er ist rechts um die Ecke. Sie können zu Fuß gehen.
Kurt:	Und die Bibliothek? Ist sie auch ziemlich nahe?
Frau Kolb:	Leider nicht. Gehen Sie an die Ecke und nehmen Sie Bus Nummer 5 (fünf)! Sie sind in zehn (10) Minuten da.

KURT GOES DOWNTOWN

Mrs. Kolb:	Tell me, what are you doing this morning, Mr. Klein?
Kurt:	I'm going downtown this morning. I'll visit the cathedral, the library, and the opera house.
Mrs. Kolb:	But you don't know the city. Do you at least have a map?
Kurt:	I'm afraid not. I really need a map. Do you have one?
Mrs. Kolb:	I have a map, but it's somewhat old. But you can use it just the same. Here it is. Why don't you take it.
Kurt:	That's very nice of you. Thanks a lot. Where is the cathedral, Mrs. Kolb? Is it far from here?
Mrs. Kolb:	Not at all. It's around the corner to the right. You can walk.
Kurt:	And the library? Is it nearby, too?
Mrs. Kolb:	I'm afraid not. Walk to the corner and take bus number 5. You'll be there in ten minutes.

Kurt: Das ist ja nicht weit. Also nehme ich den Bus. Und wo ist das Opernhaus?

Frau Kolb: Direkt gegenüber. Überqueren Sie einfach die Straße! Es ist kein Problem.

Kurt: Vielen Dank für die Auskunft. Ich gehe jetzt.

Frau Kolb: Bitte kommen Sie bald zurück!

Kurt: Auf Wiedersehen. Bis später.

Frau Kolb: Auf Wiedersehen, Herr Klein.

Kurt: That isn't very far. All right then, I'll take the bus. And where is the opera house?

Mrs. Kolb: Right opposite. Just cross the street. There's no problem.

Kurt: Thanks for the information. I'm going now.

Mrs. Kolb: Please come back soon!

Kurt: Good-by. See you later.

Mrs. Kolb: Good-by, Mr. Klein.

II. KOMBINATIONEN

Sagen Sie auf deutsch:

a. 1. What are you doing this morning?   2. What are you doing in Germany?   3. What are you doing in Cologne?

b. 1. This morning I'm going downtown.   2. This morning I'll visit the cathedral.   3. This morning I'll visit the library. 4. This morning I'll visit the opera house.

c. 1. Do you have a map of the city?   2. Do you have a letter? 3. Do you have a problem?

d. 1. I'm afraid not. I need a map.   2. Unfortunately not. I need information.   3. I'm afraid not. I need a room.

e. 1. That is very nice of you, Kurt.   2. That is nice of you, Mr. Klein.   3. Thanks a lot, Mrs. Kolb.

f. 1. Where is the cathedral? Is it far from here?   2. Where is the library? Is it far from here?   3. Where is the opera house? Is it nearby?

g. 1. Where is the taxi? Around the corner to the left?   2. Where is Mrs. Kolb's house? Across the street.   3. Where is the bus? Around the corner to the right.

h. 1. Please cross the street.   2. Please come back soon. 3. Please drive downtown.

III. SAGEN UND FRAGEN

a. *Sie sind Kurt Klein. Sie sagen:*

1. Sie fahren heute morgen in die Stadt. 2. Sie besuchen den Dom und die Bibliothek. 3. Sie besuchen auch das Opernhaus. 4. Sie kennen leider die Stadt nicht. 5. Sie brauchen einen Stadtplan. 6. Sie brauchen wirklich einen Plan. 7. Sie nehmen ihn. 8. Sie gehen zu Fuß zum Dom. 9. Sie gehen an die Ecke. 10. Sie nehmen dort den Bus. 11. Sie nehmen den Bus Nummer 5. 12. Sie sind in fünf Minuten dort. 13. Sie überqueren die Straße. 14. Sie sagen: „Vielen Dank für die Auskunft." 15. Sie kommen bald zurück. 16. Sie sagen: „Auf Wiedersehen."

b. *Sie sind Frau Kolb. Sie fragen Kurt:*

1. was er heute morgen tut (*is doing*). 2. ob er einen Stadtplan hat. 3. ob er einen Stadtplan braucht. 4. ob er an die Ecke geht. 5. ob er den Bus nimmt. 6. ob er die Straße überquert.

c. *Sie sind Kurt. Sie fragen Frau Kolb:*

1. ob sie einen Stadtplan hat. 2. ob der Dom weit von hier ist. 3. ob die Bibliothek nahe ist. 4. wo die Oper ist. 5. ob das Opernhaus nahe ist.

IV. PRONUNCIATION PRACTICE

Consonant Sounds The following consonant sounds do not exist in English:

Phoneme	Spelling
/r/	r, rr

Usually a uvular trill is made by vibrating the uvula against the back of the tongue, not unlike gargling. In final position, this sound more nearly resembles an off-glide. Pronounce: **Ehre, bitter, Reiter.**

When this phoneme is doubled between vowels, the trill is more prolonged: **Herren, Narren, mürrisch.**

Phoneme	Spelling
/x/	ch

There are two ch-sounds. The back sound follows **a, o, u, au.** It is produced by raising the back of the tongue to a position nearly

31

touching the soft palate and expelling the breath under friction: **ach, doch, Buch, Bruch, auch.**

The front sound follows (and occasionally precedes) **e, i,** umlauted vowels, **ei, eu,** and consonants. It is produced by raising the middle of the tongue to a position nearly touching the hard palate and expelling the breath under friction: **echt, ich, Löcher, durch.**

An overly energetic pronunciation of words in English beginning with *hu* will simulate this sound. Try *human, Huey, huge, Hubert.*

Uvular **r**

Repeat after your instructor or the speaker:

1.	/bri:fmarkə/	**Briefmarke**	*postage stamp*
2.	/zark/	**Sarg**	*coffin*
3.	/ra:thaws/	**Rathaus**	*town hall*
4.	/trefən/	**treffen**	*to meet*
5.	/pro:bə/	**Probe**	*rehearsal*
6.	/kindər/	**Kinder**	*children*
7.	/me:r/	**Meer**	*ocean*
8.	/ro:t/	**rot**	*red*
9.	/fa:rən/	**fahren**	*to go (by vehicle); to ride; to drive*
10.	/raysən/	**reißen**	*to tear*

Back **ch,**
after **a, o, u, au**

Repeat after your instructor or the speaker:

1.	/bax/	**Bach**	*stream*
2.	/kox/	**Koch**	*cook*
3.	/brux/	**Bruch**	*fracture*
4.	/bawx/	**Bauch**	*belly*
5.	/flax/	**flach**	*flat*
6.	/axt/	**acht**	*eight*
7.	/awx/	**auch**	*also*
8.	/fruxt/	**Frucht**	*fruit*
9.	/nox/	**noch**	*still*
10.	/flu:x/	**Fluch**	*curse*

Front **ch,**
in the immediate
vicinity of
**ä, e, i, ü, ö,
ei, eu, äu,** and
consonants

Repeat after your instructor or the speaker:

1.	/dixtər/	**Dichter**	*poet*
2.	/rexnən/	**rechnen**	*to reckon*
3.	/xi:na/	**China**	*China*
4.	/xemi:/	**Chemie**	*chemistry*
5.	/löxər/	**Löcher**	*holes*
6.	/bü:xər/	**Bücher**	*books*
7.	/rayxən/	**reichen**	*to reach*
8.	/loyxtən/	**leuchten**	*to shine*
9.	/arxitekt/	**Architekt**	*architect*
10.	/lexəln/	**lächeln**	*to smile*

V. AUFSATZ

KÖLN

Kurt ist erst einen Tag in Köln. Heute macht er eine Stadtrund-
fahrt.¹ Aber zuerst stellt er viele Fragen an Frau Kolb. Sie beantwortet sie alle. Dann gibt sie Kurt einen Stadtplan. Kurt braucht
ihn sehr. Leider ist er nicht neu.

5 Kurt geht an die Ecke. Hier wartet er auf den Bus. Aber er
kommt nicht. Plötzlich sieht Kurt einen Touristenbus.² Er steigt in
den Bus. Er bezahlt sechs (6) Mark für die Fahrt.

Zuerst besuchen sie den Dom. Kurt erkennt sofort den Baustil.³
Er ist gotisch.⁴ Kurt bewundert den Dom. Der Reiseführer erzählt

10 eine Geschichte über den Dom. Er erzählt sie auf französisch. Kurt
versteht kein Wort. Er erzählt dieselbe⁵ Geschichte auf englisch.
Natürlich versteht Kurt jetzt alles. Kurt kennt die Geschichte nicht.
Sie interessiert ihn sehr. Der Reiseführer erzählt sie noch einmal,
diesmal auf deutsch. Er spricht klar und deutlich. Kurt versteht

15 ihn perfekt.

Gerade erklärt der Reiseführer: „Auf deutsch heißt die Stadt
Köln. In England und Frankreich heißt sie ‚Cologne‘. Die Römer⁶
nannten⁷ sie ‚colonia‘, auf deutsch ‚Kolonie‘.“

Jetzt verläßt die Reisegruppe⁸ den Dom. Sie fahren alle zusam-
20 men an den Rhein. Sie bewundern die Brücke. Kurt mag die
schöne Aussicht.⁹ Er findet die Landschaft¹⁰ märchenhaft¹¹
und romantisch.

Danach fahren sie in die Neustadt.¹² Zuerst besuchen sie ein
Museum, eine Kirche, eine Volksschule¹³ und ein Gymnasium.¹⁴
25 Dann sagt der Reiseführer: „Meine Damen und Herren, Sie sind
alle müde. Ich zeige Ihnen¹⁵ nur noch das Theater. Wie das Opernhaus ist es nur ein paar Jahre alt. Dieser Stadtteil¹⁶ ist ganz neu.“

Kurt ist sehr müde. Plötzlich hat er auch Hunger. Er sieht auf
die Uhr. Es ist schon Mittag. Ein Franzose und ein Engländer
30 sammeln¹⁷ Geld für den Reiseführer und den Chauffeur. Sie
sagen: „Vielen Dank für das Trinkgeld.“¹⁸

Kurt denkt: „Ich bin froh, ich bin hier in Köln. Die Stadt ist
schön und modern. Ich mag sie sehr.“

1. city sight-seeing tour. 2. sight-seeing bus. 3. architectural style.
4. Gothic. 5. the same. 6. Romans. 7. called. 8. travel group.
9. view. 10. landscape. 11. like a fairy tale. 12. the new part of
the city. 13. elementary school. 14. (*academic*) high school.
15. you (*dative*). 16. section of the city. 17. are collecting. 18. tip.

Köln: Geschäftsstraße, nur für Fußgänger
GERMAN INFORMATION CENTER

Beantworten Sie die folgenden Fragen:

1. Was macht Kurt heute?   2. Was stellt er an Frau Kolb?
3. Was gibt sie Kurt? 4. Braucht Kurt den Stadtplan? 5. Ist er
neu? 6. Was sieht Kurt plötzlich? 7. Wieviel bezahlt er für die
Fahrt? 8. Was besuchen sie zuerst? 9. Was erzählt der Reiseführer? 10. Kennt Kurt die Geschichte? 11. Wie spricht der
Reiseführer auf deutsch? 12. Wie versteht ihn Kurt? 13. Wie
heißt Köln in England und Frankreich? 14. Wie nannten die
Römer Köln?   15. Wohin (*where*) fahren sie alle zusammen?
16. Was mag Kurt ganz besonders (*particularly*)? 17. Wie findet
er die Landschaft? 18. Wohin fahren sie danach? 19. Was besucht die Gruppe in der Neustadt? 20. Was sagt der Reiseführer? 21. Was sammeln zwei (2) Touristen für den Reiseführer? 22. Was denkt Kurt?

VI. WORTSCHATZ

	alles	everything	die Kirche	church
	also	therefore, consequently	klar	clear
			können (kann)	to be able
die	Auskunft	information	leider	unfortunately
	beantworten	to answer	die Minute	minute
	bei	at the house of	der Mittag	noon
	besuchen	to visit	modern	modern
	bewundern	to admire	mögen (mag)	to like
	bezahlen	to pay	das Museum	museum
die	Bibliothek	library	müde	tired
	brauchen	to need	nahe	near
die	Brücke	bridge	neu	new
der	Bus	bus	die Nummer	number
die	Dame	lady	das Opernhaus	opera house
	danach	afterwards, after that	paar: ein paar	a couple, few
	dann	then	perfekt	perfect
	denken	to think	der Plan	plan
	deutlich	distinct	plötzlich	suddenly
	diesmal	this time	das Problem	problem
	direkt	direct	recht	right
der	Dom	cathedral	rechts	right, to the right
	einfach	simple	die Reise	trip, journey
	einmal	once	der Reiseführer	guide
(das)	England	England	romantisch	romantic
der	Engländer	Englishman	die Schule	school
	erkennen	to recognize	sehen (sieht)	to see
	erklären	to explain	sehen auf	to look at
die	Fahrt	trip	der Stadtplan	city map
	finden	to find	steigen in	to get on
(das)	Frankreich	France	stellen	to put, place
der	Franzose	Frenchman	Fragen	to ask questions
	französisch	French	stellen an	of
	auf französisch	in French	die Straße	street
	froh	glad, happy	das Theater	theater
der	Fuß	foot	tun	to do
	ganz	quite	über	over, about
	gar nicht	not at all	überqueren	to cross
	gebrauchen	to use	die Uhr	clock, watch
	gegenüber	across, opposite	um	around
das	Geld	money	verlassen	to leave
	gerade	just	warten	to wait
die	Geschichte	story, history	weit	far
der	Hunger	hunger	wenigstens	at least
	Hunger haben	to be hungry	wirklich	really
	interessieren	to interest	das Wort	word
	ja (adverb)	certainly, you know	ziemlich	somewhat, rather
			zuerst	first, at first
	kennen	to know, be acquainted with	zurück	back

VII. ERKLÄRUNGEN UND ÜBUNGEN

1. Accusative Case Er sieht **den Dom.**   Kurt versteht **kein Wort.**
He sees the cathedral.   *Kurt doesn't understand a word.*

Kurt bewundert **die Stadt.**   Er besucht auch **eine Bibliothek.**
Kurt admires the city.   *He also visits a library.*

The accusative is the case of the direct object, the word or words toward which the action of the verb is directed.

a. Forms

Masculine	Feminine	Neuter
Nom. **der** Vater	**die** Mutter	**das** Kind
Acc. **den** Vater	**die** Mutter	**das** Kind
key sound: /n/		

Nom. **ein** Vater	**eine** Mutter	**ein** Kind
Acc. **einen** Vater	**eine** Mutter	**ein** Kind
key sound: /n/		

The forms of **kein** (*not a*) are like those of **ein:**

Nom. **kein** Vater	**keine** Mutter	**kein** Kind
Acc. **keinen** Vater	**keine** Mutter	**kein** Kind
key sound: /n/		

The 3rd-person pronouns:

Nom. **er**	*key sound:* /r/	**sie** } *key sound:*		**es** } *key sound:*	
Acc. **ihn**	*key sound:* /n/	**sie** } /i:/		**es** } /s/	
him, it		*her, it*		*it, him, her*	

Only the masculine article and pronoun differ in the accusative from the nominative; the feminine and neuter forms are identical for both cases. Learn to identify now the sound of /n/ for the masculine accusative singular.

The forms of the remaining personal pronouns are:

Nominative:	**ich**	Accusative:	**mich** (*me*)
	du		**dich** (*you,* familiar singular)
	wir		**uns** (*us*)
	ihr		**euch** (*you,* familiar plural)
	sie } *key sound:* /i:/		{ **sie** (*them*)
	Sie }		{ **Sie** (*you,* conventional form)

PRACTICE

A. *Give the accusative forms:*

1.	die Frau	11.	die Familie
2.	das Haus	12.	der Fuß
3.	ein Lehrer	13.	kein Stadtplan
4.	der Kaffee	14.	eine Mark
5.	ein Zimmer	15.	die Stadt
6.	die Fahrkarte	16.	kein Hunger
7.	ein Kind	17.	er
8.	eine Frage	18.	sie
9.	der Staat	19.	es
10.	die Post	20.	wir

B. *Answer the following questions in accordance with the example:*

Example: Kennen Sie die Stadt?
Ja, ich kenne die Stadt.
Ich kenne sie auch.

1. Bewundern Sie die Aussicht? 2. Bewundern Sie den Dom? 3. Sehen Sie den Reiseführer? 4. Verstehen Sie die Geschichte? 5. Haben Sie den Stadtplan? 6. Nehmen Sie den Bus? 7. Besuchen Sie die Bibliothek? 8. Sehen Sie die Kirche? 9. Erkennen Sie das Theater? 10. Besuchen Sie das Gymnasium?

C. *Answer the following questions negatively:*

Example: Haben Sie einen Stadtplan?
Nein, ich habe keinen Stadtplan.

1. Verstehen Sie ein Wort? 2. Haben Sie einen Koffer? 3. Erzählen Sie eine Geschichte? 4. Brauchen Sie ein Taxi? 5. Stellen Sie eine Frage? 6. Besuchen Sie eine Schule? 7. Kennen Sie einen Engländer? 8. Beantworten Sie eine Frage?

D. *Replace the nouns with pronouns:*

Example: Erkennen Sie den Baustil?
Ja, ich erkenne ihn.

1. Erkennen Sie den Dom? 2. Besuchen Sie die Oper? 3. Bewundern Sie die Aussicht? 4. Erzählen Sie die Geschichte? 5. Verstehen Sie den Reiseführer auf französisch? 6. Besuchen Sie das Museum? 7. Mögen Sie den Baustil?

E. *Say in German:*

1. He sees her. 2. I see him. 3. They admire it. 4. They know it. 5. I'll visit you, Mr. Klein. 6. They recognize us. 7. I recognize them. 8. He understands me. 9. I understand you,

Mrs. Kolb. 10. Mrs. Kolb understands me. 11. We know you (*familiar plural*).

F. *Say in German:*

1. I am visiting the cathedral, the library, and the opera house. 2. I admire the cathedral; I also admire the opera house. 3. A guide is telling a story. 4. I recognize him. 5. Kurt understands him perfectly. 6. Do you understand the story? 7. Are you visiting the new part of the city? 8. Yes, we are visiting it. 9. They have money for the guide. 10. The guide knows me. 11. He knows us all.

2. Negation
a. Nein

Fährt Kurt nach Europa? **Nein.**
Is Kurt going to Europe? No.

Nein means *no* in answer to a question. It is the negative counterpart of **ja.**

b. Nicht

Er versteht nicht.
He doesn't understand.

Kurt versteht den Reiseführer nicht.
Kurt doesn't understand the guide.

Dr. Stauffer ist **nicht sein Professor.**
Dr. Stauffer is not his professor.

Sie wohnt **nicht in Amerika.**
She doesn't live in America.

Der Bus ist **nicht an der Ecke.**
The bus isn't at the corner.

Nicht (*not*) negates a statement, word, or phrase. It tends to stand at the end of the sentence. When it negates a single item, it precedes that item.

c. Kein

Kein Student wohnt hier.
No student lives here.

Er ist **kein Reiseführer.**
He is not a guide.

Ich sehe **kein Haus** hier.
I don't see any house here.

Kein is the negative form of the article **ein** and takes the same endings as **ein.** It may mean, depending on the context, *no, not a,* or *not any.*

PRACTICE

A. *Answer the following questions with* **nein** *and a subject pronoun:*

Example: Ist Kurt in Stuttgart?
Nein, er ist nicht in Stuttgart.

1. Fährt Kurt mit dem Dampfer nach Köln? 2. Besucht Kurt zuerst Frau Kolb? 3. Ist Kurt groß und stark für sein Alter? 4. Studiert Kurt in Frankreich? 5. Ist das Studium in Deutschland teuer? 6. Fährt der Chauffeur Kurt zum Dom? 7. Ist Frau Kolb immer nett und freundlich? 8. Ist das Zimmer bei Frau Kolb sauber? 9. Erkennt Kùrt sofort den Baustil? 10. Sind das Theater und das Opernhaus alt?

B. *Respond in accordance with the example:*

Example: Hier ist ein Stadtplan.
Ich sehe keinen Stadtplan.

1. Hier ist ein Taxi. 2. Hier ist ein Bus. 3. Hier ist ein Theater. 4. Hier ist eine Kirche. 5. Hier ist ein Zug. 6. Hier ist ein Reiseführer. 7. Hier ist ein Professor. 8. Hier ist eine Uhr. 9. Hier ist ein Chauffeur. 10. Hier ist ein Museum. 11. Hier ist eine Brücke.

3. Word Order

a. Normal Word Order

S   V
Ich fahre heute in die Stadt.
I'm going downtown today.

   S   V
Viele Deutsche wohnen in Milwaukee.
Many Germans live in Milwaukee.

Normal word order in German for simple statements is: subject (S)—verb (V). This word order is also characteristic of English.

b. Inverted Word Order

  V   S
Fahren Sie heute in die Stadt? Ja.
Are you going to town today? Yes.

Subject and verb are inverted for yes-no questions. We have already practiced this word order many times.

     V   S
Heute fahre ich in die Stadt.
Today I'm going downtown.

     V   S
In Milwaukee wohnen viele Deutsche.
Many Germans live in Milwaukee.

For special emphasis or stylistic variety a word or phrase other than the subject may stand first in the sentence. The subject then follows the verb directly.

PRACTICE   *Begin each sentence with the indicated word or words:*

1. Kurt fährt *heute* in die Stadt.   2. Er sieht *zuerst* den Dom.
3. Er besucht *dann* die Bibliothek.   4. Er besucht auch *später* das Opernhaus.   5. Kurt hat *plötzlich* Hunger.   6. Er sieht *sofort* auf die Uhr.   7. Es ist *jetzt* Zeit (*time*) zum Mittagessen.[1]

4. Present Tense of haben (to have)

ich	habe	*I have, am having*
du	hast	*you have, are having*
er, sie, es	hat	*he, she, it has, is having*
wir	haben	*we have, are having*
ihr	habt	*you have, are having*
sie	haben	*they have, are having*
Sie	haben	*you have, are having*

PRACTICE   A.   *Give the correct forms of* **haben** *in accordance with the subject indicated:*

Example: Kurt hat ein Problem. (*ich*)
Ich habe ein Problem.

1. Frau Kolb.   2. Fräulein Kolb.   3. Herr Klein.   4. Wir.
5. Herr und Frau Kolb.   6. Viele Deutsche.   7. Du.   8. Ihr.

B.   *Answer the following questions, first with* **ja,** *then with* **nein:**

Example: Haben Sie eine Fahrkarte?
Ja, ich habe eine Fahrkarte.
Nein, ich habe keine Fahrkarte.

1. Haben Sie ein Haus?   2. Haben Sie ein Auto?   3. Haben Sie einen Stadtplan?   4. Haben Sie einen Brief für mich?   5. Haben Sie einen Koffer?   6. Haben Sie ein Problem?   7. Haben Sie eine Uhr?   8. Haben Sie ein Haus in Milwaukee?

C.   *Answer the same questions in exercise B with* **wir:**

Example: Haben Sie eine Fahrkarte?
Ja, wir haben eine Fahrkarte.
Nein, wir haben keine Fahrkarte.

D.   *Say in German:*

1. I have a house in America.   2. Kurt has a room in Cologne.
3. We also have a room in Cologne.   4. Do you have a letter

1. The main meal is usually eaten at midday.

from Berlin? 5. No, he has a letter from New York. 6. I have a suitcase downstairs. 7. They have money. 8. Mr. and Mrs. Kolb have mail for Kurt.

5. Imperative
a. Conventional Imperative

Bringen Sie den Koffer!
Bring the suitcase.

Gehen Sie an die Ecke!
Walk to the corner.

A conventional imperative (a command, request, or suggestion to a person or persons addressed with **Sie**) consists of the **-en** form of the verb followed by **Sie.** Note: Imperatives in German are usually followed by an exclamation mark.

b. Familiar Singular Imperative

Geh(e) in die Bibliothek, Kurt!
Go to the library, Kurt.

Bitte **bleib(e)** hier, Johann!
Please stay here, John.

The familiar singular imperative (a command, request, or suggestion to a person addressed with **du**) is formed by adding **-e** to the present stem. This **e** is often dropped in colloquial German.

Note:
trage (trag)!
carry; wear

fahre (fahr)!
drive

laufe (lauf)!
run

Verbs changing their stem vowel from **a** to **ä** and from **au** to **äu** in the 2nd and 3rd persons singular of the present tense have no umlaut in the familiar imperative.

Exceptions:
lies!
read

sprich!
talk, speak

hilf!
help

Verbs changing their stem vowel from **e** to **i** (or **ie**) in the 2nd and 3rd persons singular of the present tense also change in the familiar imperative, but never add **e**.

c. Familiar Plural
Imperative

Sprecht nur Deutsch, Kinder!
Speak only German, children.

Lauft nicht!
Don't run.

The familiar plural imperative is identical with the 2nd person plural minus **ihr.**

d. First Person
Plural Imperative

Nehmen wir Bus Nummer 5!
Let's take bus number 5!

Gehen wir zu Fuß!
Let's walk!

The first person plural imperative is the inverted **wir**-form of the verb and has the force of *let's.*

PRACTICE

A. *Form imperatives by asking Mrs. Kolb to do the following:*

Example: Deutsch sprechen
Sprechen Sie Deutsch, Frau Kolb!

1. die Post ins Zimmer tragen. 2. den Koffer ins Zimmer bringen. 3. Kurt den Brief aus Amerika geben. 4. einmal Amerika besuchen. 5. die Tür öffnen. 6. Kurt einen Stadtplan geben. 7. die schöne Aussicht bewundern. 8. mit Kurt zum Dom fahren.

B. *Tell Johann to do the things in exercise A:*

Example: Sprich Deutsch, Johann!

C. *Tell Johann and his friend Horst to do the things in exercise A:*

Example: Sprecht Deutsch, Johann und Horst!

D. *Say in German:*

1. Walk to the corner, Kurt. 2. Speak German, Kurt. 3. Ask the question. 4. Say it. 5. Buy it. 6. Learn French, John. 7. Open the door, children. 8. Please take the city map. 9. Wait for the bus. 10. Visit the museum. 11. Take the bus, Kurt.

FINAL PRACTICE

Say first, then write in German:

1. Today Kurt is going downtown. 2. First he visits the cathedral, then the library and the museum. 3. Mrs. Kolb is saying, "The cathedral is far. Take the bus, Mr. Klein." 4. Kurt walks to the corner and takes the bus. 5. Kurt says, "Thanks for the

information." 6. Kurt sees the cathedral. He recognizes the architecture; it is Gothic. 7. A guide is telling a story; he explains everything. 8. Do you know the story? Yes, I know it. 9. Do you also know the guide? No, I don't know him. 10. The guide tells the same story in French. Kurt doesn't understand a word. 11. Now he is telling it in German. Kurt understands him perfectly. 12. Here is the bridge over the Rhine. 13. Kurt admires the view. 14. They are now crossing the street. 15. Directly across they see the university. 16. They also visit the theater, the opera, and the Gymnasium. 17. Kurt has a tip for the chauffeur. 18. He thinks, "I'm glad I'm here in Cologne. The city is beautiful and modern."

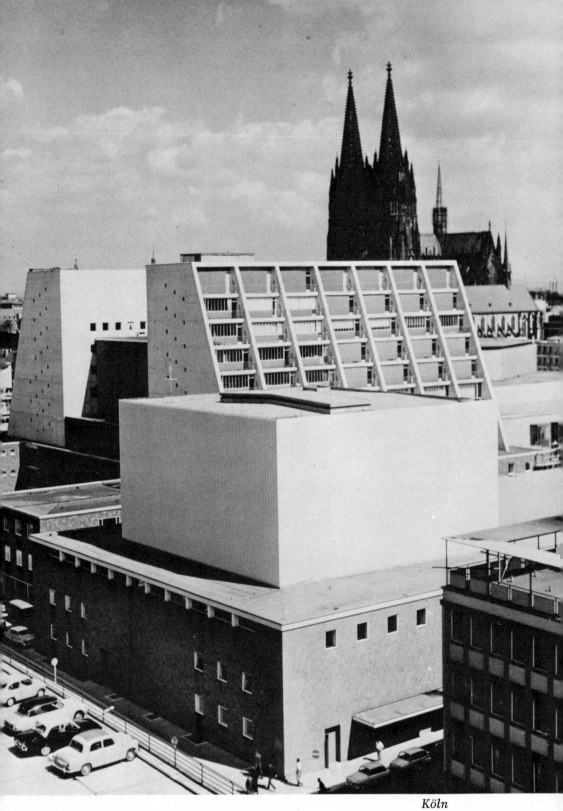

Köln
LUFTHANSA ARCHIVE

I. UNTERHALTUNG

AUF DER UNIVERSITÄT

Dekan: Sie sind also schon eine Woche in Köln. Und wie lange sind Sie schon in Deutschland?

Kurt: Ebenfalls eine Woche.

Dekan: Hoffentlich haben Sie Ihren Paß.

Kurt: Hier ist der Paß. Wo soll ich die Semestergebühren bezahlen?

Dekan: Gehen Sie bitte in das Büro gegenüber. Die Sekretärin kann Ihnen Auskunft geben. Um diese Zeit ist sie immer da.

Kurt: Noch eine Frage, Herr Dekan. Ich möchte unbedingt mein Deutsch verbessern. Wie lange soll ich hier bleiben? Können Sie mir einen Rat geben?

Dekan: Wenigstens ein Jahr, vielleicht zwei Jahre. Lesen Sie jeden Tag die Zeitung, besuchen Sie ziemlich oft das Kino oder das Theater! Suchen Sie sich auch einen Freund ohne englische Sprachkenntnisse! Kommen Sie regelmäßig in den Unterricht! Nur durch Übung können Sie lernen. Auch müssen Sie fleißig arbeiten.

AT THE UNIVERSITY

Dean: So you've been in Cologne for a week. And how long have you been in Germany?

Kurt: Also a week.

Dean: I hope you have your passport.

Kurt: Here is the passport. Where am I supposed to pay tuition for the semester?

Dean: Go to the office across the hall. The secretary can give you the information. At this time she's always in.

Kurt: One more question, sir. I definitely want to improve my German. How long should I stay here? Can you give me some advice?

Dean: At least one year, maybe two. Read the newspaper every day, go to the movies or the theater fairly often. Also find yourself a friend without any knowledge of English. Come to class regularly. Only through practice can you learn. You also have to work hard.

LESSON 3

45

Kurt: Vielen Dank für die Auskunft und die Hilfe, Herr Dekan. Auf Wiedersehen.

(Im Büro)

Kurt: Können Sie mir bitte sagen, was die Vorlesungen kosten?

Sekretärin: Sie zahlen 300 (dreihundert) Mark für das Semester. Sie studieren Literatur und Philosophie, nicht wahr?

Kurt: Ja, das stimmt.

Sekretärin: Wollen Sie privat wohnen oder im Studentenheim?

Kurt: Privat, aber ich möchte in der Mensa essen.

Sekretärin: Für eine Mahlzeit zahlen Sie zwei Mark. Viel Glück in Deutschland!

Kurt: Thanks for the information and the help, sir. Good-by.

(In the office)

Kurt: Can you tell me how much the lectures will cost (the tuition is)?

Secretary: You pay 300 marks for the semester. Am I right, you are taking up literature and philosophy?

Kurt: That's right.

Secretary: Do you want to live in a private home or in the dorm?

Kurt: In a private home, but I'd like to eat in the dining hall.

Secretary: You pay two marks per meal. Good luck in Germany!

II. KOMBINATIONEN

Sagen Sie auf deutsch:

a. 1. So you've been in Germany for a week. 2. So you've been in Cologne for a week. 3. So you've been here at the university for a week.

b. 1. How long have you been in Germany? 2. How long have you been in Cologne? 3. How long have you been in the city?

c. 1. I hope you have a passport. 2. I hope you have 300 marks. 3. I hope you have 2 marks for the bus.

d. 1. Where am I supposed to pay tuition? 2. Where am I supposed to find the secretary? 3. Where am I supposed to work?

e. 1. At this time she's always in. 2. At this time she's always at the university. 3. At this time she's over there.

f. 1. I definitely want to improve my German. 2. I definitely want to visit Hamburg. 3. I definitely want to pay my tuition now.

g. 1. Can you give me some advice? 2. Can you give Kurt some advice? 3. Can you give Mrs. Kolb some advice?

h. 1. Come to class regularly. 2. Attend the theater regularly. 3. Read the paper regularly.

i. 1. Can you tell me how much that costs? 2. Can you tell me where the dean is? 3. Can you tell me where the office is?

j. 1. Do you want to live in a private home? 2. Do you want to live in the dormitory? 3. Do you want to live in Cologne?

III. SAGEN UND FRAGEN

a. *Sie sind Kurt Klein. Sie sagen:*

1. Sie sind genau eine Woche in Köln. 2. Sie haben einen Paß. 3. Sie bezahlen die Semestergebühren. 4. Sie gehen in das Büro gegenüber. 5. Sie möchten unbedingt Ihr Deutsch verbessern. 6. Sie haben noch eine Frage. 7. Sie lesen jeden Tag die Zeitung. 8. Sie besuchen sehr oft die Oper. 9. Sie haben einen Freund ohne englische Sprachkenntnisse. 10. Sie kommen regelmäßig in den Unterricht. 11. Sie studieren Literatur und Philosophie. 12. Sie lernen besser durch Übung. 13. Sie danken für die Auskunft und die Hilfe. 14. Sie möchten wissen, wieviel das kostet. 15. Sie zahlen 300 (dreihundert) Mark für das Semester. 16. Sie wohnen privat. 17. Sie wohnen nicht im Studentenheim. 18. Sie essen in der Mensa. 19. Sie sind um die Mittagszeit zurück. 20. Sie sagen „Auf Wiedersehen".

b. *Sie sind der Dekan. Sie fragen Kurt:*

1. wie lange er schon in Deutschland ist. 2. ob er seinen Paß hat. 3. ob er einen Rat braucht. 4. ob er einen Freund in Köln hat. 5. ob er einen Freund sucht. 6. wie oft er in den Unterricht kommt. 7. ob er Literatur studiert. 8. ob er auch Philosophie studiert. 9. wie lange er in Köln bleibt. 10. ob er privat wohnen will.

IV. PRONUNCIATION PRACTICE

Consonant Sounds The following consonant sound does not exist in American English:

Phoneme	Spelling
/l/	l, ll

This sound is produced by touching the flattened tip of the tongue to the back of the upper teeth.

Pronounce:

lassen   Welle   hell   Milch

Phoneme	Spelling
/ts/	z, tz, t (*in* -tion)

This sound occurs in English, but rarely in initial position. Notice, in the following English words, the occurrence of *ts: cuts, huts, catsup, Mattson*

Now practice a few German examples:

Blitz   setzen   Nation   zu   Zeichen

Phoneme	Spelling
/pf/	pf

Pronounce both **p** *and* **f** *as in English* oomph *and then try:*

Sumpf   Apfel   Pfund   Pfeife

Front l

Repeat after your instructor or the speaker:

1.	/hel/	hell	*bright*
2.	/aləs/	alles	*everything*
3.	/brilə/	Brille	*spectacles*
4.	/layzə/	leise	*soft*
5.	/oylə/	Eule	*owl*
6.	/fi:l/	viel	*much*
7.	/falš/	falsch	*false*
8.	/blu:mə/	Blume	*flower*
9.	/last/	Last	*burden*
10.	/belən/	bellen	*to bark*

Affricate /ts/

Repeat after your instructor or the speaker:

1.	/tsa:l/	Zahl	*number*
2.	/zats/	Satz	*sentence*
3.	/katsə/	Katze	*cat*
4.	/zitsən/	sitzen	*to sit*
5.	/tsayt/	Zeit	*time*
6.	/letst/	letzt	*last*

7.	/tsvay/	**zwei**	*two*
8.	/tsvantsix/	**zwanzig**	*twenty*
9.	/hitsə/	**Hitze**	*heat*
10.	/tsu:kunft/	**Zukunft**	*future*

Affricate /pf/   *Repeat after your instructor or the speaker:*

1.	/pfayl/	**Pfeil**	*arrow*
2.	/kopf/	**Kopf**	*head*
3.	/trumpf/	**Trumpf**	*trump*
4.	/pflastər/	**Pflaster**	*plaster*
5.	/gipfəl/	**Gipfel**	*summit*
6.	/pfert/	**Pferd**	*horse*
7.	/pflu:k/	**Pflug**	*plow*
8.	/hüpfən/	**hüpfen**	*to hop*
9.	/klopfən/	**klopfen**	*to knock*
10.	/pfirzix/	**Pfirsich**	*peach*

V. AUFSATZ

ÜBER DIE UNIVERSITÄT IN DEUTSCHLAND

Kurt besucht schon einen Monat die Universität Köln. Jeden Morgen spaziert er gemütlich zur Universität. Manchmal trifft er einen Freund unterwegs.[1] Dann gehen sie zusammen in den Hörsaal.[2] Sie setzen sich nebeneinander[3] auf die Bank[4] und warten
5 geduldig[5] auf den Professor. Kurt weiß leider nicht viel über die Universität in Deutschland. Er will ein Buch über das Universitätsleben lesen.

Er liest zum Beispiel: Für die Universität in Deutschland ist die Forschung[6] oft wichtiger als[7] die Erziehung.[8] Man hat viel In-
10 teresse an der Theorie,[9] weniger[10] an der Praxis.[11] Die Universität in Deutschland ist hauptsächlich[12] bekannt für das Studium der Philosophie, Geschichte und Sprachwissenschaft.[13] Heute besteht auch Interesse für Chemie,[14] Physik[15] und Technologie.[16] Die Universität muß modern sein.

15 Kurt liest weiter. Alle Universitäten haben eine Tradition[17] und

1. on the way. 2. lecture hall. 3. **sie setzen sich nebeneinander** they sit down next to one another. 4. bench. 5. patiently. 6. research. 7. **wichtiger als** more important than. 8. education. 9. **Interesse an der Theorie haben** to be interested in the theory. 10. less. 11. practice. 12. principally. 13. philology. 14. chemistry. 15. physics. 16. technology. 17. tradition.

erhalten die Erinnerung an[18] einen großen Lehrer aufrecht, wie z.B. Kant in Königsberg oder Hegel in Berlin. Der Professor in Deutschland ist Staatsbeamter,[19] aber er denkt und darf schreiben, was er will.

20   Kurt versteht jetzt viel. Er weiß aber, er muß noch mehr lernen.

Beantworten Sie die folgenden Fragen:

1. Wie lange besucht Kurt schon die Universität?   2. Fährt er zur Universität?   3. Wen trifft er unterwegs?   4. Auf wen (*for whom*) warten Kurt und der Freund?   5. Was für ein (*what kind of*) Buch will Kurt lesen?   6. Hat eine deutsche Universität mehr Interesse für Theorie oder Praxis?   7. Für welche Fächer (*what subjects*) ist die deutsche Universität hauptsächlich bekannt?   8. Was haben alle Universitäten?   9. Was ist der Professor in Deutschland?   10. Darf er schreiben, was er denkt?

18. die Erinnerung an . . . aufrechterhalten to foster, preserve the memory of. . .   **19.** government official, civil servant.

VI.   WORTSCHATZ

arbeiten	to work	die Mahlzeit	meal
das Beispiel	example	man	one, people, you
zum Bei-	for example	manchmal	sometimes
spiel	(*e.g.*)	mehr	more
(z.B.)		die Mensa	dining hall, school cafeteria
bekannt	known		
bestehen	to exist	der Mittag	midday, noon
bringen	to bring; to take	zu Mittag	to eat the mid-
das Buch	book	essen	day meal,
das Büro	office		have lunch
der Dekan	dean	der Monat	month
ebenfalls	likewise	oft	often
fleißig	industriously	der Paß	passport
gemütlich	leisurely	die Philosophie	philosophy
das Glück	luck	privat	privately
der Freund	friend	der Professor	professor
die Freundin	girl friend	der Rat	(piece of) advice
die Hilfe	help	regelmäßig	regular
hoffentlich	it is to be hoped, I hope	schreiben	to write
		die Sekretärin	secretary
immer	always	das Semester	semester
das Interesse	interest	die Semester-	tuition, fees
das Kino	movie theater	gebühren	(*for a semester*)
kosten	to cost	(*plural*)	
das Leben	life	spazieren	to walk
lesen	to read		
die Literatur	literature		

50

die **Sprachkennt-** **nisse** (*plural*)	language ability	der **Unterricht** **verbessern** **viel**	instruction to improve much
stimmen	to be correct	**vielleicht**	perhaps
das **Studenten-** **heim**	students' home (*dormitory*)	die **Vorlesung** **weiter**	lecture further, on
treffen	to meet	die **Woche**	week
die **Übung**	practice, exercise	**zahlen**	to pay
unbedingt	absolutely	die **Zeit**	time
die **Universität**	university	die **Zeitung**	newspaper

VII. ERKLÄRUNGEN UND ÜBUNGEN

1. Prepositions with Accusative

Vielen Dank **für die Auskunft** und **die Hilfe!**
Thanks a lot for the information and the help.

Um diese Zeit ist sie immer da.
She's always there at this time.

In German, words dependent on prepositions assume certain case forms.

The following common prepositions are always followed by accusative forms:

durch	*through, by*	**gegen**	*against, toward*
für	*for*	**ohne**	*without*
	um	*around, at* (*time*)	

PRACTICE

A. Combine the following expressions with **für**:

Example: ein Haus — der Vater
ein Haus für den Vater

1. eine Garage — das Auto 2. ein Zimmer — der Professor 3. ein Problem — die Mutter 4. eine Zeitung — die Frau 5. ein Trinkgeld — der Chauffeur 6. eine Fahrkarte — die Reise 7. ein Buch — die Dame 8. eine Reise — die Familie 9. eine Uhr — das Zimmer 10. die Auskunft — der Amerikaner

B. Connect the following phrases with **für**:

Example: Ich suche ein Haus — ein Freund.
Ich suche ein Haus für einen Freund.

1. Ich bezahle die Semestergebühren — eine Freundin. 2. Ich bezahle nur zwei Mark — eine Mahlzeit. 3. Die Sekretärin

schreibt einen Brief — der Dekan. 4. Kurt bringt ein Buch — die Schwester. 5. Sie kauft einen Stadtplan — der Freund.

C. *Say in German:*

1. through (the city, the house, the cathedral, the theater)
2. without (a father, a mother, him, her, them) 3. against (the theory, the tradition, the church, the plan) 4. around (the house, the room, him, me, her) 5. for (the teacher, the professor, us, them)

2. Motion with the Accusative

Er geht **in das Büro.**
He goes into the office.

Er fährt **in die Stadt.**
He's driving into town.

Ich gehe **an die Ecke.**
I'm going to the corner.

Observe the examples above. When followed by accusative forms, certain prepositions answer the question **wohin?** (*to what place? where [to]?*). The following prepositions require accusative forms when expressing motion or direction:

an	*on, at, to, up to*[1]
auf	*on, upon, on top of*[1]
hinter	*behind, in back of*
in	*in, into*
neben	*beside, next to*
über	*over, above, about*
unter	*under, among*
vor	*before, in front of*
zwischen	*between*

Note: These prepositions always require accusative forms in a figurative sense or in certain fixed expressions:

Er spricht oft **über den Professor.**
He often talks about the professor.

Er wartet auf den Bus.
He's waiting for the bus.

1. **An** and **auf** may both mean *on*; **an** is used for vertical surfaces (**an die Tür**); **auf** is used for horizontal surfaces (**auf den Tisch**).

PRACTICE

A. Answer the following questions using the indicated phrases in your answer:

Example: Wohin gehen Sie? (*in das Zimmer*)
Ich gehe in das Zimmer.

1. Wohin reisen Sie? (an den Rhein) 2. Wohin spazieren Sie? (in den Park) 3. Wohin fahren Sie? (hinter den Dom) 4. Wohin bringen Sie das Buch? (in die Bibliothek) 5. Wohin gehen Sie heute? (in die Oper) 6. Wohin bringt Kurt den Paß? (in das Büro) 7. Wohin trägt Herr Kolb den Koffer? (in das Zimmer) 8. Wohin fährt der Chauffeur den Amerikaner? (vor mein Haus) 9. Wohin bringen Sie das Geld? (auf die Bank) 10. Wohin gehen Sie jetzt? (in die Kirche)

B. Say in German:

1. They are all going to town. 2. Kurt goes to the library. 3. Then he brings a book into the dining hall. 4. I take a book into the dormitory, but not into the dining hall. 5. We are waiting for the professor. 6. We are talking about (the) university life in Germany. 7. We're also talking about the trip. 8. We're driving to the Rhine tomorrow.

3. Accusative of Time and Space

Sie kommt **diesen Monat**.
She's coming this month.

Er bleibt **einen Tag** in Hamburg.
He's staying in Hamburg for one day.

Er geht **den ganzen Weg** zu Fuß.
He's walking the whole distance (all the way).

The accusative is used to express definite time, duration of time, and extent of space.

Note: Expressions of time precede expressions of place.

PRACTICE

A. Answer the following questions using the indicated phrases in your answers:

Example: Wann fahren Sie in die Stadt? (*diese Woche*)
Ich fahre diese Woche in die Stadt.

1. Wann fahren Sie nach Berlin? (nächsten [*next*] Monat) 2. Wie lange bleiben Sie dort? (zwei Tage) 3. Wann kommt Professor Schmidt? (diese Woche) 4. Wie lange bleibt er hier? (nur einen Tag) 5. Wann fährt er wieder nach Bremen? (den nächsten Tag)

B.   *Say in German:*

1. He is studying at the university for one year.   2. I am staying for only a month.   3. He will be (*use present tense*) in Cologne for only one day.   4. I will be here for only a week.

4. Modal Auxiliary Verbs

Modal auxiliary verbs are helping verbs followed by an infinitive which may be either expressed or understood. They do not usually express a specific action, but rather an attitude toward the action expressed by the infinitive of the verb they modify.

a. Forms

	dürfen	**können**	**mögen**
ich	darf	kann	mag
du	darfst	kannst	magst
er	darf	kann	mag
wir	dürfen	können	mögen
ihr	dürft	könnt	mögt
sie	dürfen	können	mögen
Sie	dürfen	können	mögen

	müssen	**sollen**	**wollen**
ich	muß	soll	will
du	mußt	sollst	willst
er	muß	soll	will
wir	müssen	sollen	wollen
ihr	müßt	sollt	wollt
sie	müssen	sollen	wollen
Sie	müssen	sollen	wollen

Note that the **ich** and **er** forms have no endings.

b. Meanings

dürfen expresses permission

> ich **darf:** *I am permitted to, allowed to, may*
> but
> ich **darf nicht:** *I must not*

können expresses ability

> ich **kann:** *I am able to, can, know how to*

mögen expresses liking or possibility

> ich **mag:** *I like (to), care to, may, have a mind to*

müssen expresses necessity or compulsion

ich **muß:** *I must, have to, it is necessary that I* . . .

sollen expresses moral compulsion or expectation

ich **soll:** *I am supposed to, should, shall, ought to, am to, am said to, am expected to*

wollen expresses intention or strong desire

ich **will:** *I want to, wish to, intend to, start to, claim to*

c. Word Order with Modals

Kurt darf in Deutschland **studieren.**
Kurt is permitted to study in Germany.

Sie können heute nicht hier **bleiben.**
You can't stay here today.

Wollen Sie in dem Studentenheim **wohnen?**
Do you want to live in the dorm?

An infinitive dependent on a modal auxiliary stands last in a main clause.

PRACTICE

A. Give the proper form of the modal:

1. **können**   (ich, er, wir, Sie)
2. **dürfen**   (du, ihr, sie [*singular*], sie [*plural*])
3. **mögen**   (ich, du, wir)
4. **sollen**   (wir, Sie, er, ich)
5. **wollen**   (sie [*singular*], ich, wir, Sie)
6. **müssen**   (ich, du, Sie, wir)

B. Substitute the proper present-tense form of the modal auxiliary indicated:

Example: Kurt studiert in Deutschland. (*wollen*)
Kurt will in Deutschland studieren.

1. Er bleibt ein Jahr in Köln. (sollen) 2. Er spricht besser Deutsch. (wollen)   3. Er kommt regelmäßig in den Unterricht. (müssen) 4. Er ist um zwei Uhr im Hörsaal. (sollen) 5. Ich treffe ihn da. (wollen) 6. Kurt gibt mir (*me*) ein Buch. (wollen) 7. Ich lese das Buch nicht. (können)   8. Es ist aber interessant. (sollen)

C.   *Answer the following questions with the indicated words:*

1. Wieviel muß man für eine Mahlzeit bezahlen? (zwei Mark)
2. Wie lange soll Kurt in Deutschland bleiben? (vielleicht zwei
Jahre)   3. Wem (*to whom*) soll der Dekan einen Rat geben?
(Kurt)   4. Wann darf Kurt für die Vorlesungen bezahlen?
(heute)   5. Was muß er haben? (einen Paß)   6. Wo kann Kurt
seine Semestergebühren bezahlen? (im Büro)   7. Wo will er
wohnen? (privat)   8. Wo will er essen? (in der Mensa)   9. Wohin soll Kurt regelmäßig kommen? (in den Unterricht)   10. Was
will er studieren? (Philosophie und Literatur)

5. Wissen

ich	**weiß**	I know	wir	**wissen**	we know
du	**weißt**	you know	ihr	**wißt**	you know
er	**weiß**	he knows	sie	**wissen**	they know
			Sie	**wissen**	you know

The verb **wissen** follows the conjugational pattern of the modals.

**6. Idiomatic
Present**

Sie ist schon eine Woche in Köln.
She has been in Cologne for a week.

Wie lange **wohnen Sie schon** hier?
How long have you been living here?

Use the present tense plus **schon** to express an action that began in
the past and continues into the present. Note that English uses the
present perfect.

FINAL PRACTICE   *Say first, then write in German:*

1. I hope you have a passport.   2. Without the passport you cannot study here.   3. Where am I supposed to pay the tuition fees?
4. How long should I stay here?   5. How can I learn German
better?   6. You can go to the theater or the movies.   7. Do you
care for the opera?   8. You can also go to the opera.   9. You can
learn only through practice.   10. Read the newspaper every day
and find yourself (suchen Sie sich) a friend.   11. You need a
friend without any knowledge of English.   12. You must speak
only German.   13. Many thanks for the information and the
help.   14. Where can I take the bus?   15. Can you tell me how
much it costs?   16. Does he know how much it costs?   17. Yes,

we know how much it costs. 18. Where is the library? It isn't far from here. 19. Walk to the corner, go around the corner to the left, and cross the street. 20. I want to go into the library. Must I go right or left? 21. You must go to the right. 22. But you have to walk through the city. 23. You can find the cathedral without help. 24. I want to read something about university life in Germany. 25. A German professor may think what he wants. 26. He may also write what he wants. 27. But he has to work hard.

„Alle Universitäten haben eine Tradition. . . ." Johann Wolfgang
Goethe Universität in Frankfurt
MONKMEYER

I. UNTERHALTUNG

KURT FINDET EINEN FREUND

Karl
Lenz: Entschuldigen Sie, bitte. Ich sehe Sie täglich neben mir im Hörsaal. Sind Sie Deutscher?

Kurt: Nein, ich bin Amerikaner. Man merkt es bestimmt an der Aussprache.

Karl: Aber gar nicht. Sie haben kaum einen Akzent. Wo wohnen Sie denn in den Vereinigten Staaten?

Kurt: Ich komme aus Wisconsin, ziemlich in der Mitte von Amerika. Meine Eltern besitzen ein Häuschen in einer Vorstadt von Milwaukee.

Karl: Ich muß gestehen, Wisconsin ist mir etwas fremd. Amerika interessiert mich schon seit meiner Kindheit. Aber als Kind liest man hauptsächlich von New York und dem Wilden Westen.

Kurt: Hoffentlich besuchen Sie uns bald. Heute fliegt man schon in sieben Stunden über den Atlantik.

KURT FINDS A FRIEND

Karl
Lenz: Excuse me, please. I see you next to me every day in the lecture hall. Are you German?

Kurt: No, I'm an American. You can surely tell by my pronunciation.

Karl: Not at all. You have hardly any accent. Tell me, where in the United States do you live?

Kurt: I'm from Wisconsin, pretty much in the middle of America. My parents own a little house in a suburb of Milwaukee.

Karl: I must admit Wisconsin is a bit unfamiliar to me. I've been interested in America since my childhood. But as a child one reads mostly about New York and the Wild West.

Kurt: I hope you'll visit us soon. Today you can fly across the Atlantic in just seven hours.

LESSON 4

Karl: Ja, das geht schnell. Übrigens, darf ich fragen: Gefällt es Ihnen hier?

Kurt: Ganz wunderbar. Die Leute sind sehr nett, und ich finde die Vorlesungen höchst interessant. Nur geht es nicht immer gut mit der Sprache. Manchmal verstehe ich sehr schlecht. Es ist sehr schwer.

Karl: Das braucht Zeit. Es geht bestimmt bald besser. Sind Sie hier mit Ihrer Familie?

Kurt: Nein, ich bin ganz allein. Ich bin sogar im Moment sehr unruhig. Ich höre nichts von meiner Familie.

Karl: Haben Sie Geschwister?

Kurt: Keinen Bruder, aber eine kleine Schwester — oder sagt man „Schwesterchen"? Ich schreibe ihr immer auf deutsch. Sie versteht alles. Ich schreibe auch meinen Eltern. Aber sie antworten mir nicht. Das Warten fällt schwer.

Karl: Ihre Eltern antworten Ihnen bald. Es besteht kein Grund zur Sorge. Kommen Sie doch heute abend zu uns. Wir wohnen in einem Städtchen zehn Kilometer von hier. Mit dem Auto braucht man nur eine halbe Stunde.

Kurt: Ich danke Ihnen vielmals für die Einladung. Ich komme gerne.

Karl: Yes, it's a fast trip. By the way, may I ask: Do you like it here?

Kurt: Very much. People are very nice, and I find the lectures most interesting. But I don't always do too well with the language. Sometimes I understand very poorly. It's very hard.

Karl: That takes time. It will surely be better soon. Are you here with your family?

Kurt: No, I'm all alone. In fact, I'm very worried at this moment. I have no news from my family.

Karl: Do you have any brothers and sisters?

Kurt: No brother, but a little sister—or does one say "Schwesterchen"? I always write to her in German. She understands everything. I also write to my parents. But they don't answer me. Waiting is difficult.

Karl: Your parents will be answering you soon. There's no reason to worry. Why don't you come to our house tonight? We live in a small town ten kilometers from here. It takes only half an hour by car.

Kurt: Thanks a lot for the invitation. I'll gladly come.

II. KOMBINATIONEN

Sagen Sie auf deutsch:

a. 1. Excuse me, please. Are you German? 2. Pardon me, please. Are you an American? 3. Excuse me, please. Do you live here in Cologne?

b. 1. You can tell by the pronunciation. —No, not at all. 2. You can tell by the lecture. —No, not at all. 3. You can tell by the ticket. —No, not at all.

c. 1. Where in the United States do you live? 2. Where in Germany do you live? 3. Where in Hamburg does he live?

d. 1. I must admit Wisconsin is a bit strange to me. 2. I must admit I don't know the city very well. 3. I must admit university life is a bit strange to me.

e. 1. I am interested in America. 2. I am interested in the city tour. 3. The cathedral interests me.

f. 1. As a child one reads mostly about New York. 2. As a child one reads mostly about the Wild West. 3. As a child one reads mostly about Germany.

g. 1. I hope you'll visit us soon. 2. I hope you'll come to see us soon. 3. I hope you'll write to us soon.

h. 1. Today you fly across the Atlantic in seven hours. 2. Today one drives from Bonn to Cologne in one hour. 3. Today one flies from Hamburg to Paris in two hours.

i. 1. By the way, may I ask: Do you like it here? 2. Incidentally, may I ask: Do you like it here at the university?

j. 1. Do you have brothers and sisters? —Yes, I have a brother. 2. Do you have any brothers or sisters? —Yes, I have a little sister. 3. Do you have any brothers and sisters? —Yes, I have brothers and sisters.

k. 1. Why don't you come to see us tonight. 2. Why don't you come to see us today. 3. Why don't you come to see us this morning.

l. 1. We live in a small town ten kilometers from here. 2. We live in a suburb two kilometers from here. 3. He lives in a small town in the center of Germany.

m. 1. It takes half an hour by car. 2. It takes an hour by taxi. 3. That takes time.

III. SAGEN UND FRAGEN

a. *Sie sind Karl Lenz. Sie sagen zu Kurt:*

1. Sie sehen ihn täglich neben sich (*you, yourself*) im Hörsaal. 2. Er hat kaum einen Akzent. 3. Sie merken nichts an seiner Aussprache. 4. Sie wohnen auch in einem Häuschen, nicht weit von Köln. 5. Sie müssen gestehen, Sie kennen Wisconsin nicht. 6. Sie müssen gestehen, Milwaukee ist Ihnen etwas fremd. 7. Amerika interessiert Sie schon seit Ihrer Kindheit. 8. Sie wissen, es besteht kein Grund zur Sorge. 9. Sie wissen etwas von dem Wilden Westen. 10. Er braucht nur eine halbe Stunde mit dem Auto.

b. *Sie sind immer noch Karl Lenz. Sie fragen Kurt:*

1. ob er Deutscher ist. 2. wo er in den Vereinigten Staaten wohnt. 3. ob ein Kind in Amerika von dem Wilden Westen liest. 4. ob er Sie bald besucht. 5. ob es ihm hier gefällt. 6. ob die Leute in Deutschland nett sind. 7. ob er die Vorlesungen interessant findet. 8. warum er nichts von seiner Familie hört. 9. warum die Eltern ihm nicht schreiben. 10. ob er Geschwister hat. 11. ob die kleine Schwester Deutsch spricht. 12. ob sie Deutsch versteht.

IV. PRONUNCIATION PRACTICE

Consonant Clusters The following consonant clusters do not exist in English.

Repeat after your instructor or the speaker:

Cluster	Spelling	
/gn/	gn	**Gnade, gnädig**
/kn/	kn	**Knecht, Knie, Knopf**
/kv/	qu	**Qualität, bequem, Quelle, Quittung**
/ps/	ps	**Psychologie, Psalm**
/pfl/	pfl	**pflanzen, pflücken, Pflicht**
/šv/	schw	**schweigen, schwer, schweben, schwarz**
/špr/	spr	**sprechen, springen, Sprung, Sprache**
/štr/	str	**Strecke, stricken, Streich, Strumpf**
/sts/	sz	**Szene, Szenerie, Szepter**

V. AUFSATZ

DIE GEOGRAPHIE DEUTSCHLANDS

Es ist kurz vor sieben (7:00). In einer Stunde ißt Kurt bei seinem Freund Karl zu Abend.[1] Er denkt an Karls Einladung. „Wir erwarten Sie gegen acht (8:00). Die Familie ist zu Hause, der Vater, die Mutter, und meine Schwester. Sie ist achtzehn (18)
5 Jahre alt und sehr hübsch."

Aber zuerst schreibt Kurt einen Aufsatz für die Deutschstunde. Das Thema ist die Geographie Deutschlands. Er findet die Aufgabe leicht. Er beschreibt einfach das Klima[2] und die Landschaft.[3]

„Deutschland liegt in Mitteleuropa.[4] Das Klima ist mild und im
10 allgemeinen[5] angenehm. Im Sommer ist es nicht zu heiß und im Winter nicht zu kalt. Das Wetter ist sehr veränderlich.[6] Es regnet zu jeder Jahreszeit.[7] Es ist warm im Sommer, kalt im Winter. Es schneit oft im Winter, besonders im Januar und Februar.

„Die Landschaften in Deutschland sind sehr verschieden. Im
15 Norden ist das Land flach;[8] im Süden jedoch ist es gebirgig.[9] Die Alpen[10] in Bayern[11] sind bis zu dreitausend (3000) Meter hoch. Wir nennen sie Hochgebirge.[12]

„Köln, wo ich wohne, liegt am Rhein. Die Hafenstadt[13] Hamburg liegt an der Elbe.[14] Bremen ist ebenfalls eine Hafenstadt und
20 liegt an der Weser.[15] Der Rhein, die Weser und die Elbe fließen[16] von Süden nach Norden und münden[17] in die Nordsee.[18] Die Donau[19] kommt aus dem Schwarzwald[20] und fließt nach Osten."

Kurt sieht auf die Uhr. Es ist höchste Zeit.[21] Er läuft schnell die Treppe hinunter.[22] Unten begegnet er Frau Kolb. „Gehen Sie am
25 Postamt vorbei?"[23] fragt sie ihn. „Ja? Dann darf ich Ihnen diesen Brief geben. Werfen Sie ihn bitte in den Briefkasten!"[24] Kurt tut ihr gerne diesen Gefallen.

---

1. **zu Abend essen** to eat dinner. 2. climate. 3. landscape. 4. central Europe. 5. in general. 6. changeable. 7. season. 8. flat. 9. mountainous. 10. Alps. 11. Bavaria. 12. high mountain chain. 13. seaport. 14. **die Elbe** *a major eastern German river.* 15. **die Weser** *a river in central Germany.* 16. to flow. 17. to empty. 18. North Sea. 19. Danube. 20. Black Forest. 21. **Es ist höchste Zeit** it's high time. 22. **die Treppe hinunter** down the steps. 23. **am Postamt vorbei** past the postoffice. 24. **in den Briefkasten werfen** to drop in the mailbox.

Beantworten Sie die folgenden Fragen:

1. Wo ißt Kurt in einer Stunde?   2. Wen trifft Kurt bei der Familie Lenz?   3. Wie alt ist Karls Schwester?   4. Was muß Kurt zuerst tun?   5. Wo liegt Deutschland und wie ist das Klima? 6. Regnet es viel? Wann denn?   7. Wann schneit es besonders? 8. Was nennt man Hochgebirge?   9. Nennen Sie drei (3) Flüsse (*rivers*) in Deutschland!   10. Was fragt Frau Kolb?

VI. WORTSCHATZ

der **Akzent**	accent	**laufen (läuft)**	to run
allein	alone	**leicht**	easy, light
der **Amerikaner**	American	die **Leute**	people
angenehm	pleasant	**liegen**	to lie, be situated
die **Aussprache**	pronunciation	das **Mädchen**	girl
das **Auto**	car	die **Mitte**	middle
bald	soon	**merken**	to notice
begegnen	to meet	der **Moment**	moment
beschreiben	to describe	**nennen**	to call, name
besitzen	to own, possess	der **Norden**	north
besonders	particularly	der **Osten**	east
bestimmt	surely	**regnen**	to rain
(**ein**) **Deutscher**	(a) German	**schneien**	to snow
die **Einladung**	invitation	**schnell**	fast, quick
entschuldigen	to excuse, pardon	**schwer**	hard, difficult
		schwer-	to be difficult
erwarten	to expect, await	**fallen (fällt)**	(*for someone*)
erzählen	to tell, relate	das **Schwester-**	little sister, kid
fliegen	to fly	**chen**	sister
fremd	strange, foreign	**sogar**	even
gefallen	to appeal to, be	die **Sorge**	worry, care
(**gefällt**)	pleasing to	die **Sprache**	language
der **Gefallen**	favor	die **Stunde**	hour
gern(e)	gladly	die **Deutsch-**	German class
die **Geschwister**	brothers and	**stunde**	
(*plural*)	sisters	der **Süden**	south
gestehen	to admit, confess	**täglich**	daily
der **Grund**	reason	das **Thema**	subject, topic; theme
hauptsächlich	mostly, primarily		
heiß	hot	**unruhig**	restless, worried
hoch	high	die **Vereinigten**	the United States
höchst	extremely	**Staaten**	
hören	to hear	**verschieden**	different
der **Hörsaal**	lecture hall	**vielmals**	many times, very much
hübsch	pretty		
jedoch	however	die **Vorstadt**	suburb
kalt	cold	der **Westen**	west
kaum	hardly, scarcely	das **Wetter**	weather
der **Kilometer**	kilometer	**wild**	wild
die **Kindheit**	childhood	**wunderbar**	wonderful
kurz	short(ly)	**zu**	at, to
das **Land**	land, country	**zu Hause**	at home

VII. ERKLÄRUNGEN UND ÜBUNGEN

1. Dative Case

Karl gibt **seinem Freund** eine Einladung.
Karl gives his friend an invitation.

Kurt schreibt **der Schwester** einen Brief.
Kurt writes his sister a letter.

The dative is primarily the case of the indirect object, the word or words indicating *to* or *for whom* something is done.

a. Forms

Masculine	Feminine	Neuter
Nom. **der** Vater	**die** Mutter	**das** Haus
Dat. **dem** Vater	**der** Mutter	**dem** Haus
key sound: /m/	*key sound:* /r/	*key sound:* /m/

Masculine	Feminine	Neuter
Nom. **ein** Vater	**eine** Mutter	**ein** Haus
kein Vater	**keine** Mutter	**kein** Haus
Dat. **einem** Vater	**einer** Mutter	**einem** Haus
keinem Vater	**keiner** Mutter	**keinem** Haus
key sound: /m/	*key sound:* /r/	*key sound:* /m/

The 3rd person pronouns:

Nom. **er** *key sound:* /r/	**sie** *key sound:* /iː/	**es** *key sound:* /s/
Dat. **ihm** *key sound:* /m/	**ihr** *key sound:* /r/	**ihm** *key sound:* /m/
(to) *him, it*	(to) *her, it*	(to) *it, him, her*

Note that the dative masculine and neuter forms are identical and have the key sound /m/. For the feminine the key sound is /r/. (Remember that /r/ also signifies nominative masculine singular.) The forms of the remaining personal pronouns are:

Nominative: **ich**   **du**   **wir**   **ihr**   **sie** } *key sound:* /n/   **Sie**

Dative: **mir** (*me*)
dir (*you, familiar singular*)
uns (*us*)
euch (*you, familiar plural*)
ihnen (*them*)
Ihnen (*you, conventional form*)

PRACTICE

A. *Give the dative forms:*

1. der Freund
2. das Auto
3. eine Einladung
4. die Stunde
5. das Fräulein
6. der Unterricht
7. eine Fahrkarte
8. das Zimmer
9. ein Paß
10. kein Vater

11.	das Postamt	16.	er
12.	der Winter	17.	wir
13.	keine Mutter	18.	ich
14.	der Süden	19.	sie (singular)
15.	der Norden	20.	sie (plural)

B. *Form sentences with the proper forms of the nouns:*

Example: Sie gibt (*der Vater*) die Zeitung.
Sie gibt dem Vater die Zeitung.

1. Er schreibt (der Vater, die Mutter, der Bruder, das Schwester-chen) einen Brief. 2. Gibt er (der Amerikaner, ein Freund, die Schwester) Auskunft? 3. Kurt bezahlt (der Dekan, die Sekre-tärin, das Mädchen) die Semestergebühren. 4. Er bringt (ein Freund, eine Freundin, das Schwesterchen, der Lehrer) das Buch.

C. *Complete the following sentences with the correct forms of the pronouns:*

1. Kurt gibt (er und sie [*singular*]) den Stadtplan. 2. Wir bringen (sie [*plural*] und ihr) Hilfe. 3. Sie geben (ich und du) Auskunft.

D. *Say in German:*

1. I'm writing to him tomorrow. 2. I'm giving her the book. 3. She's bringing me the mail. 4. We're writing them a letter. 5. They're paying the university two marks per meal. 6. I'm paying you (*conventional form*) more.

2. Word Order: Direct and Indirect Objects

Er schreibt **der Schwester einen Brief.**
He's writing his sister a letter.

Er schreibt **ihr einen Brief.**
He's writing her a letter.

An indirect object (*noun or pronoun*) precedes a direct noun object.

Er schreibt **ihn der Schwester.**
He's writing it to his sister.

Er schreibt **ihn ihr.**
He's writing it to her.

A direct pronoun object precedes an indirect object (*noun or pronoun*).

Learn the following combinations:

ihn mir	**sie mir**	**es mir**
ihn dir	**sie dir**	**es dir**

VII. ERKLÄRUNGEN UND ÜBUNGEN

ihn ihm	sie ihm	es ihm
ihn ihr	sie ihr	es ihr
ihn uns	sie uns	es uns
ihn euch	sie euch	es euch
ihn ihnen	sie ihnen	es ihnen
ihn Ihnen	sie Ihnen	es Ihnen

PRACTICE

A. *Answer the following questions negatively and replace the indirect noun object with the pronoun object:*

Example: Schreibt er dem Vater einen Brief?
Nein, er schreibt ihm keinen Brief.

1. Schreibt er dem Dekan einen Brief? 2. Gibt er dem Beamten einen Paß? 3. Bezahlt er der Sekretärin eine Mark? 4. Bringt er dem Professor einen Aufsatz? 5. Zeigt er dem Engländer ein Gymnasium? 6. Beschreibt er dem Amerikaner eine deutsche Landschaft? 7. Gibt er dem Kind eine Antwort? 8. Schreibt er der Schwester einen Brief?

B. *Answer the following questions by using object pronouns:*

Example: Erzählen Sie Kurt die Geschichte?
Ja, ich erzähle sie ihm.

1. Erklären Sie Kurt die Aufgabe? 2. Geben Sie dem Lehrer den Aufsatz? 3. Schreiben Sie dem Bruder einen Brief? 4. Beschreiben Sie der Schwester den Dom? 5. Erzählen Sie der Mutter die Geschichte? 6. Bringen Sie Frau Kolb das Buch? 7. Kaufen Sie der Freundin eine Fahrkarte?

3. Prepositions with the Dative

aus	from, out of	mit	with
außer	outside of, except, besides	nach	after, toward, according to
bei	at, near, at the house of	seit	since[1]
		von	from, of, about
gegenüber	opposite	zu	to, at

The prepositions above are always followed by dative forms.

1. The preposition **seit**, with or without **schon**, is often used with the present tense to express an action that began in the past and continues into the present. Example: **Sie wohnen (schon) seit einem Jahr da.** *They've been living there for a year.*

67

PRACTICE   A. *Complete the sentences with the correct forms of the indicated phrases:*

Example: Er erzählt von (*die Reise*).
Er erzählt von der Reise.

1. Er spaziert zur Universität mit (ein Freund, eine Sekretärin, ein Professor). 2. Er kommt aus (die Stadt, ein Hörsaal, ein Zimmer). 3. Sie hat keine Geschwister außer (eine Schwester und ein Bruder). 4. Er spricht von (das Universitätsleben, das Theater, das Studium) an seiner Universität. 5. Er studiert schon seit (ein Monat, eine Woche, ein Tag).

B. *Answer the following questions by replacing the dative nouns with pronouns:*

Example: Gehen Sie mit der Schwester ins Kino?
Ja, ich gehe mit ihr ins Kino.

1. Gehen Sie mit der Freundin ins Theater? 2. Gehen Sie mit Kurt in die Bibliothek? 3. Bleiben Sie heute morgen bei Frau Kolb? 4. Gehen Sie heute zu Karl? 5. Sprechen Sie heute morgen mit dem Dekan? 6. Kommen Sie gerade von der Sekretärin?

C. *Answer the following questions, using the indicated phrases:*

1. Seit wann ist Kurt in Deutschland? (seit einer Woche) 2. Bei wem wohnt Kurt? (bei einer Familie Kolb) 3. Bei wem ißt er heute zu Abend? (bei einem Freund) 4. Zu wem geht er morgen? (zu einer Freundin)

D. *Say in German:*

1. I'm going with them. 2. Are they coming with us? 3. Besides you, Kurt, we have no friend. 4. He's leaving the house with him and her. 5. After one hour he is coming back. 6. He knows something about the West. 7. He also knows something about the East.

4. Prepositions   **Er fährt in die Stadt.**   (*motion toward the city*)
with Accusative   *He's driving into the city.*
or Dative
                      Er ist schon in der Stadt.   (*location in the city*)
                      He's already in the city.

Kurt geht an die Ecke.   (*motion toward the corner*)
Kurt is walking to the corner.

Kurt wartet an der Ecke.   (*location at the corner*)
Kurt is waiting at the corner.

Er geht im Zimmer auf und ab.   (*activity within the room*)
He paces up and down (in) the room.

In Lesson 3 we listed the prepositions that require accusative forms when expressing motion or direction. The same prepositions (**an, auf, hinter, in, neben, über, unter, vor, zwischen**) require the dative if the verb indicates location or activity in a confined area. In such situations, the prepositions are used in answering the question **wo?** (*where?*)

a. Contractions

Dative Contractions		Accusative Contractions	
an dem	am	an das	ans
in dem	im	in das	ins
bei dem	beim	auf das	aufs
zu dem, zu der	zum, zur	über das	übers
von dem	vom	hinter das	hinters

Prepositions and articles are often contracted, both in the dative and accusative.

PRACTICE

A. *Answer the following questions using the indicated phrases:*

    Example: Wo wohnt Karl Lenz? (*in, eine Vorstadt*)
                 Karl Lenz wohnt in einer Vorstadt.

1. Wo arbeitet Kurt? (auf, das Zimmer)   2. Wo sind Kurt und Karl jetzt? (in, der Hörsaal)   3. Wo wartet Kurt auf den Bus? (an, die Ecke)   4. Wo ist er jetzt? (in, der Bus)   5. Wo ist Karl Lenz? (neben, der Freund)

B. *Answer the following questions using the indicated phrases:*

1. Wohin fährt Karl? (in, die Vorstadt)   2. Wohin geht Kurt? (in, das Theater)   3. Wohin fahren sie morgen? (an, die Elbe) 4. Wohin wollen sie dann reisen? (in, das Gebirge)   5. Wohin müssen sie danach gehen? (in, der Unterricht)

C. *Change the following sentences, using* **sein,** *according to the example:*

    Example: Sie gehen ins Haus.
                 Sie sind schon im Haus.

1. Sie gehen in die Bibliothek.   2. Man fährt an den Rhein.
3. Er kommt ins Büro.   4. Er geht in die Deutschstunde.   5. Sie

69

spazieren in den Park.   6. Heute abend gehen sie ins Theater.
7. Er geht an die Ecke.   8. Sie kommt in die Mensa.

D.   Say in German:

1. Kurt lives in a room at Mrs. Kolb's.   2. Mrs. Kolb is just coming into the house.   3. "Where are you going?" asks Mrs. Kolb.
4. He is going to the lecture hall.   5. Kurt walks to the corner.
6. He waits for the bus.   7. He sees the dean in front of the lecture hall.   8. They walk together into the room.

5. Verbs Requiring   **antworten**   *to answer*   **gefallen**   *to appeal to, be pleasing to*
Dative Objects   **begegnen**   *to meet*   **glauben**   *to believe*
danken   *to thank*   **helfen**   *to help*

Sie **antworten mir** nicht.
They don't answer me.

Er **begegnet ihr** auf der Straße.
He meets her on the street.

Ich **danke Ihnen.**
I thank you.

Die Stadt Köln **gefällt ihm.**
He likes the city of Cologne.
(*Cologne is pleasing to him.*)

Above are some common verbs requiring dative objects.

Note: The verb **gefallen** requires that the object in English become
the subject in German. The subject in English becomes the indirect
(dative) object in German.

PRACTICE   *A.   Change the pronouns according to the example:*

Example: Ich helfe ihm.
Er hilft mir.

1. Ich glaube ihm.   2. Ich begegne ihr.   3. Ich antworte ihnen.
4. Ich danke Ihnen.   5. Ich antworte ihm.   6. Ich begegne
ihnen.

B.   Answer the following questions:

Example: Helfen Sie mir?
Ja, ich helfe Ihnen.

1. Antworten Sie mir? 2. Glauben Sie mir? 3. Danken Sie mir? 4. Begegnen Sie ihm?

C. *Answer the following questions:*

> *Example:* Gefällt Ihnen die Stadt?
> Ja, sie gefällt mir sehr gut.
> Nein, sie gefällt mir nicht besonders.

1. Gefällt Ihnen die Oper? 2. Gefällt ihr das Haus? 3. Gefällt ihm das Buch über Amerika? 4. Gefällt Ihnen der Dom? 5. Gefällt ihr das Auto? 6. Gefällt Ihnen die Zeitung? 7. Gefällt ihnen Hamburg? 8. Gefällt ihm die Vorlesung?

D. *Say in German:*

1. He helps her often. 2. She thanks him. 3. She asks, "Do you like the room?" 4. He answers her, "I like it very much." 5. Kurt also likes the university and Cologne.

6. Inseparable Prefixes

antworten	*to answer* (intransitive)	stehen	*to stand*
beantworten	*to answer* (transitive)	bestehen	*to exist*
		entstehen	*to arise*
fangen	*to catch*	gestehen	*to admit*
empfangen	*to receive*	verstehen	*to understand*
reißen	*to tear*	suchen	*to seek*
zerreißen	*to tear to pieces*	besuchen	*to visit*
		versuchen	*to try*
schreiben	*to write*		
beschreiben	*to describe*	warten	*to wait*
		erwarten	*to expect*
sitzen	*to sit*		
besitzen	*to possess*		

Many German verbs begin with an unaccented prefix: **be-, emp-, ent-, er-, ge-, ver-, zer-.** These prefixes, though they have no meaning of their own,[1] often change the meaning of the basic verb. They always remain attached to the verb; hence they are called inseparable prefixes.

7. Word Study
a. Diminutives

die Schwester:	das Schwesterchen	*little sister*
der Bruder:	das Brüderlein	*little brother*
das Haus:	das Häuschen	*little house*

1. One exception is **zer-**, which almost always has the meaning of *all to pieces* (**brechen** to break; **zerbrechen** *to break to pieces; smash*).

The ending **-chen** (or **-lein**) forms diminutive nouns. The root vowel also umlauts where possible. Diminutives are always neuter regardless of the gender of the basic noun.

b. Compound Nouns

das Deutsch — **die Stunde:**	**die Deutschstunde** *German class*	
der Brief — **der Kasten:**	**der Briefkasten** *mailbox*	
der Rhein — **das Land:**	**das Rheinland** *Rhineland*	
fremd — **die Sprache:**	**die Fremdsprache** *foreign language*	

Compounds are characteristic of German. The gender of a compound noun is that of the final component.

c. Infinitives as Nouns

Das Warten fällt schwer.
Waiting is difficult.

Das Sprechen ist nicht immer einfach.
Speaking is not always easy.

Any infinitive may be used as a neuter noun, corresponding to English verbal nouns (gerunds).

FINAL PRACTICE *Say first, then write in German:*

1. Kurt is an American, but one can't tell by the pronunciation or the accent. 2. Karl asks, "Where in the United States do you live?" 3. Kurt answers him, "I'm from Wisconsin." 4. It's a state in the center of America. 5. "I don't know Wisconsin very well," says Karl. 6. Kurt says, "I hope you'll visit us soon." 7. Karl answers him, "I thank you. I want to come." 8. "Do you like it in Germany, Kurt?" asks Karl. 9. Kurt likes it here very much. 10. But sometimes he understands rather poorly. 11. Karl helps Kurt with a composition about the geography of Germany. 12. In the summer it is not too hot, and in winter it is

not too cold.   13. It rains a lot and snows often in January and February.   14. Tonight Kurt is eating at Karl's house.   15. He looks at the clock. It is very late.   16. He meets Mrs. Kolb at the door.   17. "Please help me," she says.   18. "Gladly," Kurt answers her.   19. "I'll gladly do you a favor."   20. Afterwards he walks to the corner and waits for the bus.

Rheinfahrt am Loreleifelsen vorbei
HENLE FROM MONKMEYER

I. UNTERHALTUNG

EINE RHEINFAHRT

Während der Mahlzeit spricht Herr Lenz, Karls Vater, mit seinem Gast aus Amerika. Kurt ist sonst immer höflich, heute aber nicht. Er hat nur Interesse für Lore Lenz, Karls Schwester. Er ist entzückt von dem Reiz und der Schönheit des Mädchens. Herr Lenz merkt nichts davon. Wovon redet er? Er redet von der Schönheit einer Rheinreise.

Herr Lenz: Aber Karl, mach doch eine Rheinfahrt mit Herrn Klein! So eine Fahrt ist doch herrlich.

Karl: Ja, das weiß ich schon. Wann finden wir aber die Zeit dafür?

Herr Lenz: Ihr findet schon mal die Zeit. Das ist kein Problem. Die Arbeit eines Studenten . . .

Karl: Glaube mir, Vater, es ist nicht wie früher. Wir sind von morgens bis abends beschäftigt.

Herr Lenz: Fahrt bald, noch während des Sommers! Auf jeden Fall vor Anfang der Kälte.

Karl: Wir versuchen es, sobald wir die Möglichkeit haben. Weißt du, wie oft die Dampfer fahren?

A TRIP DOWN THE RHINE

During the meal Mr. Lenz, Karl's father, talks with his guest from America. Kurt is usually very polite, but not today. He has eyes only for Lore Lenz, Karl's sister. He is delighted with the girl's charm and beauty. Mr. Lenz notices nothing of all this. What is he talking about? He's talking about the beauty of a Rhine excursion.

Mr. Lenz: But Karl, do take a Rhine trip with Mr. Klein. A trip like that is wonderful.

Karl: Yes, I know. But when are we going to find the time for it?

Mr. Lenz: You'll find the time all right. That's no problem. The work of a student . . .

Karl: Believe me, father, it isn't as it used to be. We are busy from morning till evening.

Mr. Lenz: Go soon, while it's still summer. In any event, before it gets cold.

Karl: We'll try it as soon as we have a chance. Do you know how often the steamers run?

LESSON 5

Herr Lenz:	Nein. Du kennst doch Herrn Schmidt nebenan. Er weiß es.
Karl:	Das stimmt, er arbeitet ja in einem Reisebüro.
Kurt:	Fräulein Lore, kommen Sie auch?
Lore:	Leider kann ich nicht, wegen meiner Prüfung.
Karl:	Komme trotz des Examens!
Lore:	Eine Rheinfahrt statt eines Examens — das wäre wirklich der Anfang vom Ende!
Herr Lenz:	(verträumt) Ein schönes Erlebnis! Auf beiden Seiten des Flusses Weinberge und Ruinen. Ja, die Legenden des Rheins. . . .
Karl:	Kurt, kennst du die Geschichte der Lorelei?
Kurt:	Du meinst das Gedicht Heines? Ich mag es sehr. Ich kann es sogar auswendig.
Herr Lenz:	Hier ist das Buch der Rheinsagen. Es ist klein gedruckt, aber lesen Sie es trotzdem!
Kurt:	Ich habe nachmittags oft Zeit zum Lesen. Recht vielen Dank, Herr Lenz.

Mr. Lenz:	No, but you know Mr. Schmidt next door. He'll know.
Karl:	That's right, he works for a travel agency.
Kurt:	Lore, are you coming too?
Lore:	Sorry, I can't because of my exam.
Karl:	Come in spite of the exam.
Lore:	A Rhine excursion instead of an exam—that would really be the beginning of the end!
Mr. Lenz:	(dreamily) A beautiful experience! On both sides of the river vineyards and ruins. Yes, the legends of the Rhine . . . .
Karl:	Kurt, do you know the story of the Lorelei?
Kurt:	You mean Heine's poem? I like it very much. I even know it by heart.
Mr. Lenz:	Here is the book of Rhine legends. It's in small print, but read it anyhow.
Kurt:	I often have time to read in the afternoon. Thank you very much, Mr. Lenz.

II. KOMBINATIONEN

Sagen Sie auf deutsch:

a. 1. Mr. Lenz is talking to his guest from America. 2. Kurt is chatting with Lore Lenz. 3. Karl is speaking with a guest from France.

b. 1. Kurt is usually polite, but not today. 2. Mrs. Kolb is always polite, but not now. 3. They are usually polite, but not today.

c. 1. Mr. Lenz notices nothing of all this. 2. Lore Lenz notices nothing of all this either. 3. We don't notice anything either.

d. 1. Such a trip is wonderful. 2. Such a conversation is wonderful. 3. Such a book is very easy.

e. 1. When do we find the time for it? 2. When do we find the money for it? 3. Where can we find the people for it?

f. 1. In any event, before it gets cold. 2. In any case, during the summer. 3. At any rate, as soon as possible.

g. 1. I'm sorry, I can't because of the exam. 2. I'm sorry, I can't because of the cold. 3. Unfortunately, we can't because of the exam.

h. 1. A trip instead of an exam—that would be the beginning of the end. 2. The opera instead of a test—that would be the beginning of the end.

i. 1. Do you know the story of the Lorelei? 2. Do you know the legend of the Rhine? 3. Unfortunately, I don't know the story of the Lorelei.

j. 1. You mean through Heine's poem? 2. He means through Shakespeare's play. 3. I mean through Schiller's poem.

k. 1. I know it by heart. 2. Do you know it by heart? 3. We know it by heart.

l. 1. I have time to read in the afternoon. 2. He has time to read in the morning. 3. We have time to read only in the evening.

III. SAGEN UND FRAGEN

a. *Sie sind Herr Lenz. Sie sagen zu Ihrem Sohn Karl (use familiar* **du** *and retain modals in your responses):*

1. Er soll eine Rheinfahrt machen. 2. Er kann die Zeit dafür finden. 3. Er muß bald fahren. 4. Er soll während des Sommers fahren. 5. Er soll Kurt die Ruinen zeigen.

b. *Sie sind Karl Lenz. Sie sagen (use* **wir***):*

1. Sie sind immer beschäftigt.   2. Sie haben Arbeit von morgens bis abends.   3. Sie versuchen es, sobald wie möglich. 4. Sie fahren vor Anfang der Kälte.   5. Sie kennen die Legenden des Rheins.   6. Sie kennen die Geschichte der Lorelei.   7. Sie haben ein Buch von Rheinsagen.   8. Sie lesen es heute nachmittag.   9. Sie haben nachmittags keine Zeit zum Lesen.   10. Sie haben nur abends Zeit dazu.

c. *Sie sind Kurt. Sie fragen Karl:*

1. ob Fräulein Lore auch kommt.   2. warum sie nicht kommt. 3. wo die Weinberge sind.   4. ob er das Gedicht Heines kennt.   5. ob er es auch auswendig kann.   6. wann Sie das Buch lesen sollen.   7. ob eine Rheinfahrt wirklich herrlich ist.

IV. PRONUNCIATION PRACTICE

Summary of Certain German Phonemes

/ŋ/, /ə/, /x/ (*back ch*) never occur in initial position.

/s/ never begins a syllable with a vowel or a diphthong.

/h/ never occurs at the end of a syllable.

/b/, /d/, /g/, /v/, /z/ never occur in final position.

Short vowels almost never occur in final position.

Repeat after your instructor or the speaker and carefully note the spellings:

1.	/ziŋən/	singen	*to sing*
2.	/zayn/	sein	*to be*
3.	/zin/	Sinn	*sense*
4.	/ze:ən/	sehen	*to see*
5.	/ap/	ab	*off*
6.	/apne:mən/	abnehmen	*to take off*
7.	/op/	ob	*whether*
8.	/gra:p/	Grab	*grave*
9.	/bant/	Band	*volume*
10.	/hunt/	Hund	*dog*
11.	/helt/	Held	*hero*
12.	/ta:k/	Tag	*day*
13.	/vekge:ən/	weggehen	*to go away*
14.	/bo:k/	bog	*bent*
15.	/moti:f/	Motiv	*motif*

16.	/bra:f/	brav	*upright, honest*
17.	/desve:gən/	deswegen	*for that reason*
18.	/morgəns/	morgens	*mornings*
19.	/karls/	Karls	*Karl's*
20.	/haysən/	heißen	*to be called*

V. AUFSATZ

AUF DEM DAMPFER

Kurt und Karl stehen an der Reling[1] des Rheindampfers. Genau wie Herr Lenz sind sie von der Schönheit der Landschaft begeistert. Nie möchten sie diese Reise vergessen. Aus diesem Grunde photographieren sie fleißig. Bei jeder Biegung[2] des Rheins wird
5 das Bild anders. Jedoch bleibt es immer gleich schön.[3]

Auf beiden Seiten des Flusses stehen Ziffern.[4] Kurt versteht die Bedeutung der Ziffern nicht. Karl erklärt sie ihm: „Schau auf die Rheinkarte! Hier steht die Nummer 550 (fünfhundertfünfzig). Daneben steht der Name der Stadt. Wir sind eben in Bonn, in der
10 Hauptstadt der Bundesrepublik.[5] Siehst du? Ein bißchen weiter ist Mehlem. Hier ist die Botschaft[6] der Vereinigten Staaten, ganz in der Nähe von Bonn. Bonn, eine Universitätsstadt, ist auch die Geburtsstadt[7] Beethovens."

Während der nächsten[8] halben[9] Stunde frühstücken Kurt und
15 Karl unten im Speisesaal des Dampfers. Sie trinken eine Tasse Kaffee und essen Brot mit Butter und etwas Marmelade darauf. Dann gehen sie wieder nach oben auf das Deck[10] zurück.

Seit dem ersten[11] Teil des 19. (neunzehnten) Jahrhunderts ist der Rhein der Lieblingsfluß[12] der deutschen Dichtung.[13] Er ist
20 auch seit derselben[14] Epoche[15] die große Straße für Touristen. Der Rhein, so sagt man oft, ist das Prunkstück[16] der deutschen Geographie.

„Was für ein Mensch ist der Rheinländer?"[17] fragt Kurt.

„Er ist besonders wegen seiner Lebensfreude[18] bekannt", ant-
25 wortet Karl. „Wie du siehst, ist er auch sehr gastfreundlich.[19] Die

1. railing. 2. bend. 3. **immer gleich schön** just as beautiful. 4. numerals. 5. Federal Republic (*of Germany*). 6. embassy. 7. native city. 8. next. 9. half. 10. deck. 11. first. 12. **der Lieblingsfluß** favorite river. 13. poetry. 14. the same. 15. epoch. 16. showpiece. 17. Rhinelander. 18. enjoyment of life. 19. hospitable.

79

Im Beethovenhaus in Bonn
MONKMEYER

Gastfreundschaft[20] des Rheinländers drückt sich in der Gemütlichkeit[21] des Menschen aus."[22]

Kurt ist mit der Auskunft zufrieden. „Ich lerne wirklich viel",
denkt er. „Aber warum ist Lore nicht bei uns?"

Beantworten Sie die folgenden Fragen:

1. Wo stehen die zwei Freunde?   2. Was möchten sie nie vergessen?   3. Was sehen sie auf beiden Seiten des Flusses?   4. Was
steht neben der Nummer 550?   5. Wo sind sie jetzt?   6. Was

20. hospitality.   21. geniality, pleasantly unhurried manner.   22.
drückt sich . . . aus expresses itself.

ist in Mehlem?   7. Was machen sie während der nächsten halben Stunde?   8. Wo frühstücken sie?   9. Was essen und trinken sie?   10. Wohin gehen sie dann zurück?   11. Seit wann ist der Rhein der Lieblingsfluß der Dichtung?   12. Was sagt Karl über den Rheinländer?

VI.   WORTSCHATZ

abends	evenings, in the evening	die **Kälte**	cold (weather)
		die **Marmelade**	jam
anders	different	das **Mädchen**	girl
der **Anfang**	beginning	**meinen**	to mean
die **Arbeit**	work	der **Mensch**	person, human being
auswendig	by heart		
die **Bedeutung**	meaning	**morgens**	mornings, in the morning
begeistert	enthusiastic		
beschäftigt	occupied, busy	**möglich**	possible
das **Bild**	picture	die **Möglichkeit**	possibility
bißchen: ein bißchen	a little	**nachmittags**	afternoons, in the afternoon
das **Brot**	bread	die **Nähe**	neighborhood, vicinity
die **Butter**	butter		
der **Dampfer**	steamship	**nebenan**	next door
eben	just, just now	**nie**	never
das **Ende**	end	**photographieren**	to photograph
entzückt (von)	delighted (with)		
das **Erlebnis**	experience	die **Prüfung**	test, examination
das **Examen**	examination	der **Reiz**	charm
der **Fall**	case, event	das **Restaurant**	restaurant
auf jeden Fall	in any case, at any rate	**schauen**	to see
		die **Schönheit**	beauty
der **Fluß**	river	**sobald**	as soon as
frühstücken	to (have) breakfast	der **Sommer**	summer
		sonst	otherwise
der **Gast**	guest	der **Speisesaal**	dining hall
das **Gedicht**	poem	die **Tasse**	cup
genau	exact	der **Teil**	part
die **Hauptstadt**	capital	**vergessen**	to forget
herrlich	splendid	**versuchen**	to try
höflich	polite	**was für (ein)**	what kind of (a)
die **Jahreszeit**	season	die **Weinberge**	vineyards
das **Jahrhundert**	century	**zeigen**	to show
		zufrieden	satisfied

VII.   ERKLÄRUNGEN UND ÜBUNGEN

1. Genitive Case   **Der Name des Mannes** ist Karl Lenz.
The man's name is Karl Lenz.

Er redet von der **Schönheit einer Rheinreise.**
He's talking about the beauty of a Rhine excursion.

Hier ist das Buch der Rheinsagen.
Here is the book of Rhine legends.

The genitive expresses possession or a close relationship between two nouns.

a. Forms

	Masculine	Feminine	Neuter
Nom.	**der Mann**	**die Frau**	**das Haus**
Gen.	**des Mannes**	**der Frau**	**des Hauses**
	key sound: /s/	*key sound:* /r/	*key sound:* /s/

	Masculine	Feminine	Neuter
Nom.	**ein Mann**	**eine Frau**	**ein Haus**
	kein Mann	**keine Frau**	**kein Haus**
Gen.	**eines Mannes**	**einer Frau**	**eines Hauses**
	keines Mannes	**keiner Frau**	**keines Hauses**
	key sound: /s/	*key sound:* /r/	*key sound:* /s/

Note that the genitive masculine and neuter forms are identical and have the key sound /s/ in both the article and the noun.

For the feminine the key sound is /r/. (Remember that /r/ also signifies nominative masculine and feminine dative singular.)

Most masculine and neuter nouns of one syllable add **es** as the genitive singular ending (**des Mannes, des Hauses, des Freundes, des Bildes**). Nouns of more than one syllable usually add. only **s** (**des Sommers, des Dampfers, des Fräuleins**). Feminine nouns add nothing.

The genitive of proper names, regardless of gender, is usually formed by adding **s** (**Kurts** Freund, **Karls** Buch, **Lores** Haus, **Deutschlands** Landschaft).

PRACTICE

A.   *Give the genitive forms:*

1.   der Gast
2.   die Freundin
3.   das Jahr
4.   der Monat
5.   ein Tag
6.   ein Rheindampfer
7.   die Zeit
8.   eine Prüfung
9.   ein Mädchen
10.   ein Mann
11.   kein Fluß
12.   keine Butter
13.   das Gedicht
14.   die Bedeutung
15.   keine Legende
16.   eine Karte
17.   die Hauptstadt
18.   das Brot

B.   *Form genitive phrases:*

Example: das Haus — der Vater
das Haus des Vaters

1. das Auto — der Freund   2. die Familie — die Sekretärin
3. die Uhr — der Professor   4. das Brot — ein Mann   5. die Tür
— das Haus   6. der Name — das Büro   7. das Problem — eine

Frau   8. die Zeit — die Prüfung   9. die Uhr — die Schwester
10. das Gedicht — der Bruder

C. *Answer the following questions negatively and then make a positive statement using the indicated expression:*

> *Example:*   Ist das das Buch des Professors? (*ein Freund*)
> Nein, es ist nicht das Buch des Professors.
> Es ist das Buch eines Freundes.

1. Ist das der Koffer des Vaters? (ein Mädchen)   2. Ist das das Problem des Professors? (der Dekan)   3. Ist das das Haus eines Amerikaners? (ein Engländer)   4. Ist das die Arbeit eines Reiseführers? (eine Sekretärin)   5. Ist das das Bild eines Mannes? (eine Frau)

D. *Say in German:*

1. This is a map of Germany.   2. Mrs. Kolb's guest takes a trip.
3. Do you see the picture of the landscape?   4. I like the beauty of the Rhine.   5. That is not the beginning of the poem.
6. Heine's poem is very beautiful.

2. Prepositions with the Genitive

anstatt (statt)	*instead of*
trotz	*in spite of*
während	*during*
wegen	*on account of, because of*

The prepositions above are followed by genitive forms.

PRACTICE

A. *Expand the following sentences by using* **während** *with the indicated expressions:*

> *Example:*   Sie sprechen (*die Mahlzeit*).
> Sie sprechen während der Mahlzeit.

1. Es schneit sehr oft (der Winter).   2. In Deutschland ist es warm (der Sommer).   3. Herr Lenz und sein Gast reden (der Abend).   4. Sie reden (die Mahlzeit).   5. Karl und Kurt sprechen zusammen (die Reise).   6. Sie photographieren fleißig (die Rheinfahrt).   7. Kurt denkt oft an Lore (der Tag).

B. *Answer the following questions using* **wegen** *with the indicated expressions:*

> *Example:*   Warum bewundert Kurt die Landschaft? (*die Schönheit*)
> Er bewundert sie wegen der Schönheit.

1. Warum ist Lore nicht hier? (die Prüfung).   2. Warum ist Kurt so begeistert? (die Lorelei).   3. Warum bleiben sie nur so

kurz? (die Arbeit). 4. Warum photographiert er so fleißig? (die Schönheit der Landschaft). 5. Warum ist die Legende so bekannt? (das Gedicht).

C. *Say in German:*

1. because of the meal; 2. in spite of the meal; 3. in spite of the day; 4. because of the season; 5. during the summer; 6. during the winter; 7. in spite of the trip; 8. because of the taxi; 9. because of the guide; 10. instead of the exam.

D. *Say in German:*

1. They take a trip to Wiesbaden instead of a trip to Berlin. 2. They leave (**verlassen**) the house in spite of the weather. 3. Kurt knows the legend because of the poem. 4. It is cold in spite of the season. 5. They are coming back during the summer. 6. Lore is staying on account of the exam.

3. Adverbial Use of the Genitive

Eines Tages findet ihr die Zeit.
One day you'll find the time.

The genitive is used adverbially to express indefinite time or the time of usual or customary action.

die Stadt Köln
the city of Cologne

eine Tasse Kaffee
a cup of coffee

der Monat Januar
the month of January

In German, nouns of quantity or place and the word **Monat** stand directly before another noun, which never has an ending.

PRACTICE

Say in German:

1. one evening; one morning; 2. the city of Düsseldorf; 3. the city of Bonn; 4. the city of Bremen; 5. the Federal Republic of Germany; 6. the month of January; 7. the month of February

4. Da- and wo- Compounds

Er weiß nichts **von der Geschichte.**
Er weiß nichts **davon.**
He knows nothing about it.

Karl spricht nicht **über die Reise.**
Karl spricht nicht **darüber.**
Karl doesn't talk about it.

Ich denke **an die Rheinfahrt.**
Ich denke **daran.**
I'm thinking of it.

When a pronoun refers to one or more things or ideas, the pronoun is replaced by **da-** (**dar-** *before a vowel*) and combined with the preposition: **dafür** (*for it, for them*), **dazu** (*to it, to them, for that purpose*), **damit** (*with it, with them*), **darin** (note the linking **r**) (*in it, in them*).

Wovon weiß er nichts?
" `does he know nothing about? (About what . . . ?)

über spricht Karl?
.at does Karl talk about? (About what . . . ?)

/oran denken Sie?
Vhat are you thinking of? (Of what . . . ?)

Wo- and **wor-** can be combined with prepositions in the same manner as **da-** and **dar-** to ask questions about objects or ideas.

PRACTICE

A. *Answer the following questions, replacing the preposition and noun with a* **da**-*compound:*

Example: Ist er mit der Auskunft zufrieden?
Ja, er ist damit zufrieden.

1. Spricht Kurt oft von Amerika? 2. Denkt er oft an seine Universität? 3. Wartet er immer auf Post? 4. Schreibt er oft für die Zeitung? 5. Fahren Sie mit dem Dampfer? 6. Sitzen Sie auf dem Deck? 7. Wollen sie mit dem Zug fahren? 8. Versteht Kurt viel von der Geschichte? 9. Erkennt man ihn an seinem Akzent?

B. *Replace the repeated noun and preposition in the question with a* **da**-*compound:*

Example: Hier ist ein Zimmer. Wohnen Sie in dem Zimmer?
Hier ist ein Zimmer. Wohnen Sie darin?

1. Dort ist ein Restaurant. Ist ein Studentenheim neben dem Restaurant? 2. Das Mittagessen ist gut. Müssen wir viel für das Mittagessen bezahlen? 3. Hier ist ein Brief aus Amerika. Sehen Sie keine Adresse auf dem Brief? 4. Die Frage ist schwer. Haben Sie keine Antwort auf die Frage? 5. Das Problem ist nicht leicht. Soll ich nichts über das Problem sagen? 6. Physik? Hat sie kein Interesse für Physik?

C. *Change the questions in Exercise A by substituting a* **wo**-*compound for the prepositional phrase:*

Example: Ist er mit der Auskunft zufrieden?
Womit ist er zufrieden?

D. *Say in German:*

1. Are you paying for the meal? 2. Yes, I'm paying for it. 3. With what are you paying for the meal? 4. Kurt is satisfied with the meal, but I'm not satisfied with it. 5. What are you not satisfied with? 6. By the way, does Lore have the time for a trip? 7. No, she has no time for it. 8. Are you going on (**mit**) the train? 9. Yes, I'm going on it. 10. Is the suitcase in the car? 11. Yes, it's already in there. 12. What are you waiting for? 13. I'm waiting for the mail. 14. Are you waiting for it, too?

5. Declension of the Interrogatives <u>wer</u> and <u>was</u>

Nom.	**wer?**	*who?*	**was?**	*what*
Gen.	**wessen?**	*whose?*		
Dat.	**wem?**	*whom?, to whom?*		
Acc.	**wen?**	*whom?*	**was?**	*what*

The declension of **wer** is complete with all four cases, but **was** has no forms in the genitive or dative. Remember that **wo-** (**wor-** before a vowel) plus preposition is the equivalent of English preposition plus *what.*

Wer wohnt bei Frau Kolb?
Who resides at Mrs. Kolb's?

Was ist in der Schachtel?
What is in the box?

Wessen Gedicht kann Karl auswendig?
Whose poem does Karl know by heart?

Wem schreibt Kurt immer auf deutsch?
(To) whom does Kurt always write in German?

Auf wen wartet Lore?
For whom is Lore waiting?

Was studiert Kurt an der Universität in Bonn?
What does Kurt study at the university in Bonn?

6. Kennen Wissen Können

Ich kenne das Mädchen.
I know (am acquainted with) the girl.

Wir kennen Berlin.
We know Berlin.

Kennen Sie das Buch?
Do you know the book?

In German there are three verbs "to know." Use **kennen** to express acquaintanceship with a person, place, or thing.

Ich weiß, wann er kommt.
I know when he's coming.

Sie wissen, wo er wohnt.
You know where he lives.

Wissen is usually followed by a clause.

Er weiß nichts (. . . alles, . . . etwas).
He knows nothing (. . . everything, . . . something).

Das wissen wir nicht.
That we don't know.

Wissen is used with **alles, etwas, nichts,** and other indefinite words.

Er kann Schi laufen.
He knows how to ski.

Sie können lesen.
They know how to read.

Können means "to know how to" do something.

Können Sie Englisch?
Can you speak (do you know) English?

Können is also used to express knowledge of a language.

PRACTICE

A. *Complete the sentences below with the appropriate form of* **kennen, wissen,** *or* **können.**

> *Example:* Ich _____ den Mann.
> Ich kenne den Mann.

1. _____ Sie Frau Kolb? 2. Ich _____ sie schon lange. 3. _____ Sie, ob er kommt? 4. Wir _____ alles. 5. Du _____ ihn gut. 6. Er _____ Deutsch. 7. Ich _____, was das ist. 8. _____ Sie das Gedicht von Heine? 9. _____ Sie, wo Kurt wohnt? 10. Leider _____ ich nichts. 11. Ich _____ den Dekan. 12. _____ Sie Französisch?

B. *Say in German:*

1. He can read well. 2. Do you know how to drive a car? 3. I speak German. 4. She already knows how to write. 5. They can write, can't they? 6. Do you know English?

FINAL PRACTICE *Say first, then write in German:*

1. Whose father is talking with Kurt during the meal?   2. Karl is busy from morning till evening.   3. Who is delighted with the girl's beauty and charm?   4. Karl can't find the time for a Rhine trip.   5. "You can find the time for it during the summer," says Mr. Lenz.   6. Lore can't come. A trip instead of an exam; that would be the beginning of the end.   7. Karl isn't happy because of the weather.   8. They are now standing at the railing of the Rhine steamer.   9. Kurt doesn't understand the significance of the numerals.   10. They are on the bank (an dem Ufer) of the river.   11. To whom does Karl explain the numerals? "Do you see the numeral 550? Next to it is the name of the city."   12. You have the Rhine map. What can you see on it?   13. They are now eating in the dining hall.   14. They are eating bread with some marmalade on it.   15. They are also drinking a cup of tea.

1. ORAL PRACTICE

A. *LEARN THIS DIALOGUE:*

Kurt: Guten Tag. Ich bin Kurt Klein.
Herr Lenz: Sind Sie nicht Karls Freund aus Indiana?
Kurt: Das stimmt nicht ganz. Ich komme aus Wisconsin.
Herr Lenz: Entschuldigen Sie, bitte! Von Geographie verstehe ich nicht viel.
Kurt: Darf ich fragen: Kommt Karl bald wieder zurück? Er will mir die Stadt zeigen.
Herr Lenz: So? Er kennt sie aber selbst nicht gut.
Kurt: Wie lange wohnen Sie schon in Köln?
Herr Lenz: Erst seit einem Jahr.
Karl: Ach, Kurt, du bist schon hier. Papa, kennst du Kurt Klein?
Herr Lenz: Ja, wir kennen uns (*each other*) schon. Er wartet auf dich. Du bist heute der Reiseführer!

B. *COMPLETE APPROPRIATE RESPONSES BY KARL:*

Kurt: Was besuchen wir denn in der Stadt?
Karl: Wir _____, _____ und _____.
Kurt: Hast du einen Stadtplan?
Karl: Leider _____. Ich brauche _____.
Kurt: Ist der Dom sehr weit von hier?
Karl: Aber _____. Wir können _____.
Kurt: Ist die Bibliothek auch nahe?
Karl: Nein, wir _____.
Kurt: Wo ist das Opernhaus?
Karl: Direkt _____. Wir _____ einfach die Straße.
Kurt: Vielen Dank für die Auskunft.
Karl: _____.

C. *EXPRESS THE FOLLOWING IN GERMAN:*

Kurt: Where am I to pay tuition?
Secretary: Please go to the office across the hall. May I ask? How long have you been here?

Kurt:	A week. Yes, it's been a week today.
Secretary:	You speak German very well.
Kurt:	I've been speaking German for a long time.
Secretary:	I can tell. You have hardly any accent.
Kurt:	I'm living at Mrs. Kolb's. But I would like to eat lunch in the dining hall.
Secretary:	Very well. By the way, do you like it here in Cologne?
Kurt:	The people are very nice, and the city is beautiful.

D. COMPLETE THE SENTENCES:

1. Es besteht kein Grund zur _____ .
2. Mit dem Auto _____ man nur eine halbe _____ .
3. Vielen Dank für die _____ .
4. Kurt findet die Vorlesungen _____ interessant.
5. Während der _____ hat Kurt nur Interesse _____ Lore Lenz.
6. Karl kann nicht reisen. Er ist von morgens bis _____ _____ .
7. Auf jeden _____ machen die Freunde ihre (*their*) Reise vor Januar.
8. Sie versuchen es, sobald _____ _____ .

2. STRUCTURAL PRACTICE

A. COMPLETE WITH APPROPRIATE ENDINGS:

1. Kurt arbeitet für d— Vater in ein— Stadt in Amerika. 2. Er hat ein— Schwester, aber kein— Bruder. 3. Er möchte mit d— Flugzeug nach Europa fliegen. 4. Er möchte an d— Universität Köln Literatur studieren. 5. Ein— Tag— trifft er d— Dekan auf d— Straße. 6. „Kommen Sie morgen in— Büro!" sagt d— Dekan. 7. Ein— Sekretärin sitzt neben d— Dekan während d— Unterhaltung. 8. Kurt zeigt d— Sekretärin d— Paß. 9. Nach d— Unterhaltung geht er in d— Bibliothek. 10. Dort begegnet er ein— Freund. 11. Sie gehen zusammen durch d— Bibliothek

in d— Hörsaal. 12. Sie warten auf d— Professor. 13. Statt d— Professor— kommt ein— Mädchen. 14. Wegen ein— Erkältung (*f.*) kann der Professor nicht kommen.

B. REPLACE THE INDICATED WORDS WITH PRONOUNS:

1. Er kommt nicht ohne *seinen Freund.*
2. Gehen Sie bitte mit *Ihrem Vater!*
3. Kennen Sie *Frau Kolb?*
4. Nein, ich kenne nur *Herrn Kolb.*
5. Wir kennen *die Kolbs* sehr gut.
6. Durch *Karl und Lore* trifft Kurt nette Leute.
7. Warum wohnt Kurt nicht bei *Karl Lenz?*
8. Heute muß Kurt *seiner Mutter* schreiben.
9. Er schickt *den Eltern* ein Bild.
10. Er bringt *der Sekretärin* seinen Paß.

C. REPEAT THE SENTENCES USING THE INDICATED PRONOUNS:

1. Ich bin Amerikaner. (Sie)
2. Ich wohne in der Mitte von Amerika. (wir)
3. Ich arbeite in einer Bibliothek. (er)
4. Ich muß morgen früh in die Stadt fahren. (wir)
5. Ich verlasse das Haus um sieben Uhr. (sie, *feminine*)
6. Ich treffe Frau Kolb vor dem Haus. (er)
7. Ich spreche mit ihr. (ihr)
8. Ich lese ein Buch im Bus. (sie, *feminine*)
9. Ich soll auf den Vater warten. (du)
10. Ich sehe ihn. (er)
11. Ich gehe ins Büro. (er)
12. Ich schreibe einen Brief. (er)

D. REPEAT THE SENTENCES WITH THE INDICATED MODALS:

1. Der Brief ist für Sie. (müssen)
2. Er spricht fabelhaft Deutsch. (sollen)
3. Was tun Sie heute morgen? (wollen)

4. Sie gebrauchen den Stadtplan. (können)
5. Gehen wir zu Fuß? (können)
6. Überqueren wir die Straße? (müssen)
7. Wo bezahlt er die Semestergebühren? (sollen)
8. Er verbessert seine Aussprache. (können)
9. Sie haben keinen Akzent. (sollen)
10. Der Student liest das Buch über Deutschland. (müssen)

E. *USE APPROPRIATE FORMS OF THE IMPERATIVE TO COMPLETE THE COMMANDS:*

1. _____ bitte, Frau Kolb! (entschuldigen)
2. _____ uns bald, Kinder! (besuchen)
3. _____ doch, Kurt! (fliegen)
4. _____ nicht so unruhig, Frau Lenz! (sein)
5. _____ mir bitte, Herr Klein! (antworten)
6. _____ Karl für die Einladung, Kurt! (danken)
7. _____ nicht davon, Herr Kolb! (reden)
8. _____ bitte die Geschichte, Karl! (lesen)
9. _____ sie auch, Herr Lenz! (lesen)
10. _____ es sobald wie möglich, Herr Klein! (versuchen)

F. *SAY IN GERMAN:*

1. I have to read a story. 2. You are supposed to read it, too. 3. May I read the letter from America? 4. You may read it. 5. Why aren't you eating, Kurt? 6. Kurt is eating, but I'm not eating. 7. He is giving me the suitcase. 8. I don't want to take it.

G. *WRITE IN GERMAN:*

1. He's coming to our house (*to us*) with a friend. 2. Together they drive through the city. 3. They are now at Karl's house. 4. They want to speak with Mr. Lenz. 5. Mr. Lenz asks, "What

can I do for you?"   6. Kurt answers him, "You can help me."
7. "How can I help you?" 8. "You can explain this map to me."
9. It's a map of the Rhine. 10. Karl says to his sister, "Come
with us!" 11. "I can't come with you; I have an exam." 12. They
have to take the trip without her.   13. Kurt doesn't like this.
14. She doesn't like it either. 15. An exam instead of a trip? Do
you like that?

Die „Krone", bekanntes Gasthaus in Aßmannshausen
HENLE FROM MONKMEYER

I. UNTERHALTUNG

IM HOTEL IN ASSMANNSHAUSEN

Kurt: Karl, wach auf! Wir müssen uns beeilen.

Karl: (schläfrig) Was ist los? Warum . . . ?

Kurt: Du mußt aufstehen. Der Dampfer fährt um zehn Uhr ab.

Karl: (richtet sich auf und reibt sich die Augen) Laß ihn abfahren! Ich lege mich wieder hin.

Kurt: Nein, bitte! Du kannst dich nicht mehr hinlegen. Steh bitte auf!

Karl: Kann ich ins Bad? Bist du fertig?

Kurt: Ich muß mich noch rasieren.

Karl: Ich brauche wenigstens zehn Minuten. Ich muß mich waschen und kämmen.

Kurt: Rasierst du dich nicht?

Karl: (sieht sich im Spiegel an) Nein, ich glaube nicht. (Besinnt sich) Ach, wie ärgerlich! Ich habe keine Zahnpasta mehr.

Kurt: Ärgere dich nicht darüber! Nimm meine! Aber beeile dich jetzt!

Karl: Mach dir keine Sorgen! Wir verspäten uns nicht.

IN THE HOTEL AT ASSMANNSHAUSEN

Kurt: Karl, wake up! We have to hurry.

Karl: (sleepily) What's the matter? Why . . . ?

Kurt: You have to get up. The steamer leaves at ten.

Karl: (sits up and rubs his eyes) Let it leave! I'm going back to sleep again.

Kurt: Please don't! You can't lie down again. Please get up.

Karl: Can I get into the bathroom? Are you finished?

Kurt: I still have to shave.

Karl: It'll take me at least ten minutes. I still have to wash up and comb my hair.

Kurt: Aren't you going to shave?

Karl: (looks at himself in the mirror) No, I don't think so. (Remembers) Oh, how maddening! I don't have any more toothpaste.

Kurt: Don't fret about that. Take mine. But hurry up now.

Karl: Don't worry. We're not going to be late.

Karl steht auf, streckt sich und geht ins Bad. Die beiden Freunde unterhalten sich weiter durch die offene Tür.

Kurt: Wann sollen wir in Wiesbaden ankommen?

Karl: Ich weiß nicht genau. Ich erkundige mich später.

Kurt: Ich glaube, wir sollen um sieben Uhr ankommen.

Karl: Du irrst dich. Wir landen kurz vor acht in Biebrich.

Kurt: In Biebrich? Steigen wir nicht in Wiesbaden aus?

Karl: Wiesbaden liegt nicht am Rhein. Wir fahren mit dem Bus nach Wiesbaden. Oder wir bestellen uns ein Taxi.

Kurt: Ein Taxi? Ich kann mir das nicht leisten. Ich muß mir einen Pullover kaufen.

Karl: Bist du knapp an Geld? Ich kann dir etwas leihen.

Kurt: Danke. Ich erwarte einen Scheck von zu Hause. Bist du fertig?

Karl: Ich muß mich noch anziehen. Gehe runter[1] und bestelle Frühstück für zwei!

Karl gets up, stretches and goes into the bathroom. The two friends keep conversing through the open door.

Kurt: When are we supposed to get to Wiesbaden?

Karl: I don't know exactly. I'll inquire later.

Kurt: I think we're supposed to arrive at seven o'clock.

Karl: You're mistaken. We disembark at Biebrich shortly before eight.

Kurt: At Biebrich? Don't we get off in Wiesbaden?

Karl: Wiesbaden isn't on the Rhine. We'll take the bus to Wiesbaden. Or we order a cab.

Kurt: A cab? I can't afford that. I have to buy a sweater.

Karl: Are you short on cash? I can lend you some money.

Kurt: Thanks, but I expect a check from home. Are you finished in the bathroom?

Karl: I still have to dress. You go downstairs and order breakfast for two.

II. KOMBINATIONEN

Sagen Sie auf deutsch:

a. 1. Wake up, Karl.   2. Please wake up, Kurt.   3. Please wake up, Mr. Lenz.

b. 1. You have to get up, Karl.   2. We have to get up.   3. He wants to get up.

1. While **runter** is the abbreviated form of **herunter** (*down*[*stairs*], *toward speaker*), it is often used colloquially for both **herunter** and **hinunter** (*down*[*stairs*], *away from speaker*). In the above context **runter** is used in place of **hinunter**.

c. 1. It takes me at least ten minutes.   2. It takes me at least an hour.   3. It takes us at least a day.

d. 1. I have to wash.   2. I have to comb my hair.   3. I want to wash.   4. I want to comb my hair.

e. 1. How maddening! I don't have any more toothpaste.   2. How maddening! I don't have any more money.   3. How maddening! We don't have any more time.

f. 1. Don't fret about that, Karl.   2. Hurry up now, Karl!   3. Don't worry, Karl.

g. 1. When are we supposed to arrive in Wiesbaden?   2. When are you supposed to disembark at Biebrich?   3. We are supposed to arrive at eight o'clock.

h. 1. I'll inquire later.   2. I'll inquire tomorrow.   3. We'll inquire tonight.

i. 1. Aren't we getting off in Wiesbaden?   2. Aren't they getting off in Bremen?   3. Aren't you getting off in Aßmannshausen?

j. 1. I can't afford that.   2. I can't afford a cab.   3. I can't afford the trip.

k. 1. I have to buy myself a sweater.   2. I still have to buy (myself) toothpaste.   3. I still have to buy a ticket.

l. 1. I expect a check from home.   2. Do you expect a check from America?   3. I'm expecting money from my father.

III.   SAGEN UND FRAGEN

a. *Sie sind Kurt Klein. Sie sagen zu Karl:*

1. Er soll aufwachen. (*Use imperative*)   2. Er muß aufstehen.   3. Er kann sich nicht mehr hinlegen.   4. Sie müssen sich noch rasieren.   5. Er soll sich nicht ärgern.   6. Er soll Ihre Zahnpasta nehmen. (*Use imperative*)   7. Er soll sich beeilen. (*Use imperative*)   8. Sie kommen um sieben Uhr in Wiesbaden an.   9. Sie können sich das nicht leisten.   10. Sie müssen sich einen Pullover kaufen.   11. Sie erwarten einen Scheck von zu Hause.

b. *Sie sind Karl. Sie sagen zu Kurt:*

1. Sie legen sich wieder hin.   2. Sie wollen ins Bad.   3. Sie müssen sich waschen und kämmen.   4. Sie haben keine Zahnpasta mehr.   5. Er soll sich keine Sorgen machen.

6. Sie verspäten sich nicht. 7. Sie erkundigen sich später.
8. Er irrt sich. 9. Sie steigen nicht in Wiesbaden aus. 10. Sie
bestellen sich ein Taxi. 11. Sie können Kurt Geld leihen.
12. Sie müssen sich noch anziehen. 13. Er soll runter gehen.
(*Use imperative*) 14. Er soll Frühstück für zwei bestellen.
(*Use imperative*)

c. *Sie sind Karl. Sie fragen Kurt:*

1. was los ist. 2. ob Sie ins Bad können. 3. ob er sich
nicht rasiert. 4. wann Sie in Wiesbaden ankommen sollen.
5. ob er knapp an Geld ist. 6. ob er im Bad fertig ist.

IV. AUFSATZ

DIE SEHENSWÜRDIGKEITEN[1]

Kurt und Karl amüsieren sich großartig. Tagsüber besuchen sie
dieses oder jenes Schloß, manchmal auch eine Kirche oder gar[2]
ein Museum. Immer wieder[3] sagt Karl: „Der Reiseführer gibt hier
eine Ruine[4] an. Wir müssen uns die Ruine ansehen." Am näch-
5 sten Tag heißt es:[5] „Diese Kirche ist weltberühmt.[6] Die[7] sollten[8]
wir uns auch ansehen." Oder Karl sagt: „Das Museum in dem
Städtchen ist sehenswert.[9] Ich möchte[10] es dir zeigen."

Kurt interessiert sich natürlich für alles. Heute ist er jedoch
müde. Er möchte sich einfach ausruhen, in einem Café sitzen und
10 die schöne Natur genießen.

Kurt schlägt das Reisebuch auf. „Jeder Teil Deutschlands kann
dem Reisenden[11] etwas bieten. Welchen Teil des Landes wollen
Sie besuchen? Das kommt ganz auf Sie an. Sind Sie Bergsteiger[12]
oder Schifahrer?[13] Dann fahren Sie nach Bayern oder Österreich.
15 Schwimmen Sie gerne und ziehen Sie das Meer vor? Dann begeben
Sie sich[14] an den Strand[15] der Nord- oder Ostsee![16] Sind Sie erschöpft[17] und müssen sich erholen? Jede Gegend in Deutschland
hat einen Kurort[18] oder ein Heilbad."[19]

Der junge Student liest das Kapitel genau durch. Dann überlegt

---

1. sights (*e.g.: of a city*). 2. even. 3. **immer wieder** again and again.
4. ruin. 5. . . . **heißt es** this is the way it goes. 6. world-famous.
7. That (*demonstrative*). 8. should. 9. worth seeing. 10. would
like. 11. traveler. 12. mountain climber. 13. skier. 14. **begeben
Sie sich** betake yourself. 15. shore. 16. **die Ostsee** Baltic Sea. 17. exhausted. 18. health resort. 19. spa.

20 er sich: Wohin soll er während der Weihnachtsferien fahren? Im
Stillen[20] entschließt er sich: die Weihnachtsferien verbringt er in
Bayern. Er wird Wintersport treiben[21] und sich dabei — wie immer
— erkälten.

Beantworten Sie die folgenden Fragen:

1. Wie amüsieren sich die Freunde?   2. Was sagt Karl an einem
Tage?   3. Und was sagt er am nächsten Tag?   4. Warum will
Kurt sich heute nichts ansehen?   5. Was möchte er einfach tun?
6. Kann jeder Teil Deutschlands dem Touristen etwas bieten?
7. Welchen Teil des Landes soll man besuchen?   8. Wohin
fahren Sie als Bergsteiger oder Schifahrer?   9. Sie schwimmen
sehr gerne. Wo sollen Sie hinfahren?   10. Sie sind müde und
erschöpft. Wo können Sie sich erholen?   11. Wohin will der
junge Student während der Weihnachtsferien fahren?   12. Was
wird er in Bayern tun?   13. Erkältet er sich oft im Winter?

20. silently, to himself.   21. **Wintersport treiben** to engage in winter
sports.

V. WORTSCHATZ

ab/fahren	to leave, depart	**sich besinnen**	to remember
sich amüsieren	to have a good time	**bestellen**	to order
		bieten	to offer
an/geben	to indicate, specify	**das Café**	café
		dabei	at the same time, in the process
an/kommen	to arrive		
an/kommen auf + *accusative*	to depend on	**dieser, diese, dieses**	this
das kommt auf Sie an	that depends on you	**durch/lesen**	to read through
		sich entschließen	to decide
sich an/sehen	to take a look at	**sich erholen**	to recuperate, recover
sich an/ziehen	to get dressed		
ärgerlich	annoying, provoking	**sich erkälten**	to catch cold
		sich erkundigen	to inquire
sich ärgern über	to fret, worry about	**erschöpft**	exhausted
		fertig	ready, done, finished
sich auf/richten	to raise oneself, sit upright	**das Frühstück**	breakfast
		die Gegend	area, section, region
auf/schlagen	to open (*a book*)		
auf/stehen	to get up	**genießen**	to enjoy
auf/wachen	to wake up	**gern(e)** + *any verb*	to like to do something
sich aus/ruhen	to take a rest	**großartig**	marvelous
aus/steigen	to get off	**herunter**	down(stairs) (*toward speaker*)
das Bad	bath		
sich beeilen	to hurry		

sich hin/legen	to lie down	**runter**	downstairs
sich interessie**ren**	to be interested	der **Scheck**	check
für	in	**schläfrig**	sleepy
sich irren	to be mistaken	das **Schloß**	castle
jeder, jede,	each, every	**schwimmen**	to swim
jedes		der **Spiegel**	mirror
jener, jene,	that	**sich strecken**	to stretch
jenes		**tagsüber**	in the day time
das **Kapi**t**el**	chapter	**sich überlegen**	to ponder, reflect,
sich kämmen	to comb one's		think about
	hair	**sich unterhalten**	to converse
knapp	scarce, short (on)	**verbringen**	to spend, pass
landen	to land		(time)
leihen	to lend	**vergehen**	to pass, slip away
sich leisten	to afford		(time)
los	loose	**sich verspäten**	to be late
Was ist	What's the	**vor/ziehen**	to prefer
los?	matter?	**sich waschen**	to wash, take a
	What's wrong?		bath
das **Meer**	ocean	die **Weihnachts-**	Christmas vaca-
die **Nat**u**r**	nature	**ferien**	tion
offe**n**	open	(*plural*)	
(das) **Österreich**	Austria	**welcher,**	which
der **Pull**o**ver**	sweater	**welche,**	
sich rasie**ren**	to shave	**welches**	
reiben	to rub	die **Zahnpasta**	toothpaste

VI. ERKLÄRUNGEN UND ÜBUNGEN

1. Separable
Prefixes

a.

Verbs like **abfahren** (*to leave* [*by vehicle*]), **aufstehen** (*to get up*), **zurückkommen** (*to come back*) consist of a prefix and a verb. Unlike the inseparable prefixes, **ab-, auf-, zurück-** have an independent meaning. Common separable prefixes are: **ab-, an-, auf-, aus-, mit-, vor-, zurück-**. The separable prefix ˙carries the main stress. *Pronounce:* **auf/schlagen, vor/ziehen, zurück/gehen.**

b.

Er fährt morgen früh ab.
He's leaving tomorrow morning.

Wir kommen bald zurück.
We're coming back soon.

Kommen Sie bitte mit!
Please come along.

Separable prefixes are separated from the verb in the present tense and the imperative and stand last in the clause.

c.

Er will morgen abfahren.
He wants to leave tomorrow.

Wir müssen bald zurückkommen.
We have to come back soon.

In the infinitive, separable prefixes remain prefixed to the verb.

PRACTICE

A. Answer the following questions, first affirmatively, then negatively:

> *Example:* Steht Karl auf?
> Ja, er steht auf.
> Nein, er steht nicht auf.

1. Wacht Karl bald auf?   2. Stehen die Freunde früh auf?
3. Fahren sie ab?   4. Steigen sie in Aßmannshausen aus?
5. Lassen sie den Dampfer abfahren? 6. Legt Karl sich wieder hin?   7. Sollen sie um acht in Wiesbaden ankommen?
8. Kommen sie um sieben in Biebrich an?   9. Muß Karl sich noch anziehen?   10. Zieht Kurt sich an?

B. Answer the following questions using the indicated expressions:

> *Example:* Wann steht Kurt auf? (*sehr früh*)
> Kurt steht sehr früh auf.

1. Wann fährt er ab? (früh) 2. Wo steigt er ein? (in Wiesbaden) 3. Wo steigt er aus? (in Heidelberg) 4. Wann kommt er zurück? (am nächsten Tag) 5. Wer kommt nicht mit? (Fräulein Lore) 6. Wann wacht Karl auf? (bald) 7. Was fährt um zehn Uhr ab? (der Dampfer) 8. Wer steigt in Biebrich aus? (die Freunde) 9. Was geht immer weiter? (die Unterhaltung)

C. Change the following sentences to imperatives:

> *Example:* Ich fahre früh ab.
> Fahre früh ab!
> Fahren Sie früh ab!

1. Ich steige in Köln ein.   2. Ich komme um sieben an.   3. Ich

gebe das zu (*to admit*). 4. Ich fahre morgen zurück. 5. Ich stehe nicht auf. 6. Ich steige in Wiesbaden aus.

D. Respond to the following commands using the modal indicated:

    Example: Kommen Sie bitte mit! (*können*)
                 Ich kann nicht mitkommen.

1. Kommen Sie bitte mit! (dürfen)   2. Fahren Sie bitte früh ab! (sollen)   3. Steigen Sie jetzt ein! (können)   4. Gehen Sie morgen zurück! (müssen)   5. Lesen Sie das Buch durch! (wollen) 6. Stehen Sie bitte auf! (dürfen)   7. Fahren Sie zurück! (können)

E. Say in German:

1. Lore is waking up.   2. Karl is hurrying.   3. Kurt is coming along tomorrow.   4. Please come back today, Kurt!   5. I have to leave early.   6. Can you get off at Bonn?   7. I have to get off at Bonn.   8. Do you arrive tomorrow?   9. Kurt goes downstairs. 10. Open the book, please.

2. Reflexive Pronouns

Reflexive pronouns are either direct objects (accusative) or indirect objects (dative):

Subject	Accusative Reflexive	Dative Reflexive
ich	mich	mir
du	dich	dir
er	sich	sich
sie	sich	sich
es	sich	sich
wir	uns	uns
ihr	euch	euch
sie	sich	sich
Sie	sich	sich

The reflexive pronouns are identical with the personal pronouns except in the 3rd person and conventional address where the pronoun is always **sich,** no matter whether accusative or dative, singular or plural.

a. Reflexive Verbs with the Accusative

Reflexive verbs always take a pronoun object in the accusative or dative corresponding to the subject. Most reflexive verbs have accusative reflexive pronouns. The following are some common accusative reflexive verbs:

sich ausziehen	*to get undressed*
sich entschließen	*to decide*
sich freuen über + accusative	*to be happy about*
sich freuen auf + accusative	*to look forward to*
sich setzen	*to sit down*

Learn the following model conjugation for a reflexive verb with direct object pronouns

ich	wasche mich	*I am washing (myself)*
du	wäschst dich	*you are washing (yourself)*
er		*he*
sie	wäscht sich	*she* } *is washing (herself)*
es		*it* (itself)
wir	waschen uns	*we are washing (ourselves)*
ihr	wascht euch	*you are washing (yourselves)*
sie	waschen sich	*they are washing (themselves)*
Sie	waschen sich	*you are washing (yourself, yourselves)*

b. Reflexive Verbs with the Dative

ich	helfe mir	*I help myself*
du	hilfst dir	*you help yourself*
er		*he helps himself*
sie	hilft sich	*she helps herself*
es		*it helps itself*
wir	helfen uns	*we help ourselves*
ihr	helft euch	*you help yourselves*
sie	helfen sich	*they help themselves*
Sie	helfen sich	*you help yourself, yourselves*

Any transitive verb may be reflexive even if its object is in the dative.

c. Dative of Interest

Ich kaufe ihr etwas.
I'm buying something for her.

Er ist mir ein lieber Freund.
He is a dear friend of mine (to me.)

Die Zeit verging ihnen schnell.
Time passed quickly for them.

The dative of interest indicates for whom or to whose advantage something is done, exists, or happens.

d. Possession with Dative Pronouns

Ich wasche mir das Gesicht. (*preferred to:* **Ich wasche mein Gesicht.**)
I'm washing my face.

Er kämmt sich das Haar.
He's combing his hair.

Ich ziehe mir den Pullover an.
I'm putting my sweater on.

When the emphasis is on the person rather than on proprietorship, the definite article is used before nouns designating parts of the body or articles of clothing. The use of the indirect reflexive pronoun clearly identifies the possessor.

e. Reciprocal Reflexives

Wir sehen uns oft.
Wir sehen einander oft.
We see each other (one another) often.

Sie erzählen sich oft Geschichten.
Sie erzählen einander oft Geschichten.
They often tell each other (one another) stories.

The reflexive pronouns or the invariable **einander** may be used reciprocally. **Einander** is preferred to avoid ambiguity.

PRACTICE

A. *Answer the following questions affirmatively:*

Example: Amüsieren Sie sich?
Ja, ich amüsiere mich.

1. Ruhen Sie sich aus? 2. Zieht sie sich an? 3. Beeilen sie sich? 4. Entschließt ihr euch? 5. Setzt er sich? 6. Unterhalten sie sich? 7. Helfen Sie sich? 8. Erholst du dich? 9. Hilft er sich? 10. Erkälten Sie sich?

B. *Say in German:*

1. Kurt is getting dressed. 2. He is washing his face and hands. 3. Karl is taking a rest. 4. They have to hurry. 5. Are you angry? 6. Now Karl is putting his sweater on. 7. Is he catching a cold? 8. Lore is also interested in a Rhine trip. 9. Do you write each other letters (**Briefe**)?

3. Present Tense of werden (*to become, get*)

ich	**werde**	*I am becoming, getting*
du	**wirst**	*you are becoming, getting*
er, sie, es	**wird**	*he, she, it is becoming, getting*
wir	**werden**	*we are becoming, getting*
ihr	**werdet**	*you are becoming, getting*
sie	**werden**	*they are becoming, getting*
Sie	**werden**	*you are becoming, getting*

PRACTICE

A. *Change the sentences by using the subjects indicated:*

> *Example:* Er wird alt. (*ich*)
> Ich werde alt.

1. Ich werde müde. (*Sie*) 2. Sie wird nicht jünger. (*ihr auch nicht*) 3. Unsere Nachbarn werden immer freundlicher. (*Ihre auch?*) 4. Glauben Sie, daß Hans bald fertig wird? (*ich*) 5. Ihr solltet nicht ärgerlich werden. (*du*)

FINAL PRACTICE

Say first, then write in German:

1. Karl has to get up. 2. The steamer leaves at 10 o'clock. 3. Karl doesn't want to get up. 4. Kurt still has to shave. 5. Karl has to wash up and comb his hair. 6. He needs at least ten minutes. 7. Karl doesn't have any more toothpaste. 8. Kurt says, "Take mine, but hurry up now." 9. They are supposed to arrive in Biebrich shortly before eight. 10. They don't get off at Wiesbaden. 11. Wiesbaden is not on the Rhine. 12. Kurt and Karl take a bus to Wiesbaden. 13. Kurt wants to buy himself a sweater. 14. Karl can lend him some money. 15. Kurt is expecting a check from home. 16. Karl gets dressed. 17. Kurt goes downstairs and orders breakfast. 18. They don't see one another very often.

Weinberg und Schloß am Rhein
HENLE FROM MONKMEYER

I. UNTERHALTUNG

NACH DER RHEINREISE

Kurt: Dein Vater hatte recht. Die Rheinreise war einfach herrlich.

Karl: Wir hatten auch Glück. Das Wetter war wunderbar.

Kurt: Nur am Schluß wurde es trüb.

Karl: Das hat dich nicht gestört. Du hast trotzdem viel photographiert.

Kurt: Ja, ich habe viele Aufnahmen gemacht. Ich habe mich fast geschämt.

Karl: Geschämt? Warum?

Kurt: Ich habe das Knipsen immer kritisiert. Jetzt habe ich es selbst so gemacht.

Karl: Du hast doch nicht nur photographiert.

Kurt: Das ist wahr. Ich habe mit vielen Leuten geplaudert.

Karl: Sag mal, wer war der große Herr? Er hat Zigarren geraucht. War er vielleicht Bayer?

Kurt: Woher hast du das gewußt?

Karl: Ich habe es an seiner Aussprache gemerkt. Und wer war der Franzose?

AFTER THE TRIP DOWN THE RHINE

Kurt: Your father was right. The Rhine trip was simply marvelous.

Karl: We were also lucky. The weather was wonderful.

Kurt: Only toward the end it turned cloudy.

Karl: That didn't bother you. You took a lot of pictures in spite of it.

Kurt: Yes, I took a lot of pictures. I was almost ashamed.

Karl: Ashamed? Why?

Kurt: I've always criticized (*indiscriminate*) picture taking. Now I've done the same thing.

Karl: But you didn't just take pictures.

Kurt: That is true. I chatted with a lot of people.

Karl: Tell me, who was the tall man? He smoked cigars. Was he a Bavarian?

Kurt: Yes. How did you know that?

Karl: I could tell by his pronunciation. And who was the Frenchman?

LESSON 7

Kurt: Er war Maler und hat viel von sich erzählt. Er hat mir sogar seine Skizzen gezeigt.

Karl: Vielleicht ist er bekannt. Weißt du, wie er heißt?

Kurt: Keine Ahnung. Ich weiß, er hat in Paris studiert, in Rom gelebt und ist durch ganz Deutschland gereist.

Karl: Der Herr war sehr gesprächig, oder du warst sehr neugierig.

Kurt: Beides. Ich habe Fragen gestellt und er hat sie beantwortet.

Karl: Du hast viel auf der Reise gelernt.

Kurt: Also bin ich nicht der typische Tourist.

Karl: Bestimmt nicht. Du interessierst dich für Menschen, nicht nur für Vergnügen.

Kurt: He was a painter and talked a good deal about himself. He even showed me his sketches.

Karl: Perhaps he's well known. Do you know what his name is?

Kurt: No idea. I know he studied in Paris, lived in Rome, and has traveled through all of Germany.

Karl: The gentleman was very talkative or you were very inquisitive.

Kurt: Both. I asked questions and he answered them.

Karl: You learned a lot on the trip.

Kurt: Then I'm not the typical tourist.

Karl: Definitely not. You're interested in people, not merely in fun.

II. KOMBINATIONEN

Sagen Sie auf deutsch:

a. 1. Your father was right.   2. Your teacher was right. 3. Was he right?

b. 1. We were lucky too; the trip was simply marvelous.   2. I was lucky too; the weather was beautiful.   3. They were lucky; it got cloudy only at the end.

c. 1. I've always criticized picture-taking.   2. I've criticized the weather.   3. I haven't criticized the hotel.

d. 1. I chatted with many people.   2. I chatted with an American.   3. I chatted with a professor from New York.

e. 1. Who was the man? —He smoked a lot.   2. Who was the

man? —Was he perhaps a Bavarian?   3. Who was the man?
—Was he perhaps from Hamburg?

f.   1. Do you know what his name is?   2. Do you know where
he lives?   3. Do you know why he travels?

g.   1. I know he studied in Paris.   2. I know he's lived in Rome.
3. I know he's traveled a lot.

h.   1. The gentleman was talkative and he was nice.   2. You
were talkative or you were inquisitive.   3. He was talkative
or you were inquisitive.

i.   1. You're interested in people.   2. I'm interested in people,
too.   3. They are not interested in fun.

III. SAGEN UND FRAGEN

a.   *Sie sind Kurt Klein. Sie sagen zu Karl:*

1. Sein Vater hatte recht.   2. Sie hatten beide Glück.   3. Sie
haben viel geknipst.   4. Sie haben sechzig Aufnahmen
gemacht.   5. Sie waren typische Touristen.   6. Sie haben
sich fast geschämt.   7. Sie haben das Knipsen oft kritisiert.
8. Sie haben es selbst so gemacht.   9. Sie haben mit vielen
Leuten geplaudert.   10. Sie haben viele Fragen gestellt.
11. Sie interessieren sich nicht nur für Vergnügen.

b.   *Sie sind Karl. Sie sagen zu Kurt:*

1. Das Wetter hat ihn nicht.gestört.   2. Er hat trotzdem viel
photographiert.   3. Er hat doch nicht nur photographiert.
4. Sie haben alles an der Aussprache gemerkt.   5. Sie glauben,
der Maler ist bekannt.   6. Er (*Kurt*) war neugierig.   7. Er
hat viel auf der Reise gelernt.   8. Er ist kein typischer Tourist.
9. Er interessiert sich für Menschen.   10. Er interessiert sich
aber auch für Vergnügen.

c.   *Sie sind Karl. Sie fragen Kurt:*

1. wie viele Aufnahmen er gemacht hat.   2. ob der große
Herr Bayer war.   3. ob der andere (*other*) Herr Franzose
war.   4. ob der Franzose gesagt hat, wo er wohnt.   5. ob er
auch gesagt hat, wie er heißt.   6. ob das Wetter gut war.
7. ob es später trüb wurde.

IV. AUFSATZ

FILM UND BÜHNE

Während seines Aufenthalts in Deutschland hat sich Kurt hauptsächlich mit kulturellen bzw.[1] literarischen Dingen beschäftigt. In der Architektur, wie auch auf anderen Gebieten,[2] hat das Land große Fortschritte[3] gemacht. Im Gegensatz dazu[4] haben

5 nur wenige Filme Kurt beeindruckt. Sehr viele sind romantisch und sentimental, sogar ein bißchen kitschig.[5] Sie haben das Leben und die Liebe verschönert[6] und romantisiert. Nur ein paar haben sich mit wichtigen Themen befaßt.[7] Kurt hatte sich von den Filmen des Auslands[8] eine bessere Meinung gebildet.[9] Die Re-

10 gisseure[10] Frankreichs, Italiens und Japans z.B. haben vorzügliche[11] Filme gedreht.[12]

Das Theater hat in der Geschichte Deutschlands immer eine große Rolle gespielt. Es hat aber seine frühere Höhe[13] noch nicht wieder erreicht. Man hat zwar die Jahre über viele Theater gebaut,

15 sogar während der Nachkriegszeit;[14] aber Gebäude ersetzen[15] keine Dichter.

Was hat man also in den letzten[16] Jahren aufgeführt?[17] Man bevorzugt[18] die Dramatiker[19] der Vergangenheit, wie Lessing, Goethe, Schiller und Hauptmann. Auch die Meisterwerke[20] des

20 Auslands hat man inszeniert,[21] wie z.B. Stücke von Tennessee Williams und Jean Anouilh. Die deutschen Dramatiker der Nachkriegszeit[22] dagegen[23] haben nicht sehr viel geleistet. Gewiß haben sie der Bühne neue Schauspiele geliefert, aber diese Werke haben keinen besonderen Wert. Weder im Film noch im Theater kommt

25 man den Leistungen der Vorkriegsjahre[24] nahe.[25]

---

1. **bzw.** = **beziehungsweise** respectively, or.   2. **auf anderen Gebieten** in other areas.   3. progress.   4. **im Gegensatz dazu** in contrast (to that).
5. junky, silly, cheap.   6. **verschönern** to embellish.   7. **sich befassen mit** to be concerned with, treat.   8. **das Ausland** foreign countries.
9. **bilden** to form.   10. (film) director.   11. outstanding, excellent.
12. **drehen** *here:* to produce, turn out.   13. **seine frühere Höhe** its earlier heights.   14. postwar years.   15. to replace.   16. recent.   17. **aufführen** to perform.   18. **bevorzugen** to favor.   19. dramatists.   20. masterpieces.   21. **inszenieren** to put on (a play).   22. postwar period.
23. on the other hand.   24. prewar years.   25. **nahekommen** to approach, come close to.

Beantworten Sie die folgenden Fragen:

1. Womit hat sich Kurt hauptsächlich beschäftigt? 2. Auf welchen Gebieten hat das Land große Fortschritte gemacht? 3. Warum haben so wenige Filme Kurt beeindruckt? 4. Wovon hatte er sich eine bessere Meinung gebildet? 5. Was hat in der Geschichte Deutschlands immer eine große Rolle gespielt? 6. Was hat man sogar während der Nachkriegsjahre getan? 7. Welche Dramatiker bevorzugt man jetzt? 8. Nennen Sie zwei Dramatiker aus dem Ausland! 9. Wer hat nicht sehr viel geleistet? 10. Was haben sie der Bühne geliefert?

V. WORTSCHATZ

die **Ahnung**	presentiment, idea	die **Liebe**	love
der **Aufenthalt**	stay, sojourn	**liefern**	to furnish, supply
die **Aufnahme,** die **Aufnahmen** [1]	photo, snapshot	der **Maler**	painter
		mehrere	several
bauen	to build	die **Meinung**	opinion
der **Bayer**	Bavarian	**neugierig**	curious
beeindrucken	to impress	**plaudern**	to chat
sich **beschäftigen**	to busy oneself, be occupied	**rauchen**	to smoke
		recht haben	to be right
die **Bühne**	stage	die **Rolle**	role
der **Dichter,** die **Dichter**	poet, writer	eine **Rolle spielen**	to play a role, a part
das **Ding,** die **Dinge**	thing	sich **schämen**	to be ashamed
		das **Schauspiel,** die **Schauspiele**	drama
erreichen	to attain, reach		
der **Film,** die **Filme**	film, movie	**schlecht**	bad
das **Gebäude,** die **Gebäude**	building	der **Schluß**	end, conclusion
		selbst	myself, himself, etc.
gesprächig	talkative	die **Skizze,** die **Skizzen**	sketch
Glück haben	to be lucky		
(das) **Italien**	Italy	**stören**	to disturb
(das) **Japan**	Japan	das **(Theater)- stück,** die **(-)stücke**	(stage) play
das **Knipsen**	picture taking, shooting of snapshots		
		trotzdem	nevertheless
der **Krieg**	war	**trüb**	gloomy, cloudy
kritisieren	to criticize	**typisch**	typical
leben	to live, reside	die **Vergangenheit**	past
leisten	to achieve		
die **Leistung**	achievement, performance	das **Vergnügen**	pleasure
		wahr	true

1. Starting with this *Wortschatz*, most nouns will be accompanied by their nominative plural forms.

weder . . .	neither . . . nor	**wichtig**	important
noch		**die Zigarre, die**	cigar
wenige	few	**Zigarren**	
das Werk, die	work	**zwar**	to be sure, it is
Werke			true,
der Wert	value		admittedly

VI. ERKLÄRUNGEN UND ÜBUNGEN

1. Regular and Irregular Verbs

In English and German there are two main classes of verbs, regular (sometimes called weak) and irregular (sometimes called strong). Regular verbs add endings to the present stem to form past tenses (infinitive: *learn;* simple past: *learned;* past participle: *learned*). Irregular verbs alter the stem vowel (infinitive: *ring;* simple past: *rang;* past participle: *rung*).

2. Simple Past of Regular Verbs

a. Forms

ich sagte	*I said, was saying, used to say*[1]
du sagtest	*you said, were saying, used to say*
er sagte	*he said, was saying, used to say*
wir sagten	*we said, were saying, used to say*
ihr sagtet	*you said, were saying, used to say*
sie sagten	*they said, were saying, used to say*
Sie sagten	*you said, were saying, used to say*

The past stem is formed by suffixing **-t-** to the present stem of the infinitive:

sag-t-

When the present stem ends in **-d** or **-t,**[2] **-et** is suffixed:

land-et-   arbeit-et-   öffn-et-

To this stem are added the personal endings of the past indicative:

	Singular	Plural
1st person	**-e**	**-en**
2nd person	**-est**	**-et**
3rd person	**-e**	**-en**
	conventional form	**-en**

1. The English *I used to* + *infinitive* is generally rendered in German colloquial speech by adding **immer** (in the sense of *usually*) to the verb expressing the action or event. Example: *My mother used to say* . . . **Meine Mutter sagte immer** . . . .
2. Or -chn, -ckn, -dn, -fn, -gn, -tm.

112

b. Use

Er plauderte immer mit den Leuten.
He was always chatting (used to chat) with the people.

Ich wohnte lange in Paris.
I lived in Paris for a long time.

Der Maler **erzählte** viel von sich, **zeigte** Kurt seine Skizzen und **beantwortete** viele Fragen.
The painter talked a good deal about himself, showed Kurt his sketches, and answered many questions.

The simple past, especially in written German, is used for actions which are customary, continued, sequential, or simultaneous.

c. Simple Past of haben, sein, werden

Learn the simple past forms of the following important verbs:

haben	sein	werden
ich hatte (*had*)	ich war (*was*)	ich wurde (*became*)
du hattest	du warst	du wurdest
er hatte	er war	er wurde
wir hatten	wir waren	wir wurden
ihr hattet	ihr wart	ihr wurdet
sie hatten	sie waren	sie wurden
Sie hatten	Sie waren	Sie wurden

d. Simple Past of Modal Auxiliary Verbs

Modals with umlaut in the infinitive drop the umlaut in the simple past. Otherwise, they are to be treated like regular verbs:

können	müssen	dürfen
ich konnte	ich mußte	ich durfte
du konntest	du mußtest	du durftest
er konnte	er mußte	er durfte
wir konnten	wir mußten	wir durften
ihr konntet	ihr mußtet	ihr durftet
sie konnten	sie mußten	sie durften
Sie konnten	Sie mußten	Sie durften

sollen	wollen
ich sollte	ich wollte
du solltest	du wolltest
er sollte	er wollte
wir sollten	wir wollten
ihr solltet	ihr wolltet
sie sollten	sie wollten
Sie sollten	Sie wollten '

Note the additional change in this modal:

mögen

ich mochte
du mochtest
er mochte
wir mochten
ihr mochtet
sie mochten
Sie mochten

Also, observe the special forms for **wissen:**

ich wußte
du wußtest
er wußte
wir wußten
ihr wußtet
sie wußten
Sie wußten

e. Separable Prefixes in the Simple Past

Er legte sich hin.
He lay down.

Man führte das Schauspiel auf.
They put on the play.

Separable prefixes stand last in a main clause when the verb is in the simple past.

PRACTICE

A. Conjugate in the simple past:

1. sagen   2. machen   3. arbeiten   4. dürfen   5. müssen
6. haben   7. sein   8. werden

B. Give the simple past of the following verbs in the specified persons:

1. **wir** (sagen, spielen, bilden, einführen, arbeiten, sein)
2. **er** (haben, werden, gehören, können, wollen, müssen)
3. **Sie** (sein, besuchen, bewundern, werden, führen, sich erholen)
4. **sie** (sing.) (warten, glauben, hören, begegnen, werden)
5. **ich** (müssen, haben, spielen, leben, beantworten)

C. Change to simple past:

1. Herr Lenz hat recht.   2. Die Rheinreise ist herrlich.   3. Die zwei Freunde haben Glück.   4. Sie haben gutes Wetter.   5. Es

114

wird immer besser. 6. Nichts stört sie. 7. Sie machen viele Aufnahmen. 8. Kurt kritisiert das Knipsen nicht. 9. Er photographiert oft. 10. Ein Herr redet ihn an. 11. Dieser Herr raucht eine Zigarre. 12. Er ist Bayer. 13. Karl merkt es an der Aussprache. 14. Kurt stellt viele Fragen. 15. Der Herr beantwortet sie.

D. *Change the verbs (and pronouns) to appropriate plural forms:*

1. Ich machte eine Rheinreise.
2. Sie konnte nicht mitkommen.
3. Ich ärgerte mich darüber.
4. Ich plauderte mit einem Herrn.
5. Er war sehr gesprächig.

E. *Change each statement by substituting the items indicated:*

> *Example:* Herr Lenz war gestern in Bonn. (*die Freunde — in Wiesbaden*)
> Die Freunde waren gestern in Wiesbaden.

1. Herr Lenz hatte schlechtes Wetter. (die Freunde — gutes Wetter)
2. Die Freunde machten viele Aufnahmen. (der Franzose — wenige)
3. Der Franzose war Maler. (Kurt und Karl — Studenten)
4. Der Maler lebte in Paris. (Seine Familie — Deutschland)
5. Kurt studierte in Köln. (Mehrere Freunde — Göttingen)
6. Kurt wollte die Rheinreise machen. (Karl — müssen)

F. *Say in German, using the simple past:*

1. The weather was beautiful. 2. We took a trip. 3. I talked to a Bavarian. 4. He was smoking a cigar. 5. He was living in Munich. 6. I didn't know his name. 7. I learned a lot.

3. Compound Past of Regular Verbs
a. Forms

German past participles add the prefix **ge-** and the suffix **-t** to the present stem. Verbs with stem **-ier-** do not prefix **ge-**:

gearbeitet	*worked*	**gelernt**	*learned*
gefragt	*asked*	**geliefert**	*furnished; delivered*

but: **studiert** *studied*

Learn these patterns of the compound past of regular verbs:

USING **haben** AS THE AUXILIARY

ich	**habe gesagt**	*I said, have said*
du	**hast gesagt**	*you said, have said*
er, sie, es	**hat gesagt**	*he, she, it said, has said*

115

wir	haben gesagt	*we said, have said*
ihr	habt gesagt	*you said, have said*
sie	haben gesagt	*they said, have said*
Sie	haben gesagt	*you said, have said*

USING sein AS THE AUXILIARY

ich	bin gereist	*I traveled, have traveled*
du	bist gereist	*you traveled, have traveled*
er, sie, es	ist gereist	*he, she, it traveled, has traveled*
wir	sind gereist	*we traveled, have traveled*
ihr	seid gereist	*you traveled, have traveled*
sie	sind gereist	*they traveled, have traveled*
Sie	sind gereist	*you traveled, have traveled*

Verbs that are intransitive and express a change of position or condition require **sein** as the auxiliary in the compound past. Note also that **bleiben, begegnen, werden,** and **sein** itself are conjugated with **sein** in the compound past.

WITH A REFLEXIVE PRONOUN

ich	habe mich interessiert	*I was (have been) interested*
du	hast dich interessiert	*you were (have been) interested*
er, sie, es	hat sich interessiert	*he, she, it was (has been) interested*
wir	haben uns interessiert	*we were (have been) interested*
ihr	habt euch interessiert	*you were (have been) interested*
sie	haben sich interessiert	*they were (have been) interested*
Sie	haben sich interessiert	*you were (have been) interested*

In normal word order the reflexive pronoun follows the finite verb. In inverted word order it follows the subject: **Habe ich mich** nicht dafür **interessiert?**

b. Use

Ich habe viele Aufnahmen gemacht.
I took many pictures.

Das Theater hat immer eine große Rolle gespielt.
The theater has always played an important part.

Du hast dich für Menschen interessiert.
You were interested in people.

The compound past expresses a single, definite, past action which connects the past with the present. It is the customary conversational past tense. The compound past may be equivalent in meaning to both the simple past and present perfect in English. In form, the compound past is in many ways like English, except that in German the past participle stands last in a main clause.

c. Compound Past of <u>haben</u>, <u>sein</u>, <u>werden</u>

haben

ich	habe gehabt	I (have) had
du	hast gehabt	you (have) had
er, sie, es	hat gehabt	he, she, it (has) had
wir	haben gehabt	we (have) had
ihr	habt gehabt	you (have) had
sie	haben gehabt	they (have) had
Sie	haben gehabt	you (have) had

sein

ich	bin gewesen	I have been, I was
du	bist gewesen	you have been, you were
er, sie, es	ist gewesen	he, she, it has been, he, she, it was
wir	sind gewesen	we have been, we were
ihr	seid gewesen	you have been, you were
sie	sind gewesen	they have been, they were
Sie	sind gewesen	you have been, you were

werden

ich	bin geworden	I have become, I became
du	bist geworden	you have become, you became
er, sie, es	ist geworden	he, she, it has become, he, she, it became
wir	sind geworden	we have become, we became
ihr	seid geworden	you have become, you became
sie	sind geworden	they have become, they became
Sie	sind geworden	you have become, you became

d. Past Participle of Verbs with Inseparable Prefix

besuchen	besucht
erwarten	erwartet

The prefix **ge-** is omitted in the past participles of verbs with inseparable prefix.

e. Past Participle of Verbs with Separable Prefix

aufführen	aufgeführt
anschauen	angeschaut

Past participles of verbs with separable prefix have **-ge-** between the separable prefix and the verb stem.

PRACTICE

A. *Conjugate in the compound past:*

1. machen   2. leisten   3. bauen   4. sein   5. haben   6. sagen
7. werden

B. *Give the compound past of the following verbs in the specified persons:*

1. **wir** (sagen, spielen, bilden, einführen, arbeiten)
2. **er** (haben, werden, bauen, gehören)
3. **Sie** (sein, führen, sich interessieren, besuchen)
4. **ich** (machen, beantworten, sich erholen, werden)

C. *Change from simple past to compound past:*

Example: Der Maler machte Skizzen.
Der Maler hat Skizzen gemacht.

1. Der Mann arbeitete in Deutschland. 2. Wir besuchten ihn. 3. Ich stellte Fragen. 4. Kurt reiste durch Deutschland. 5. Er bewunderte die Landschaft. 6. Sie war wirklich schön.

D. *Make the following sentences negative and substitute pronouns wherever possible:*

Example: Der Film hat Kurt sehr beeindruckt.
Nein, er hat ihn nicht beeindruckt.

1. Die Rheinreise ist herrlich gewesen. 2. Das Wetter ist wunderbar gewesen. 3. Das Wetter ist trüb geworden. 4. Das hat Kurt gestört. 5. Karl hat sich amüsiert. 6. Kurt und Karl haben viel gelernt.

E. *Express the following sentences in the compound past:*

1. Er schaut sich viele Filme an. 2. Wenige Filme beeindrucken Kurt. 3. Kurt bildet sich eine bessere Meinung. 4. Die Regisseure drehen gute Filme. 5. Sie befassen sich mit wichtigen Themen. 6. Man baut viele Theater. 7. Viele Deutsche (*Germans*) besuchen das Theater. 8. Man führt moderne Stücke auf. 9. Das Theater spielt immer eine große Rolle. 10. Das Land macht viele Fortschritte.

F. *Form questions with the expressions indicated:*

Example: Ich habe lange in Köln gewohnt. (*wie lange?*)
Wie lange haben Sie in Köln gewohnt?

1. Ich habe den Professor oft besucht. (wie oft?) 2. Ich habe mich bei ihm amüsiert. (wann?) 3. Ich habe gute Fortschritte in seiner Klasse gemacht. (wo?) 4. Ich habe seine Vorlesungen (*lectures*) bewundert. (warum?) 5. Ich habe mich für seine Arbeit interessiert. (warum?) 6. Ich habe ihm viel über Amerika erzählt. (worüber?) 7. Im September bin ich durch das Rhein-

land gereist. (wohin?) 8. Ich bin nicht gerne nach Hause zurückgereist. (wohin?)

FINAL PRACTICE   *Say first, then write in German:*

1. Karl's father was right.   2. The trip was splendid.   3. Kurt and Karl were lucky.   4. The weather became overcast only at the end.   5. That did not disturb them.   6. Kurt took pictures on the trip.   7. Are you critical of taking snapshots?   8. Kurt talked with a gentleman (**Herrn**).   9. The gentleman was (a) Bavarian and was smoking a cigar.   10. Could you tell it from his accent? 11. The Frenchman was (a) painter.   12. He studied in New York and has traveled a lot.   13. I was very talkative and asked questions.   14. Are you interested only in fun?   15. Kurt occupied himself with literature.   16. But the theater did not impress him much.

„Ich habe früher nichts von Rheinwein verstanden. Jetzt kenne ich mich schon aus."
GREGOR KIERBLEWSKY

I. UNTERHALTUNG

KURT BERICHTET ÜBER SEINE REISE

Frau Kolb: Sie sind lange fort gewesen.
Kurt: Wir haben uns gemütlich den Rhein angesehen.
Frau Kolb: Sie sehen sehr gebräunt aus.
Kurt: Ich war viel im Freien. Anfang der Woche war ich noch dunkler.
Frau Kolb: Sie sind wohl mit dem Dampfer gefahren?
Kurt: Nur auf der Hinfahrt. Auf der Rückfahrt reisten wir im Auto.
Frau Kolb: Mit dem Auto? Ist das nicht teuer?
Kurt: Im Gegenteil. Karl traf zufällig einen Freund. Er hat uns mitgenommen.
Frau Kolb: Dann hat es Sie ja gar nichts gekostet.
Kurt: Die Reise war wirklich billig. Wir haben meistens in Jugendherbergen übernachtet.
Frau Kolb: Haben Sie auch gut gegessen?
Kurt: Gut gegessen und getrunken. Ich habe sogar alte Rheinlieder gesungen.
Frau Kolb: Das gehört dazu, gerade wie der Rheinwein.

KURT REPORTS ON HIS TRIP

Mrs. Kolb: You've been away a long time.
Kurt: We took a leisurely look at the Rhine.
Mrs. Kolb: You look very tanned.
Kurt: I was outdoors a lot. At the beginning of the week I was even more tanned.
Mrs. Kolb: I suppose you traveled by steamer?
Kurt: Only on the way down. On the way back we came by car.
Mrs. Kolb: By car? Isn't that expensive?
Kurt: Just the opposite. Karl happened to meet a friend. He took us along.
Mrs. Kolb: Then it didn't cost you anything.
Kurt: The trip was really inexpensive. We spent the night mostly in youth hostels.
Mrs. Kolb: Did you eat well?
Kurt: Ate and drank well. I even sang old Rhine songs.
Mrs. Kolb: That's part of it, just like the Rhine wine.

Kurt: Ich habe früher nichts von Rheinwein verstanden.
          Jetzt kenne ich mich schon aus.

Frau Kolb: Ich habe es beinahe vergessen: man hat Sie öfter
           angerufen.

Kurt: Wissen Sie, woher der Anruf kam?

Frau Kolb: Ein Herr hat nach Ihnen gefragt, aber seinen Namen
           nicht angegeben.

Kurt: Kam Post für mich, Frau Kolb? Mein Scheck sollte
          schon gestern hier sein.

Frau Kolb: Er ist gestern angekommen. Ich erkannte sofort den
           Umschlag.

Kurt: Hatte ich sonst noch Post?

Frau Kolb: Ja, zwei, drei Briefe und eine Ansichtskarte. Ich habe
           alles auf Ihr Zimmer gebracht.

Kurt: Recht vielen Dank.

Frau Kolb: Bitte. Keine Ursache.

Kurt: I never knew anything about Rhine wines before. Now I
          feel pretty expert.

Mrs. Kolb: I almost forgot. Somebody called you several times.

Kurt: Do you know where the call came from?

Mrs. Kolb: A gentleman asked for you, but didn't give his name.

Kurt: Was there any mail for me, Mrs. Kolb? My check was sup-
          posed to be here yesterday.

Mrs. Kolb: It arrived yesterday. I recognized the envelope right away.

Kurt: Did I have any other mail?

Mrs. Kolb: Yes, two or three letters and a picture postcard. I took
           everything up to your room.

Kurt: Thanks a lot.

Mrs. Kolb: You're welcome. Don't mention it.

II. KOMBINATIONEN

Sagen Sie auf deutsch:

a. 1. You've been away a long time. 2. No, I haven't been
away long.   3. My brother has been away a long time.

b. 1. You look tanned. 2. Mr. Lenz doesn't look very tanned.
3. At the beginning of the week, I was even more tanned.

c. 1. I suppose you came by steamer. 2. He probably came by car. 3. They probably came by bus.

d. 1. Just the opposite. —The trip was very expensive. 2. Just the opposite. —Karl met a friend. 3. On the contrary, the friend took us along.

e. 1. Then it didn't cost you anything at all. 2. It didn't cost him anything at all. 3. No, it didn't cost them anything at all.

f. 1. You ate well? —That's part of it. 2. You sang Rhine songs? —That's part of it, too. 3. You drank Rhine wine? —That's part of it.

g. 1. I almost forgot. —Somebody called you several times. 2. Mrs. Kolb almost forgot. —A man asked for Kurt. 3. Kurt almost forgot. —His check was supposed to be here.

h. 1. I recognized the envelope. 2. Can Mrs. Kolb recognize the envelope? 3. Should she know the envelope?

i. 1. I took everything to your room. 2. She only took the mail to his room. 3. She didn't take the postcard to his room.

j. 1. Thank you. —You are welcome. 2. Thank you, Mrs. Klein. —Don't mention it. 3. Thank you, Mrs. Kolb. —You're welcome, Mr. Klein.

III. SAGEN UND FRAGEN

a. *Sie sind Frau Kolb. Sie sagen zu Kurt:*

1. Er ist lange fort gewesen. 2. Er sieht sehr gebräunt aus. 3. Sie haben es beinahe vergessen. Man hat ihn öfter angerufen. 4. Ein Herr hat nach ihm gefragt. 5. Sein Brief ist gestern angekommen. 6. Sie erkannten sofort den Umschlag. 7. Sie haben alle Post auf sein Zimmer gebracht.

b. *Sie sind Kurt. Sie sagen zu Frau Kolb:*

1. Sie haben sich gemütlich den Rhein angesehen. 2. Sie waren Anfang der Woche noch dunkler. 3. Sie sind auf der Hinfahrt mit dem Dampfer gefahren. 4. Sie reisten auf der Rückfahrt im Auto. 5. Für Sie war die Reise sehr billig.

6. Sie haben meistens in Jugendherbergen übernachtet. 7. Sie haben gut gegessen und getrunken. 8. Sie haben früher von Rheinwein nichts verstanden. 9. Sie kennen sich aber jetzt schon gut aus. 10. Ihr Scheck sollte schon gestern hier sein.

c. *Sie sind Frau Kolb. Sie fragen Kurt:*

1. ob er mit dem Dampfer gefahren ist. 2. ob ein Privatauto nicht teuer ist. 3. ob er gut gegessen hat. 4. ob eine Rheinreise billig ist.

d. *Sie sind Kurt. Sie fragen Frau Kolb:*

1. ob sie weiß, woher Ihr Anruf kam. 2. ob Post für Sie kam. 3. ob Sie sonst noch Post bekommen haben. 4. wo die Post jetzt ist.

IV. AUFSATZ

SCHULE UND LAUFBAHN[1]

Kurt plaudert gern. Vor einer Woche hat er neben einem Herrn im Café gesessen. Dieser[2] stellte sich vor: Dr. Hans Greiber, Gymnasiallehrer.[3] „Ich unterhalte mich immer gerne mit Amerikanern", sagte Dr. Greiber. „Ich bin ein Jahr in Amerika gewesen und es
5 hat mir gut dort gefallen."
„Warum sind Sie nicht länger geblieben?" erkundigte sich Kurt.
„Unser Kultusministerium[4] hatte mich nach Amerika geschickt", erklärte Dr. Greiber. „Ich sollte dort das Erziehungswesen[5] studieren. Dafür hat man mich auf ein Jahr beurlaubt."[6]
10 „Ich bin schon fünf (5) Wochen hier, verstehe aber das Schulsystem und die Ausbildungsmöglichkeiten[7] noch nicht."
„Es kommt auf die Wahl des Berufes an", erklärte Dr. Greiber. „Nehmen wir an, Sie sind Bäcker. Sie sind im Alter von sechs (6) Jahren in die Volksschule[8] eingetreten. Sie sind acht (8) Jahre

---

1. career. 2. the latter. 3. *teacher in a Gymnasium (secondary school roughly equivalent to high school plus junior college).* 4. State Department of Education. 5. educational system. 6. **beurlauben** to grant a leave. 7. educational possibilities. 8. elementary school.

15 dort geblieben. Mit vierzehn (14) Jahren haben Sie die Volksschule
verlassen. Dann sind Sie Bäckerlehrling[9] geworden. Als Lehrling[10]
besuchten Sie drei (3) Jahre lang mehrere Male in der Woche eine
Berufsschule.[11] Nach dem dritten[12] Jahr mußten Sie eine Gesellenprüfung[13] machen. Nach einigen[14] weiteren Jahren im Beruf
20 haben Sie Ihre Meisterprüfung[15] gemacht. Heute haben Sie Ihre
eigene Bäckerei."

„Und Sie?" lachte Kurt. „Sie sind ja nicht Handwerker,[16] sondern Akademiker."[17]

„Ich bin auch mit sechs Jahren in die Volksschule gegangen.
25 Mit zehn (10) bin ich ins Gymnasium gekommen. Mit neunzehn
(19) Jahren habe ich das Abitur[18] gemacht, das heißt[19] die
Schlußprüfung[20] in einem Gymnasium. Danach habe ich mein
Studium an der Universität begonnen. Ich habe in Heidelberg und
Tübingen Philosophie studiert und meine Examen[21] in Heidelberg
30 abgelegt.[22] Ich habe gut abgeschnitten[23] und kurz danach meine
Doktorarbeit[24] geschrieben. Die Behörden[25] haben mich zum Studienassessor[26] ernannt. Ich bin jetzt in Köln angestellt."

Dr. Greiber und Kurt sind zusammen an die Haltestelle gegangen. Zuerst aber haben sie ihre[27] Adressen und Telefonnum-
35 mern ausgetauscht.[28]

Beantworten Sie die folgenden Fragen:

1. Wo hat Kurt gestern abend gesessen? 2. Wen hat er dort
getroffen? 3. Was ist Dr. Greiber von Beruf? 4. Wie lange ist
Dr. Greiber in Amerika gewesen? 5. Wie hat es ihm dort gefallen? 6. Wer hat ihn nach Amerika geschickt? 7. Was versteht Kurt noch gar nicht? 8. Mit wieviel Jahren ist der Bäcker
in die Volksschule eingetreten? 9. Wie lange ist er dort geblieben? 10. Mit wie vielen Jahren hat er die Volksschule verlassen?
11. Was ist er dann geworden? 12. Was für Prüfungen mußte
er machen? 13. Was für eine Schule mußte er als Lehrling besuchen? 14. Ist Dr. Greiber Handwerker? 15. In welche Schule
ist er mit zehn Jahren gekommen? 16. Wann hat er das

9. apprentice to a baker. 10. apprentice. 11. trade school. 12. third.
13. test for journeyman. 14. some, several. 15. (trade) master's
examination. 16. craftsman. 17. academician. 18. *final examination in a Gymnasium.* 19. **das heißt** that is. 20. final examination.
21. examinations. 22. **Examen ablegen** to take an examination.
23. **abschneiden** to make out (*on an examination*). 24. doctoral dissertation. 25. authorities. 26. *academic rank in a Gymnasium.*
27. their. 28. **austauschen** to exchange.

Abitur gemacht? 17. An welchen Universitäten hat er studiert?
18. Wo hat er seine Examen abgelegt? 19. Wo ist er jetzt angestellt? 20. Wohin sind Kurt und Dr. Greiber gegangen? 21.
Was haben die beiden (*two*) ausgetauscht?

V. WORTSCHATZ

an/nehmen, nahm an, angenommen, er nimmt an	to assume; to accept	im Freien	outside, in the open
		gebräunt	tanned
		im Gegenteil	on the contrary
der Anruf	telephone call	die Haltestelle	bus or streetcar stop
an/rufen, rief an, angerufen	to call (up)	die Hinfahrt	the way there
		die Jugendherberge, die Jugendherbergen	youth hostel
die Ansichtskarte	picture postcard		
an/stellen	to employ	lachen	to laugh
sich aus/kennen, kannte sich aus, sich ausgekannt	to know one's way around	das Mal	time (in sequence)
		meistens	mostly
aus/sehen, sah aus, ausgesehen, er sieht aus	to look, appear	mit/nehmen, nahm mit, mitgenommen, er nimmt mit	to take along
der Bäcker	baker	öfter	rather often, several times
die Bäckerei	bakery	die Rückfahrt	the trip back
beginnen, begann, begonnen	to begin	schicken	to send
		singen, sang, gesungen	to sing
beinahe	almost	das Telefon	telephone
bekommen, bekam, bekommen	to get, receive	übernachten	to spend the night
der Beruf	occupation, profession, trade	der Umschlag	envelope
		die Ursache	cause
dunkel	dark	keine Ursache	don't mention it
eigen	own		
ein/treten, trat ein, ist eingetreten, er tritt ein	to enter	sich vor/stellen	to introduce oneself
		die Wahl	choice; election
		der Wein	wine
		woher	where . . . from
ernennen, ernannte, ernannt	to appoint, designate	wohl	probably, I suppose
fort	away	zufällig	accidentally, by chance

VI. ERKLÄRUNGEN UND ÜBUNGEN

1. Simple Past of Irregular Verbs

a. Forms

ich trank	*I drank, I was drinking*
du trankst	*you drank, you were drinking*
er trank	*he drank, he was drinking*
wir tranken	*we drank, we were drinking*
ihr trankt	*you drank, were drinking*
sie tranken	*they drank, they were drinking*
Sie tranken	*you drank, you were drinking*

Irregular verbs change the internal stem vowel in the simple past:

Infinitive	Past Stem
essen	aß
lesen	las
nehmen	nahm
schreiben	schrieb
trinken	trank
kommen	kam[1]
leiden	litt[1]

To the past stem are added the following personal endings:

	Singular	Plural
1st person	-	**-en**
2nd person	**-(e)st**[2]	**-(e)t**[2]
3rd person	-	**-en**
	Sie form	**-en**

PRACTICE

A. Give the simple past of the following verbs in the persons indicated:

1. essen (er, wir) 2. schreiben (ich, ihr) 3. trinken (ich, sie [sing.]) 4. mitnehmen (er, ihr) 5. lesen (du, Sie) 6. kommen (sie [plural], wir)

B. Conjugate in all persons of the simple past:

1. ich schrieb 2. ich blieb 3. ich fuhr 4. ich aß 5. ich kam an 6. ich las 7. ich sang 8. ich nahm 9. ich litt 10. ich trank

1. Occasionally, the final consonant(s) will be changed.
2. Stems ending in **-d, -t,** etc. have **-est** and **-et.** If the stem ends in **-s** or **-ß,** usually only **-t** is added to form the 2nd person singular and plural.

127

2. Compound Past of Irregular Verbs

a. Forms

The compound past of irregular verbs consists of an auxiliary (**haben** or **sein**) and a past participle. The past participle often has a different stem vowel from the infinitive and the simple past:

Infinitive	Simple Past	Past Participle
lesen	**las**	**gelesen**
trinken	**trank**	**getrunken**
nehmen	**nahm**	**genommen**

The past participle is formed by adding the prefix **ge-** and the suffix **-en** to the past-participle stem:

ge-trunk-en	**getrunken**
ge-schrieb-en	**geschrieben**
ge-nomm-en	**genommen**

Learn these patterns of the compound past of irregular verbs:

USING **haben** AS THE AUXILIARY

ich habe getrunken	*I drank, I have drunk*
du hast getrunken	*you drank, you have drunk*
er hat getrunken	*he drank, he has drunk*
wir haben getrunken	*we drank, we have drunk*
ihr habt getrunken	*you drank, you have drunk*
sie haben getrunken	*they drank, they have drunk*
Sie haben getrunken	*you drank, you have drunk*

USING **sein** AS THE AUXILIARY

ich bin gekommen	*I came, I have come*
du bist gekommen	*you came, you have come*
er ist gekommen	*he came, he has come*
wir sind gekommen	*we came, we have come*
ihr seid gekommen	*you came, you have come*
sie sind gekommen	*they came, they have come*
Sie sind gekommen	*you came, you have come*

b. Verbs with Inseparable Prefix

ich habe verstanden
ich habe bekommen

Verbs with inseparable prefix do not require the prefix **ge-**.

c. Verbs with Separable Prefix

ich habe angerufen
ich bin angekommen

The separable element is prefixed to the past participle.

PRACTICE

A. Give the compound past of the following verbs in the persons indicated:

1. lesen (wir, Sie) 2. essen (er, du) 3. schreiben (ich, ihr)
4. ankommen (sie [sing.], sie [plural]) 5. trinken (er, wir)
6. mitnehmen (er, ich)

B.   Conjugate in all persons of the compound past:

1. ich habe genommen   2. ich habe geschrieben   3. ich habe gelesen 4. ich habe mitgenommen 5. ich habe getrunken 6. ich habe vorgelesen   7. ich habe bekommen   8. ich habe angerufen   9. ich habe vergessen   10. ich habe gesungen

3. Principal Parts

Infinitive	Simple Past	Auxiliary	Participle	3rd Person Singular
Regular:				
sagen	**sagte**		**gesagt**[1]	
eilen	**eilte**	**ist**	**geeilt**	
Irregular:				
singen	**sang**		**gesungen**[1]	
fahren	**fuhr**	**ist**	**gefahren**	**fährt**

The principal parts of a verb are so called because all tenses can be formed from them.

Practice the following principal parts of verbs you have already learned. (Verbs with similar stem changes are grouped together in classes for ease of memorization.) Note especially the principal parts of reflexive verbs and of separable-prefix verbs:

I. **bleiben** (*to stay, remain*)   **blieb**   ist geblieben
   leihen (*to lend*)   **lieh**   geliehen
   schreiben (*to write*)   **schrieb**   geschrieben
   (**beschreiben** [*to describe*])[2] **beschrieb**   beschrieben
   steigen (*to climb*)   **stieg**   ist gestiegen
   (**aus/steigen** [*to get off*])   **stieg aus**   ist ausgestiegen

II. **bieten** (*to offer*)   **bot**   geboten
    fliegen (*to fly*)   **flog**   ist geflogen
    genießen (*to enjoy*)   **genoß**   genossen
    sich entschließen (*to decide*) **entschloß sich** sich entschlossen

III.

a. **finden** (*to find*)   **fand**   gefunden
   singen (*to sing*)   **sang**   gesungen
   trinken (*to drink*)   **trank**   getrunken

b. **beginnen** (*to begin*)   **begann**   begonnen
   sich besinnen (*to remember*)   **besann sich**   sich besonnen

1. **haben** (**hat**) to be used as the auxiliary with all verbs not conjugated with **sein** (**ist**).
2. Verbs formed from simple verbs by the addition of a prefix always have the same stem changes as the simple verbs from which they are formed.

| helfen (*to help*) | half | geholfen | er hilft |
| schwimmen (*to swim*) | schwamm | ist geschwommen | |

IV. kommen (*to come*)	kam	ist gekommen	
(bekommen [*to get*])	bekam	bekommen	
(an/kommen [*to arrive*])	kam an	ist angekommen	
sprechen (*to speak*)	sprach	gesprochen	er spricht
treffen (*to meet*)	traf	getroffen	er trifft

V. ein/treten (*to enter*)	trat ein	ist eingetreten	er tritt ein
geben (*to give*)	gab	gegeben	er gibt
(an/geben [*to specify*])	gab an	angegeben	er gibt an
lesen (*to read*)	las	gelesen	er liest
(durch/lesen [*to read through*])	las durch	durchgelesen	er liest durch
liegen (*to lie*)	lag	gelegen	
sehen (*to see*)	sah	gesehen	er sieht
(an/sehen [*to look at*])	sah an	angesehen	er sieht an
(aus/sehen [*to look*])	sah aus	ausgesehen	er sieht aus
vergessen (*to forget*)	vergaß	vergessen	er vergißt

VI. auf/schlagen (*to open [a book]*)	schlug auf	aufgeschlagen	er schlägt auf
fahren (*to drive, ride, go*)	fuhr	ist gefahren	er fährt
(ab/fahren [*to depart*])	fuhr ab	ist abgefahren	er fährt ab
tragen (*to carry, wear*)	trug	getragen	er trägt
sich waschen (*to wash, bathe*)	wusch sich	sich gewaschen	er wäscht sich

VII. gefallen (*to appeal to*)	gefiel	gefallen	es gefällt
heißen (*to be called*)	hieß	geheißen	
lassen (*to leave, let*)	ließ	gelassen	er läßt
(verlassen [*to leave*])	verließ	verlassen	er verläßt
laufen (*to run*)	lief	ist gelaufen	er läuft
an/rufen (*to call up*)	rief an	angerufen	
behalten (*to keep, hold*)	behielt	behalten	er behält
sich unterhalten (*to converse*)	unterhielt sich	sich unterhalten	er unterhält sich

4. Verbs with Additional Irregularities

essen (*to eat*)	aß	gegessen	er ißt
gehen (*to go, walk*)	ging	ist gegangen	
haben (*to have*)	hatte	gehabt	er hat
nehmen (*to take*)	nahm	genommen	er nimmt
(an/nehmen [*to assume*])	nahm an	angenommen	er nimmt an
(mit/nehmen [*to take along*])	nahm mit	mitgenommen	er nimmt mit
sein (*to be*)	war	ist gewesen	er ist
sitzen (*to sit*)	saß	gesessen	
(besitzen [*to own*])	besaß	besessen	
stehen (*to stand*)	stand	gestanden	
(bestehen [*to exist*])	bestand	bestanden	
(gestehen [*to admit*])	gestand	gestanden	
(verstehen [*to understand*])	verstand	verstanden	
tun (*to do, make*)	tat	getan	

werden (*to become*)	**wurde**	**ist geworden**	**er wird**
ziehen (*to pull*)	**zog**	**gezogen**	
(sich an/ziehen [*to get dressed*])	**zog sich an**	**sich angezogen**	
(vor/ziehen [*to prefer*])	**zog vor**	**vorgezogen**	

Some verbs, like those above, have irregularities besides changes in the stem vowel, and others form their past and past participle in unpredictable patterns. Give your special attention to the principal parts of such verbs.

5. Mixed Verbs

bringen	(*to bring, take*)	**brachte**	**gebracht**
denken	(*to think*)	**dachte**	**gedacht**
brennen	(*to burn*)	**brannte**	**gebrannt**
kennen	(*to know*)	**kannte**	**gekannt**
rennen	(*to run*)	**rannte**	**ist gerannt**
nennen	(*to name*)	**nannte**	**genannt**
wenden	(*to turn*)	**wandte**	**gewandt**
senden	(*to send*)	**sandte**	**gesandt**

Mixed verbs have some of the characteristics of both regular and irregular verbs, as well as other irregularities. Like regular verbs, mixed verbs have -t- in the simple past and, like irregular verbs, vowel change in the simple past and the past participle. The mixed verbs **bringen** and **denken** have still other irregularities.

6. Aber and sondern

Ein Herr hat angerufen, aber er hat seinen Namen nicht angegeben.
A gentleman called, but he didn't give his name.

Diese Prüfung ist nicht sehr lang, aber sie ist schwer.
This test is not very long, but it is difficult.

Das Haus ist nicht grün, sondern weiß.
The house is not green, but white.

Aber and **sondern** both mean *but*; **sondern** is used after a negative to express a contrary fact. Note the expression **nicht nur . . . sondern auch** (*not only . . . but also*):

Diese Prüfung ist nicht nur lang, sondern auch schwer.
This test is not only long, but also difficult.

131

LESSON 8

PRACTICE

A. *Give the present, simple past, and compound past of the following verbs in the person indicated:*

Example: ich (*essen*)
ich esse, ich aß, ich habe gegessen

1. er (mitnehmen)
2. wir (bleiben)
3. sie (sing.) (laufen)
4. du (lesen)
5. ich (fliegen)

6. ich (aussteigen)
7. du (treffen)
8. Sie (trinken)
9. er (ansehen)
10. ich (gehen)

B. *Change the following sentences to (a) simple past; (b) compound past:*

1. Er kommt in Bayern an. 2. Es wird schön dort. 3. Er steigt in München aus. 4. Wir reisen nach Köln. 5. Fahren Sie mit dem Dampfer? 6. Er schreibt einen Brief an seine Eltern. 7. Das kostet nichts. 8. Ich bin lange fort.

C. *Answer the following questions using the words or phrases indicated:*

Example: Wann haben Sie Ihre Arbeit begonnen? (*um zehn Uhr*)
Ich habe sie um zehn Uhr begonnen.

1. Wann sind Sie abgefahren? (um acht Uhr) 2. Wann sind Sie angekommen? (um zehn Uhr) 3. Wo haben Sie gegessen? (in einem Restaurant) 4. Was haben Sie getrunken? (Kaffee und Milch) 5. Neben wem haben Sie im Café gesessen? (einem Lehrer) 6. Wo hat er seine Doktorarbeit geschrieben? (in Heidelberg) 7. Wo sind Sie auf der Rückfahrt ausgestiegen? (in Köln)

D. *Say in German:*

1. I went to Cologne. 2. I was away a long time. 3. I went by ship. 4. My parents lived in Cologne for many years. 5. I went to elementary school there. 6. I came to America at the age of fourteen (**vierzehn**). 7. My brother and I both went to the University in America.

FINAL PRACTICE *Say first, then write in German:*

1. Kurt is talking with Mrs. Kolb. 2. He's been away for a long time. 3. He and Karl were taking a look at the Rhine. 4. Kurt

is very tanned. Mrs. Kolb noticed that.   5. He was outside a good bit.   6. They went down by ship, but they came back by car.   7. It was not very expensive.   8. Karl's friend took them along in his car.   9. Karl and Kurt spent the night in youth hostels.   10. They ate and drank very well.   11. Kurt even sang.   12. He drank Rhine wine and now he knows his way around.   13. Somebody (**jemand, man**) called Kurt several times.   14. Kurt also received some mail.   15. His check arrived yesterday.   16. Mrs. Kolb recognized the envelope right away.   17. She took everything up to Kurt's room.

Eine Tasse Kaffee im Freien
GERMAN INFORMATION CENTER

I. UNTERHALTUNG

NACH DEM EXAMEN

Kurt: War das Chemieexamen wirklich so schwer?
Lore: Ja, wirklich. Ich habe Angst vor dem Resultat.
Kurt: Machen Sie sich keine Sorgen darüber!
Lore: Das wird nicht leicht sein.
Kurt: Worüber sorgen Sie sich?
Lore: Ich frage mich immer wieder: Ist Chemie das richtige Fach für mich?
Kurt: Sie haben doch immer gute Noten bekommen.
Lore: Na ja, aber die letzten Arbeiten waren ziemlich schlecht. Ich bin sehr unzufrieden.
Kurt: Sie müssen sich ein wenig entspannen. Haben Sie Lust auf eine Tasse Kaffee?
Lore: Ja, aber erst muß ich einige Besorgungen machen. Können Sie ein paar Minuten warten?
Kurt: In welches Geschäft gehen Sie? Ich fahre Sie gerne hin.
Lore: Es lohnt sich kaum. Das Warenhaus ist nur drei Straßen von hier.
Kurt: Ich fahre Sie trotzdem. Steigen Sie ein!
Lore: Diesen Wagen habe ich noch nie gesehen.

AFTER THE EXAM

Kurt: Was the chemistry exam really that hard?
Lore: It really was. I'm afraid of the result.
Kurt: Don't worry about it.
Lore: That won't be easy.
Kurt: What are you worried about?
Lore: I keep asking myself: Is chemistry the right field for me?
Kurt: You've always gotten good grades.
Lore: Yes, but the last few tests were pretty bad. I'm very dissatisfied.
Kurt: You need to relax a bit. Are you in the mood for a cup of coffee?
Lore: Yes, but first I have to run some errands. Can you wait a few minutes?
Kurt: What store are you going to? I'll be glad to drive you there.
Lore: It's hardly worth it. The department store is only three blocks from here.
Kurt: I'll drive you just the same. Get in.
Lore: I haven't seen this car before.

LESSON 9

135

Kurt: Er gehört nicht mir. Ich habe ihn mir geliehen. Übrigens, wo ist das Warenhaus?

Lore: In der Mozartstraße. Biegen Sie links ein!

Kurt: Ich kenne dieses Warenhaus. Am Anfang mußte ich fast jeden Tag hingehen.

Lore: Wieso denn?

Kurt: Man bringt nicht immer die richtigen Sachen mit.

Lore: Wir sind schon da. Wo parken Sie?

Kurt: Ich werde schon einen Platz finden. Ich warte auf Sie am Eingang.

10 Minuten später

Kurt: Das ging aber schnell.

Lore: Ich wußte genau, was ich suchte: Abteilung, Marke, Preislage.

Kurt: Jetzt können wir endlich unseren Kaffee trinken. Wollen Sie ins Continental?

Lore: Was gefällt Ihnen so gut an diesem Café?

Kurt: Die Terrasse. Ich sitze gern im Freien.

Lore: Mir ist alles recht. Ich will nur nicht an das Examen denken.

Kurt: It doesn't belong to me. I borrowed it. By the way, where is the department store?

Lore: On Mozart Street. Turn left.

Kurt: I know that store. In the beginning I had to go there almost daily.

Lore: How come?

Kurt: You don't always bring the right things along.

Lore: We're here. Where are you going to park?

Kurt: I'll find a place. I'll wait for you at the entrance.

10 minutes later

Kurt: That went pretty fast.

Lore: I knew exactly what I was looking for: department, brand, price range.

Kurt: Now we can finally drink our coffee. Do you want to go to the Continental?

Lore: What do you like so much about that café?

Kurt: The terrace. I like the open air.

Lore: Anything's okay with me. I just don't want to think about the exam.

II. KOMBINATIONEN

Sagen Sie auf deutsch:

a. 1. I'm afraid of the result.   2. He's afraid of the exam. 3. We're afraid of the work.

b. 1. Don't worry about it, Mr. Lenz.   2. Don't worry about it, Karl.   3. What are you worried about?

c. 1. That won't be easy.   2. That won't be hard.   3. Won't that be possible?

d. 1. I keep asking myself: Is chemistry the right field for me? 2. She keeps asking herself: Is history the right field for her? 3. I kept asking myself: Was the exam really so hard?

e. 1. You've always gotten good grades.   2. You're right; I've always gotten good grades.   3. Did he really get good grades?

f. 1. You have to relax a bit.   2. I have to relax a bit.   3. We have to relax a bit.

g. 1. Are you in the mood for a cup of coffee?   2. I'm in the mood for a beer.   3. She's in the mood for a cup of tea.

h. 1. I have to run a few errands. Can you wait a few minutes? 2. My mother has to run a few errands; we can't wait.   3. Oh, you can wait a few minutes.

i. 1. I'll be glad to drive you there.   2. He'll be glad to drive me there.   3. Will you drive me there? —It's hardly worth it.

j. 1. The car doesn't belong to me.   2. I borrowed the car. 3. I've never seen the car before.

k. 1. I knew exactly what I was looking for.   2. I found everything: department, brand, price range.   3. I never know what I'm looking for.

l. 1. What do you like so much about this café?   2. What does he like so much about the café?   3. What do they like so much about this theater?

m. 1. I just don't want to think about this exam.   2. She just doesn't want to think about chemistry.   3. She just doesn't want to think about the result.

III. SAGEN UND FRAGEN

a. *Sie sind Kurt. Sie sagen zu Lore:*

1. Sie soll sich keine Sorgen machen (*use imperative*).   2. Sie hat immer gute Noten bekommen.   3. Sie muß sich ein

wenig entspannen. 4. Sie fahren sie gerne ins Geschäft.
5. Sie soll einsteigen (*use imperative*). 6. Der Wagen gehört
Ihnen nicht. 7. Sie haben ihn sich geliehen. 8. Sie mußten
am Anfang oft in dieses Warenhaus. 9. Sie werden schon
einen Parkplatz finden. 10. Sie warten auf sie (Lore) am
Eingang. 11. Sie wollen jetzt Ihren Kaffee trinken. 12. Sie
sitzen gern im Freien.

b. *Sie sind Lore. Sie sagen zu Kurt:*

1. Sie haben das Examen schwer gefunden. 2. Sie haben
wirklich Angst vor dem Resultat. 3. Sie machen sich Sorgen
darüber. 4. Ihre letzten Arbeiten waren ziemlich schlecht.
5. Sie müssen noch einige Besorgungen machen. 6. Sie
haben diesen Wagen noch nie gesehen. 7. Sie wußten genau,
was Sie suchten. 8. Sie haben die Abteilung gleich gefunden.
9. Ihnen ist alles recht. 10. Sie wollen nicht ans Examen
denken.

c. *Sie sind Kurt. Sie fragen Lore:*

1. ob das Examen wirklich so schwer war. 2. ob sie vor dem
Resultat Angst hat. 3. warum sie sich sorgt. 4. ob sie Lust
auf eine Tasse Kaffee hat. 5. in welches Geschäft sie geht.
6. wo das Warenhaus ist. 7. ob sie ins Continental will.

d. *Sie sind Lore. Sie fragen Kurt:*

1. ob Chemie das richtige Fach für Sie ist. 2. ob er einige
Minuten warten kann. 3. ob dieser Wagen neu ist. 4. wieso
er am Anfang so oft ins Warenhaus gehen mußte. 5. wo er
jetzt parken wird. 6. was ihm so gut am Continental gefällt.

IV. AUFSATZ

DEUTSCHE CAFÉS UND WIRTSCHAFTEN

Kurt und Lore saßen gemütlich auf der Terrasse des Cafés Continental, tranken langsam eine Tasse Kaffee, hörten Musik und
blickten auf den Rhein hinaus. Nebenan unterhielten sich zwei
Damen auffallend laut über Schönheitsmittel[1] und die neuesten
5 Moden.[2] „Diese Damen scheinen schon mehrere Stunden hier zu
sitzen", bemerkte Kurt endlich. „Seit unserer Ankunft haben sie

1. cosmetics. 2. fashions, styles.

kaum etwas verzehrt.[3] Der Kaffeeklatsch[4] mag angenehm für die Damen sein, aber er bedeutet schlechtes Geschäft für den Besitzer. Wird sie denn niemand hinauswerfen?"

10 „Nein, sie haben einen Kaffee bestellt, und das genügt", erklärte Lore. „Das verleiht[5] ihnen das Recht, die schöne Landschaft zu genießen und weiter zu plaudern. Einige Herren und Damen kommen fast jeden Tag in dieses Lokal, bestellen eine Tasse Kaffee oder Tee und unterhalten sich stundenlang mit ihren Kollegen 15 oder Freundinnen. Natürlich kommen manche Leute allein und verlangen dann noch Zeitungen oder Zeitschriften, um[6] sich zu beschäftigen. Insgesamt[7] zahlen sie recht wenig für einen angenehmen Nachmittag."

„Gibt es[8] solche Cafés auch auf dem Land?"

20 „Viel weniger", erwiderte Lore. „In den Dörfern bleiben die Frauen meistens zu Hause bei den Kindern. Die Männer machen sich das Leben leicht.[9] Sie gehen abends aus, in ein Gasthaus oder in eine Wirtschaft. Sie besuchen dasselbe Wirtshaus jahraus, jahrein[10] und werden Stammgäste[11] des Lokals. Man reserviert 25 ihnen also einen Stammtisch,[12] denn sie wollen immer mit ihren Freunden zusammensitzen."

„Ich kann mir das ganz gut vorstellen", sagte Kurt. „Gerade wie die Damen neben uns, haben auch diese Herren ihre Lieblingsthemen.[13] Sie diskutieren politische Fragen, beschweren sich über die 30 Steuern und ihre Familien und spielen Karten. Dabei serviert man ihnen eine Maß[14] Bier oder ein Glas Wein."

„Ja, auf dem Land und in der Kleinstadt[15] ist das die Regel", sagte Lore. „Bei einer Flasche Wein und einer Zigarre vergeht[16] die Zeit sehr schnell für die Väter. Die Mütter und Töchter hinge- 35 gen sitzen zu Hause . . ."

„. . . und amüsieren sich auf ihre Art",[17] lachte Kurt. „Vielleicht fahre ich dieses Wochenende mal aufs Land und sehe mir so eine Gaststätte an. Man soll da gut und billig zu essen bekommen. Das ist das richtige für mich."

40 Plötzlich sah Kurt auf seine Uhr. Beide erschraken, weil es schon spät geworden war.[18] Sie hatten um 5 Uhr Verabredungen. Kurt rief den Kellner. „Herr Ober, zahlen, bitte", sagte er. Der

3. **verzehren** to consume.   4. *a get-together for coffee and cake.* 5. gives, confers (upon).   6. **um . . . zu** in order to . . . .   7. in all, all together.   8. **gibt es?** are there?   9. **sich das Leben leicht machen** to make life pleasant for oneself, to take it easy.   10. **jahraus, jahrein** year in, year out.   11. *regular guests at a public eating and drinking place.* 12. *table reserved for regular guests.*   13. favorite topics.   14. stein. 15. small town (*city under 100,000*).   16. **vergehen** to pass (*time*). 17. **auf ihre Art** in their fashion.   18. **war geworden** had gotten.

Am Stammtisch
GREGOR KIERBLEWSKY

Kellner schrieb die Rechnung. Kurt legte einen Zehnmarkschein[19] auf den Tisch, und der Kellner gab ihm auf zehn Mark heraus.[20] Dann standen sie auf und verließen das Café.

Beantworten Sie die folgenden Fragen:

1. Was machten Kurt und Lore auf der Terrasse? 2. Wie unterhielten sich die zwei Damen nebenan? 3. Worüber unterhielten sie sich? 4. Was bedeutet der Kaffeeklatsch für den Besitzer? 5. Warum? 6. Welches Recht verleiht die Tasse Kaffee? 7. Was verlangen manche Leute? 8. Wieviel zahlen die Gäste für

19. ten-mark note. 20. **herausgeben** to give change.

einen angenehmen Nachmittag? 9. Warum gibt es weniger Cafés auf dem Lande? 10. Wie machen die Männer sich das Leben leicht? 11. Wie werden sie Stammgäste des Lokals? 12. Warum reserviert man ihnen einen Tisch? 13. Worüber diskutieren die Herren? 14. Was serviert man ihnen dabei? 15. Wo sitzen die Mütter und Töchter? 16. Was will Kurt dieses Wochenende tun? 17. Warum erschraken Kurt und Lore? 18. Warum rief Kurt den Kellner? 19. Was schrieb der Kellner? 20. Was legte Kurt auf den Tisch? 21. Was machte der Kellner?

V. WORTSCHATZ

die **Abteilung, -en**	department	die **Flasche, -n**	bottle
die **Angst**	fear	das **Gasthaus, ‥er**	inn
Angst haben	to be afraid	die **Gaststätte, -n**	inn
		genügen	to be enough, suffice
die **Ankunft, ‥e**	arrival	das **Geschäft, -e**	store, business
auffallend	conspicuous(ly), noticeably	**hinaus/ blicken auf** + *ac-*	
aus/gehen, ging aus, ist ausgegangen	to go out	*cusative*	to look out upon
		hinaus/wer- fen, warf hinaus, hinaus/ geworfen, wirft hinaus	to throw out
bedeuten	to mean, signify		
bemerken	to notice		
sich **beschweren**	to complain		
der **Besitzer, -**	owner	**hin/fahren, fuhr hin, ist hin/ge- fahren**	to drive, go there (*by vehicle*)
die **Besorgung, -en**	errand		
das **Bier**	beer		
das **Dorf, ‥er**	village	**hingegen**	on the other hand
ein/biegen, bog ein, ist eingebogen	to turn	**hin/gehen, ging hin, ist hin/ge- gangen**	to go there (*usu- ally: to walk*)
der **Eingang, ‥e**	entrance		
ein/steigen, stieg ein, ist einge- stiegen	to get in	die **Karte, -n**	card, map
		der **Kellner, -**	waiter
		das **Kind, -er**	child
endlich	finally	der **Kollege, -n**	colleague
sich **entspannen**	to relax	das **Land**	country
erschrecken, erschrak, ist erschrocken, erschrickt	to be frightened, alarmed	**auf dem Land(e)**	in the country
		aufs Land	to the country
		langsam	slow
erwidern	to reply	**laut**	loud
essen	to eat	**legen**	to lay
zu essen bekommen	to get (some- thing) to eat	sich **lohnen**	to be worthwhile
		die **Lust**	inclination, de- sire
das **Fach, ‥er**	subject, field (*of study*)		

	Lust haben auf (zu)	to be in the mood for	die Steuer, -n	tax
die	Marke, -n	brand, make	stundenlang	for hours
	mit/bringen, brachte mit, mit/gebracht	to take along	der Tee	tea
			die Terrasse, -n	terrace
			der Tisch, -e	table
die	Note, -n	grade, mark	die Tochter, ⸚	daughter
der	Ober, -	waiter	die Treppe, -n	step, stairs
	parken	to park	die Verabredung, -en	appointment
der	Platz, ⸚e	place	verlangen	to demand, insist upon
die	Preislage, -n	price range	sich (dative) vor/stellen	to imagine
die	Rechnung, -en	bill, check, tab	der Wagen, -	car
	die Rechnung schreiben	to make out the bill	das Warenhaus, ⸚er	department store
das	Recht, -e	right, privilege	die Wirtschaft, -en	tavern
die	Regel, -n	rule	das Wochenende, -n	weekend
	reservieren	to reserve	die Zeitschrift, -en	magazine
das	Resultat	result	zusammen/sitzen, saß zusammen, zusammengesessen	to sit together
	richtig	correct		
die	Sache, -n	thing, matter		
	scheinen, schien, geschienen	to seem, appear		
sich	sorgen	to worry		

VI. ERKLÄRUNGEN UND ÜBUNGEN

1. Der-Words

	Masculine	Feminine	Neuter	Plural (all genders)	
	der	die	das	die	*the*
	dieser	diese	dieses	diese	*this, that*
	jeder	jede	jedes	alle	*each, every*
	jener[1]	jene	jenes	jene	*that*
	mancher[2]	manche	manches	manche	*many a, some*
	solcher[2]	solche	solches	solche	*such a*
	welcher	welche	welches	welche	*which, what*
	aller	alle	alles	alle	*all*

Words declined like the definite article are adjectives called **der-words**.

1. **Jener** is seldom used in the spoken language. To express, for example, *that man*, use **der Mann (da)**, or **dieser Mann (da)**.
2. **Mancher** and **solcher** in the singular are usually replaced in the spoken language by **manch ein** and **solch ein** (*also:* **so ein**).

Model declension of a **der**-word:

Masculine	Feminine	Neuter	Plural
N. **dieser Mann**	**diese Frau**	**dieses Zimmer**	**diese Eltern**
G. **dieses Mannes**	**dieser Frau**	**dieses Zimmers**	**dieser Eltern**
D. **diesem Mann**	**dieser Frau**	**diesem Zimmer**	**diesen Eltern**
A. **diesen Mann**	**diese Frau**	**dieses Zimmer**	**diese Eltern**

2. Der-Words as Pronouns

Welcher Wagen gehört Ihnen? **Dieser** hier.
Which car belongs to you? This one here.

Welche Besorgungen müssen Sie heute machen? Nur **diese**.
Which errands do you have to run today? Only these.

In **welches Geschäft** gehen Sie? In **dieses**.
What store are you going in? In this one.

Der-words used as pronouns or as adjectives have identical endings.

PRACTICE

A. *Give the nominative singular form of the **der**-word below with each noun indicated:*

1. **dies-** (Reise, Warenhaus, Mädchen, Schwester, Wagen, Examen)
2. **welch-** (Kind, Tag, Vater, Tisch, Arbeit, Haus)
3. **jed-** (Student, Professor, Entschuldigung, Aufgabe, Buch)

B. *Answer the following questions with the proper form of the **der**-word indicated:*

Example: Welches Examen war so schwer? (*dies-*)
Dieses.

1. Welche Besorgungen müssen Sie machen? (dies-) 2. In welches Warenhaus geht sie? (dies-) 3. Welchem Freund schreiben Sie einen Brief? (jed-) 4. Welchem Studenten helfen Sie? (nicht jed-) 5. Welchen Lehrern danken Sie für ihre Hilfe? (all-)

C. *Answer the following questions by using the proper form of j**ader**:*

Example: Hat dieses Mädchen ein Auto?
Ja, jedes Mädchen hat ein Auto.

1. Hat dieser Lehrer eine Tasse Kaffee? 2. War dieses Examen schwer? 3. Waren diese Semesterarbeiten schlecht? 4. Ist diese Wirtschaft Ihnen recht? 5. Gefällt Ihnen dieses Café?

D. *Say in German:*

1. This café is well known. 2. He says every café is well known. 3. Which student said that? 4. This student here. 5. Which subject are you studying? 6. Every student asks: Which

subject is right for me?   7. Some students study chemistry.
8. Such students work hard.

3. Plurals of Nouns

Unlike plurals in English, German plurals are not formed according to one general rule, but according to one of the following patterns:

	Singular	Plural	Vocabulary Listing[1]
no ending	**der Bruder**	**die Brüder**	**der Bruder, ─**
	die Mutter	**die Mütter**	**die Mutter, ─**
	das Theater	**die Theater**	**das Theater, -**
-(n)(e)n	**der Professor**	**die Professoren**	**der Professor, -en**
	die Frau	**die Frauen**	**die Frau, -en**
	die Aufgabe	**die Aufgaben**	**die Aufgabe, -n**
	die Freundin	**die Freundinnen**	**die Freundin, -nen**
-e	**der Brief**	**die Briefe**	**der Brief, -e**
	die Stadt	**die Städte**	**die Stadt, ─e**
	das Jahr	**die Jahre**	**das Jahr, -e**
-er	**der Mann**	**die Männer**	**der Mann, ─er**
	das Bild	**die Bilder**	**das Bild, -er**
-s	**der Park**	**die Parks**	**der Park, -s**
	das Auto	**die Autos**	**das Auto, -s**

Note: All German nouns end in **n** in the dative plural, except nouns which already end in **n** or end in **s**:

Nom.	**die Brüder**	**die Städte**	**die Jahre**	**die Wagen**	**die Autos**
Dat.	**den** Brüdern	**den** Städten	**den** Jahren	**den** Wagen	**den** Autos

a. Plurals with No Ending

Most masculine and neuter nouns in **-el**, **-en**, and **-er** add no ending to form the plural. Some masculine nouns umlaut the vowel:

Masculine

Singular	Plural
der Spiegel	**die Spiegel**
der Wagen	**die Wagen**
der Ober	**die Ober**
der Bruder	**die Brüder**

Neuter

Singular	Plural
das Kapitel	**die Kapitel**
das Essen	**die Essen**
das Theater	**die Theater**

1. Beginning with this lesson, all plurals of nouns are indicated in the **Wortschatz**. Because of the variety of German plural endings, try to learn the plural along with each noun you encounter.

To this group belong also two feminine nouns:

die Mutter   die Mütter
die Tochter   die Töchter

All nouns ending in -chen and -lein are neuter and add nothing to form the plural:

das Mädchen   die Mädchen
das Fräulein   die Fräulein

b. Plurals in -n, -en, -nen

Most feminine nouns and some masculine and neuter nouns add -n, -en, or -nen to form the plural:

der Professor	die Professoren
die Arbeit	die Arbeiten
die Aufgabe	die Aufgaben
die Familie	die Familien
die Frau	die Frauen
die Lehrerin	die Lehrerinnen
die Schwester	die Schwestern
die Tür	die Türen
die Uhr	die Uhren
das Auge	die Augen

PRACTICE

A. *Give the nominative plural of the following nouns:*

1.	der Dampfer	9.	das Theater
2.	die Treppe	10.	die Tochter
3.	der Sommer	11.	der Vater
4.	die Straße	12.	die Kirche
5.	das Schwesterchen	13.	der Bruder
6.	der Besitzer	14.	die Bedeutung
7.	der Koffer	15.	das Mädchen
8.	die Mutter	16.	der Handwerker

B. *Decline in the plural:*

    Example: die Theater, diese Theater

            N. die Theater   diese Theater
            G. der Theater   dieser Theater
            D. den Theatern   diesen Theatern
            A. die Theater   diese Theater

1. die Kapitel, diese Kapitel;   2. die Koffer, diese Koffer;   3. die Vorlesungen, welche Vorlesungen;   4. die Büchlein, diese Büchlein;   5. die Väter, manche Väter;   6. die Ober, solche Ober;   7. diese Briefkästen, alle Briefkästen;   8. die Reisen, alle Reisen

C. *Express in the plural:*

1. mit dem Mädchen;   2. in dem Wagen;   3. nach der Tradition;   4. auf dem Dampfer;   5. mit dieser Tochter;   6. auf dem

Spiegel;   7. bei manchem Bruder;   8. bei welchem Amerikaner;
9. mit jedem Mädchen;   10. während dieser Zeit

D. Say in German:

1. I am interested in your schools.   2. Which universities have
women students?   3. All schools have many girls.   4. They often
become women teachers.   5. How many semesters do you have?
6. Do the students have many examinations during the year?
7. Do the professors help you much?

4. Future Tense

a.		
ich werde sie anrufen	*I will call her*	
du wirst sie anrufen	*you will call her*	
er wird sie anrufen	*he will call her*	
wir werden sie anrufen	*we will call her*	
ihr werdet sie anrufen	*you will call her*	
sie werden sie anrufen	*they will call her*	
Sie werden sie anrufen	*you will call her*	

The future tense consists of the appropriate form of the auxiliary
werden plus the infinitive of the main verb. The infinitive always
stands last in the clause.

b. **Es wird wohl wahr sein.**
It's probably true.

The future may express probability in present time. Such a probability statement often contains adverbs such as **wohl** (*probably*),
wahrscheinlich (*probably*), and **vielleicht** (*perhaps*).

c. **Wir fahren morgen in die Stadt.**
We're going to town tomorrow.

Even more frequently than in English, the present tense is used
in German to express future action, especially when an expression
of time clearly indicates future.

PRACTICE

A. Change to future:

1. War das Examen wirklich so schwer?   2. Das ist nicht leicht
gewesen.   3. Du hast schlechte Noten bekommen.   4. Seid ihr
in die Stadt gefahren?   5. Warten Sie auf mich?   6. Das ging
schnell.   7. Es lohnt sich kaum.

B. Say in German:

1. Will your sisters be here tomorrow?   2. I'll show you the
rooms.   3. They'll like it here.   4. Will your father come, too?
5. I'll find Mrs. Kolb.   6. She's probably at home.

5. Hin and her

Ich fahre Sie gerne hin.
I'll be glad to drive you there.

Sie blickten auf den Rhein hinaus.
They looked out at the Rhine.

Komm her!
Come here.

Wohin gehen Sie?
or
Wo gehen Sie **hin?**
Where are you going?

Woher kommst du?
or
Wo kommst du her?
Where do you come from?

Hin and **her** are directional adverbs. They may be used alone or with other adverbs or separable prefixes and generally stand last in a main clause. **Hin** indicates motion away from the position of the speaker; **her,** motion toward the position of the speaker.

PRACTICE

Select the appropriate directional adverb from the following list and complete the sentences below:

her, hin; herab, herauf, heraus, herein;
hinab, hinauf, hinaus, hinein

1. Er geht die Treppe (up, *away from speaker*) _____.
2. Er kommt die Treppe (up, *toward speaker*) _____.
3. Bringen Sie es mir (down, *toward speaker*) _____!
4. Werfen Sie sie (out, *away from speaker*) _____!
5. Er ist (here) _____ gekommen.
6. Ich bin (there) _____ gegangen.
7. Kommen Sie bitte (in, *toward speaker*) _____!

FINAL PRACTICE   *Say first, then write in German:*

1. The chemistry exam was really not very hard.   2. I'm not afraid of the result.   3. Are you worried about your exam?   4. No, but many of my grades were bad.   5. Are you going to run a few errands today?   6. I'll gladly drive you downtown.   7. I have to buy some things in a department store.   8. We sat on the terrace and drank a cup of coffee.   9. Some ladies were sitting next to us and talking about cosmetics.   10. They didn't eat much.   11. Other people were reading newspapers and magazines.   12. They don't pay much for a pleasant afternoon. 13. Lore said: "You won't find such cafés in the country."   14. "At least you won't find as many."   15. But I know everybody discusses political questions and complains about taxes.   16. They probably also play cards a lot.   17. But it was getting very late. 18. Lore and Kurt both had appointments.   19. The waiter wrote the bill and gave it to Kurt.   20. Kurt said: "Waiter, the check, please!"

„Unser Familienleben in Deutschland ist sehr eng
GERMAN INFORMATION CENTER

I. UNTERHALTUNG

DIE SEMESTERARBEIT

Lore: Sie sehen sehr traurig aus. Wieder keine Nachrichten von zu Hause?

Kurt: Im Gegenteil. Ich hatte zwei Briefe von meinen Eltern.

Lore: Nun, warum die schlechte Laune?

Kurt: Ich mache keine Fortschritte bei meiner Semesterarbeit.

Lore: Für Ihr Seminar? Worüber schreiben Sie?

Kurt: Über das Theater von Bertolt Brecht. Ich muß zehn Stücke lesen.

Lore: Das ist doch nicht schwer.

Kurt: Es dauert aber lange. Ich muß so viele Wörter nachschlagen.

Lore: Ich leihe Ihnen gerne mein Wörterbuch.

Kurt: Danke. Ich bin mit meinem deutsch-englischen Wörterbuch zufrieden. Bisher hatte ich keine Probleme damit.

Lore: Kann ich irgendwie behilflich sein?

Kurt: Leider muß ich die Bücher selbst lesen.

Lore: Vielleicht kann ich hie und da eine Stelle erklären.

Kurt: Ja, das wäre sehr nett. Aber es ist eigentlich nicht das Lesen.

THE TERM PAPER

Lore: You look very sad. Again no news from home?

Kurt: On the contrary. I had two letters from my parents.

Lore: Then why the bad mood?

Kurt: I'm not making any headway with my term paper.

Lore: For your seminar? What are you writing about?

Kurt: About the theater of Bertolt Brecht. I have to read ten plays.

Lore: That isn't so hard.

Kurt: But it takes a long time. I have to look up so many words.

Lore: I'll be happy to lend you my dictionary.

Kurt: Thanks. I'm satisfied with my German-English dictionary. Up to now I've had no problems with it.

Lore: Can I help in any way?

Kurt: Unfortunately, I have to read the books myself.

Lore: Maybe I can explain a passage to you now and then.

Kurt: Yes, that would be very nice. But it actually isn't the reading.

LESSON 10

Lore: Sie müssen Ihre Arbeit wohl auf deutsch schreiben.
Kurt: Gewiß. Stellen Sie sich vor, wie viele Fehler . . . !
Lore: Seien Sie nicht so pessimistisch! Sie haben doch Freunde.
Kurt: Freunde? Was können Freunde tun?
Lore: Ihre Arbeit korrigieren.
Kurt: Sie meinen, Sie würden meine Fehler verbessern?
Lore: Ich würde mein Bestes tun.
Kurt: Merken Sie, meine Stimmung hat sich schon gebessert?

Lore: You probably have to write your paper in German.
Kurt: Exactly. Just imagine how many mistakes . . . !
Lore: Don't be so pessimistic. You do have friends.
Kurt: Friends? What can friends do?
Lore: Correct your paper.
Kurt: You mean you'd correct my errors?
Lore: I'd do my best.
Kurt: Do you notice how my mood has already improved?

II. KOMBINATIONEN

Sagen Sie auf deutsch:

a. 1. You look very sad. 2. He looks very happy. 3. No, he looked very sad.

b. 1. Then why the bad mood? 2. Then why the good mood? 3. Then why this sad mood?

c. 1. I'm making no headway with my term paper. 2. Karl was making headway with his paper. 3. This student was making no headway either.

d. 1. What are you writing about? —About the theater of Brecht. 2. What is he writing about? —About the history of Germany. 3. What are they writing about? —About three plays by Goethe.

e. 1. But it takes a long time. 2. It doesn't take long at all. 3. Did it really take long?

f. 1. I have to look up so many words. 2. Why do you have to look up so many words? 3. Every American has to look up very many words.

g. 1. Up to now I've had no problems with my dictionary.

2. Up to now I've had no problems with it. 3. Have you had problems with your dictionary?

h. 1. Can I help in any way? 2. Can I help you in any way? 3. Everybody wants to help us.

i. 1. Maybe I can explain a passage here and there. 2. Lore explained a passage to him now and then. 3. Shall I explain a passage to you?

j. 1. Don't be so pessimistic. You have friends. 2. Don't be so sad. We want to help you. 3. Don't be so happy. You have to read ten plays!

k. 1. You mean you would correct my errors? 2. You mean you would explain this play to me? 3. You mean you would correct my paper?

l. 1. I would do my best. 2. She would do her best. 3. I would correct your paper.

III. SAGEN UND FRAGEN

a. *Sie sind Lore und sagen zu Kurt:*

1. Er sieht sehr traurig aus. 2. Sie leihen ihm gerne Ihr Wörterbuch. 3. Sie wollen hie und da eine Stelle erklären. 4. Er soll nicht so pessimistisch sein. 5. Sie wollen seine Arbeit korrigieren. 6. Sie würden Ihr Bestes tun.

b. *Sie sind Kurt und sagen zu Lore:*

1. Sie hatten zwei Briefe von Ihren Eltern. 2. Sie machen keine Fortschritte bei Ihrer Arbeit. 3. Sie schreiben eine Arbeit für Ihr Seminar. 4. Sie sind mit Ihrem deutsch-englischen Wörterbuch zufrieden. 5. Sie hatten bisher keine Probleme damit. 6. Sie müssen leider die Bücher selbst lesen.   7. Sie müssen Ihre Arbeit auf deutsch schreiben. 8. Ihre Stimmung hat sich schon gebessert.

c. *Sie sind Lore und fragen Kurt:*

1. ob er wieder keine Nachrichten von zu Hause hat. 2. worüber er für das Seminar schreibt. 3. warum er so viele Wörter nachschlagen muß. 4. ob er mit seinem Wörterbuch zufrieden ist. 5. ob Sie irgendwie behilflich sein können. 6. warum er so pessimistisch ist. 7. ob er denn keine Freunde hat.

d. *Sie sind Kurt und fragen Lore:*

1. ob sie sich vorstellen kann, wie viele Fehler Sie machen.
2. was Freunde denn für Sie tun können.   3. ob sie wirklich
Ihre Fehler verbessern würde.   4. ob sie Ihre Arbeit korrigieren würde.

IV. AUFSATZ

DAS FAMILIENLEBEN

Kurt und sein Freund Karl sind am Bahnhof. Sie haben den Tag
in Aachen verbracht und fahren jetzt wieder nach Hause. Sie
lösen ihre Fahrkarten, kaufen sich ein paar Zeitschriften und
steigen zusammen in den Zug. Sie hören wiederholt[1] den Laut-
5 sprecher:[2] „Achtung! Achtung! Der Personenzug[3] in Richtung
Köln fährt sogleich ab. Bitte einsteigen und die Türen schließen!"

Karl möchte ruhig seine Illustrierte[4] lesen, aber Kurt unterbricht ihn immer wieder. Er stellt seinem Freund allerlei Fragen
über das Familienleben in Deutschland. Zuerst spricht Karl von
10 seinem Vater und seiner Mutter, dann von seinen Großeltern; zu
guter Letzt[5] erwähnt er auch seine Schwester Lore.

Karl erklärt seinem Freund: „Unser Familienleben in Deutschland ist sehr eng und die Familie als Gemeinschaft[6] ist sehr
wichtig. In vielen Familien herrscht[7] immer noch die Autorität
15 des Vaters. Auf der andern Seite[8] hat sich vieles geändert, und die
Jugend trifft jetzt oft ihre eigenen Entscheidungen. In meiner
Familie bestimmt[9] der Vater über ziemlich alles: über Lores und
meine Erziehung, unsere Berufsausbildung,[10] unsere Geldausgaben.[11] Unsere Mutter kümmert sich nicht viel um diese Fragen.
20 Natürlich ist auch mein Vater, wie die meisten[12] deutschen Väter,
der Ernährer[13] seiner Familie. Unsere Frauen sind noch nicht so
frei wie eure Frauen in Amerika. Meine Mutter steht dem Haushalt vor;[14] sie macht die Hausarbeit, kocht und widmet sich[15] den
Kindern.

25   „Der deutsche Vater ist das Familienoberhaupt. Er spielt ge-

---

1. repeatedly.   2. loudspeaker.   3. local train.   4. picture magazine.
5. **zu guter Letzt** finally, as a fitting conclusion.   6. social unit.   7. pre-
vails.   8. **auf der andern Seite** on the other hand.   9. **bestimmen über** to
have a say about.   10. professional (occupational) training.   11. expenditures.   12. **die meisten** most.   13. breadwinner.   14. **dem Haushalt vorstehen** to run the house.   15. **sich widmen** (+ *dative*) to devote
oneself (to).

wöhnlich nicht mit seinen Kindern. Er ist sozusagen[16] nicht der Kamerad[17] seiner Kinder, sondern ihr Vorgesetzter.[18] Er verlangt Respekt und Gehorsam."[19]

Der Schaffner ruft aus: „Nächste Station Köln." Karl sagt:
30 „Genug geredet. Es ist Zeit auszusteigen."[20]

Beantworten Sie die folgenden Fragen:

1. Wo sind Kurt und sein Freund jetzt? 2. Wo haben sie den Tag verbracht? 3. Was machen sie am Bahnhof? 4. Was hören die zwei Freunde? 5. Worüber stellt Kurt Fragen? 6. Wie ist das Familienleben in Deutschland? 7. Inwiefern (*in what respect*) hat sich vieles geändert? 8. Worüber bestimmt der Vater? 9. Wer ist der Ernährer in Karls Familie? 10. Worum kümmert sich die Mutter? 11. Was tut der deutsche Vater gewöhnlich nicht? 12. Was verlangt der Vater von den Kindern? 13. Wer ruft jetzt aus: „Nächste Station Köln?" 14. Was müssen die Freunde tun?

16. so to speak. 17. comrade. 18. superior. 19. obedience. 20. **Es ist Zeit auszusteigen** It's time to get off.

V. WORTSCHATZ

achten	to respect	die **Großeltern**	grandparents
die **Achtung**	attention; respect	die **Hausarbeit**	housework
Achtung!	Attention!	der **Haushalt**	household
allerlei	all kinds of	**hie und da**	now and then, here and there
sich **ändern**	to change		
aus/rufen,	to call out, ex-	**irgendwie**	in any way, somehow
rief aus,	claim		
ausgerufen		**jedermann**	everybody
der **Bahnhof, ⸚e**	railroad station	die **Jugend**	youth
behilflich	helpful, of assistance	**korrigieren**	to correct
		sich **kümmern um**	to be concerned with
sich **bessern**	to get better		
bisher	up to now	die **Laune**	mood
dauern	to take, last	**lösen**	to solve
eigentlich	actually	**eine Fahr-**	to buy a ticket
eng	close, narrow	**karte lösen**	(*for the train*)
erwähnen	to mention		
die **Erziehung**	education, upbringing	die **Nachricht, -en**	news; report
das **Familienober-**	head of the	**nach/schla-**	to look up
haupt, ⸚er	family	**gen, schlug nach, nach-**	
der **Fehler, -**	error, mistake	**geschlagen**	
frei	free	**reden**	to talk, speak
gewiß	certainly	die **Richtung, -en**	direction
gewöhnlich	usually		

153

der **Schaffner,** -	conductor	**traurig**	sad, melancholy
schließen, **schloß, ge-** **schlossen** **(aus)**	to close, shut; conclude (from)	**treffen: Ent-** **scheidungen** **treffen**	to make decisions
die **Semester-** **arbeit, -en**	term paper	**tun: sein** **Bestes tun**	to do one's best
das **Seminar, -e**	seminar	**unterbrechen,** **unterbrach,**	to interrupt
sogleich	right away, immediately	**unterbro-** **chen, un-**	
die **Station, -en**	station	**terbricht**	
die **Stelle, -n**	passage, place; position	**vieles**	many things
		das **Wörterbuch,**	dictionary
die **Stimmung**	mood	**∸er**	

VI. ERKLÄRUNGEN UND ÜBUNGEN

1. Ein-Words

Masculine	Feminine	Neuter	Plural	*(all genders)*
ein	**eine**	**ein**	—	*a, one*
kein	**keine**	**kein**	**keine**	*no, not a, not any*
mein	**meine**	**mein**	**meine**	*my*
dein	**deine**	**dein**	**deine**	*your* (familiar singular)
sein	**seine**	**sein**	**seine**	*his, its*
ihr	**ihre**	**ihr**	**ihre**	*her, its*
unser	**unsere**	**unser**	**unsere**	*our*
euer	**eure**	**euer**	**eure**	*your* (familiar plural)
ihr	**ihre**	**ihr**	**ihre**	*their*
Ihr	**Ihre**	**Ihr**	**Ihre**	*your* (conventional form)

Words declined like the indefinite article are adjectives called **ein-**words. The **ein**-words consist of **ein** itself and **kein** and all the possessive adjectives.

Model declensions of **ein**-words:

	Masculine	Feminine	Neuter	Plural
N.	**mein** Bruder	**meine** Schwester	**mein** Haus	**meine** Eltern
G.	**meines** Bruders	**meiner** Schwester	**meines** Hauses	**meiner** Eltern
D.	**meinem** Bruder	**meiner** Schwester	**meinem** Haus	**meinen** Eltern
A.	**meinen** Bruder	**meine** Schwester	**mein** Haus	**meine** Eltern
N.	**ihr** Bruder	**ihre** Schwester	**ihr** Haus	**ihre** Eltern
G.	**ihres** Bruders	**ihrer** Schwester	**ihres** Hauses	**ihrer** Eltern
D.	**ihrem** Bruder	**ihrer** Schwester	**ihrem** Haus	**ihren** Eltern
A.	**ihren** Bruder	**ihre** Schwester	**ihr** Haus	**ihre** Eltern

Note that **ein**-words, unlike **der**-words, have no ending (and thus no key sound) in the masculine nominative singular and neuter nominative and accusative singular.

PRACTICE

A. *Decline in the singular and plural:*

1. Ihr Ober;   2. meine Fahrkarte;   3. sein Onkel;   4. ihre Hausarbeit;   5. unser Theater;   6. kein Kapitel;   7. dein Mann; 8. eure Aufgabe

B. *Using the appropriate ending of the possessive adjective, complete the following* (Repeat the entire sentence each time.):

1. Wo ist unser- (Haus, Zimmer, Schule, Freund)?
2. Hier sind mein- (Eltern, Schwestern, Freunde, Aufgaben).
3. Da steht Ihr- (Zug, Mutter, Wagen, Haus).
4. Ich bewundere ihr- (Museum, Wintersport, Meinung, Arbeit).
5. Das ist dein- (Mann, Uhr, Geld, Tasse).

C. *Answer the following questions using the appropriate form of* **mein** *and* **sein:**

Example: Ist das Ihr Koffer?
             Nein, das ist nicht mein Koffer. Es ist sein Koffer.

1. Ist das Ihre Tasse Kaffee?   2. Ist das Ihr Vater?   3. Ist das Ihr Hotel?   4. Ist das Ihre Aufnahme?   5. Ist das Ihr Fehler? 6. Ist das Ihre Meinung?   7. Ist das Ihr Geld?   8. Ist das Ihr Tisch?   9. Ist das Ihre Uhr?   10. Ist das Ihre Mutter?

D. *Answer the following questions using the appropriate form of* **unser:**

Example: Ist das Ihr Koffer?
             Ja, das ist unser Koffer.

1. Ist das Ihr Hotel?   2. Ist das Ihr Wagen?   3. Ist das Ihr Haus?   4. Ist das Ihre Arbeit?   5. Ist das Ihr Auto?   6. Ist das Ihre Tochter?   7. Ist das Ihr Stadtplan?

E. *Using the appropriate endings of the* **ein**-*words, complete the following sentences:*

1. Er bringt unser- Sachen herunter.   2. Mein- Koffer ist nicht da.   3. Ist er auf Ihr- Zimmer?   4. Vielleicht ist er auf sein- Zimmer.   5. Wo ist denn unser- Kellner?   6. Wann bringt er uns unser- Kaffee?   7. Unser- Familien besuchen einander oft. 8. Unser- Familienleben ist eng.   9. Ich suche ein- Taxi, aber ich

finde kein- Taxi.   10. Diese Dame fährt mit uns in unser- Zug.
11. Sie spricht mit mein- Freund Karl.   12. Kurt hat Lore, die
Schwester sein- Freundes, gern.   13. Mein- Freund löst jetzt sein-
Fahrkarte.   14. Er steigt in sein- Zug.   15. Er kauft sich ein-
Zeitschrift.

F.   *Say in German:*

1. Kurt has to write a term paper.   2. "Don't you have any news
from home?" asks Lore.   3. Kurt has had only one letter from
his parents.   4. Kurt has to read a play by Brecht.   5. Kurt is
satisfied with his dictionary.   6. Do you like your dictionary?   7.
Lore will do her best.   8. She can explain a passage here and
there.   9. "May I correct your errors?" she asks.   10. She notices
his mood has improved.

2. Plurals of Nouns, continued

a. Plurals in -e

Most monosyllabic nouns add **-e** to form the plural. All the feminines also umlaut; most of the masculines do.

Masculine

Singular	Plural
der Brief	**die Briefe**
der Hund (*dog*)	**die Hunde**
der Dom	**die Dome**
der Fuß	**die Füße**
der Grund	**die Gründe**
der Krieg	**die Kriege**
der Satz (*sentence*)	**die Sätze**
der Tag	**die Tage**
der Teil	**die Teile**
der Tisch	**die Tische**
der Zug	**die Züge**

Feminine

Singular	Plural
die Hand (*hand*)	**die Hände**
die Stadt	**die Städte**
die Wand (*wall*)	**die Wände**

Neuter

Singular	Plural
das Jahr	**die Jahre**
das Schiff (*ship*)	**die Schiffe**
das Stück	**die Stücke**
das Werk	**die Werke**

b. Plurals in -er Other monosyllabic neuters have **-er** as plural ending with umlaut where possible.

das Bild	die Bilder
das Buch	die Bücher
das Dorf	die Dörfer
das Feld (*field*)	die Felder
das Geld	die Gelder
das Glas	die Gläser
das Haus	die Häuser
das Kind	die Kinder
das Land	die Länder
das Lied (*song*)	die Lieder
das Wort	die Wörter[1]

c. Plurals in -s A small number of nouns, mostly neuter and of non-German origin, add **-s** to form the plural.

das Auto	die Autos
das Hotel	die Hotels
das Kino	die Kinos
der Park	die Parks
das Radio	die Radios
das Restaurant	die Restaurants
das Taxi	die Taxis

PRACTICE

A.   Give the nominative plural of the following nouns:

1. der Tag;   2. der Teil;   3. das Jahr;   4. die Stadt;   5. das Werk;   6. der Zug;   7. die Hand;   8. das Buch;   9. der Bahnhof;   10. das Beispiel;   11. der Freund;   12. der Fluß;   13. das Glas;   14. der Monat;   15. der Film;   16. das Geschäft;   17. die Wand;   18. das Kino;   19. der Fortschritt;   20. der Sohn (*son*);   21. das Feld;   22. der Mann

B.   Change the following phrases to plural:

1. in das Glas   2. mit dem Geld   3. in dem Werk   4. aus der Hand   5. wegen meines Buches   6. außer diesem Lied   7. in dem Park   8. aus dem Dorf   9. für den Mann   10. ins Kino   11. ohne das Kind   12. auf dem Bild   13. mit ihrem Freund   14. bei seiner Semesterarbeit   15. während des Krieges   16. auf dem Buch   17. mit seinem Wörterbuch   18. in unserem Teil   19. in dem Restaurant   20. auf eurem Tisch   21. in die Stadt   22. unter deinem Haus.

1. **Wort** has a second plural, **Worte**, used to refer to words in connected discourse.

C. Say in German:

1. Do your friends visit you often?   2. Yes, my friends visit me often.   3. We have many rooms in our house.   4. Is your suitcase in your room?   5. My suitcase is not in my room.   6. Our waiter is bringing us our coffee.   7. Lore is talking with her friend Kurt.   8. Kurt likes his friend's sister.   9. They buy their tickets and get on their train.

FINAL PRACTICE *Say first, then write in German:*

1. Kurt looks sad.   2. Didn't his parents write?   3. He had two letters from them today.   4. Unfortunately, he's making no headway with his term paper.   5. He had to read many plays by Brecht for the paper.   6. It took a long time.   7. He had to look up so many words.   8. Lore will lend him her dictionary.   9. But Kurt is satisfied with his dictionary.   10. Up to now he had no problems.   11. Lore wants to correct his errors.   12. Kurt thanks her.   13. His mood has already improved.   14. Where are Kurt and his friend Karl?   15. They are at the railroad station and are buying their tickets.   16. They also bought some magazines. 17. Now they are on a train and are traveling to Cologne. 18. Kurt asks Karl all sorts of questions about family life in Germany.   19. Karl is also interested in family life in America. 20. Karl says: "My father is the head of our family.   21. He didn't play with his children often.   22. But we had respect for him."

1. ORAL PRACTICE

A. LEARN THIS DIALOGUE:

Kurt: Bitte beeile dich! Du mußt sofort aufstehen.
Karl: Aufstehen? Schon wieder? Ich bin noch viel zu müde.
Kurt: Bitte wach auf! Sonst fährt der Dampfer ohne uns.
Karl: Laß ihn nur abfahren! Und laß mich schlafen!
Kurt: Leg dich nicht wieder hin! Du mußt dich noch waschen und rasieren.
Karl: Mach dir keine Sorgen! Ich stehe schon auf. Aber ich habe keine Zahnpasta mehr.
Kurt: Du kannst diese Zahnpasta haben. Übrigens, wann kommen wir in Wiesbaden an?
Karl: Wir sollen gegen 7 ankommen.
Kurt: Ich glaube, du irrst dich. Wir kommen um 7 in Biebrich an.
Karl: Von da ist es nur eine halbe Stunde. Wir bestellen uns ein Taxi.
Kurt: Kannst du dir das leisten? Ich warte noch immer auf meinen Scheck.
Karl: Bist du knapp an Geld? Ich kann dir Geld leihen.

B. COMPLETE THE SENTENCES:

Kurt: Herr Lenz hatte _____. Die Rheinreise war einfach _____.
Karl: Ja, wir hatten auch _____. Das Wetter war _____.
Kurt: Nur am _____ wurde es _____.
Karl: Das hat dich nicht gestört. Du hast doch viele _____ gemacht.
Kurt: Habe ich zu viel _____?
Karl: Du hast doch auch mit vielen Leuten _____.
Kurt: Woher hast du _____, daß der Herr Bayer war?
Karl: Ich habe es an seiner _____ _____. Und wer war der Franzose?
Kurt: Er war _____. Er hat viel von sich _____. Er hat mir auch seine Skizzen _____. Er hat in Paris _____ und in Rom _____. Jetzt ist er durch ganz Deutschland _____.

159

REVIEW 2

Karl: War der Herr so _____ oder warst du nur
_____ ?

Kurt: Beides. Ich habe viele _____ gestellt und er hat
sie _____ .

C. EXPRESS THE FOLLOWING IN GERMAN:

Frau Kolb: You've been away a long time and you look very
tanned.

Kurt: I was outdoors a lot. At the beginning of the week I
looked even more tanned.

Frau Kolb: Did you travel by ship?

Kurt: Only on the way down. In Heidelberg Karl happened
to meet a friend from Cologne. He took us along.

Frau Kolb: Then it didn't cost much.

Kurt: It was really quite inexpensive. We slept mostly in
hostels.

Frau Kolb: I almost forgot. Somebody called you several times.

Kurt: Do you happen to know where the call came from?

Frau Kolb: The gentleman didn't give his name. By the way, your
check came. I recognized the envelope.

Kurt: Did I have any other mail?

Frau Kolb: A picture postcard. I took everything up to your room.

D. COMPLETE APPROPRIATE RESPONSES BY LORE:

Kurt: War das Chemieexamen wirklich so schwer?

Lore: Ich _____ .

Kurt: Machen Sie sich keine Sorgen darüber!

Lore: Ich frage mich immer wieder: _____ ?

Kurt: Sie müssen sich entspannen. Haben Sie Lust zu einem
Kaffee?

Lore: Ja, aber erst _____ .

E. COMPLETE APPROPRIATE RESPONSES BY KURT:

Lore: Sie sehen traurig aus. Wieder keine Nachrichten von zu
Hause?

Kurt: _____ . Ich hatte zwei Briefe.

Lore: Warum denn die schlechte Laune?

Kurt:	Ich mache _____ Semesterarbeit.
Lore:	Warum finden Sie das so schwer?
Kurt:	Ich muß _____.
Lore:	Ich leihe _____.
Kurt:	Danke. Ich bin _____ zufrieden.
Lore:	Kann ich _____ sein?
Kurt:	Vielleicht können Sie _____ erklären.

2. STRUCTURAL PRACTICE

A. REPEAT THE SENTENCES USING THE INDICATED MODALS IN THE SIMPLE PAST:

1. Er kommt nicht mit. (können)
2. Ich steige in Bonn aus. (sollen)
3. Er gibt das zu. (müssen)
4. Wir fahren bald zurück. (wollen)
5. Er sieht sich den Dom an. (wollen)

B. CHANGE THE FOLLOWING SENTENCES TO IMPERATIVES:

1. Du steigst in Köln ein, Kurt.
2. Sie stehen jetzt auf, Herr Lenz.
3. Du liest das Buch durch, Karl.
4. Ihr fahrt erst um acht Uhr ab, Kinder.
5. Du legst dich jetzt hin, Lore.
6. Ihr amüsiert euch gut, Kinder.
7. Du fährst jetzt in die Stadt, Karl.

C. REPEAT THE FOLLOWING SENTENCES USING THE INDICATED PRONOUNS:

1. Ich ruhe mich gut aus. (Sie)
2. Er stellt sich vor. (wir)
3. Erholst du dich gut? (ihr)
4. Er muß sich helfen. (wir)

5. Du beeilst dich nicht. (ich)
6. Erkälten Sie sich nicht? (er)
7. Du setzt dich hin. (Sie)
8. Er zieht sich an. (sie [*plural*])

D. CHANGE THE FOLLOWING SENTENCES TO (A) SIMPLE PAST, (B) COMPOUND PAST:

1. Herr Lenz hat recht.
2. Die Rheinreise ist herrlich.
3. Das Wetter wird trübe.
4. Die Freunde machen viele Aufnahmen.
5. Warum ärgert sich der Bayer?
6. Lore kommt leider nicht mit.
7. Der Franzose reist durch ganz Deutschland.
8. Kurt weiß nicht, wie er heißt.
9. Der Franzose zeigt ihm seine Skizzen.
10. Sie interessieren ihn sehr.
11. Kurt bleibt sehr lange fort.
12. Er trifft zufällig einen Freund.
13. Wo singt er die Rheinlieder?
14. Essen sie gut?
15. Ich kenne mich schon aus.
16. Das vergißt er nicht.
17. Ein Herr ruft öfter an.
18. Warum gibt er seinen Namen nicht an?
19. Sie bringt den Brief auf sein Zimmer.
20. Wann rasierst du dich?
21. Die Ansichtskarte kommt bald an.
22. Wie lange warten Sie schon darauf?
23. Ich schreibe heute noch meine Arbeit.
24. Kurt und Karl gehen zusammen ins Hotel.
25. Sie trinken ein Glas Wasser.

E. SUPPLY THE CORRECT ENDING:

1. Wir gehen sehr oft in dies— Café. 2. Ich treffe dort mein— Freundin. 3. Wir setzen uns in ein— Ecke. 4. Es ist kein— großes Café. 5. Essen Sie auch in dies— Café? 6. Nein, wir essen in ein— Restaurant. 7. Geht Ihr— Freund oft mit Ihnen?

8. Dies— Essen schmeckt ausgezeichnet.   9. Mit welch— Maler haben Sie sich dort unterhalten?   10. Ich kenne sein— Sohn und sein— Tochter.   11. Jetzt gehen wir in ein— Geschäft.   12. In welch— Geschäft möchten Sie gehen?   13. Dies— Warenhaus ist nicht weit.   14. Ich fahre Sie in mein— Wagen hin.   15. Lore macht Besorgungen für ihr— Mutter.   16. Macht sie dies— Besorgungen jed— Tag?   17. Werden Sie ein— Parkplatz für Ihr— Wagen finden?   18. Jetzt habe ich Lust zu ein— Tasse Kaffee.

F.   CHANGE THE FOLLOWING SENTENCES TO THE PLURAL:

1. Auf dem Tisch sehe ich kein Glas.
2. Dieses Warenhaus ist ganz in der Nähe.
3. Gehört ihm dieses Radio?
4. Macht diese Studentin immer ihre Arbeit?
5. Sein Lehrer ist mit ihm nicht zufrieden.
6. Lernt das Mädchen besser?
7. Unsere Tochter macht regelmäßig ihre Aufgabe.
8. Ihre Lehrerin ist mit ihrer Prüfung zufrieden.

G.   SAY, THEN WRITE IN GERMAN:

1. We were driving to a restaurant near the Rhine.   2. Some men and women were sitting next to us.   3. The gentlemen didn't eat or drink much.   4. Their wives were talking about cosmetics. 5. The men were asking them questions, but they didn't answer. 6. Lore ordered a cup of coffee.   7. I saw three waiters, but they were busy.   8. They usually don't work very much.   9. Suddenly Lore looked very sad.   10. "I am worried about my exam," she said.   11. She often wonders: "Is chemistry the right subject for me?"   12. She's also interested in literature.   13. Every friend admires her for that.

„Ich habe dir ein kleines Zimmer reserviert, in einem sehr ruhigen Hotel."

HENLE FROM MONKMEYER

I. UNTERHALTUNG

EINE NETTE ÜBERRASCHUNG

Kurt: Was für eine nette Überraschung!

Vater: Hast du mein Telegramm nicht erhalten?

Kurt: Doch, aber erst vor einer halben Stunde. Ich freue mich außerordentlich über deinen Besuch.

Vater: Du siehst glänzend aus. Deutschland scheint dir zu bekommen.

Kurt: Wie geht's Mutti? Und der Kleinen?

Vater: Ausgezeichnet. Natürlich wollte Mutti mitkommen. Leider ist es aber eine teure Reise.

Kurt: Du mußtest deine Reise nicht selbst bezahlen?

Vater: Nein. Ich bin ja geschäftlich hier. Wir haben seit Oktober eine Bonner Filiale.

Kurt: Geht sie gut?

Vater: Bisher ja. Ein junger Deutscher hat die Leitung übernommen. Ich soll ihm neue Anweisungen geben. . . . Das hübsche Mädchen da. Wartet es auf dich?

Kurt: Das ist Lore Lenz. Habe ich sie nicht in meinem letzten Brief erwähnt?

A PLEASANT SURPRISE

Kurt: What a pleasant surprise!

Father: Didn't you get my telegram?

Kurt: I did, but only half an hour ago. I'm terribly happy about your visit.

Father: You look terrific. Germany seems to agree with you.

Kurt: How's Mom? And the kid sister?

Father: They're fine. Of course, Mother wanted to come along. Unfortunately however, it's an expensive trip.

Kurt: You didn't have to pay for the trip yourself?

Father: No, I'm here for business reasons. We've had a branch in Bonn since October.

Kurt: Is it working out well?

Father: So far, yes. A young German has taken over the management. I'm supposed to give him new instructions . . . . That pretty girl over there. Is she waiting for you?

Kurt: That's Lore Lenz. Didn't I mention her in my last letter?

165

Vater: Nicht nur im letzten, sondern auch im ersten, zweiten und dritten . . .

Kurt: Vater, darf ich bekanntmachen? Fräulein Lore Lenz.

Lore: Guten Tag, Herr Klein.

Vater: Guten Tag, Fräulein Lenz. Bitte nehmen Sie Platz!

Lore: Wie war Ihre Überfahrt?

Vater: Zuerst war das Wetter stürmisch, dann wurde es besser. Ich konnte nur wenig schlafen.

Kurt: Ich habe dir ein kleines Zimmer reserviert, in einem sehr ruhigen Hotel.

Lore: Kurt sagt, Sie bleiben drei Tage hier. Meine Eltern würden sich freuen, Ihre Bekanntschaft zu machen.

Vater: Ich würde mich auch freuen. Vielleicht wird es möglich sein.

Father: Not only in the last letter, but also in the first, second, and third . . .

Kurt: Father, may I introduce Miss Lore Lenz?

Lore: How do you do, Mr. Klein.

Father: How do you do, Miss Lenz. Please sit down.

Lore: How was your trip over?

Father: At first the weather was stormy, then it got better. I could sleep only very little.

Kurt: I've reserved a small room for you, in a very quiet hotel.

Lore: Kurt says you're staying here for three days. My parents would be pleased to meet you.

Father: I would also enjoy it. Perhaps it will be possible.

II. KOMBINATIONEN

Sagen Sie auf deutsch:

a. 1. What a pleasant surprise! 2. What a pleasant trip! 3. What a pleasant conversation!

b. 1. Didn't you get my telegram? 2. Didn't you get my letter? 3. I got your telegram and your letter.

c. 1. I'm terribly happy about your visit. 2. I'm terribly happy about your pleasant surprise. 3. We're terribly happy about the telegram.

d. 1. How are Mother and the kid sister? 2. How is Kurt's kid sister? 3. They're fine.

e. 1. Of course, Mother wanted to come along. 2. Of course, your sister wanted to come along. 3. Why didn't they come along?

f. 1. I'm here on business. 2. Men often travel on business. 3. Did Kurt's father really come on business?

g. 1. A young German has taken over the management. 2. A Frenchman has taken over the management of the Paris branch. 3. An American is supposed to take over the management in October.

h. 1. I'm supposed to give him new instructions. 2. He is to receive new instructions. 3. He has already gotten new instructions.

i. 1. Didn't I mention her in my last letter? 2. Yes, you mentioned her in your last letter. 3. You also mentioned her family in every letter.

j. 1. Not only in the last letter, but also in the first. 2. Not only in the first letter, but also in the second. 3. Not only in the second, but also in the third.

k. 1. I reserved a small room for you. 2. I reserved it in a quiet hotel. 3. You can sleep in a quiet hotel.

l. 1. My parents would like to meet you. 2. Karl would like to meet you. 3. I would also like to meet your parents.

III. SAGEN UND FRAGEN

a. *Sie sind Kurt. Sie sagen zu Ihrem Vater:*

1. Sein Besuch ist eine nette Überraschung. 2. Sie haben sein Telegramm vor einer Stunde erhalten. 3. Sie freuen sich außerordentlich über seinen Besuch. 4. Sie haben ihm ein Zimmer in einem ruhigen Hotel reserviert. 5. Sie hoffen, er kann schlafen.

b. *Sie sind der Vater. Sie sagen zu Kurt:*

1. Er sieht glänzend aus. 2. Deutschland scheint ihm zu bekommen. 3. Sie sind geschäftlich hier. 4. Ihre Firma hat seit Oktober eine Bonner Filiale. 5. Sie sollen dem jungen Deutschen neue Anweisungen geben. 6. Ihre Überfahrt war zuerst stürmisch. 7. Sie haben nur wenig geschlafen. 8. Sie bleiben drei Tage hier. 9. Sie würden sich auch freuen, die Familie Lenz kennenzulernen. 10. Sie hoffen, es wird möglich sein.

c. *Sie sind Kurt und fragen den Vater:*

1. wie es der Mutter geht.   2. wie es der Kleinen geht.
3. ob er seine Reise nicht selbst bezahlen mußte.   4. ob die
Bonner Filiale gut geht.   5. ob Sie Lore Lenz in einem Brief
erwähnt haben.   6. ob Sie bekanntmachen dürfen? Fräulein
Lore Lenz.

d. *Sie sind der Vater und fragen Kurt:*

1. ob er Ihr Telegramm erhalten hat.   2. ob das junge
Mädchen auf ihn wartet.   3. wo er ein Zimmer reserviert
hat.   4. ob es in einem ruhigen Hotel ist.

IV. AUFSATZ

BEI DER FAMILIE LENZ

„Das war ein ausgezeichnetes Essen, Frau Lenz", sagte Herr
Klein. Dann wandte er sich an Herrn Lenz. „Ihre Frau ist eine
hervorragende Köchin. Die deutsche Küche hat mir immer vorzüglich geschmeckt, aber die Mahlzeit heute abend war besonders
5 gut."

„Sie haben ja unseren kleinen Nachtisch noch nicht versucht",
sagte Frau Lenz bescheiden. „Vielleicht werden Sie dann Ihre
Meinung ändern."

„Das bezweifle ich", lächelte Herr Klein. „Den leckeren[1] Sauer-
10 braten[2] werde ich so schnell nicht vergessen. Und auch die Bratkartoffeln[3] waren erstklassig."

„Und jetzt zum Nachtisch bekommen Sie frische Erdbeeren."
Nach dem Essen setzten sich die Herren gemütlich ins Wohnzimmer. (Währenddessen[4] spülten die armen Frauen das Geschirr
15 in der Küche ab.[5]) Bald waren sie in ein interessantes Gespräch
vertieft.

Herr Lenz bemerkte: „Ihr Kurt hat prima Deutsch gelernt. Er
macht ab und zu noch einen grammatischen Fehler, besonders mit
den Endungen der Adjektive,[6] aber er hat seinen amerikanischen
20 Akzent fast ganz verloren. Unser Karl spricht rheinländisches
Deutsch. Kurt wird reines Hochdeutsch sprechen."

„Hochdeutsch?" fragte Kurt.

1. delicious.   2. **der Sauerbraten** *a dish made of beef or pork marinated
in vinegar before cooking.*   3. fried potatoes.   4. meanwhile.   5. **ab-
spülen (das Geschirr)** to wash (the dishes).   6. **das Adjektiv, -e** adjective.

„Ja“, erwiderte Herr Lenz. „Dieser Begriff[7] ist für den Ausländer oft verwirrend.[8] Er bezeichnet die Sprache von Ober-[9]
25 und Mitteldeutsch[10] im Gegensatz zu Nieder- oder Plattdeutsch.[11]
Aber er bezeichnet auch die deutsche Schriftsprache[12] im Gegensatz zu den Mundarten[13] und der Umgangssprache.“[14]

„Deutsch“, fuhr Herr Lenz fort, „zeigt viel Verwandtschaft
mit anderen modernen westlichen Sprachen. Deutsch hat aber
30 mehr Formen als Französisch, Spanisch oder Italienisch, denn man
dekliniert alle Substantive, Adjektive und Pronomen. Die Verben hingegen sind leicht — Deutsch teilt sie nicht in Konjugationen ein wie die romanischen Sprachen. Die Verben zeigen
oft eine enge Verwandtschaft mit dem Englischen.“

35 In diesem Augenblick kamen die Damen aus der Küche. „Will
jemand mehr Kaffee oder vielleicht ein Gläschen Wein?“ erkundigte sich Frau Lenz.

Alle lehnten mit Dank ab. „Möchtet ihr euch jetzt nicht zu uns
setzen?“[16] fragte Herr Lenz seine Gattin und Tochter.

40 „Gerne“, antwortete Lore sofort.

Beantworten Sie die folgenden Fragen:

1. Was sagte Herr Klein über das Abendessen? 2. Was für eine
Köchin ist Frau Lenz? 3. Wie war die Mahlzeit? 4. Was hat
Herr Klein noch nicht versucht? 5. Was serviert Frau Lenz als
Nachtisch? 6. Wohin setzen sich die Herren nach dem Abendessen? 7. Und was machen die Frauen? 8. Was für Fehler
macht Kurt noch immer? 9. Wer wird richtiges Hochdeutsch
sprechen, Karl oder Kurt? 10. Welcher Begriff ist verwirrend
für den Ausländer? 11. Warum sind die Verben leicht? 12. Mit
welcher Sprache zeigen die Verben eine enge Verwandtschaft?
13. Wie viele wollten Kaffee oder Wein? 14. Was fragte Herr
Lenz seine Frau und Tochter?

7. concept. 8. confusing. 9. **das Oberdeutsch** Upper German.
10. **das Mitteldeutsch** Middle German. 11. **das Niederdeutsch, das Plattdeutsch** Low German. 12. written language. 13. **die Mundart, -en**
dialects. 14. everyday language. 15. **das Substantiv, -e** substantive,
noun. 16. **sich zu jemandem setzen** to sit down with someone.

V. WORTSCHATZ

ab und zu	now and then	der **Augenblick,**	moment
ab/lehnen	to decline	**-e**	
die **Anweisung,**	instruction, or-	**ausgezeich-**	excellent
-en	der, direction	**net**	
arm	poor	**außerordent-**	extraordinary,
		lich	exceptional

der Ausländer, -	foreigner	mit/kommen,	to come along
bekannt/	to introduce,	kam mit,	
machen	make known	ist mitge-	
die Bekanntschaft	acquaintance	kommen	
bescheiden	modest	der Nachtisch, -e	dessert
der Besuch, -e	visit	nehmen:	to sit down, take
bezeichnen	to designate,	Platz	a seat
	refer to	nehmen	
bezweifeln	to doubt (*a fact*)	prima	first-rate
(das) Deutsch	German (*lan-*	rein	pure, clean
	guage)	scheinen:	to seem to agree
ein/teilen	to divide, classify	jemandem	with someone
die Endung, -en	ending	zu bekom-	
(das) Englisch	English (*lan-*	men	
	guage)	scheinen	
die Erdbeere, -n	strawberry	schlafen,	to sleep
erhalten, er-	to receive	schlief, ge-	
hielt, erhal-		schlafen,	
ten, erhält		schläft	
erstklassig	first-class	schmecken	to taste
die Filiale, -n	branch, affiliate	(das) Spanisch	Spanish
die Form, -en	form		(*language*)
fort/fahren,	to continue	stürmisch	stormy
fuhr fort,		das Telegramm,	telegram
ist fortge-		-e	
fahren,		die Überfahrt,	crossing, trip
fährt fort		-en	across (*the*
(das) Französisch	French (*language*)		*ocean*)
sich freuen über	to be happy	übernehmen,	to take over
+ *accusa-*	about	übernahm,	
tive		übernom-	
frisch	fresh	men, über-	
die Gattin,-nen	wife	nimmt	
geschäftlich	on business, re-	die Überra-	surprise
	lating to busi-	schung, -en	
	ness	verlieren, ver-	to lose
das Gespräch, -e	talk, conversa-	lor ver-	
	tion	loren	
glänzend	splendid, terrific	vertieft	engrossed, ab-
hervorragend	outstanding		sorbed
(das) Italienisch	Italian (*language*)	die Verwandt-	relationship
kennen/	to become ac-	schaft	
lernen	quainted with,	vorzüglich	excellent
	get to know	sich wenden,	to turn
die Köchin, -nen	cook	wandte	
die Küche, -n	kitchen; cuisine	sich, sich	
lächeln	to smile	gewandt	
die Leitung	management	westlich	western
die Mahlzeit, -en	meal	das Wohnzim-	living room
		mer, -	

VI. ERKLÄRUNGEN UND ÜBUNGEN

1. Adjective Endings

Der-words, **ein**-words, and descriptive adjectives have certain endings which indicate their relationship to each other and to the nouns they modify. The key sound indicates the gender, number, and case of the noun that the adjective modifies.

a. Adjectives Following Der-Words

Masculine				Neuter
N. der kleine Mann	/r/		/s/	das kleine Zimmer
G. des kleinen Mannes		/s/		des kleinen Zimmers
D. dem kleinen Mann(e)		/m/		dem kleinen Zimmer
A. den kleinen Mann	/n/		/s/	das kleine Zimmer

Feminine				Plural (*all genders*)
N. die kleine Frau		/i:/		die kleinen Mädchen
G. der kleinen Frau		/r/		der kleinen Mädchen
D. der kleinen Frau	/r/		/n/	den kleinen Mädchen
A. die kleine Frau		/i:/		die kleinen Mädchen

Adjectives after **der**-words[1] have the following endings:

(1) **-e** in the nominative singular of all genders and the accusative feminine and neuter singular;

(2) **-en** everywhere else in both the singular and plural.

Since the **der**-words carry the key sounds, **-e** and **-en** are neutral suffixes.

PRACTICE

A. Decline in all cases, singular and plural:

1. der große Bruder; 2. die kleine Schwester; 3. das neue Haus

B. Complete the following:

1. die nett— Überraschung
2. der arm— Mann
3. das gut— Wetter
4. die klein— Schwester
5. diese ruhig— Zimmer
6. die stürmisch— Reise
7. solche groß— Häuser
8. die neu— Filiale
9. des lang— Briefes
10. wegen solcher schön— Mädchen
11. mit den neu— Anweisungen
12. für den jung— Bruder
13. alle gut— Kinder
14. dieses wichtig— Telegramm
15. welche frei— Stunde
16. diesem lieb— Kind
17. jedes gut— Hotel
18. den gut— Mann
19. welches klein— Kind
20. der letzt— Brief
21. der gut— Frau
22. der lieb— Eltern
23. in diesem ruhig— Zimmer
24. aller gut— Kaffee
25. die lang— Stunden
26. diesem interessant— Gespräch

C. Say in German:

1. this good meal?; 2. which small house?; 3. small houses;
4. new instructions; 5. this expensive trip; 6. the last visit;

1. The invariable ending **-er** is used on all city names to form adjectives. For example:

die Bonner Filiale(n) **Münchner Bier**
the Bonn branch(es) *Munich beer*

7. in the big room; 8. the first crossing; 9. that pretty girl; 10. all young mothers; 11. for the poor man; 12. on account of these last letters; 13. which little mistake?; 14. such bad weather

D. *Answer the following questions using the phrases indicated:*

   Example: Was hat Kurt erhalten? (*das kurze Telegramm*)
   Er hat das kurze Telegramm erhalten.

1. Worüber freut sich Kurt? (der nette Besuch) 2. Was mußte der Vater nicht selbst bezahlen? (die teure Reise) 3. Was hat ein junger Deutscher übernommen? (die neue Leitung — die Bonner Filiale) 4. Wer wartet auf Kurt? (das hübsche Mädchen da) 5. Wann hat Kurt Lore erwähnt? (in, der letzte Brief) 6. Wo wird der Vater schlafen? (in, das neue Hotel)

b. Adjectives Following Ein-Words

Masculine			Neuter
N. ein kleiner Mann	/r/	/s/	ein kleines Zimmer
G. eines kleinen Mannes		/s/	eines kleinen Zimmers
D. einem kleinen Mann(e)		/m/	einem kleinen Zimmer
A. einen kleinen Mann	/n/	/s/	ein kleines Zimmer

Feminine			Plural (*all genders*)
N. eine kleine Frau		/ə/	keine kleinen Mädchen
G. einer kleinen Frau		/r/	keiner kleinen Mädchen
D. einer kleinen Frau	/r/	/n/	keinen kleinen Mädchen
A. eine kleine Frau		/ə/	keine kleinen Mädchen

Adjectives after **ein-**words have the following endings:

(1) When the **ein-**word has no ending, as in the nominative masculine and neuter singular and accusative neuter singular, the adjective or adjectives following the **ein-**word carry the key sound. The key sounds must always be preserved.

(2) Except for **-e** on adjectives in the nominative and accusative feminine singular, the neutral suffix **-en** is used everywhere else in both the singular and plural.

PRACTICE

A. *Decline in all cases, singular and plural:*

1. **kein guter Freund;** 2. **keine alte Schule;** 3. **kein großes Zimmer**

B. *Complete the following:*

1. eine nett— Überraschung
2. ein arm— Mann
3. kein gut— Wetter
4. meine klein— Schwester
5. keine ruhig— Zimmer
6. eine stürmisch— Reise
7. eure groß— Häuser
8. eine neu— Filiale
9. seines lang— Briefes
10. wegen unserer nett— Studentinnen
11. mit keinen neu— Anweisungen
12. für ihren jung— Bruder
13. in ein klein— Dorf

172

14.	**keiner klein— Mädchen**	21.	**ein letzt— Brief**
15.	**ein wichtig— Telegramm**	22.	**meine gut— Frau**
16.	**keine frei— Stunde**	23.	**meiner lieb— Eltern**
17.	**einem lieb— Kind**	24.	**in einem ruhig— Zimmer**
18.	**unser neu— Hotel**	25.	**gegen deinen lang— Besuch**
19.	**einen gut— Mann**	26.	**meine lieb— Freunde**
20.	**Ihr klein— Kind**	27.	**keine gut— Gründe**

C. Say in German:

1. a good meal; 2. no small house; 3. my new instructions; 4. an expensive trip; 5. his last visit; 6. in our big room; 7. her first crossing; 8. their pretty daughter; 9. no young mothers; 10. for a poor man; 11. on account of your last letters; 12. a little mistake; 13. your bad weather; 14. in my long letter; 15. a big house; 16. a little room; 17. a little woman

D. Answer the following questions using the phrases indicated:

> *Example:* Wann hat Kurt das Telegramm bekommen?
> (*vor, eine halbe Stunde*)
> Er hat das Telegramm vor einer halben Stunde bekommen.

1. Wer hat die Leitung der Bonner Filiale übernommen? (ein junger Deutscher) 2. Von wem hat Kurt oft geschrieben? (das schöne Mädchen) 3. Wie beschreibt er Lore? (als, ein hübsches Mädchen) 4. Was für ein Zimmer hat Kurt reserviert? (ein schönes, ruhiges Zimmer) 5. Wo hat Kurt dem Vater ein Zimmer reserviert? (in, ein neues Hotel) 6. Was für eine Köchin ist Frau Lenz? (eine ausgezeichnete Köchin) 7. Was für ein Essen hat Frau Lenz serviert? (ein vorzügliches Essen)

2. Unpreceded Adjectives

Masculine				Neuter
N. **guter Kaffee**	/r/		/s/	**gutes Wasser**
G. **guten Kaffees**		/s/		**guten Wassers**
D. **gutem Kaffee**		/m/		**gutem Wasser**
A. **guten Kaffee**	/n/		/s/	**gutes Wasser**
Feminine				Plural (*all genders*)
N. **gute Milch**		/ə/		**gute Erdbeeren**
G. **guter Milch**		/r/		**guter Erdbeeren**
D. **guter Milch**	/r/		/n/	**guten Erdbeeren**
A. **gute Milch**		/ə/		**gute Erdbeeren**

The endings on unpreceded adjectives are the key sounds since neither a **der**-word nor an **ein**-word precedes. Again, the key sounds must be preserved in order to indicate gender, number, and case. The only exceptions are the masculine and neuter genitive singular, where the key sound is in the noun and the adjective has the neutral suffix **-en.**

PRACTICE

A. Decline in all cases:

1. **heißer Tee;** 2. **frische Milch;** 3. **gutes Essen;** 4. **kleine Kinder**

B. Complete the following:

1. **nett— Überraschungen** (*nominative*)
2. **frei— Zeit** (*nominative*)
3. **stürmisch— Reisen** (*accusative*)
4. **groß— Häuser** (*genitive*)
5. **frisch— Wassers**
6. **aus gut— Gründen**
7. **wegen alt— Männer**
8. **kalt— Kaffees**
9. **bei klein— Kindern**
10. **neu— Anweisungen** (*dative*)
11. **frisch— Milch** (*genitive*)
12. **bei gut— Wetter**

C. Say in German:

1. little houses; 2. of new instructions; 3. good beer; 4. bad weather; 5. in bad weather; 6. little mistakes; 7. with little children; 8. of cold water; 9. fresh strawberries; 10. in warm coffee (*dative*); 11. in hot coffee (*accusative*)

D. Answer the following questions using the phrases indicated:

> *Example:* Was für Wasser soll er bringen? (*heißes Wasser*)
> Er soll heißes Wasser bringen.

1. Was für Anweisungen soll der Vater geben? (neue Anweisungen) 2. Was für Wetter hatte der Vater auf der langen Reise? (gutes Wetter) 3. Was für Deutsch spricht Karl? (rheinländisches Deutsch) 4. Und Kurt? (reines Hochdeutsch) 5. Was für Fehler macht Kurt noch immer? (kleine Fehler)

3. Adjectives Used as Nouns

der Deutsche
the German (*man*)

die Deutsche
the German (*woman*)

die Armen
the poor (*people*)

das Alte
the old

Altes und Neues
old (*things*) *and new* (*things*)

ein Deutscher
a German (*man*)

eine Deutsche
a German (*woman*)

A descriptive adjective may be used as a noun by capitalizing it and suffixing the appropriate ending, depending on whether a **der**-word, an **ein**-word, or nothing precedes. Masculine and feminine adjective-nouns refer to people, whereas neuters refer to things or abstractions.

Note also these expressions:

etwas Kaltes
something cold

nichts Neues
nothing new

viel Interessantes
much (that is) interesting

wenig Schönes
little (that is) beautiful

but: **alles Gute**
everything good

Remember that of the above group only **alles** is a **der**-word. Adjectives following **alles** thus have neutral suffixes. The other adjective-nouns, being unpreceded, carry the key sounds.

PRACTICE

A. Translate:

1. etwas Schönes   2. alles Neue   3. eine Arme   4. der Alte
5. die Deutschen   6. die Kleine   7. nichts Warmes   8. alles Mögliche   9. das Neue   10. wenig Kaltes

B. Express in German, using adjective-nouns:

1. the beautiful woman   2. nothing good.   3. something interesting   4. much that is easy   5. something nice   6. something having to do with business   7. a German man   8. a sad man   9. everything new   10. nothing old

4. Adverbs

Lore **ist schön.**
Lore ist schön.

Das Kind **ist gut.**
The child is good.

Lore **singt schön.**
Lore sings beautifully.

Das Kind **singt gut.**
The child sings well.

Most adjectives may be used also as adverbs without any change in form and without any ending whatsoever.

FINAL PRACTICE

Say first, then write in German:

1. Kurt has a nice surprise.   2. He had just a half hour ago received a short telegram from his father.   3. He is very happy about his father's visit.   4. Mr. Klein says: "You look terrific!"
5. Germany seems to agree with Kurt.   6. Kurt asks about his mother and kid sister.   7. His mother wanted to come along, but it is an expensive trip.   8. "This is a business trip," says Kurt's father.   9. "We have a new Bonn branch."   10. "A young German has taken over the management."   11. "I suppose you have to give him new instructions," says Kurt.   12. A pretty girl is waiting for Kurt.   13. It is Lore Lenz.   14. Kurt has mentioned her in many letters to his parents.   15. Mr. Klein tells Lore about the stormy weather during his crossing.   16. He could not sleep much.   17. Kurt has reserved a quiet room for his father.
18. He will visit him in his hotel later.

Das neue Opernhaus in Köln
GERMAN INFORMATION CENTER

I. UNTERHALTUNG

KURT BEGLEITET SEINEN VATER

Vater: Du hast mir jetzt manches gezeigt. Nur eins nicht—
mein Hotel.

Kurt: In diesem Stadtviertel sind alle Hotels, auch deins.

Vater: Ich bin wirklich erschöpft. Bitte laß mich ein paar
Stunden schlafen.

Einige Stunden später

Kurt: Hast du gut geschlafen?

Vater: Ich fühle mich wieder erfrischt. Ich würde heute abend
ganz gerne ausgehen.

Kurt: Ich weiß, du liebst die Oper. Aber die Vorstellung war
schon ausverkauft.

Vater: Schade. Und morgen abend?

Kurt: Es gibt noch einige sehr teure Plätze.

Vater: Für so etwas Schönes zahle ich gern.

Kurt: Für heute abend habe ich Karten für ein anderes Programm. Ich weiß nicht, ob es dir gefallen wird.

Vater: Komm schon heraus damit!

Kurt: Elektronische Musik. Sehr viele Studenten interessieren
sich dafür.

KURT ACCOMPANIES HIS FATHER

Father: You've now shown me quite a few things. Only one thing
you haven't—my hotel.

Kurt: All hotels are in this section, including yours.

Father: I'm really exhausted. Please let me sleep a few hours.

A few hours later

Kurt: Did you sleep well?

Father: I feel refreshed. I wouldn't mind going out tonight.

Kurt: I know you love opera. But the performance was sold out.

Father: What a shame. And tomorrow night?

Kurt: There are a few very expensive seats left.

Father: I don't mind paying for something as fine as that.

Kurt: For tonight I have tickets for a different program. I don't
know whether you'll care for it.

Father: Come on, let's have it!

Kurt: Electronic music. Very many students are interested in it.

LESSON 12

177

Vater: Ist diese Musik nicht hauptsächlich für junge Leute? Kann meine Generation so etwas verstehen?

Kurt: Man muß es probieren. Also abgemacht. Heute moderne Musik, morgen Oper — und übermorgen?

Vater: Was hältst du von der Einladung der Familie Lenz?

Kurt: Ich denke, du solltest sie annehmen. Sie sind sehr nett und aufmerksam.

Vater: Also rufe an, danke ihnen und frage, wann sie uns erwarten. Aber dann gehen wir essen. Ich habe großen Hunger.

Father: Isn't this music mainly for young people? Can my generation understand something like that?

Kurt: You have to try it. All right then. Today modern music, tomorrow opera—and day after tomorrow?

Father: What do you think of the Lenz's invitation?

Kurt: I think you ought to accept it. They are very nice and helpful.

Father: Well, call them, thank them, and ask when they expect us. But after that let's go eat. I'm terribly hungry.

II. KOMBINATIONEN

Sagen Sie auf deutsch:

a. 1. All hotels are in this section.   2. All department stores are in this section.   3. My house is in this section.

b. 1. I am really exhausted.   2. Kurt's father even looks exhausted.   3. After work we're all exhausted.

c. 1. Please let me sleep a few hours.   2. Please let me rest a few minutes.   3. I want to sleep a few hours.

d. 1. I feel completely refreshed.   2. Kurt's father feels refreshed.   3. Do you now feel refreshed?

e. 1. I wouldn't mind going out tonight.   2. We would all like to go out tonight.   3. Kurt's father wouldn't mind going to the opera.

f. 1. I don't mind paying for something as fine as that.   2. He wouldn't pay even for something as fine as that.   3. He would pay for something stupid (Dummes).

g. 1. Many students are interested in it.   2. Young people are mainly interested in it.   3. Are you interested in it?

h. 1. Can my generation understand something like that? 2. Can young people understand something like that? 3. Everybody can understand something like this.

i. 1. One has to try it. 2. Everyone has to try it. 3. We ought to try it.

j. 1. What do you think of the Lenz family's invitation? 2. What do you think of Lore's invitation? 3. I think you should accept them.

k. 1. Call them and thank them. 2. Ask them when they expect us. 3. Tell them I'm very hungry.

III. SAGEN UND FRAGEN

a. *Sie sind der Vater und sagen zu Kurt:*

1. Er hat Ihnen jetzt manches gezeigt. 2. Er hat Ihnen aber das Hotel nicht gezeigt. 3. Sie sind wirklich sehr müde. 4. Sie wollen einige Stunden schlafen. 5. Sie fühlen sich wieder erfrischt. 6. Sie würden heute abend ganz gerne ausgehen. 7. Sie zahlen gerne für etwas Schönes. 8. Er soll schon damit (mit der Wahrheit) herauskommen (*use imperative*). 9. Er soll die Familie Lenz anrufen (*use imperative*). 10. Er soll ihnen für die Einladung danken (*use imperative*). 11. Er soll fragen, wann sie Sie erwarten (*use imperative*). 12. Sie haben großen Hunger.

b. *Sie sind Kurt und sagen zu Ihrem Vater:*

1. Alle Hotels sind in diesem Stadtviertel—auch seins. 2. Sie wissen, er liebt die Oper. 3. Sie haben angerufen: die Vorstellungen sind ausverkauft. 4. Sie haben aber Karten für ein anderes Programm. 5. Sie wissen nicht, ob es ihm gefallen wird. 6. Sie hören gern elektronische Musik. 7. Er soll es einmal probieren. 8. Er sollte die Einladung der Familie Lenz annehmen.

c. *Sie sind Kurt und fragen den Vater:*

1. ob er gut geschlafen hat. 2. ob er sich erfrischt fühlt. 3. ob er noch immer die Oper liebt. 4. ob er soviel für die Oper ausgeben will. 5. ob ihm die elektronische Musik gefallen wird. 6. wohin er morgen abend gehen will. 7. ob er die Einladung annehmen will. 8. wann er zur Familie Lenz gehen möchte.

IV. AUFSATZ

PERSÖNLICHE ANZEIGEN

Nach mehreren Stunden kehrte Kurt ins Hotel zurück. Sein Vater saß bequem in einem Ledersessel[1] und war wach und munter. Auf dem Tisch neben ihm lagen einige Zeitungen und auch etliche Illustrierte.[2]

5 „Eines kann ich immer noch nicht verstehen", bemerkte Herr Klein. „Sieh dir dieses Blatt an! Die deutschen Zeitungsausgaben[3] sind im allgemeinen viel dünner als unsere und doch bringen sie so viele Nachrichten über Außen- und Innenpolitik,[4] Wirtschaftsprobleme[5] und Lokalangelegenheiten[6] wie bei uns. Und sieh dir

10 auch diese Spalten[7] an mit persönlichen Anzeigen!"

Kurt lachte. „Du meinst gewiß die vielen Geburts-, Verlobungs-, Vermählungs- und Todesanzeigen.[8] Wie zum Beispiel hier: ‚Die Geburt unseres ersten Sohnes Heinz zeigen wir hocherfreut[9] an.‘[10] Oder diese andere: ‚Statt Karten. Wir vermählen uns

15 am . . .‘ Oder: ‚Gestern abend verschied[11] nach langem Leiden[12] unser lieber Großvater Friedrich Müller.‘ Ich finde das alles ganz nett und sehr geschmackvoll."

„Und was hältst du hiervon?"[13] fragte der Vater und fing zu lesen an. „ ‚Hübsche kultivierte Witwe,[14] heitere Natur, zuverläs-

20 siger Charakter, attraktive Erscheinung, sucht neues Eheglück[15] mit gebildetem, gut aussehendem Herrn im Alter bis 58 Jahre. Vertraulich . . .‘ "

Kurt hatte viele solche Anzeigen gesehen. Zuerst fand er sie lächerlich, sogar grotesk. „Das verstößt[16] doch gegen den guten

25 Geschmack!" hatte er sich öfter gesagt. Dann dachte er: „Andere Länder, andere Sitten."

Der Vater hatte unterdessen eine andere Anzeige entdeckt: „Wie gefällt dir diese Anzeige? ‚Ich danke der Feuerwehr und allen Nachbarn, die[17] so tapfer mitgeholfen haben, den großen

30 Brand[18] bei mir zu löschen.‘[19] Und dann steht der Name und die Adresse des Bauern."

1. leather chair. 2. **etliche Illustrierte** some picture magazines. 3. newspaper editions. 4. **Außen- und Innenpolitik** foreign and domestic policy. 5. economic problems. 6. local affairs. 7. **die Spalte, -n** column (*in a newspaper*). 8. **Geburts-, Verlobungs-, Vermählungs- und Todesanzeigen** birth, engagement, marriage, and death announcements. 9. joyfully. 10. **anzeigen** to announce. 11. **verscheiden, verschied, ist verschieden** to depart (*to die*). 12. **das Leiden,-** suffering. 13. **halten (hier)von** to think of (*this*). 14. **die Witwe, -n** widow. 15. conjugal bliss. 16. **verstoßen, verstieß, verstoßen** to go against. 17. who (*relative pronoun*). 18. fire, conflagration. 19. to put out, extinguish.

„Warum nicht?" fragte Kurt. „Auf diese Art und Weise[20] sprechen die Deutschen oft ihren Dank aus[21] oder teilen ihren Bekannten ihre Familienereignisse mit. Natürlich haben manche Leute besseren Geschmack als andere. Und das ist überall so."

35

Beantworten Sie die folgenden Fragen:

1. Wann kehrte Kurt ins Hotel zurück? 2. Was machte Kurts Vater? 3. Was lag auf dem Tisch neben dem Sessel? 4. Was kann Herr Klein immer noch nicht verstehen? 5. Welche Nachrichten enthalten die deutschen Zeitungen? 6. Was für persönliche Anzeigen fand Herr Klein in der Zeitung? 7. Wie haben solche Anzeigen Kurt gefallen? 8. Was hatte er sich öfter gesagt? 9. Was wollte die Witwe in der Anzeige? 10. Wofür dankte der Bauer seinen Nachbarn und der Feuerwehr? 11. Was teilen die Deutschen ihren Bekannten mit in diesen persönlichen Anzeigen?

20. **auf diese Art und Weise** in this way. 21. **aussprechen** to express.

V. WORTSCHATZ

abgemacht	settled, agreed	die **Feuerwehr, -en**	fire department
an/fangen, fing an, angefangen, fängt an	to begin	**sich fühlen**	to feel
		gebildet	educated
		die **Generation, -en**	generation
die **Anzeige, -n**	ad, announcement	der **Geschmack, ∺e**	taste
aufmerksam	helpful, attentive	**geschmackvoll**	tasteful, in good taste
ausverkauft	sold out	**heiter**	cheerful
der **Bauer, -n, -n**	farmer	**hiervon**	of this
der **Bekannte, -n, -n**	acquaintance	**lächerlich**	ridiculous
bequem	comfortable	**lieben**	to love
das **Blatt, ∺er**	leaf, sheet, newspaper	**meinen**	to mean, say, think
dünn	thin	**mit/helfen, half mit, mitgeholfen, hilft mit**	to assist, cooperate
entdecken	to discover		
enthalten, enthielt, enthalten, enthält	to contain		
das **Ereignis, -se**	event	**mit/teilen**	to communicate, inform
erfrischt	refreshed	**munter**	merry
die **Erscheinung, -en**	appearance	die **Musik**	music
		die **Oper, -n**	opera
		persönlich	personal

181

der **Platz, ⁔e** (*theater, etc.*)	seat	**unterdessen**	meanwhile
		sich vermählen	to get married, marry
probieren	to try	**vertraulich**	confidential
das **Programm, -e**	program	die **Vorstellung, -en**	performance
schade	too bad, a pity		
die **Sitte, -n**	custom	**wach**	awake
der **Sohn, ⁔e**	son	**zurück/kehren**	to return
das **Stadtviertel, -**	section (of town)	**zuverlässig**	reliable, dependable
tapfer	brave		
übermorgen	day after tomorrow		

VI. ERKLÄRUNGEN UND ÜBUNGEN

1. Indefinite Numerical Adjectives

Es gibt noch **einige teure Plätze.**
There are still some expensive seats.

Viele junge Studenten interessieren sich für diese Musik.
Many young students are interested in this music.

Es gibt nur **wenige gute Plätze** für diese Vorstellung.
There are only a few good seats for this performance.

The indefinite numerical adjectives **andere** (*other*), **einige** (*some*), **mehrere** (*several*), **viele** (*many*), **wenige** (*few*) have the endings of unpreceded adjectives, as do all adjectives following them.

PRACTICE

A. *Decline in the plural:*

1. **einige gute Hotels;** 2. **viele gute Männer;** 3. **wenige gute Studentinnen**

B. *Fill in the blanks with the proper adjective endings:*

1. **einige nett— Leute**
2. **für viele jung— Männer**
3. **andere schön— Bilder**
4. **wenige gut— Köchinnen**
5. **mehrerer interessant— Bücher**
6. **einige stürmisch— Überfahrten**
7. **in vielen klein— Zimmern**
8. **viele teur— Plätze**
9. **neben ander— groß— Häusern**
10. **wenige interessant— Leute**

C. *Say in German:*

1. some German girls
2. in several old books
3. other interesting programs
4. for many other reasons
5. many nice students
6. several good hotels
7. few good rooms
8. of other new houses

D. *Answer the following questions using the indicated words:*

> *Example:* Was für Plätze gibt es noch? (*viele gut-*)
> Es gibt noch viele gute Plätze.

1. Gibt es gute Hotels in dieser Stadt? (einige sehr gut-) 2. Wie viele Leute wohnen hier? (mehrere jung-) 3. Was für Bücher haben Sie dieses Semester gelesen? (einige interessant-) 4. Kennen Sie die zwei großen Männer? (mehrere groß-) 5. Gibt es viele billige Karten? (nur wenige teuer-)

2. Ein-Words as Pronouns

Sie haben mir manches gezeigt, nur **ein(e)s** nicht.
You've shown me lots of things, except for one thing.

Hier sind alle Karten, auch **deine.**
All tickets are here, yours too.

Wessen Platz ist das? Das ist **meiner.**
Whose seat is that? That is mine.

Ein-words may be used independently as pronouns and have the same endings as **der-**words used as adjectives.

PRACTICE

A. *Ask a question based on each of the following statements, in accordance with the example:*

> *Example:* Hier ist mein Hotel. (*Ihr*)
> Und wo ist Ihres?

1. Hier ist dein Zimmer. (sein) 2. Hier ist Ihr Hotel. (unser) 3. Hier ist ihr Platz. (Ihr) 4. Hier sind unsere Karten. (Ihr) 5. Hier ist meine Einladung. (dein) 6. Hier ist mein Koffer. (ihr) 7. Hier ist ihre Zeitschrift. (mein)

B. *Complete the following:*

1. Ihr Haus und mein—. 2. Ihr Auto und unser—. 3. Sein Vater und mein—. 4. Seine Arbeit und unser—. 5. Unsere Plätze und sein—. 6. Meine Eltern und Ihr—.

C. *Express in German:*

1. That is my book, not yours. 2. I have a car. Do you also have one? 3. Here is my suitcase. Where is yours? 4. Kurt has a magazine, but Karl doesn't have any. 5. Do you have your ticket? I have mine. 6. Where is your train? I see mine.

3. Irregular Nouns

a.

der Assistent	des Assistenten	die Assistenten
der Christ	des Christen	die Christen
der Deutsche	des Deutschen	die Deutschen
der Franzose	des Franzosen	die Franzosen

der Herr	des Herrn	die Herren
der Junge	des Jungen	die Jungen
der Komponist	des Komponisten	die Komponisten
der Mensch	des Menschen	die Menschen
der Prinz	des Prinzen	die Prinzen
der Russe	des Russen	die Russen
der Soldat	des Soldaten	die Soldaten
der Student	des Studenten	die Studenten
der Tourist	des Touristen	die Touristen

A number of masculine nouns, mostly denoting human beings, have **-(e)n** as the plural as well as **-(e)n** in the genitive, dative, and accusative singular.

Model Declensions

Singular	Plural
N. **der** Junge	N. **die** Jungen
G. **des** Jungen	G. **der** Jungen
D. **dem** Jungen	D. **den** Jungen
A. **den** Jungen	A. **die** Jungen

Singular	Plural
N. **der** Herr	N. **die** Herren
G. **des** Herrn	G. **der** Herren
D. **dem** Herrn	D. **den** Herren
A. **den** Herrn	A. **die** Herren

Singular	Plural
N. **der** Student	N. **die** Studenten
G. **des** Studenten	G. **der** Studenten
D. **dem** Studenten	D. **den** Studenten
A. **den** Studenten	A. **die** Studenten

b.
der Doktor	die Doktoren[1]
der Professor	die Professoren[1]
der Nachbar	die Nachbarn[2]
der Staat	die Staaten

Masculine nouns of non-German origin ending in **-or**, as well as a few others, have **-(e)n** in the plural only.

Model Declension

Singular	Plural
N. **der** Doktor	N. **die** Doktoren
G. **des** Doktors	G. **der** Doktoren
D. **dem** Doktor	D. **den** Doktoren
A. **den** Doktor	A. **die** Doktoren

1. Note that the stress changes in the plural.
2. Genitive **Nachbarn** is now preferred in the singular.

	Singular	Plural
c.	N. **der Gedanke**	N. **die Gedanken**
	G. **des Gedankens**	G. **der Gedanken**
	D. **dem Gedanken**	D. **den Gedanken**
	A. **den Gedanken**	A. **die Gedanken**

	Singular	Plural
	N. **der Name**	N. **die Namen**
	G. **des Namens**	G. **der Namen**
	D. **dem Namen**	D. **den Namen**
	A. **den Namen**	A. **die Namen**

	Singular	Plural
	N. **das Herz**	N. **die Herzen**
	G. **des Herzens**	G. **der Herzen**
	D. **dem Herzen**	D. **den Herzen**
	A. **das Herz**	A. **die Herzen**

The nouns **der Gedanke, der Name, das Herz** are irregular in the singular.

PRACTICE

A.   Decline the following irregular nouns in the singular:

1. **der Gedanke**   4. **das Herz**
2. **der Komponist**   5. **der Staat**
3. **der Name**   6. **der Soldat**

B.   Say in German:

1. with the name   2. the name of the boy   3. the professor's neighbors   4. the students' books   5. the gentleman's pretty wife
6. in spite of the name   7. in your heart   8. on account of this soldier

FINAL PRACTICE   *Say first, then write in German:*

1. Kurt showed his father a great many things.   2. Only one thing he didn't show him—his hotel.   3. Mr. Klein is exhausted and wants to sleep a few hours.   4. Kurt and his father are going out this evening.   5. They will visit Lore's family.   6. Tomorrow evening they will probably go to the opera.   7. This evening the performance was sold out.   8. The name of the opera is „Lohengrin" by Wagner.   9. On Friday they will hear electronic music. 10. There are still a few very expensive seats left.   11. Can Mr. Klein's generation understand electronic music?   12. This music is mainly for young people.   13. Kurt says you have to try it.   14. It is settled. Today they will hear modern music.   15. What does Kurt think of the invitation from the Lenz family?   16. He thinks his father should accept it.   17. What kind of people are the Lenzes?   18. They are very nice and helpful people.   19. Kurt calls up the Lenz family and accepts the invitation.   20. Kurt and his father then go and eat.   21. Mr. Klein is very hungry.

185

Auf der Autobahn
GERMAN INFORMATION CENTER

I. UNTERHALTUNG

DER VATER BESUCHT DIE FAMILIE LENZ

Vater:	Ich muß morgen schon in aller Frühe nach Bonn.
Frau Lenz:	Ach, das ist schade. Können Sie wirklich nicht länger bleiben?
Vater:	Es ist leider nicht möglich. Ich muß spätestens übermorgen im Büro sein.
Kurt:	Vater will mit dem Bus nach Bonn. Was halten Sie davon, Herr Lenz?
Herr Lenz:	Ich würde lieber mit dem Zug fahren. Es geht schneller und ist sicherer.
Frau Lenz:	Es ist auch viel einfacher. Der Verkehr auf der Autobahn wird immer stärker.
Herr Lenz:	Und gleichzeitig auch gefährlicher. Besonders auf dieser Strecke.
Frau Lenz:	Wir haben die besten Autostraßen — und auch die meisten Unfälle.
Karl:	Ich fürchte, wir kommen vom Thema ab. Um wieviel Uhr möchten Sie abfahren, Herr Klein?
Vater:	Das weiß ich eben nicht. Wann muß ich weg, um gegen neun in Bonn zu sein?

FATHER VISITS THE LENZ FAMILY

Father:	I have to leave bright and early tomorrow for Bonn.
Mrs. Lenz:	That's a pity. You really can't stay any longer?
Father:	Unfortunately it's not possible. I have to be in the office day after tomorrow at the latest.
Kurt:	Dad wants to go to Bonn by bus. What do you think of this, Mr. Lenz?
Mr. Lenz:	I'd rather go by train. It's faster and safer.
Mrs. Lenz:	It's also much simpler. Traffic on the highway keeps getting heavier.
Mr. Lenz:	And at the same time more dangerous. Especially on this stretch.
Mrs. Lenz:	We have the best highways—and also the most accidents.
Karl:	I'm afraid we're getting off the subject. At what time would you like to leave, Mr. Klein?
Father:	That's what I don't know yet. When do I have to leave to get to Bonn around nine?

Karl:	Um Punkt sieben geht ein Zug, glaube ich.
Vater:	Da muß ich aber früh aufstehen.
Kurt:	Und es ist schon elf Uhr. Wir sollten jetzt ins Hotel zurück.
Vater:	Vielen Dank für den netten Abend.
Karl:	Wußten Sie, daß es regnet, Herr Klein?
Vater:	Es regnet?
Kurt:	Ja, wir hatten ein Gewitter. Es hat gedonnert und geblitzt.
Vater:	Ich habe wirklich nichts gehört.
Karl:	Ja, ihr wart alle so ins Gespräch vertieft und habt nichts gemerkt.
Vater:	Hier ist der Beweis: Ich habe mich ausgezeichnet mit Ihnen unterhalten.

Karl:	There's a train at seven sharp, I think.
Father:	Oh, but then I have to get up early.
Kurt:	And it's already eleven. We ought to get back to the hotel now.
Father:	Thank you very much for a pleasant evening.
Karl:	Did you know that it's raining, Mr. Klein?
Father:	It's raining?
Kurt:	Yes, we had a thunderstorm. There was thunder and lightning.
Father:	I really didn't hear anything.
Karl:	Yes, you were all so immersed in your conversation that you didn't notice anything.
Father:	Here is the proof: I had a marvelous chat with you.

II. KOMBINATIONEN

Sagen Sie auf deutsch:

a. 1. I have to be in Bonn bright and early tomorrow. 2. He has to be in Frankfurt bright and early tomorrow. 3. They have to get up bright and early tomorrow.

b. 1. That's a pity. You really can't stay any longer? 2. That's a pity. You really have to get up at seven? 3. That's a pity. He has to be in Bonn at nine.

c. 1. Unfortunately it's not possible. He has to be in the office day after tomorrow. 2. It really isn't possible. We have to be home tomorrow at the latest. 3. Why isn't it possible?

d. 1. Father wants to go by bus. What do you think of this? 2. He can't stay any longer. What do you think of that? 3. I have to leave very early. What does he think of that?

e. 1. I would rather go by train. 2. He would rather go by bus. 3. We would rather stay home.

f. 1. Traffic on the highway keeps getting heavier. 2. Traffic is getting more dangerous. 3. At the same time, it's getting faster.

g. 1. We have the best highways. 2. We have the most accidents. 3. Did you have very many accidents?

h. 1. I'm afraid we're getting off the subject. 2. Are we getting off the subject? 3. I'm afraid you're right.

i. 1. When do I have to leave to be in Bonn around nine? 2. Why do we have to leave now in order to be there at ten? 3. You have to leave at seven sharp.

j. 1. Did you know it is raining? 2. Did you know we had a thunderstorm? 3. Did he know there was thunder and lightning?

III. SAGEN UND FRAGEN

a. *Sie sind der Vater. Sie sagen:*

1. Sie müssen in aller Frühe nach Bonn. 2. Sie können nicht länger bleiben. 3. Sie müssen spätestens übermorgen im Büro sein. 4. Sie müssen sehr früh aufstehen. 5. Sie danken für den netten Abend. 6. Sie wußten nicht, daß es regnet. 7. Sie haben nichts gehört. 8. Hier ist der Beweis: Sie haben sich ausgezeichnet unterhalten.

b. *Sie sind Herr Lenz. Sie sagen:*

1. Sie würden lieber mit dem Zug fahren. 2. Sie finden, daß es sicherer ist. 3. Sie finden, daß der Verkehr stärker wird. 4. Sie glauben, daß er auch gefährlicher wird. 5. Sie haben hier die besten Autostraßen. 6. Sie haben leider auch die meisten Unfälle.

c. *Sie sind Karl. Sie fragen Herrn Klein:*

1. ob er nicht länger bleiben kann. 2. wann er zurück sein muß. 3. um wieviel Uhr er abfahren will. 4. ob er weiß, daß es geregnet hat. 5. ob er weiß, daß es gedonnert hat.

6. ob er weiß, daß es geblitzt hat.   7. ob er wirklich nichts gehört hat.   8. ob er so ins Gespräch vertieft war.   9. ob er wirklich nichts gemerkt hat.

IV. AUFSATZ

HABEN DIE AMERIKANER ES BESSER?

Die Unterhaltung hatte sich gestern abend lange um Unterschiede zwischen dem Leben in Deutschland und Amerika gedreht. Im Laufe[1] des Abends hatte Herr Lenz oft mit dem Kopf genickt.[2] „Ja, Goethe hatte recht", hat er immer wiederholt. „Er hatte
5 zweifellos recht." Kurts Vater hatte entweder nicht richtig achtgegeben oder die Bemerkung nicht verstanden, denn er hatte gar nicht darauf reagiert.

Auch Kurt hatte sie nicht richtig verstanden. Goethe war Deutschlands größter und bekanntester Dichter, und Kurt hatte
10 seine besten Gedichte und berühmtesten Stücke gelesen. Diese Bemerkung konnte er sich aber nicht erklären, solange er auch[3] darüber nachdachte. Womit hatte Goethe recht? Endlich konnte er sich nicht mehr bezähmen[4] und gab seine Verlegenheit zu.

Karl lachte: „Goethe schrieb einmal ein Gedicht, ‚Amerika, du
15 hast es besser'. Als mein Vater deinem Vater zuhörte, dachte er besonders an Goethes Worte. Er kennt ja Goethe in- und auswendig,[5] und sogar ich kann mich an die erste Strophe[6] erinnern":
　　　Amerika, du hast es besser
　　　Als unser Kontinent, der alte.
20 　　　Hast keine verfallenen[7] Schlösser
　　　Und keine Basalte.[8]

„Verstehe ich ihn richtig?" fragte Kurt. „Amerikaner sind weniger an die Tradition gebunden."[9]

„Sie haben dadurch weniger Vorurteile als die Europäer", fügte
25 Karl hinzu. „Unsere politischen Einrichtungen z.B. sind vielleicht veraltet,[10] und wir sind deshalb nicht in der Lage, so rasche Fortschritte[11] zu machen."

„Aber haben wir es heute wirklich besser?" fragte Kurt.

1. **im Laufe** (+ *genitive*) in the course (of).   2. **mit dem Kopf nicken** to nod.   3. **solange . . . auch** no matter how long . . .   4. **sich bezähmen** to control oneself.   5. **in- und auswendig** in and out, thoroughly.   6. **strophe,** stanza.   7. delapidated.   8. basalt, heavy volcanic rock.   9. **an die Tradition gebunden** bound by tradition.   10. outmoded.   11. **so rasche Fortschritte** (*pl.*) such rapid progress.

„Vielen Deutschen kommt das so vor", sagte Karl. „Für sie ist
30 Amerika immer noch das Land der reichen Leute und der unbegrenzten[12] Möglichkeiten. Amerika hat schon über hundert Jahre
keinen Krieg auf eigenem Boden[13] geführt.[14] Sie wissen, wie stark
die Schwerindustrie[15] ist und wie sie das Leben des einzelnen
Menschen beeinflußt hat. Aber viel mehr noch bewundern und
35 beneiden sie die schönen, modernen Wohnungen in den amerikanischen Filmen: Wohnungen mit den neuesten Einrichtungen
und Geräten. Alle Amerikaner scheinen wenigstens ein Auto zu
besitzen und viele Leute aus dem Mittelstand[16] sogar zwei. Das
Leben der amerikanischen Hausfrau scheint viel leichter zu sein
40 als das unserer Frauen. Siehst du, Kurt, meinen Eltern geht es
prima für deutsche Verhältnisse, viel besser als den meisten Deutschen. Aber im Vergleich[17] zum amerikanischen Leben . . ."

„Ihr habt doch seit dem Kriege viele Amerikaner kennengelernt. Sind sie glücklicher oder zufriedener als ihr? Ich wieder-
45 hole: geht es uns wirklich besser?"

Karl mußte lachen, denn Kurt verlangte anscheinend eine
direkte Antwort. „Die Unterschiede zwischen den Ländern werden
kleiner und unwichtiger", sagte er, „aber eines wird immer
schwieriger, mein Freund."

50 „Und was ist das?"

„Der Unterschied zwischen Mythus[18] und Wirklichkeit. Und
dies ist vielleicht unser Hauptproblem."

Beantworten Sie die folgenden Fragen:

1. Worum hat sich die Unterhaltung gestern abend gedreht?
2. Was hat Herr Lenz immer wiederholt? 3. Warum hat Herr
Klein nicht auf die Bemerkung reagiert? 4. Was hatte Kurt von
Goethe gelesen? 5. Was konnte Kurt sich gar nicht erklären?
6. Was gab er endlich zu? 7. Was kennt Herr Lenz in- und auswendig? 8. Woran sind Amerikaner weniger gebunden? 9. Was
ist Amerika immer noch für viele Deutsche? 10. Seit wann hat
Amerika keinen Krieg auf eigenem Boden geführt? 11. Was hat
die Großindustrie stark beeinflußt? 12. Was beneiden viele
Deutsche aber am meisten? 13. Wie scheint das Leben der
amerikanischen Hausfrau zu sein? 14. Wie geht es Kurts Eltern
für deutsche Verhältnisse? 15. Was für eine Antwort verlangte
Kurt? 16. Wie werden die Unterschiede zwischen den Ländern?
17. Was wird immer schwieriger?

12. unlimited. 13. **auf eigenem Boden** on its own soil. 14. **Krieg führen**
to wage war. 15. heavy industry. 16. middle class(es). 17. **im
Vergleich** in comparison. 18. myth.

V. WORTSCHATZ

ab/kommen, kam ab, ist abgekommen	to deviate from, get off (*a subject*)	nach/denken über, dachte nach, nachgedacht	to think about, reflect over
acht/geben auf, gab acht, achtgegeben, gibt acht	to pay attention to, take care of	der Punkt, -e um Punkt sieben	point, period, dot at seven sharp
anscheinend	apparently	reich	rich
		schwierig	difficult
die Autobahn, -en	autobahn, super highway	sicher	sure, safe
die Autostraße, -n	highway	spätestens	at the latest
		die Strecke, -n	stretch
beeinflussen	to influence	der Unfall, ⸚e	accident
beneiden	to envy	der Unterschied, -e	difference
der Beweis	proof	das Verhältnis, -se	condition, circumstance
blitzen	to lighten		
donnern	to thunder	der Verkehr	traffic
sich drehen um	to deal with, hinge upon; to turn about	die Verlegenheit	embarrassment, difficulty, dilemma
die Einrichtung, -en	institution, facility	vertieft in + *accusative*	immersed in
einzeln	individual	vor/kommen, kam vor, ist vorgekommen	to seem, appear, happen
der Europäer, -	European		
die Frühe	early morning, early hour		
in aller Frühe	bright and early, first thing in the morning	das Vorurteil, -e weg wiederholen	prejudice away to repeat
fürchten	to fear	die Wirklichkeit	reality
gefährlich	dangerous	die Wohnung, -en	dwelling, apartment
das Gewitter, -	thunderstorm		
gleichzeitig	at the same time	zu/geben, gab zu, zugegeben, gibt zu	to admit, confess
glücklich	happy, fortunate		
halten von, hielt, gehalten, hält	to think of		
		zu/hören	to listen to
das Hauptproblem, -e	main problem	zweifellos	doubtless, without a doubt
hinzu/fügen	to add		

VI. ERKLÄRUNGEN UND ÜBUNGEN

1. Comparison
a. Predicate Adjectives and Adverbs

Marie ist schön.
Marie is pretty.

Trudi ist schöner.
Trudi is prettier.

Der Bus fährt schnell.
The bus travels fast.

Der Zug fährt schneller.
The train travels faster.

Lore **ist am schönsten.**   Das Flugzeug **fährt am schnellsten.**
Lore is prettiest.   *The plane travels fastest.*

Mein Zimmer **ist dunkel.**
My room is dark.

Ihr Zimmer **ist dunkler.**
Your room is darker.

Sein Zimmer **ist am dunkelsten.**
His room is darkest.

To form the comparative of predicate adjectives and all adverbs, add **-er** to the positive form of the word regardless of length. (Adjectives ending in **-er, -el** customarily drop **e** in the comparative **teuer, teurer; dunkel, dunkler**). The superlative consists of **am** plus the adjective or adverb with ending **-(e)sten.**[1]

b. Attributives

Das ist **ein kleines Zimmer.**
That's a small room.

Das ist **ein kleineres Zimmer.**
That's a smaller room.

To form the comparative of adjectives modifying a noun (attributives), add **-er** and the appropriate ending.

Ist dieses Zimmer das kleinste (Zimmer) im Haus?
Is this room the smallest (room) in the house?

Ja, es ist das kleinste.
Yes, it's the smallest.

To form the superlative, use the proper form of the definite article plus **-(e)st** and the appropriate ending. Where the noun is clearly understood, the superlative in the predicate is also in attributive form.

c. so . . . wie; als

Mein Zimmer ist **so klein wie Ihres.**
My room is as small as yours.

Sein Zimmer ist **kleiner als ihres.**
His room is smaller than hers.

In comparisons, **so . . . wie** (*as . . . as*) expresses equality, whereas **als** (*than*) expresses inequality.

1. If the adjective or adverb ends in **d, t,** or an s-sound (**s, ß, z, tz**), add **-est-** to form the superlative: **am härtesten.**

d. immer +
Comparative

Der Verkehr wird **immer stärker.**
The traffic is getting heavier and heavier.

Es wird **immer dunkler.**
It is getting darker and darker.

Immer plus comparative is equivalent in English to the comparative expressed twice.

Note that the idiomatic phrase **immer wieder** is rendered in English by *again and again.* Example:

Es hat **immer wieder** gedonnert.
It thundered again and again.

PRACTICE

A. *Change all predicate adjectives and adverbs in the following sentences first to comparative and then to superlative:*

1. Dieses Haus ist schön. 2. Aber die Zimmer sind klein. 3. Man fährt schnell mit dem Zug. 4. Fährt man sicher mit diesem Wagen? 5. Ist diese Strecke gefährlich? 6. Die Autobahn ist nicht gefährlich. 7. Es war gemütlich bei Ihnen. 8. Diese Erdbeeren sind frisch. 9. Arbeiten Sie schwer? 10. Meine Arbeit ist leicht.

B. *Change all attributive adjectives first to comparative and then to superlative:*

1. schnelle Züge 2. sichere Autos 3. über die gefährliche Strecke 4. die schönen Frauen 5. angenehme Hotels 6. in ruhigen Zimmern 7. passende Bücher 8. trotz schwerer Arbeit 9. einsame Autostraßen 10. von interessanten Lehrern

C. *Answer the following questions negatively using a comparative:*

Example: Ist der Zug so schnell wie das Flugzeug?
Nein, das Flugzeug ist schneller als der Zug.

1. Ist die Reise so einfach mit dem Zug wie mit dem Auto? 2. Ist der Verkehr auf der Autobahn so gefährlich wie auf dieser Strecke? 3. Fährt man so sicher mit dem Auto wie mit dem Zug? 4. Sind diese Karten so teuer wie die anderen? 5. Findet man die billigen Plätze so bequem wie die teuren? 6. Ist dieser Zug so schnell wie der nächste?

D. *Say in German:*

1. I've said that again and again. 2. Marie is prettier than my sister. 3. But Lore is prettiest. 4. Kurt doesn't speak German as well as Karl. 5. Kurt understands more quickly than many American students. 6. The train is safer than the bus. 7. It

194

also goes faster and is simpler.   8. The train is much more comfortable than a car.   9. And the traffic on the autobahn keeps getting heavier and heavier.   10. On this stretch it is most dangerous.   11. We have the most accidents despite the best highways.

2. Irregular Comparison
a. Monosyllabics

Positive	Comparative	Superlative Adverbial	Superlative Attributive
alt	älter	am ältesten	der (die, das) älteste
arm	ärmer	am ärmsten	der (die, das) ärmste
dumm	dümmer	am dümmsten	der (die, das) dümmste
grob	gröber	am gröbsten	der (die, das) gröbste
klug	klüger	am klügsten	der (die, das) klügste
krank	kränker	am kränksten	der (die, das) kränkste
kurz	kürzer	am kürzesten	der (die, das) kürzeste
lang	länger	am längsten	der (die, das) längste
stark	stärker	am stärksten	der (die, das) stärkste
warm	wärmer	am wärmsten	der (die, das) wärmste

Many monosyllabic adjectives with **a**, **o**, or **u** add umlaut in the comparative and superlative.

b. Very Irregular Monosyllabics

Positive	Comparative	Superlative Adverbial	Superlative Attributive
groß	größer	am größten	der (die, das) größte
gut	besser	am besten	der (die, das) beste
hoch[1]	höher	am höchsten	der (die, das) höchste
nahe	näher	am nächsten[2]	der (die, das) nächste[2]
viel	mehr	am meisten	der (die, das) meiste

A few common adjectives have irregular comparatives and superlatives.

c. gern, lieber, am liebsten

Er **fährt gern** mit dem Auto.
He likes to travel by car.

Sie **fährt lieber** mit dem Zug.
She prefers to travel by train.

Sie **fliegen am liebsten** mit dem Flugzeug.
They like best to travel by plane.

The adverb **gern(e)** has irregular comparative and superlative forms. Note the English meanings.

1. The **c** of **hoch** is dropped in the positive when endings are added: **ein hohes Haus.**
2. Note that a **c** is added in the superlative.

PRACTICE

A. Change all adjectives and adverbs first to comparative and then to superlative:

1. Der alte Mann ist Herr Schmidt.   2. Er ist krank.   3. Er sitzt gern zu Hause.   4. Kurts Vater bleibt lange.   5. Seine Reise ist kurz.   6. Es gibt gute Autobahnen in Deutschland.   7. Amerika hat große Autostraßen.   8. Hier ist der Verkehr immer stark. 9. Wir haben viele Autos in Amerika.   10. Wohin fahren Sie gern?

B. Answer the following questions using the indicated words in accordance with the example:

Example: Trinken Sie lieber Kaffee als Tee? (*Milch*)
            Ja, aber ich trinke am liebsten Milch.

1. Lernen Sie lieber Deutsch als Französisch? (Englisch)
2. Fahren Sie lieber mit dem Zug als mit dem Auto? (Bus)
3. Singen Sie lieber auf französisch als auf englisch? (auf deutsch)
4. Fahren Sie lieber nach Bonn als nach Köln? (München)
5. Sprechen Sie lieber mit jungen als mit alten Leuten? (Kinder)

C. Say in German:

1. Do you like to eat in a restaurant?   2. I prefer to eat at home. 3. Mr. Klein is much taller than Mr. Lenz.   4. He prefers a larger car.   5. Kurt wants to see the most powerful car here. 6. The Klein family always likes to travel by car.   7. They travel more often than the Lenzes.

3. Impersonal Verbs and Expressions

a.

Es amüsiert mich.
I'm amused.

Es interessiert mich.
It interests me.

Es ärgert mich.
I'm angry.

Es ist mir nicht gut.
I'm not feeling well.

Es blitzt.
It's lightening.

Es ist mir übel.
I am (feeling) sick.

Es donnert.
It's thundering.

Es ist mir recht.
It's all right with me.

Es freut mich.
I'm pleased.

Es gefällt mir.
I like it.

Es friert.
It's freezing.

Es geht mir gut.
I'm fine.

Es friert mich.
I'm cold.

Es gelingt mir.
I succeed.

Es ist schade.
It's a pity.

Es tut mir leid.
I'm sorry.

Es regnet.
It's raining.

Es tut mir weh.
It hurts me.

Es schneit.
It's snowing.

Like English, German has a number of verbs which always or frequently take an impersonal subject.[1] Many of them deal with weather conditions.

b.

Es gibt viele Autos auf der Autobahn.
There are many cars on the highway.

Es gibt heute **Schnee.**
There's snow today.

Es ist nur **ein Student** hier.
There's only one student here.

Es sind jetzt **drei Studenten** im Zimmer.
There are now three students in the room.

Es gibt takes an accusative object and is used to make a general statement expressing existence. **Es ist, es sind** are followed by the nominative case and are used for making more specific statements.

PRACTICE

A. *Answer the following questions in accordance with the example:*

Example: Tut es Ihnen leid?
Nein, es tut mir nicht leid.

1. Amüsiert es Sie? 2. Ging es ihm gut? 3. Ist es ihr recht? 4. Friert es dich? 5. Hat es ihnen weh getan? 6. Wird es sie interessieren? 7. Ist es Ihnen gelungen, ihn zu sprechen? 8. War es ihm übel?

B. *Make each question in A above negative and then give an affirmative answer:*

Example: Tut es Ihnen nicht leid?
Doch, es tut mir leid.

1. Some verbs can take either an impersonal or a personal subject. For example: **Er** amüsiert mich. *He amuses me;* or: **Sie** interessiert ihn. *She interests him;* or **Er** tut mir leid. *I feel sorry for him.*

197

C. *Say in German:*

1. It's lightening. 2. It won't snow tomorrow. 3. Do you think it will rain? 4. I am glad. 5. Are you glad? 6. I don't feel well. 7. Don't they feel well either? 8. Were you sorry? 9. I wasn't sorry. 10. They weren't angry. 11. I wasn't angry either. 12. It doesn't interest him. 13. That's a pity. 14. She always succeeds.

D. *Complete each of the following sentences with* **ist, sind,** *or* **gibt:**

1. Heute _____ es Regen. 2. Gestern _____ es Schnee. 3. Es _____ zwei Männer im Haus. 4. _____ es solche Leute? 5. _____es so etwas? 6. Es _____ wenige gute Studenten hier. 7. Es _____ viele Probleme auf der Welt.

4. Special Constructions

a. Infinitive Phrases

Er hofft, morgen zu uns zu kommen.
He hopes to come to our house tomorrow.

Anstatt mit dem Bus zu fahren, fährt Herr Klein mit dem Zug.
Instead of going by bus, Mr. Klein travels by train.

Karl redete, **ohne vom Thema abzukommen.**
Karl talked without getting off the subject.

Herr Klein muß um 7 Uhr weg, **um gegen 9 in Bonn zu sein.**
Mr. Klein has to leave at 7:00 in order to be in Bonn around 9:00.

The infinitive stands last in an infinitive phrase. The expressions **(an)statt . . . zu** (*instead of . . .*), **ohne . . . zu** (*without . . .*), and **um . . . zu** (*in order to . . .*) are always followed by an infinitive.

b. Verbs Similar to Modals

Er **hört** sie **singen.**
He hears her singing.

Er **läßt** sie **kommen.**
He has her come. He lets her come.

Er **sieht** sie **kommen.**
He sees her coming.

Hören, lassen, and **sehen** follow the same pattern as the modal auxiliaries and take a dependent infinitive without **zu.** Note that **lassen** frequently expresses causative action.

PRACTICE

A. *Combine the following pairs of sentences by means of the indicated word:*

Example: Er fährt jetzt ab. (*um*) Er kommt gegen 9 an.
Er fährt jetzt ab, um gegen 9 anzukommen.

1. Herr Klein muß bald gehen. (um) Er ist morgen in Bonn. 2. Er will länger bleiben. (anstatt) Er fährt nach Bonn. 3. Der

Verkehr wird immer größer. (ohne) Er wird sicherer. 4. Man kommt vom Thema ab. (anstatt) Man spricht von Herrn Kleins Reise. 5. Der Vater sollte ins Hotel zurück. (um) Er steht früh auf. 6. Herr Klein sprach. (ohne) Er hört das Gewitter.

B. Say in German:

1. We have to go now in order to be there bright and early. 2. Instead of going with us, Kurt stayed home. 3. Mr. Klein had to take the train in order to get to Bonn quickly. 4. He had Kurt call the railroad station. 5. He did not leave without thanking the Lenz family. 6. He hoped to get to the station on time. 7. He saw the train arrive.

FINAL PRACTICE   *Say first, then write in German:*

1. Mr. Klein and his son Kurt visited the Lenz family one evening. 2. They had a very good time. 3. They wanted to stay longer, but they couldn't. 4. Mr. Klein had to be in Bonn bright and early the next day. 5. Mr. Lenz said: "I would prefer to go by train." 6. Traffic is heavy everywhere today. 7. On the autobahn in Germany it gets more and more dangerous. 8. The stretch between Cologne and Bonn is especially dangerous. 9. The Germans have the best roads—and also the most accidents. 10. Mr. Klein will leave at 7 o'clock in order to be in Bonn before 9:00. 11. He has to get up very early then. 12. It was 11 o'clock, and Kurt and his father had to return to the hotel. 13. Mr. Klein thanked Mr. and Mrs. Lenz for the nice evening. 14. Mr. Klein didn't know it had been thundering and lightening. 15. He had a marvelous chat with the Lenzes.

Bonn am Rhein
GERMAN INFORMATION CENTER

I. UNTERHALTUNG

VOR DEM EXAMEN

Kurt wartet auf Lore im Wohnzimmer der Familie Lenz. Herr Lenz verläßt gerade das Haus. Er erblickt Kurt und unterhält sich kurz mit ihm.

Herr Lenz: Ist Ihr Vater rechtzeitig abgereist?

Kurt: Nein, mit Verspätung. Er hat den Zug leider verpaßt.

Herr Lenz: Na, wie ist denn das passiert? Hat er sich verschlafen?

Kurt: Nein, er war schon um fünf aufgestanden, und ich habe ihn pünktlich abgeholt.

Herr Lenz: Ja, und dann?

Kurt: Es war furchtbar neblig und ich habe ganz langsam fahren müssen.

Herr Lenz: Da war eben nichts zu machen. Hat er lange auf den nächsten Zug warten müssen?

Kurt: Zum Glück nicht, nur eine halbe Stunde. Er hat natürlich sofort mit Bonn telefoniert.

Herr Lenz: Dann ist ja wohl alles in Ordnung.

Lore Lenz kommt herein. Der Vater verläßt das Haus.

BEFORE THE EXAM

Kurt is waiting for Lore in the living room of the Lenz family. Mr. Lenz is just leaving the house. He sees Kurt and chats briefly with him.

Mr. Lenz: Did your father leave on time?

Kurt: No, he was late. Unfortunately, he missed the train.

Mr. Lenz: Well, how did that happen? Did he oversleep?

Kurt: No, he'd gotten up at five, and I picked him up on time.

Mr. Lenz: Yes, and then?

Kurt: It was terribly foggy, and I had to drive very slowly.

Mr. Lenz: You couldn't help that. Did he have to wait long for the next train?

Kurt: Fortunately not, only half an hour. Of course, he immediately phoned Bonn.

Mr. Lenz: Then I suppose everything is okay.

Lore Lenz enters. Her father leaves the house.

LESSON 14

Lore: Sie kommen mir ziemlich nervös vor. Stehen Sie vor einem Examen?

Kurt: Leider ja. Ich konnte mich nicht richtig vorbereiten. Und schließlich wollte ich meinem Vater die Stadt zeigen.

Lore: Hat man die Prüfung rechtzeitig angesagt?

Kurt: Der Professor hatte schon vorige Woche davon gesprochen.

Lore: Dann ist es natürlich Ihre Schuld! Sie dürfen eigentlich nicht klagen.

Kurt: Ich will es ja nur erklären. Vaters Besuch war unerwartet.

Lore: Sie werden das Examen schon bestehen.

Kurt: Bisher habe ich mich vor Examen nie gefürchtet. Aber gestern abend habe ich nicht einschlafen können.

Lore: Vielleicht haben Sie zu viel Kaffee getrunken.

Kurt: Nein, mir sind alle Fragen durch den Kopf gegangen.

Lore: Nach dem Examen geht es Ihnen bestimmt besser.

Lore: You seem kind of nervous to me. Do you have an exam ahead of you?

Kurt: Yes, I'm sorry to say. I couldn't properly prepare for it. And after all, I wanted to show Dad the city.

Lore: Did they announce the exam early enough?

Kurt: The professor had already talked about it last week.

Lore: Then it's obviously your fault! You really shouldn't complain.

Kurt: I only want to explain it. Dad's visit was unexpected.

Lore: You'll surely pass the exam.

Kurt: Up to now I've never been scared of exams. But last night I couldn't get to sleep.

Lore: Maybe you drank too much coffee.

Kurt: No, all the questions kept passing through my mind.

Lore: After the exam you'll undoubtedly feel better.

II. KOMBINATIONEN

Sagen Sie auf deutsch:

a. 1. Kurt is waiting for Lore in the living room. 2. Lore is waiting for Mr. Lenz. 3. We are waiting for Mr. Klein in Bonn.

b. 1. Mr. Lenz is just leaving the house. 2. I'm just leaving my hotel. 3. She's just leaving town.

c. 1. Did your father leave on time? 2. Did he leave late? 3. Yes, he left late.

d. 1. Unfortunately, he missed the train. 2. Unfortunately, he overslept. 3. Unfortunately, it was raining.

e. 1. He had gotten up at five. 2. I had gotten up at four. 3. I picked him up on time.

f. 1. It simply couldn't be helped. 2. It simply can't be helped. 3. Why couldn't it be helped?

g. 1. Then I suppose everything is okay. 2. Then I suppose everything was okay. 3. Then I suppose everything will be okay.

h. 1. You seem kind of nervous to me. 2. Kurt seems kind of nervous to Lore. 3. Kurt has been very nervous all morning.

i. 1. Do you have an exam ahead of you? 2. Yes, I have an exam ahead of me. 3. I had an exam ahead of me.

j. 1. I couldn't prepare properly. 2. We couldn't prepare properly because of the weather. 3. He couldn't prepare properly; he wanted to show the city to his father.

k. 1. Then it is obviously your fault. 2. Then it was obviously his fault. 3. Then it is obviously our fault.

l. 1. You really mustn't complain. 2. I'm not complaining; I'm explaining. 3. Why mustn't I complain?

m. 1. All the questions passed through my mind. 2. I couldn't fall asleep; everything passed through my mind. 3. Why couldn't you get to sleep?

III. SAGEN UND FRAGEN

a. *Sie sind Kurt. Sie sagen zu Herrn Lenz oder Lore:*

1. Ihr Vater ist mit Verspätung abgereist. 2. Ihr Vater hat leider den Zug verpaßt. 3. Sie haben Ihren Vater pünktlich abgeholt. 4. Sie haben langsam fahren müssen. 5. Zum Glück haben Sie nicht lange warten müssen. 6. Sie haben sofort mit Bonn telefoniert. 7. Sie konnten sich nicht richtig vorbereiten. 8. Jetzt stehen Sie vor dem Examen. 9. Sie

wollten ja Ihrem Vater die Stadt zeigen.   10. Sie wollen nicht klagen; Sie wollen nur erklären.   11. Sie haben sich bisher nie vor Examen gefürchtet.   12. Gestern haben Sie nicht einschlafen können.   13. Sie haben nicht zu viel Kaffee getrunken.   14. Alle Fragen sind Ihnen durch den Kopf gegangen.

b.   *Sie sind Lore Lenz. Sie sagen zu Kurt:*

1. Er kommt Ihnen nervös vor.   2. Es ist seine Schuld. 3. Er darf eigentlich nicht klagen.   4. Er wird das Examen schon bestehen.   5. Er hat vielleicht zu viel Kaffee getrunken.   6. Es geht ihm besser nach dem Examen.

c.   *Sie sind Herr Lenz. Sie fragen Kurt:*

1. ob sein Vater rechtzeitig abgereist ist.   2. warum er mit Verspätung abgereist ist.   3. ob er den Zug verpaßt hat. 4. ob er sich verschlafen hat.   5. ob er früh genug aufgestanden ist.   6. ob er lange hat warten müssen.

d.   *Sie sind Lore Lenz und fragen Kurt:*

1. warum er so nervös ist.   2. ob er vor einem Examen steht.   3. warum er sich nicht richtig vorbereiten konnte. 4. ob man das Examen rechtzeitig angesagt hatte.   5. warum er sich vor dem Examen fürchtet.   6. ob er sich immer davor gefürchtet hat.

IV. AUFSATZ

EINE REISE NACH BONN

„Ein Ferngespräch", rief Frau Kolb am Spätnachmittag. Ihre Stimme klang etwas erregt. In ihrem ganzen Leben hatte sie nur drei Ferngespräche bekommen, und alle drei hatten mit traurigen Nachrichten zu tun.

5   Kurts Vater, Herr Klein, war am Apparat. Es war ihm gelungen, den geschäftlichen Teil seiner Reise früher als erwartet abzuschließen.[1] Könnte[2] Kurt nach Bonn kommen? Sie würden[3] zusammen eine Stadtrundfahrt machen und am Abend vielleicht nach Bad Godesberg fahren. Herr Klein war mit einem Sekretär

1. **abschließen** to conclude.   2. Could.   3. would.

10 der amerikanischen Botschaft[4] befreundet,[5] und dieser Herr mit
einem so verantwortungsvollen[6] Posten hatte sie zum Abendessen
eingeladen. Kurt war noch immer mißgestimmt[7] wegen der
Prüfung und wollte sich zerstreuen.

Also hielt er kurz nach vier vor dem Büro der amerikanischen
15 Firma.[8] Der Vater hatte längere[9] Zeit auf ihn gewartet und war
unruhig geworden, denn der Verkehr auf der Autobahn war
äußerst stark. Jetzt stellte er Kurt stolz seinen Kollegen vor. Dann
verabschiedeten sie sich, um ihre Stadtrundfahrt zu machen.

Sie fuhren zusammen durch die Hauptstadt. Sie fanden sie
20 hübsch, friedlich[10] und ruhig, aber waren doch ein bißchen enttäuscht. Sie fragten sich, ob so ein kleines, anscheinend unbedeutendes Städtchen wirklich die Hauptstadt eines großen Landes sein
könnte.[11] Herr Klein hatte Berlin früher sehr gut gekannt und
zog[12] immer wieder Vergleiche.

25 Nein, Bonn war doch so verschieden von Berlin! Hier gab es
keine historischen Denkmäler wie das Brandenburger Tor,[13] keine
herrlichen Straßen wie den Kurfürstendamm,[14] verhältnismäßig[15]
wenige Kinos, keine Untergrundbahnen[16] und auch weniger
Tageszeitungen, Konzertsäle[17] und Kaufhäuser[18] als in vielen
30 anderen deutschen Städten. Außerdem ist Berlin heute noch eine
der größten deutschen Industriestädte mit großer wirtschaftlicher
Bedeutung. Mit der Entstehung[19] des vereinigten deutschen
Reiches[20] im Jahre 1871 ist es auch weltpolitisch immer wichtiger
geworden. Zur gleichen Zeit hat sich die preußische[21] Hauptstadt
35 zu einem kulturellen Zentrum entwickeln können. Aber Berlin
ist heute von der Bundesrepublik geographisch getrennt[22] und
selbst in zwei Teile gespalten.[23] Es eignet sich also nicht mehr
zur Hauptstadt der Bundesrepublik.

„Ja, warum gerade Bonn?" fragte der Vater. „Gab es keine
40 anderen Städte? Warum hat sich Frankfurt oder Köln nicht dazu
geeignet?"

Karl hatte Kurt seine Ansichten über diese Frage dargelegt.[24]
Man hatte Bonn vornehmlich[25] aus praktischen Gründen gewählt.
Größere Städte waren zerstört. Man hatte Sorgen genug damit,
45 Wohnungen zu bauen und konnte die Städte nicht mit solchen

4. embassy.　5. **mit . . . befreundet** friends with . . . .　6. responsible.
7. out of sorts.　8. firm.　9. **länger** rather long.　10. peaceful.　11. **ob
so ein . . . Städtchen wirklich . . . sein könnte** whether such a little town
really could be . . . .　12. **zog . . . Vergleiche** made comparisons.　13. **das
Brandenburger Tor** the Brandenburg Gate.　14. **der Kurfürstendamm** *the
major business thoroughfare in Berlin.*　15. relatively.　16. subways.
17. **der Konzertsaal, die Konzertsäle** concert hall.　18. department stores.
19. *here:* creation.　20. empire.　21. Prussian.　22. separated.
23. split.　24. stated, set forth.　25. particularly.

Problemen belasten.[26] In Bonn war auch manches zerstört, aber es gab noch reichlich[27] Platz zur Errichtung[28] von neuen Regierungsgebäuden.[29] Auch hatte es den Politikern[30] und Diplomaten[31] sehr gut gefallen, daß[32] man von Bonn aus[33] herrliche Fahrten unter-
50 nehmen konnte und eine schöne Aussicht auf den Rhein und das Siebengebirge[34] hatte.

„Weißt du, Vater, vor dem Krieg wohnten hier weniger als 20 000 Leute, meistens Beamte, Universitätsprofessoren und Studenten. Jetzt ist die Einwohnerzahl auf 141 000 gestiegen."
55 Vater und Sohn hatten die Hauptstraßen besichtigt, auch das Beethovenhaus[35] und das Rathaus. Das Bundeshaus war schon geschlossen. Herr Klein telefonierte mit der amerikanischen Botschaft. Man erwartete sie gegen acht Uhr, sagte der Sekretär, und Kurt und Herr Klein machten sich sofort auf den Weg.[36]

Beantworten Sie die folgenden Fragen:

1. Wie klang Frau Kolbs Stimme? 2. Wer war am Apparat? 3. Was war Herrn Klein gelungen? 4. Was würden Vater und Sohn zusammen tun? 5. Wohin wollten sie am Abend fahren? 6. Mit wem war Herr Klein sehr befreundet? 7. Was für einen Posten hatte dieser Herr? 8. Warum wollte Kurt sich zerstreuen? 9. Warum war der Vater unruhig geworden? 10. Wie stellte er Kurt vor? 11. Wie fanden sie Bonn? 12. Was fragten sie sich? 13. Warum zog der Vater Vergleiche mit Berlin? 14. Was hatte Bonn nicht? 15. Wann ist Berlin politisch wichtig geworden? 16. Wann hat sich Berlin zu einem kulturellen Zentrum entwickelt? 17. Aus welchen Gründen wurde Bonn zur Hauptstadt gewählt? 18. Was waren diese praktischen Gründe? 19. Was hat den Diplomaten besonders gut gefallen? 20. Was berichtet Kurt über die Einwohnerzahl der Bundesstadt?

26. **belasten** to burden. 27. plenty of. 28. erection. 29. government buildings. 30. **der Politiker, -** politician. 31. **der Diplomat, -en, -en** diplomat. 32. that (*subordinating conjunction requiring verb at end of clause*). 33. **von Bonn aus** from Bonn. 34. **das Siebengebirge** the Seven Hills (*on the right bank of the Rhine near Bonn*). 35. *house in which Beethoven was born.* 36. **sich auf den Weg machen** to set out.

V. WORTSCHATZ

das **Abendessen**	dinner, evening meal	der **Apparat, -e**	apparatus, telephone
ab/holen	to fetch, pick up	**außerdem**	moreover
ab/reisen	to depart, leave	**äußerst**	extremely
an/sagen	to announce	die **Aussicht, -en**	view
die **Ansicht, -en**	view, opinion	der **Beamte, -n, -n**	official

besichtigen	to take a look at, inspect	der Nachmittag, -e	afternoon
bestehen, bestand, bestanden	to pass (an examination)	neblig	foggy
		nervös	nervous
		die Ordnung	order
das Bundeshaus	Parliament Building	passieren	to happen
		der Posten	post, position
das Denkmal, ⸚er	monument	das Rathaus	city hall
sich eignen	to be suited for	rechtzeitig	on time
ein/laden, lud ein, eingeladen, lädt ein	to invite	rufen, rief, gerufen	to call, cry out
		schließlich	after all
		die Schuld	fault, guilt
ein/schlafen, schlief ein, ist eingeschlafen, schläft ein	to fall asleep	sofort	immediately
		die Stimme, -n	voice
		stolz	proud
		die Tageszeitung, -en	daily newspaper
die Einwohnerzahl	total population	telefonieren (mit jemandem)	to telephone someone
enttäuscht	disappointed	unbedeutend	insignificant
entwickeln	to develop	unerwartet	unexpected
erblicken	to see, catch sight of	unternehmen, unternahm, unternommen, unternimmt	to undertake
erregt	excited		
das Ferngespräch, -e	long-distance call		
furchtbar	awful	sich verabschieden	to say good-by
sich fürchten vor + dative	to be afraid of	vereinigt	united
		verpassen	to miss
gelingen, gelang, ist gelungen	to succeed	sich verschlafen, verschlief, verschlafen, verschläft	to oversleep
gleich	right away		
halten, hielt, gehalten, hält	to stop	die Verspätung	delay
		sich vor/bereiten	to prepare oneself
herein/kommen, kam herein, ist hereingekommen	to come in, enter	vorig	last, previous
		wählen	to choose, elect
		der Weltkrieg, -e	world war
		wirtschaftlich	economic
klagen	to complain	das Zentrum, die Zentren	center, focal point
klingen, klang, geklungen	to sound	zerstören	to destroy
		sich zerstreuen	to amuse oneself

VI. ERKLÄRUNGEN UND ÜBUNGEN

1. Modal Constructions **a. Principal Parts**	Infinitive	Past	Participles	3rd Singular
	dürfen	durfte	**gedurft (dürfen)**	darf
	können	konnte	**gekonnt (können)**	kann
	mögen	mochte	**gemocht (mögen)**	mag

müssen	mußte	gemußt (müssen)	muß
sollen	sollte	gesollt (sollen)	soll
wollen	wollte	gewollt (wollen)	will

All modals have two past participles. The regular past participle is formed like the past participle of any weak verb, but without umlaut. The second past participle is identical with the infinitive. Each is used in specific situations.

b. Double-Infinitive Construction

Ich habe ganz langsam fahren müssen.
I had to drive very slowly.

Das habe ich gemußt.
I had to (do that).

Er hat nicht einschlafen können.
He couldn't get to sleep.

Er hat es nicht gekonnt.
He couldn't.

When a compound tense of a modal has a dependent infinitive, the second past participle of the modal is used. This construction is called a "double infinitive" and always stands last in any clause. But, like English, German also has abbreviated sentences where the modal is used without any expressed infinitive. Frequently, there is a neuter pronoun in such constructions.

c. Compound Tenses of lassen, hören, sehen

Sie hat ihn gehen lassen.
She let him go.

Sie hat ihn gehen hören.
She heard him go.

Sie hat ihn gehen sehen.
She saw him go.

Like the modals, **lassen, hören,** and **sehen** also have a second past participle identical with the infinitive and used with a dependent infinitive.

PRACTICE

A. *Supply the correct past participle of the indicated modal:*

1. Er hat um fünf Uhr aufstehen _____ (müssen).
2. Hat er es wirklich _____ (müssen)?
3. Ich habe ihn pünktlich abholen _____ (wollen).
4. Aber ich habe es nicht _____ (können).
5. Ich habe langsam fahren _____ (müssen).
6. Er hat es eigentlich nicht machen _____ (dürfen).
7. Warum hat er es nicht _____ (dürfen)?
8. Niemand hat das tun _____ (sollen).

B. *Change the following sentences to compound past:*

Example: Kurts Vater wollte rechtzeitig abreisen.
Kurts Vater hat rechtzeitig abreisen wollen.

1. Er wollte den Zug nicht verpassen. 2. Er mußte um fünf Uhr aufstehen. 3. Kurt sollte ihn abholen. 4. Man konnte nicht

208

schnell fahren. 5. Es ließ sich nichts machen. 6. Aber Herr Klein mußte nicht lange warten. 7. Kurt durfte wieder nach Hause fahren.

C. *Say in German, using double-infinitive construction where possible:*

1. Kurt couldn't prepare for the exam. 2. Why couldn't he? 3. He had to show his father the city. 4. Did he have to? 5. Didn't he have to study? 6. I had to. 7. Didn't you want to pass every exam? 8. I did.

2. Past Perfect	**ich hatte gesagt**	I had said
	du hattest gesagt	you had said
	er hatte gesagt	he had said
	wir hatten gesagt	we had said
	ihr hattet gesagt	you had said
	sie hatten gesagt	they had said
	Sie hatten gesagt	you had said

	ich war gereist	I had traveled
	du warst gereist	you had traveled
	er war gereist	he had traveled
	wir waren gereist	we had traveled
	ihr wart gereist	you had traveled
	sie waren gereist	they had traveled
	Sie waren gereist	you had traveled

The past perfect tense consists of the simple past of **haben** or **sein** and the past participle. Its use is the same as in English.

Remember that all modals are conjugated with **haben: ich hatte es gemußt.**

PRACTICE

A. *Supply the correct form of* **haben** *or* **sein** *to make each sentence past perfect:*

1. Kurt _____ auf Lore im Wohnzimmer gewartet. 2. Herr Lenz _____ das Haus verlassen müssen. 3. Aber er _____ sich kurz mit Kurt unterhalten wollen. 4. Kurts Vater _____ nicht rechtzeitig abgereist. 5. Er _____ es aber gewollt. 6. Kurt und sein Vater _____ sehr früh aufgestanden. 7. Der Zug _____ aber nicht auf sie gewartet.

B. *Change the following sentences to past perfect:*

Example: Kurt sollte seinen Vater um sechs Uhr abholen.
Kurt hatte seinen Vater um sechs Uhr abholen sollen.

1. Herr Klein wollte den Zug nicht verpassen. 2. Er konnte damit leider nicht nach Bonn fahren. 3. Er mußte den nächsten

209

Zug nehmen.   4. Er mußte nicht lange warten.   5. Kurt wollte nicht schneller fahren.   6. Er durfte es eigentlich nicht.   7. Man mußte natürlich mit Bonn telefonieren.

C. *Say in German:*

1. Kurt had seemed rather nervous to Lore.   2. He had an exam ahead of him.   3. He hadn't been able to prepare for it.   4. After all, he'd wanted to show his father the city.   5. Had Kurt's professor already talked about the exam?   6. Yes, he had announced it on time.   7. Then it was Kurt's fault.

3. Future Perfect **Er wird sich** bald für das Examen **vorbereitet haben.**
He will have soon prepared himself for the exam.

Herr Klein wird wohl rechtzeitig **abgereist sein.**
Mr. Klein probably left on time.

As in English, the future perfect is rarely used. In German, it is used chiefly to express probability in the past (second example). When signifying probability, **wohl** or **schon** is usually added for emphasis.

PRACTICE *Answer the following questions to express probability in the past:*

> *Example:*   Ist Herr Klein rechtzeitig abgereist?
> Er wird wohl rechtzeitig abgereist sein.

1. Hat er den Zug verpaßt?   2. Hat er sich verschlafen? 3. Hat Kurt vor einem Examen gestanden?   4. Hat er sich nicht vorbereitet?   5. Hat man die Prüfung rechtzeitig angesagt?

FINAL PRACTICE *Say first, then write in German:*

1. Did your father leave on time this morning?   2. He probably missed the train.   3. Why did that happen?   4. We hadn't overslept.   5. We both had gotten up very early, and I picked him up on time.   6. It was just very foggy.   7. We couldn't drive fast. 8. But you couldn't help that.   9. Luckily, Mr. Klein was able to leave on the next train.   10. He had had to wait only half an hour.   11. Naturally, he had telephoned Bonn.   12. Everything

was probably okay. 13. Kurt seemed nervous to Lore. 14. He hadn't been able to prepare for a test. 15. It was his fault all right. 16. The professor had announced the test last week. 17. Kurt really shouldn't complain. 18. He had only wanted to explain it to Lore. 19. Kurt had never been afraid of exams before, but he couldn't get to sleep last night. 20. He had not drunk too much coffee. 21. Many questions were going through his head. 22. After the exam he'll feel better for sure.

Blick auf München; im Vordergrund das Rathaus
HENLE FROM MONKMEYER

I. UNTERHALTUNG

KURT BRAUCHT EINEN ANZUG

Karl: Worüber lachst du so? Hat deine Mutter etwas Lustiges geschrieben?

Kurt: Lies diesen Brief! Mutter schreibt aus Amerika, daß ich einen neuen Anzug brauche.

Karl: Das ist wirklich komisch.

Kurt: Sie weiß, daß ich auf meine Sachen nicht achtgebe. Ich merke nie, wenn sie schlecht aussehen.

Lore: Bei Frauen kommt so was kaum vor.

Karl: Bei dir gewiß nicht, Lore. Du gibst zu viel für Kleider aus. Vater hat sich noch gestern darüber beschwert.

Lore: Hast du vergessen, wie er über dich geklagt hat? Über deine Ausgaben?

Karl: Ich kaufe etwas Neues, wenn das Alte kaputt ist. Du dagegen, wenn es nicht mehr modisch ist.

Kurt: Sobald euer Streit vorüber ist, möchte ich euch um einen Gefallen bitten.

Karl: Dann hören wir sofort auf.

KURT NEEDS A SUIT

Karl: Why are you laughing so? Did your mother write something amusing?

Kurt: Read this letter! Mother writes from America that I need a new suit.

Karl: That's really funny.

Kurt: She knows that I don't take care of my things. I never notice when they look bad.

Lore: That sort of thing hardly ever happens with women.

Karl: Certainly not in your case, Lore. You spend too much for clothes. Dad was just complaining about it yesterday.

Lore: Have you forgotten how he was complaining about you and your expenditures?

Karl: I buy new things when the old ones are no longer good. You, on the other hand, when they're no longer in style.

Kurt: As soon as your quarrel is over, I'd like to ask you a favor.

Karl: Then we'll stop right away.

213

Kurt: Ich möchte wissen, wo man hier einen Anzug preiswert kaufen kann.

Karl: Es kommt darauf an, was du preiswert nennst.

Kurt: Wenn es möglich ist, möchte ich nur 200 (zweihundert) Mark ausgeben.

Karl: Ich glaube, daß du dafür etwas finden kannst.

Kurt: Darf ich fragen, wo du deinen letzten Anzug gekauft hast?

Karl: Ich habe ihn gekauft, als wir noch in Frankfurt wohnten.

Lore: Seitdem wir hier wohnen, kauft Vater seine Sachen bei Müller am Dom.

Karl: Ich kann dieses Konfektionsgeschäft hoch empfehlen.

Kurt: Weißt du, Karl, ob es irgendwo einen Ausverkauf gibt?

Karl: Keine Ahnung. Die Eltern sind gut informiert, weil sie die Anzeigen studieren.

Lore: Bis wann wollen Sie das wissen?

Kurt: Ich gehe entweder Freitagmittag oder Sonnabendmorgen.

Karl: Dann haben wir keine Eile.

Kurt: I'd like to know where you can get a suit at a reasonable price here.

Karl: It depends on what you call a reasonable price.

Kurt: If possible, I'd like to spend only 200 marks.

Karl: I think you can find something for that.

Kurt: May I ask where you bought your last suit?

Karl: I bought it when we were still living in Frankfurt.

Lore: Since we've been living here, Dad has been buying his clothes at Müller's near the cathedral.

Karl: I can recommend this clothing store highly.

Kurt: Do you know whether there's a sale anywhere, Karl?

Karl: I have no idea. My parents are well informed because they study the ads.

Lore: By when do you want to know?

Kurt: I'll go either Friday noon or Saturday morning.

Karl: Then there's no hurry.

II. KOMBINATIONEN

Sagen Sie auf deutsch:

a. 1. Why are you laughing so? Did your father write something amusing? 2. Why are you laughing so? Did your brother say something amusing? 3. Why is he laughing so? Did I say something stupid?

b. 1. Read this letter! She writes that I need a car. 2. Read this telegram! He says I don't need money. 3. Read this letter! Mother says I need a new suit.

c. 1. She knows that I don't take care of my things. 2. Everybody knows that he doesn't take care of his clothes. 3. Everybody knows that Lore takes care of her things.

d. 1. That sort of thing hardly ever happens with women. 2. That sort of thing seldom happens with Americans. 3. That sort of thing always happens with boys.

e. 1. Certainly not in her case. Lore spends too much for clothes. 2. Certainly not in my case. I never spend too much for clothes. 3. Certainly not in our case. We never spend very much for food.

f. 1. Men buy new things when the old ones are no longer good. 2. Women buy new things when the old ones are no longer in style. 3. Kurt buys something new when he has the money.

g. 1. I'd like to know where you can get clothes at a good price. 2. I'd like to know where you can get a car at a good price. 3. He'd like to know where he can get a suit at a good price.

h. 1. It depends on what you call a good price. 2. It depends on what you call cheap. 3. It depends on what you call expensive.

i. 1. If possible, Kurt would like to spend only 200 marks. 2. If possible, we would like to spend only 3 marks. 3. I'd like to spend very little, if possible.

j. 1. I bought my last suit when we were living in Munich. 2. Did you buy your last suit when you were still living in Frankfurt? 3. We bought our last car when we were living in Cologne.

k. 1. Since they've been living in Cologne, they've been buying their clothes at Schmidt's. 2. Since I've been living here, I've been buying my suits at Müller's. 3. Where have you been buying your clothes since you've been living here?

l. 1. Do you know whether there's a sale at Müller's? 2. Does he know whether there's a sale in Munich? 3. Do you know whether there will be a sale today?

III. SAGEN UND FRAGEN

a. *Sie sind Kurt. Sie sagen zu Karl:*

1. Er soll diesen Brief lesen. (*Use imperative*) 2. Ihre Mutter schreibt, daß Sie einen neuen Anzug brauchen. 3. Sie

weiß, daß Sie auf Ihre Sachen nicht achtgeben. 4. Sie merken nie, wenn Ihre Kleider schlecht aussehen.

b. *Sie sind Karl. Sie sagen zu Lore:*

1. Sie gibt zu viel für neue Kleider aus. 2. Sie kaufen etwas Neues, wenn das Alte kaputt ist. 3. Sie kauft etwas Neues, wenn das Alte nicht mehr modisch ist.

c. *Sie sind Karl. Sie sagen zu Kurt:*

1. Sie hören sofort auf. 2. Es kommt darauf an, was er preiswert nennt. 3. Sie glauben, er kann etwas für 200 (zweihundert) Mark finden. 4. Sie haben den letzten Anzug gekauft, als Sie in Frankfurt wohnten. 5. Sie können dieses Geschäft nur empfehlen. 6. Sie haben keine Ahnung, ob es irgendwo einen Ausverkauf gibt. 7. Ihre Eltern sind gut informiert, weil sie die Anzeigen studieren. 8. Sie haben keine Eile.

d. *Sie sind Kurt. Sie fragen Karl:*

1. ob er weiß, wo man einen preiswerten Anzug kaufen kann. 2. ob es möglich ist, einen guten Anzug für 200 (zweihundert) Mark zu kaufen. 3. wo er seinen letzten Anzug gekauft hat. 4. ob es irgendwo einen Ausverkauf gibt.

IV. AUFSATZ

EINE EINLADUNG NACH BAYERN

Es war schon nach neun Uhr abends, als es bei Kolbs klingelte. Zuerst achtete Kurt nicht darauf, weil Herr Kolb oft spät Gäste zum Kartenspiel empfing. Aber dann hörte Kurt Schritte auf der Treppe, und er wußte, daß er jetzt Besuch bekommen würde.[1]
5 Ganz verlegen fuhr er sich schnell mit dem Kamm durch das Haar,[2] öffnete die Tür und war überrascht, als er die Geschwister Lenz erblickte.

„Was wollt ihr denn so spät?" fragte er, ohne zu merken, wie unhöflich das klang.

---

1. would. 2. **fuhr er . . . Haar** ran his comb quickly through his hair.

Mittenwald in den Bayrischen Alpen
GIDAL FROM MONKMEYER

10 „So heißt du uns willkommen?" Karl schien fast beleidigt zu
sein. „Nun, dann brauchen wir dir auch nichts von der Einladung
zu sagen."

„Einladung? Davon höre ich immer gern."

Albert Lorreng, ein alter Freund von Karl Lenz, hatte vor einer
15 halben Stunde angerufen und Karl und Lore eingeladen, mit ihm
zum Schilaufen in die Bayrischen Alpen[3] zu fahren. Er hatte noch
Platz in seinem großen Wagen und Kurt konnte selbstverständlich
mitkommen.

Kurt hatte immer den Wunsch gehabt, einmal Bayern zu be-
20 suchen. Eigentlich wußte er nicht warum, denn er interessierte
sich recht wenig[4] für Schilaufen. Seitdem er vor langer Zeit in
Colorado gestürzt war[5] und sich das Bein gebrochen hatte, hatte
er fast alles Interesse für diesen Sport verloren. Jetzt dachte er, daß
er vielleicht ein zu starkes Vorurteil gegen einen Sport hatte, der
25 jetzt bei der Jugend so beliebt war. Er sollte ihn doch wieder
probieren, da er ja inzwischen älter und reifer geworden war.

Nachdem die Freunde ihn wieder verlassen hatten, nahm Kurt
ein Reisebuch über Bayern von seinem Bücherregal.[6] „Obwohl es
heute Fabriken in den Städten gibt", las er leise vor sich hin,
30 „bleibt Bayern doch ein Agrarland,[7] ein Land mit Höfen[8] und
Feldern, Weiden[9] und Wäldern." Kurt blätterte[10] weiter. „Der
Bayer ist kein Träumer;[11] er ist Realist und liebt deshalb nur das
Echte." Kurt dachte: „Wie komisch, daß diese Reisebücher immer
alles verallgemeinern."

35 Dann kam er zu dem Kapitel „Wintersport". Er las weiter:
„Wenn Sie nach Garmisch-Partenkirchen kommen, dem bekanntesten Wintersportplatz Bayerns, dann bewundern Sie nicht nur
seine Lage am Fuße der Alpen. Nein, Sie werden staunen, daß
Garmisch trotz seiner Berühmtheit[12] seinen ländlichen[13] Charak-
40 ter bewahren[14] konnte. Ideal für Sportler[15] sind die Schilifte,[16]
Bergbahnen,[17] und das große Eisstadion.[18] Neben dem Schilaufen
können Sie Ausflüge machen in die vielen kleinen, idyllisch gelegenen[19] Dörfer, die Sie überall in den Bayrischen und Österreichischen Alpen finden."

45 Ein anderes Kapitel handelte von der Geschichte Bayerns und
betonte, daß Bayern immer ein Grenzland[20] war, daß seine Macht

---

3. **die Bayrischen Alpen** the Bavarian Alps.   4. **recht wenig** very little.
5. **stürzen** to fall, take a plunge.   6. bookshelf.   7. agricultural province.   8. **der Hof,** ⸚e farm.   9. meadows.   10. **blättern** to turn over
pages, leaf through.   11. dreamer.   12. fame.   13. rural, rustic.
14. **bewahren** to keep, preserve.   15. **der Sportler, -** sportsman.   16. **der
Schilift, -e** skilift.   17. **die Bergbahn, -en** alpine railway.   18. **das Eisstadion, -stadien** ice stadium.   19. situated.   20. border province.

Eiermarkt in Nürnberg
HENLE FROM MONKMEYER

durch den Dreißigjährigen Krieg²¹ größer wurde, daß seine Hauptstädte — wie München und Nürnberg — viel im Zweiten Weltkrieg
gelitten hatten, und daß es seitdem²² einen starken Zustrom²³
50 von Flüchtlingen²⁴ gab. Kurt wollte noch die Kapitel über München
und Nürnberg lesen, merkte jedoch, wie er immer müder wurde.
Endlich legte er das Buch nieder. Als er am Einschlafen war,
dachte er: „Komisch, ich habe nicht mal gefragt, wann wir abfahren. Nun, ich hoffe nur, daß wir fahren . . . ."

Beantworten Sie die folgenden Fragen:

1. Warum achtete Kurt nicht darauf, daß es klingelte?   2. Wann
wußte er, daß man ihn besuchen wollte?   3. Wen erblickte er,
als er die Tür öffnete?   4. Warum schien Karl fast beleidigt?
5. Warum konnte Albert Lorreng auch Kurt einladen?   6. Welchen Plan hatte Kurt schon lange?   7. Wann hatte er sein Interesse für Schilaufen verloren?   8. Bei wem war dieser Sport
besonders beliebt?   9. Warum sollte er Schilaufen doch wieder
probieren?   10. Wo war das Reisebuch über Bayern?   11. Was
für ein Land ist Bayern trotz seiner Fabriken?   12. Was für ein
Mensch ist der Bayer?   13. Was findet Kurt komisch an den
meisten Reisebüchern?   14. Welches Kapitel las er danach?
15. Wie heißt der bekannteste Wintersportplatz?   16. Worüber
wird der Sportler staunen?   17. Was ist ideal für ihn?   18. Wohin kann er Ausflüge machen?   19. Was hat er in dem Kapitel
über Bayerns Geschichte gelesen?   20. Woran dachte Kurt, als er
am Einschlafen war?

21. **der Dreißigjährige Krieg** the Thirty Years' War.   22. since that time,
ever since.   23. influx.   24. **der Flüchtling, -e** refugee.

V. WORTSCHATZ

abgetragen	worn-out, thread-bare	der Ausverkauf	clearance sale
achten auf + *accusative*	to pay attention to	(das) Bayern	Bavaria
		beleidigen	to insult
der Anzug, ⸚e	suit	beliebt	popular
auf/hören	to stop, cease	betonen	to stress, emphasize
der Ausflug, ⸚e	excursion		
die Ausgabe, -n	expenditure	bilden	to form
aus/geben, gab aus, ausgegeben, gibt aus	to spend	bitten um, bat, gebeten	to ask for
		brechen	to break
		sich ein Bein brechen	to break one's leg

220

dagegen	on the other hand	das	**Konfektions-geschäft, -e**	ready-to-wear store
deshalb	therefore	die	**Lage, -n**	situation, location
echt	real, genuine			
Eile haben	to be in a hurry		**leiden, litt, gelitten**	to suffer
empfangen, empfing, empfangen, empfängt	to receive		**lustig**	merry, gay, amusing
		die	**Macht, ⁻e**	power
			modisch	in style
empfehlen, empfahl, empfohlen, empfiehlt	to recommend		**österreichisch**	Austrian
			preiswert	at a reasonable price, worth the price
entweder . . . oder	either . . . or		**reif**	mature
		das	**Schilaufen**	skiing
die	**Fabrik, -en**	factory	der	**Schritt, -e**	step
das	**Feld, -er**	field	der	**Sonnabend**	Saturday
der	**Freitag**	Friday	der	**Sport**	sport
	handeln von	to deal with, treat of		**staunen**	to be surprised
			der	**Streit, -e**	quarrel
	informieren	to inform		**überrascht**	surprised
	inzwischen	meanwhile		**unhöflich**	impolite
	irgendwo	somewhere, anywhere		**verallge-meinern**	to generalize
	kaputt	broken, torn, unusable		**verlegen**	embarrassed
				vorüber	past, over
das	**Kartenspiel, -e**	card game	der	**Wald, ⁻er**	forest, woods
die	**Kleider**	clothes		**willkommen heißen**	to welcome
	klingeln	to ring			
	komisch	funny, comical	der	**Wunsch, ⁻e**	wish, desire

VI. ERKLÄRUNGEN UND ÜBUNGEN

1. Coordinating Conjunctions

Ich brauche einen Anzug, **aber ich gebe** nur 200 Mark aus.
I need a suit, but I'll spend only 200 marks.

Meine Eltern sind gut **informiert, denn sie lesen** die Anzeigen.
My parents are well informed, for they read the ads.

Coordinating conjunctions have no effect on word order. The coordinating conjunctions are:

aber	*but*	**sondern**	*but (on the contrary)*
denn	*for, because*		
oder	*or*	**und**	*and*

PRACTICE

Combine the following sentences by means of the indicated conjunctions:

1. (denn) Kurt und Karl lachen. Sie lesen etwas Lustiges.
2. (aber) Kurt braucht einen neuen Anzug. Er will keinen.

3. (denn) Karl kauft auch etwas Neues. Seine alten Kleidungs-stücke sind kaputt.   4. (oder) Man muß manchmal neue Kleider kaufen. Man sieht schlecht aus.   5. (und) Wir gehen zu Müller. Du kannst mitkommen.   6. (denn) Herr Lenz hat das Geschäft empfohlen. Ihre Konfektion ist preiswert.

2. Dependent Clauses

A clause is "dependent" because it depends on a main clause to complete its meaning. Dependent clauses are introduced by subordinators: subordinating conjunctions, interrogative pronouns and adjectives, indefinite pronouns, and relative pronouns.

a. Subordinating Conjunctions

als	*when*	ob	*whether, if*
bevor	*before*	obgleich	*although*
bis	*until*	obwohl	*although*
da	*since (reason)*	seitdem	*since (time)*
damit	*in order that, so that*	sobald	*as soon as*
daß	*that*	während	*while*
ehe	*before*	wann	*when*
falls	*in case, in the event that*	weil	*because*
nachdem	*after*	wenn	*if, when, whenever*

This list contains the important subordinating conjunctions.

b. Dependent Word Order

We have been using two of the three word-order possibilities in German:

Normal Word Order

S   V

Ich kaufe einen Anzug bei Müller.

Inverted Word Order

V   S

Bei Müller kaufe ich einen Anzug.

These two types occur in independent (main) clauses. The third type occurs in dependent (subordinate) clauses:

Dependent Word Order

S   V

Ich weiß, **daß er** einen Anzug bei Müller **kauft.**

The order of elements in all three is basically the same; only the relative position of subject and verb is altered.

c. Word Order Synopses in Dependent Clauses

Verb without Separable Prefix

Ich weiß, **daß Kurt** heute einen neuen Anzug **kauft.**
              kaufte.
              gekauft hat.
              gekauft hatte.
              kaufen wird.

Verb with Separable Prefix

Ich weiß, **daß Kurt** heute sehr früh **aufsteht.**

aufstand.
aufgestanden ist.
aufgestanden war.
aufstehen wird.

Verb with Modal Auxiliary

Ich weiß, **daß Kurt** heute einen neuen Anzug **kaufen will.**

kaufen wollte.
hat kaufen wollen.
hatte kaufen wollen.
wird kaufen wollen.

In dependent clauses, the inflected (*finite*) form of the verb always stands last, except when a double-infinitive construction is present. Separable prefixes are always attached to their verb in dependent clauses.

d. als, wann, wenn

Ich habe den Anzug gekauft, als wir noch in Frankfurt wohnten.
I bought the suit when we still lived in Frankfurt.

Wissen Sie, wann Kurt einen neuen Anzug kaufen wird?
Do you know when Kurt is going to buy a new suit?

Er merkt nie, wenn sein Anzug schlecht aussieht.
He never notices when(ever) his suit looks bad.

Als, wann, and **wenn** all mean *when*. **Als** is used to refer to a single, definite, past action; **wann** is used for indirect (*and direct*) questions; **wenn** is used in time clauses, often with the meaning of *whenever*.[1]

e. Inversion in Main Clause

Vater kauft seine Kleider bei Müller, seitdem wir hier wohnen.
Seitdem wir hier wohnen, kauft Vater seine Kleider bei Müller.
Father has been buying his clothes at Müller's since we've been living here.

Ich kaufe etwas Neues, wenn das Alte abgetragen ist.
Wenn das Alte abgetragen ist, kaufe ich etwas Neues.
I buy new things when the old ones are worn out.

If the subordinate clause precedes the main clause, the subject and finite verb of the main clause are inverted.

---

1. In conditional clauses, **wenn** always corresponds to English *if*: **Wenn der Zug heute rechtzeitig ankommt, sind wir um fünf Uhr dort.** *If the train arrives on time today, we'll be there at 5 o'clock.*

f. Omission of da\u00df   **Ich glaube, da\u00df du** etwas f\u00fcr 200 Mark **findest.**
I think that you'll find something for 200 marks.

Ich glaube, du findest etwas f\u00fcr 200 Mark.
I think you'll find something for 200 marks.

The subordinating conjunction **da\u00df** may be omitted. Normal word order is then used in the dependent clause.

g. Omission of wenn   **Wenn Sie** einen guten Anzug **kaufen wollen,** gehen Sie zu M\u00fcller.
Wollen Sie einen guten Anzug **kaufen, so** (**dann**) gehen Sie zu M\u00fcller.
If you want to buy a good suit, go to M\u00fcller's.

Wenn meaning *if* may be omitted, but the finite verb then starts the clause. The main clause is often introduced by **so** or **dann.**

PRACTICE   *A. Combine the following sentences by means of the indicated subordinating conjunctions:*

Example: Mutter schreibt. (*da\u00df*) Ich brauche einen neuen Anzug.
Mutter schreibt, da\u00df ich einen neuen Anzug brauche.

1. Meine Mutter wei\u00df. (da\u00df) Ich gebe nicht acht auf meine Sachen.   2. Ich merke nie. (wenn) Meine Kleidung sieht schlecht aus.   3. Lore versteht das nicht. (da) Sie gibt viel f\u00fcr Kleider aus.   4. Herr Lenz hat sich dar\u00fcber beschwert. (da\u00df) Lore hat viele Kleider gekauft.   5. Karl kauft etwas Neues. (nur wenn) Das Alte ist kaputt.   6. Lore kauft sich etwas Neues. (ehe) Sie braucht es.   7. Karl und Lore h\u00f6ren zu sprechen auf. (da) Kurt will um einen Gefallen bitten.

B. Combine the following sentences by means of the indicated subordinating conjunctions:

Example: (*da*) Kurt brauchte einen Anzug. Er mu\u00dfte ein Gesch\u00e4ft finden.
Da Kurt einen Anzug brauchte, mu\u00dfte er ein Gesch\u00e4ft finden.

1. (ehe) Er fuhr in die Stadt. Er sprach mit Lore.   2. (obgleich) Er hatte viel Geld. Er wollte nur 200 Mark f\u00fcr den Anzug ausgeben.   3. (seitdem) Karl und Lore wohnen hier. Ihr Vater kauft seine Kleider bei M\u00fcller.   4. (ob) Es gibt irgendwo einen Ausverkauf. Karl wei\u00df nicht.   5. (weil) Die Eltern studieren die Anzeigen. Sie sind gut informiert.   6. (da) Kurt braucht die Auskunft nicht sofort. Man hat keine Eile.

224

C. *Combine the following sentences, using subordinating question words:*

Example: Karl will wissen. Worüber lacht Kurt so?
Karl will wissen, worüber Kurt so lacht.

1. Karl will wissen. Wer hat den Brief geschrieben? 2. Kurt zeigt ihm. Was stand in dem Brief? 3. Karl kann nicht verstehen. Warum hat Frau Klein den Brief geschrieben? 4. Lore weiß. Worüber spricht Kurts Mutter? 5. Lore kauft sich immer alles. Was braucht sie? 6. Karl weiß. (wie) Hat sich sein Vater beschwert?

D. *Complete the following with* **als, wann,** *or* **wenn:**

1. _____ Kurt von seiner Mutter hörte, zeigte er seinen Freunden den Brief. 2. _____ sie schreibt, schreibt sie immer etwas Lustiges. 3. Sie scheint zu wissen, _____ Kurt etwas braucht. 4. Kurt merkt nie, _____ seine Kleider schlecht aussehen. 5. _____ er Lore und Karl über Kleider fragte, begann ein kleiner Streit. 6. Lore und Karl wollen wissen, _____ Kurt seinen neuen Anzug kaufen will. 7. Er weiß nicht, _____ er einen braucht. 8. _____ kommen Sie?

E. *Repeat the following sentences without* **daß:**

Example: Ich glaube, daß Kurt einen neuen Anzug braucht.
Ich glaube, Kurt braucht einen neuen Anzug.

1. Karl denkt, daß der Brief von Frau Klein komisch ist. 2. Frau Klein weiß, daß Kurt nicht auf seine Sachen achtgibt. 3. Lore sagt, daß so was bei Frauen kaum vorkommt. 4. Aber Karl glaubt, daß Lore zu viel für neue Kleider ausgibt. 5. Wir sind der Meinung, daß Karl auch viele Ausgaben hat.

F. *Repeat the following sentences by omitting* **wenn:**

Example: Wenn Sie einen guten Anzug wollen, gehen Sie zu Müller.
Wollen Sie einen guten Anzug, so gehen Sie zu Müller.

1. Wenn ich das Geld bekomme, kaufe ich einen neuen Anzug. 2. Wenn es nicht regnet, gehe ich zu Müller. 3. Wenn ihr mitkommt, helfe ich euch auch eines Tages. 4. Wenn Müller etwas Preiswertes hat, kaufe ich es. 5. Wenn es euch gefällt, freue ich mich.

FINAL PRACTICE   *Say first, then write in German:*

1. Karl wants to know why Kurt is laughing.   2. Kurt has received a letter from his mother.   3. Mrs. Klein writes that her son needs a new suit.   4. Karl thinks it's funny that Mrs. Klein has written such a letter.   5. Kurt should really buy a new suit, for his old one looks bad.   6. Lore always notices when her clothes look bad.   7. Her brother thinks she has always spent too much for clothes.   8. Her father was even complaining about it yesterday.   9. But Karl had forgotten how his father had complained about his expenditures.   10. Karl says he only buys something new after the old is worn out.   11. Lore, on the other hand, buys something new as soon as the old is no longer in style.   12. But Lore and Karl stop right away since Kurt wants to ask something.   13. He wants to know where you can buy a suit at a good price.   14. He wants to spend no more than 200 marks, if that is possible.   15. Karl bought a nice suit when the family used to live in Frankfurt.   16. Since they've been here, his father has bought his clothes at Müller's near the cathedral.   17. Karl recommends this shop, but doesn't know whether there's a sale there.   18. Kurt will wait until he gets more information from Karl's parents.   19. There is no particular hurry.

1. ORAL PRACTICE

A. COMPLETE THE SENTENCES:

Kurt: Was für eine nette _____ !

Vater: Hast du mein Telegramm nicht _____ ?

Kurt: Doch, aber _____ vor einer halben _____.
Ich freue mich _____ über deinen _____.

Vater: Du siehst _____ aus. Deutschland scheint dir zu _____.

Kurt: Warum konnte Mutti nicht _____ ?

Vater: Du weißt, es ist eine _____ Reise. Ich bin ja _____ hier und mußte meine Reise nicht selbst _____.

Kurt: Seit wann habt ihr denn die Bonner _____ ?

Vater: Seit Oktober. Ein junger Deutscher hat die _____ übernommen und ich soll ihm neue _____ geben.

Kurt: Vater, hier ist Lore Lenz. Darf ich _____ ?
Meine Freundin, Lore Lenz.

Vater: Bitte, nehmen Sie _____ , Fräulein Lenz.

Lore: Wie war Ihre _____ ?

Vater: Ich konnte wegen des stürmischen Wetters wenig _____. Ich bin wirklich _____.

Kurt: Ich habe dir ein Zimmer in einem sehr _____ Hotel _____. Du kannst dich da _____.

B. EXPRESS THE FOLLOWING IDEAS IN GERMAN:

Kurt: Did you sleep well?

Father: I feel refreshed. I wouldn't mind going out tonight.

Kurt: I called the opera. The performance was almost sold out.

Father: What a shame!

Kurt: Wait! They have a few expensive seats left.

Father: You know I don't mind paying for something nice like that.

Kurt: I also have a ticket for tomorrow night. Maybe you won't care for that program.

Father: Come on, let's have it!

REVIEW 3

Kurt: Have you ever heard of electronic music?

Father: Electronic music? Isn't that for young people?

Kurt: You should try it, too. By the way, what do you think of the Lenz family's invitation?

Father: I think we should accept it. But now let's go eat. I'm terribly hungry.

C. ANSWER THE FOLLOWING QUESTIONS IN GERMAN:

1. Warum muß der Vater in aller Frühe nach Bonn?
2. Wann muß er spätestens im Büro sein?
3. Warum empfiehlt Herr Lenz den Zug?
4. Wie wird der Verkehr auf der Autobahn?
5. Was haben die Deutschen außer den besten Autostraßen?
6. Wann muß der Vater wegfahren, um gegen neun Uhr in Bonn zu sein?
7. Warum haben die Herren nichts vom Gewitter gemerkt?
8. Wofür ist das ein Beweis?
9. Warum ist der Vater mit Verspätung abgereist?
10. Um wieviel Uhr ist er aufgestanden?
11. Warum hat Kurt langsam fahren müssen?
12. Wie lange hat der Vater auf den nächsten Zug warten müssen?

2. STRUCTURAL PRACTICE

A. FILL IN THE APPROPRIATE ADJECTIVE ENDINGS:

1. Vor einer halb— Stunde hatte Kurt ein länger— Telegramm von seinem Vater erhalten. 2. Am nächst— Tage sollte sein Vater in Köln ankommen. 3. Für Kurt war das ein unerwartet— Besuch. 4. Seine lieb— Mutter konnte nicht mitkommen, weil es immer noch eine teur— Reise ist. 5. Herr Klein sollte dem jung— Leiter neu— Anweisungen geben. 6. Sonst stand nichts Neu— in dem Telegramm. 7. Kurz nach des Vaters Ankunft stellte Kurt ihm seine hübsch— Freundin vor. 8. Kurt hatte Lore in allen sein— Briefen erwähnt. 9. Wegen des stürmisch—

Wetters hatte Herr Klein wenig auf der lang— Überfahrt geschlafen. 10. Kurt hatte ihm ein schön—, klein— Zimmer in einem ruhig— Hotel bestellt. 11. Nach mehrer— Stunden fühlte sich der älter— Herr erfrischt. 12. Er wollte sich noch am selb— Abend eine deutsch— Oper oder sonst etwas Interessant— ansehen. 13. Leider gab es nur noch teur— Plätze. 14. Aber für so etwas Schön— zahlte der Vater gern. 15. Morgen abend wollte er seinen Vater zu einem ander— Programm einladen. 16. Würde sich sein alt— Herr (*old man*), ein Mann aus einer ander— Generation, für elektronisch— Musik interessieren? 17. „Modern— Musik ist nur für jung— Leute", sagte der Vater. 18. Herr Klein würde lieber die nett— Einladung der deutsch— Familie annehmen. 19. Jetzt will er in ein gut—Restaurant gehen, denn er hat groß— Hunger. 20. Morgen muß er in all— Frühe aufstehen; für ihn ist das aber nichts Neu—.

B. COMBINE THE FOLLOWING SENTENCES BY MEANS OF A CONJUNCTION:

1. Der Vater hat den Zug verpaßt. (obwohl) Er war früh aufgestanden. 2. Er war um fünf aufgestanden. (und) Kurt hat ihn pünktlich abgeholt. 3. Kurt hat langsam fahren müssen. (da) Es war sehr neblig. 4. Der Vater hat mit Bonn telefoniert. (nachdem) Sie kamen am Bahnhof an. 5. Alles war in Ordnung. (weil) Er hat früh genug angerufen. 6. Sein Vater hatte den Zug verpaßt. (und) Kurt war vielleicht deshalb nervös. 7. Er war so nervös. (weil) Er stand vor einem Examen. 8. Er zeigte dem Vater die Stadt. (bevor) Er hatte sich richtig vorbereitet. 9. Kurt sollte nicht klagen. (denn) Der Professor hatte die Prüfung angesagt. 10. Kurt hatte sich nie vor Examen gefürchtet. (aber) Er hat gestern nicht einschlafen können. 11. Er konnte nicht einschlafen. (weil) Er machte sich Sorgen. 12. Kurt wird das Examen bestehen. (wenn) Er arbeitet heute nachmittag.

C. REVERSE THE CLAUSES:

1. Kurt mußte laut lachen, als er den Brief seiner Mutter las.
2. Seine Sachen sehen schlecht aus, weil er nicht auf sie achtgibt.
3. Bei Frauen kommt so etwas nicht vor, da sie sich oft neue

229

Kleider kaufen.   4. Herr Lenz beschwerte sich sehr, als Lore mit neuen Kleidern nach Hause kam.   5. Kurt will nicht viel ausgeben, wenn es möglich ist.   6. Er kann sich nicht viel leisten, während er in Deutschland wohnt.   7. Er kauft sich etwas Neues, wenn das Alte kaputt ist.   8. Er kann überhaupt nichts kaufen, bis er seinen Scheck bekommt.

D. GIVE, IN THE PERSON INDICATED, THE PRESENT, SIMPLE PAST, COMPOUND PAST, PAST PERFECT, AND FUTURE PERFECT OF THE FOLLOWING VERBS:

1. warten (ich)
2. abholen (er)
3. müssen (ich)
4. erklären (wir)
5. trinken (Sie)
6. gehen (du)

E. SUPPLY THE CORRECT PARTICIPLE OF THE INDICATED MODAL:

1. Ich hatte ihm schreiben _____. (sollen)
2. Er hat mir nicht antworten _____. (wollen)
3. Warum hat er es nicht _____? (wollen)
4. Ich habe lange auf seine Antwort warten _____. (müssen)
5. Haben Sie es _____? (müssen)

F. SAY, THEN WRITE IN GERMAN:

1. Mr. Klein's trip was more expensive than ours.   2. He looked younger than Mr. Lenz.   3. Kurt's father was as old as mine. 4. I know no prettier girl than Lore.   5. Everyone thinks that she is the prettiest girl in the class.   6. But she is not the best student.   7. Karl gets better marks than she.   8. Why couldn't Kurt find a quieter hotel?   9. Mr. Klein prefers traveling by train. 10. He has to be home tomorrow at the latest.   11. I don't understand why this stretch is the most dangerous.   12. The most accidents are here.   13. Yes, the traffic is getting heavier.

G. WRITE IN GERMAN:

1. Karl did not forget how his father had complained about him.
2. Why did he have to spend so much money?   3. He wasn't
sure that he needed so much.   4. Of course, it all depends on
what you call "much."   5. Your suit is certainly more stylish and
also less expensive than mine.   6. I don't know why you think
so.   7. It is just as expensive as yours.   8. Did you buy it before
you came to Germany?   9. I can't remember when I bought it.
10. A student's expenses are always high, but they are highest in
September.   11. Last September I bought nothing new because I
had seen nothing interesting.

Franz Kafka
DR. KLAUS WAGENBACH

I. UNTERHALTUNG

KURT UND LORE DUZEN EINANDER

Kurt: Ich weiß eigentlich nicht, wie ich dieses Thema anschneiden soll . . . Ich möchte etwas vorschlagen.

Lore: Bitte, sagen Sie offen, was Sie sagen wollen! Schließlich kennen wir uns schon eine Zeitlang.

Kurt: Das ist es eben. Junge Leute, die sich gut kennen, duzen sich. Als Ausländer bin ich aber nicht sicher, wer den Vorschlag machen soll.

Lore: Kümmern wir uns nicht darum! Duzen wir uns einfach!

Kurt: „Du" und „Sie"—das ist ein Unterschied, den es im Englischen nicht gibt.

Lore: Es gibt dafür andere Schwierigkeiten.

Kurt: Ja, das schon. Also Lore, möchtest du dir . . . Entschuldige, das „du" klingt zuerst etwas komisch.

Lore: Aber dann gewöhnt man sich daran. Was wolltest du fragen?

Kurt: Möchtest du dir morgen abend eine Operette ansehen?

Lore: Darf ich fragen, was man spielt?

Kurt: „Die lustige Witwe" von Franz Lehar. Du hast sie vielleicht schon gesehen.

KURT AND LORE SAY "DU" TO EACH OTHER

Kurt: I really don't know how to tackle this subject. . . . I'd like to make a suggestion.

Lore: Please feel free to say what's on your mind. After all, we've known each other for some time.

Kurt: That's just it. Young people who know each other well use "du." But as a foreigner I am not sure who is supposed to make the suggestion.

Lore: Let's not worry about it. We'll simply say "du" to each other.

Kurt: "Du" and "Sie"—that's a difference that doesn't exist in English.

Lore: There are other difficulties to make up for that.

Kurt: That's for sure. All right then, Lore, would you like . . . Pardon, but this "du" sounds funny at first.

Lore: But then you get used to it. What did you want to ask?

Kurt: Would you like to see an operetta tomorrow night?

Lore: May I ask what's playing?

Kurt: "The Merry Widow" by Franz Lehar. Maybe you've already seen it.

LESSON 16

Lore: Sehr oft. Ich finde die Musik altmodisch. Ein Bühnenstück wie „Die Dreigroschenoper" gefällt mir besser. Erinnerst du dich an das Lied von Mackey Messer?

Kurt: Mackey Messer? Ich habe noch nie davon gehört.

Lore: Tatsächlich? Man singt das Lied gleich am Anfang.

Kurt: Ach, du meinst „Mack the Knife".

Lore: „Mack the Knife"? Entschuldige, aber darüber muß ich lachen.

Kurt: Wieso denn?

Lore: „Mack the Knife." Das klingt nun wirklich nach einem Gangster.

Kurt: Das war er auch. Ein Verbrecher, der viel Böses getan hatte.

Lore: Das stimmt. Übrigens, was hältst du von der Musik?

Kurt: Na, man muß sich erst daran gewöhnen.

Lore: Aber man vergißt sie nie.

Kurt: Also, wenn „Die Dreigroschenoper" wieder gespielt wird, sehen wir sie uns an.

Lore: Quite often. I find the music old-fashioned. A stage production like "The Three-Penny Opera" appeals to me more. Do you remember the song about Mackey Messer?

Kurt: Mackey Messer? I've never heard of that.

Lore: Honestly? It's the song that they sing right at the beginning.

Kurt: Oh, you mean "Mack the Knife."

Lore: "Mack the Knife?" Pardon me, but I have to laugh.

Kurt: But why?

Lore: "Mack the Knife." That really sounds like a gangster.

Kurt: That's what he was. A criminal who did a lot of bad things.

Lore: That's true. By the way, what do you think of the music?

Kurt: Well, you first have to get used to it.

Lore: But you never forget it.

Kurt: All right then, when "The Three-Penny Opera" is playing again, we'll go to see it.

II. KOMBINATIONEN

Sagen Sie auf deutsch:

a. 1. I really don't know how to tackle this subject. 2. He really doesn't know how to tackle this topic. 3. We really don't know how to tackle this subject.

b. 1. Please tell us frankly what you want to say. 2. After all, we've known each other for a while.   3. After all, they've known each other for a while.

c.   1. That's just it. People who know each other well use "du."
2. That's just it. Say frankly what's on your mind.   3. That's just it. As a foreigner one isn't sure.

d.   1. Du and Sie—that's a difference that doesn't exist in English.
2. Large and small—that's a difference that exists in all languages.   3. That's just it. We'll simply say "du" to each other.

e.   1. At first it sounds funny, but then you get used to it.
2. That's just it. At first it sounds strange.   3. Does it really sound strange?

f.   1. Would you like to see an operetta tomorrow?   2. Would you like to see a movie tonight?   3. Would they like to see an opera next week?

g.   1. Do you remember the Merry Widow?   2. Do you remember the song of Mackey Messer?   3. I don't remember it; I've never heard of it.

h.   1. He was a criminal who did a lot of bad things.   2. He was a nice man who did a lot of good things.   3. He doesn't sound like a gangster.

i.   1. By the way, what do you think of the music?   2. Incidentally, what do you think of the Three-Penny Opera?   3. By the way, what does he think of this poem?

III.   SAGEN UND FRAGEN

a.   *Sie sind Kurt und sagen zu Lore:*

1. Sie wissen nicht, wie Sie dieses Thema anschneiden sollen.
2. Als Ausländer wissen Sie nicht, wann man „du" sagt. 3. Sie sind froh, daß es diesen Unterschied im Englischen nicht gibt.   4. Sie finden, daß „du" etwas komisch klingt. 5. Sie haben noch nie von Mackey Messer gehört. 6. Sie wissen, daß Mack ein Verbrecher war.   7. Sie finden, daß man sich an die Musik gewöhnen muß.   8. Sie werden die Musik nie vergessen.   9. Sie sehen sich die Dreigroschenoper an, wenn sie gespielt wird.

b.   *Sie sind Lore und sagen zu Kurt:*

1. Er soll offen sagen, was er sagen will. (*Use imperative*)
2. Sie kennen sich schließlich schon mehrere Monate. 3. Sie

wissen nicht, wer den Vorschlag machen soll. 4. Sie kümmern sich nicht darum. Sie duzen sich. 5. Sie wissen nicht,
ob Sie sich die Operette ansehen wollen. 6. Sie finden die
Musik altmodisch. 7. Sie glauben, Mackey Messer ist das
Lied gleich am Anfang. 8. Sie müssen lachen, weil das nach
einem Gangster klingt. 9. Sie haben vergessen, daß er
Gangster war.

c. *Sie sind Lore und fragen Kurt:*

1. was er wirklich sagen will. 2. wie lange Sie sich schon
kennen. 3. ob es nicht andere Schwierigkeiten im Englischen
gibt. 4. was er fragen wollte. 5. ob er tatsächlich nicht
von Mackey Messer gehört hat. 6. was er von der Musik
hält.

IV. AUFSATZ

FRANZ KAFKA

Kurt war die Brechtarbeit satt, an der er schon so lange arbeitete. Er mußte eine Zeitlang damit aussetzen,[1] um mehr Abstand[2] von der Sache zu gewinnen. In der Zwischenzeit wollte er
aber nicht faulenzen.[3] Hier war die Gelegenheit, nach der er sich
5 so lange gesehnt hatte, nämlich einige Werke von Franz Kafka zu
lesen. Dieser Schriftsteller, der ihm bisher nur durch ein paar
kurze Erzählungen bekannt war, hatte schnell sein Interesse geweckt. Vor allen Dingen[4] hatte „Die Verwandlung"[5] einen sehr
großen Eindruck auf ihn gemacht. Eine unglaubliche Geschichte:
10 Ein Geschäftsreisender, der immer seine Pflicht getan hatte, findet
sich eines Morgens in ein Insekt verwandelt![6] Kurt hatte keinerlei
Probleme gehabt, diese Erzählung zu interpretieren.

Als er nun zweihundert Seiten von Kafkas „Der Prozeß"[7] gelesen hatte, sah er plötzlich ein, daß er daraus nicht klug werden
15 konnte.[8] Dieser Roman, dessen Stil[9] er bewunderte, dessen Handlung[10] er jedoch nicht zu deuten[11] wußte, schien ihm ein Rätsel
zu sein.

---

1. **aussetzen** to pause, to take a break. 2. **der Abstand** distance, perspective. 3. **faulenzen** to be idle. 4. **vor allen Dingen** above all. 5. **Die
Verwandlung** (*title of a short story*) The Metamorphosis. 6. trans-
formed, changed. 7. **Der Prozeß** (*title of a novel*) The Trial. 8. **aus
etwas klug werden** to understand, make head or tail of something.
9. style. 10. *here:* plot. 11. **deuten** to interpret.

Bei anderen Schriftstellern hatte ihm der Lebenslauf manchmal einige Anhaltspunkte[12] gegeben. Jetzt las er: „Kafka, Franz. In
20 Prag geboren,[13] studierte Jura[14] in Prag und München. Begann früh mit schriftstellerischen[15] Arbeiten. Danach Angestellter an einer Versicherungsanstalt[16] in Prag. Unternahm verschiedene Auslandsreisen. Zog 1923 nach Berlin; im folgenden Jahr in Wien im Alter von 41 Jahren gestorben."
25 „Das hilft nicht viel", dachte Kurt. „Ich muß wohl eine ganze Biographie lesen." Und dann stellten sich mehrere interessante Tatsachen heraus.[17]

Denn hier fand er endlich Kafkas großes Problem: sein Verhältnis zu seinem Vater. Der junge Schriftsteller sah in seinem
30 Vater all das verkörpert[18], was er selbst werden wollte, aber was er nie sein konnte. Er fühlte sich von ihm unterdrückt[19] und mißverstanden.[20] Kafka, der an einem furchtbaren Minderwertigkeitsgefühl[21] litt, fand es unmöglich, mit seinem Vater zu brechen. So unsicher fühlte er sich, daß er sich zweimal verlobte, aber es nie
35 wagte, zu heiraten. Dieser schöpferische[22] Schriftsteller, dessen Werk in alle Kultursprachen[23] übersetzt ist und Gegenstand akademischer Studien bleibt, hatte in seinem Nachlaß[24] verfügt,[25] daß man nach seinem Tode alle Manuskripte verbrennen sollte. Kafkas Freund, der Schriftsteller Max Brod, weigerte sich, im
40 Sinne Kafkas zu handeln,[26] und ließ seine Manuskripte veröffentlichen.

Angst vor aller Autorität — Vater, Polizei, Gericht, Staat; Selbstbefreiung[27] von Schuldgefühl;[28] der modellhafte[29] Mensch, der sich nicht behaupten[30] kann — hier waren Themen in Kafkas
45 Leben, die auch im Roman vorhanden waren. Jetzt konnte Kurt zu seiner Lektüre zurückkehren. Diesmal las er den Roman fertig[31] und hatte das Gefühl, ihn viel besser zu verstehen.

Beantworten Sie die folgenden Fragen:

1. Woran arbeitete Kurt schon so lange? 2. Warum mußte er eine Zeitlang damit aussetzen? 3. Nach welcher Gelegenheit hatte er sich lange gesehnt? 4. Wodurch war Kafka Kurt bekannt? 5. Welche Erzählung von Kafka hat einen großen Ein-

---

12. **der Anhaltspunkt, -e** foothold. 13. born. 14. the law. 15. literary. 16. insurance concern. 17. **sich heraus/stellen** to come out, be revealed. 18. embodied. 19. suppressed. 20. misunderstood. 21. inferiority complex. 22. creative, original. 23. civilized languages. 24. legacy, literary remains. 25. **verfügen** to order, decree. 26. **im Sinne . . . zu handeln** to carry out Kafka's intentions. 27. self-liberation. 28. guilt feelings. 29. model (*adjective*). 30. to assert. 31. **fertig/lesen** to read (something) through, to completion.

druck auf ihn gemacht? 6. Wovon handelt diese Erzählung?
7. Was sah Kurt plötzlich ein, nachdem er viele Seiten von Kafkas
,,Der Prozeß" gelesen hatte? 8. Wo studierte Kafka? 9. Wo
arbeitete er? 10. Wie alt war er, als er starb? 11. Was war
Kafkas großes Problem? 12. Was sah der junge Schriftsteller in
seinem Vater? 13. Woran litt Franz Kafka? 14. Warum hat er
nie geheiratet? 15. Was verfügte Kafka in seinem Nachlaß?
16. Hat man das getan? Erklären Sie! 17. Nennen Sie einige
Themen in Kafkas Werken!

V. WORTSCHATZ

altmodisch	old-fashioned	der Lebenslauf	career, life
der Angestellte, -n, -n	employee	die Lektüre, -n	reading
		das Lied, -er	song
an/schneiden, schnitt an, angeschnitten	to tackle, broach (*a subject*)	nämlich	namely
		nun	now, well (*interjection*)
böse	angry, bad, mean	die Operette, -n	operetta
das Bühnenstück, -e	stage performance, stage play	die Pflicht, -en	duty
		die Polizei	police
		(das) Prag	Prague
duzen	to say "du"	das Rätsel, -	riddle
der Eindruck, ⁓e	impression	der Reisende, -n, -n	traveler, traveling salesman
ein/sehen, sah ein, eingesehen, sieht ein	to perceive, comprehend, realize	der Geschäftsreisende	traveling salesman
		der Roman, -e	novel
		satt	satisfied, satiated
sich erinnern an + accusative	to remember (*something*)	etwas satt haben *or* sein	to have had enough of something
die Erzählung, -en	tale, story	der Schriftsteller, -	writer
das Gefühl, -e	feeling	die Schwierigkeit, -en	difficulty
der Gegenstand, ⁓e	object	sich sehnen nach	to long for
die Gelegenheit, -en	opportunity	die Seite, -n	side, page
		spielen	to play
das Gericht, -e	court	sterben, starb, ist gestorben, stirbt	to die
gewinnen, gewann, gewonnen	to win, gain		
		die Tatsache, -n	fact
sich gewöhnen an + accusative	to get accustomed to	tatsächlich	actually
		der Tod	death
		unglaublich	unbelievable
handeln	to act	übersetzen	to translate
heiraten	to marry	der Verbrecher, -	criminal
keinerlei	of no sort, not any	verbrennen, verbrannte, verbrannt	to burn (up)

238

sich verloben	to become en- gaged	**sich weigern**	to refuse
veröffent- lichen	to publish	**(das) Wien**	Vienna
		die Zeitlang	while
vorhanden	present, on hand	**ziehen, zog, ist gezo- gen**	to move
der **Vorschlag, ∸e**	suggestion		
wagen	to dare	**die Zwischenzeit**	intervening time, meantime
wecken	to wake		

VI. ERKLÄRUNGEN UND ÜBUNGEN

1. Relative Pronouns

a. Forms

	Masculine	Feminine	Neuter	Plural	
Nom.	**der**	**die**	**das**	**die**	*who, which, that*
Gen.	**dessen**	**deren**	**dessen**	**deren**	*whose, of which*
Dat.	**dem**	**der**	**dem**	**denen**	*(to) whom, which, that*
Acc.	**den**	**die**	**das**	**die**	*whom, which, that*

While there are three relative pronouns in English, German has only one to refer to both people and things.[1] This pronoun is identical with the definite article except for all genitive forms and the dative plural.

b. Agreement

Ein Verbrecher, der viel Böses getan hatte, ...
A criminal who had done much evil ...

Kurt, dessen Eltern in Amerika sind, ...
Kurt, whose parents are in America, ...

Die Dame, der er die Karte gibt, ...
The lady to whom he gives the ticket ...

Lore, die Sie gut kennen, ...
Lore, whom you know well, ...

Junge Leute, die sich gut kennen, ...
Young people who know each other well ...

Die Touristen, denen wir helfen, ...
The tourists (whom) we help ...

A relative pronoun agrees in gender and number with its ante-

1. Forms of **welcher, welche, welches** are also used as relatives in all cases but the genitive. These forms are far less common:

	Masculine	Feminine	Neuter	Plural
Nom.	**welcher**	**welche**	**welches**	**welche**
Gen.	—	—	—	—
Dat.	**welchem**	**welcher**	**welchem**	**welchen**
Acc.	**welchen**	**welche**	**welches**	**welche**

cedent (a noun in the main clause to which it relates), but its case is determined by its function in the subordinate clause. Contrary to English, the relative pronoun may never be omitted in German.

The finite form of the verb stands last in a relative clause. Relative clauses are always set off by commas.

PRACTICE

A. *Form relative clauses:*

> *Example:* Kurt,
> Er fährt in die Stadt.
> Kurt, der in die Stadt fährt,

1. Kurt,
a. Er geht ins Theater.
b. Er geht mit Lore.
c. Er kennt die Sitten nicht.
d. Er will sie lernen.

2. Lore,
a. Sie begleitet Kurt.
b. Sie bewundert Brecht.
c. Sie hat die Stücke von Brecht gelesen.
d. Sie kennt die Literatur.

3. Das Opernhaus,
a. Es ist groß.
b. Es ist alt.
c. Es ist in der Stadt.
d. Es ist teuer.

4. Die Deutschen,
a. Sie reisen viel.
b. Sie mögen Operetten nicht.
c. Sie siezen (*say* **Sie** *to*) einander.
d. Sie haben schon die Vereinigten Staaten besucht.

5. Kurt,
a. Sein Vater war in Deutschland.
b. Seine Mutter ist zu Hause.
c. Sein Vater ist Geschäftsmann.
d. Die Schwester seines Freundes heißt Lore.

6. Lore,
a. Ihr Auto ist ein Volkswagen.
b. Ihre Mutter kann gut kochen.
c. Ihr Bruder ist Student auf der Universität.
d. Ihr Vater arbeitet fleißig.

240

7. Die Deutschen,
a. Wir studieren ihre Literatur.
b. Wir lesen ihre Geschichte.
c. Ihr Land ist in Europa.
d. Ihre Probleme sind kompliziert.

B. *Combine the following sentences:*

Example: Das ist ein Theaterstück. Es ist sehr berühmt.
Das ist ein Theaterstück, das sehr berühmt ist.

1. „Die lustige Witwe" ist eine Operette. Sie ist altmodisch.
2. Mackey Messer ist ein nettes Lied. Es gefällt mir sehr. 3. Kurt zeigt Lore die Eintrittskarten. Er hat sie schon gestern gekauft. 4. Kurt beobachtet viele fremde Sitten. Er kann sie nicht verstehen. 5. Dort ist ein Amerikaner. Ein Deutscher erklärt ihm die Sitten. 6. Kurt duzt Lore. Er kennt sie gut. 7. Das ist ein Unterschied. Es gibt ihn nicht im Englischen.

2. Relative Pronouns as Objects of Prepositions

Das ist **Musik, für die** Lore sich interessiert.
That's music in which Lore is interested.

Mackey Messer ist ein **Lied, von dem** Kurt noch nie gehört hat.
Mack the Knife is a song Kurt has never heard of.

Das sind die **Leute, bei denen** sie wohnt.
Those are the people at whose house she lives.

Relative pronouns that are objects of a preposition must have the proper case form required by the preposition.[1]

PRACTICE

A. *Supply the appropriate relative pronoun in each sentence:*

1. Das Hoftheater ist das Theater, in _____ wir gehen wollen.
2. Kurt gibt Lore das Programm, für _____ er ziemlich viel bezahlt hat. 3. Das Stück, über _____ sie oft gesprochen haben, war wirklich spannend. 4. Kennst du die Studentin, mit _____ Kurt ins Theater ging? 5. Die deutsche Bühne, an _____ man früher Interessantes gespielt hat, hat heute wenig Gutes. 6. Diese Musik, über _____ wir uns öfter unterhalten haben, klingt komisch. 7. Das sind Sitten, an _____ Kurt sich nicht gewöhnen kann. 8. Ja, das sind auch Sachen, mit _____ ich nicht bekannt bin. 9. Das ist das Brechtstück, von _____ wir nie gesprochen haben. 10. Er ist ein Dramatiker, für _____ wir uns interessiert haben.

---

1. Prepositions plus relative pronoun referring to things are occasionally replaced by **wo**-compounds (**wo**- *or* **wor**- + *preposition*): Das ist **Musik, wofür** Lore sich interessiert. Mackey Messer ist ein **Lied, wovon** Kurt noch nie gehört hat.

B. Say in German:

1. This is a question which I can't answer.   2. This is a custom to which I can't get accustomed.   3. One says "du" to a person whom one knows well.   4. Kurt now says "du" to Lore, whom he has invited to the opera house.   5. The operetta they want to see is by Kurt Weill.   6. The song they sing at the beginning is called "Mack the Knife."

3. Wer and Was
   as Relative
   Pronouns

a.

Es kommt darauf an, wer der Maler ist.
It depends on who the painter is.

Wer nicht lachen kann, ist nicht glücklich.
He who can't laugh isn't happy.

Das ist **etwas, was** ihm gefallen wird.
This is something that he will like.

Er sagte **nichts, was** mich interessiert hat.
He said nothing that interested me.

Wer and **was** are sometimes used as indefinite relative pronouns referring to general or unspecified antecedents. **Wer** as a relative pronoun means *whoever* or *he who*. **Was** as a relative pronoun means *what, that, that which*. **Was** is used when no definite antecedent exists or where the antecedent is an indefinite neuter like **alles** (*all, everything*), **etwas** (*something*), **nichts** (*nothing*), **vieles** (*much, a great deal*).

b.

Das ist **das Schönste, was** ich gesehen habe.
This is the nicest thing (that) I have seen.

Sie sagt, ihr gefällt diese Musik, was ich aber nicht glaube.
She says she likes this music, something that I don't believe.

Was is also used when the antecedent is a neuter superlative adjective-noun and when the antecedent is a whole clause, with **was** meaning *a fact that, something that*.

PRACTICE

Say in German:

1. He who goes to Europe must have money.   2. Whoever goes first will arrive first.   3. He who doesn't work will fail.   4. Whoever bought this car will sell it soon.   5. Whoever has read this book will understand the problem.   6. I know what he said.   7. I know what he means.   8. Do you understand what he heard? 9. This is something he bought.   10. This is something he wrote.

11. This is something he has read.   12. This is nothing that will please him.   13. He said everything that we wanted to hear. 14. He wrote everything that was important.   15. This is the most interesting thing I have learned.   16. He says this is true, something that I can't believe.   17. They say he wrote the play, which is not true.

4. Derjenige; derselbe

Er ist **derjenige, der** die Oper **geschrieben hat.**
He is the one who wrote the opera.

Ich schreibe **demjenigen, der** mich am besten **versteht.**
I'll write to the one who understands me best.

Es ist **dasselbe Stück, das er** schon **gesehen hat.**
It's the same play he has already seen.

Derjenige (*the one*) and **derselbe** (*the same*) are common antecedents of relative pronouns. They consist of the definite article plus **-jenig-** or **-selb-,** with appropriate adjective endings.

PRACTICE

Supply the appropriate form of **derjenige** *or* **derselbe:**

1. Ist er _____, dessen Stück man heute im Theater spielt?   2. Ist das _____ Operette, die du in Köln gesehen hast?   3. Ja, sie ist _____, die dir nicht gefallen hat.   4. Sprechen Sie mit _____, der Ihnen am meisten helfen kann!   5. Sie sprechen immer mit _____ Leuten.

FINAL PRACTICE

Say first, then write in German:

1. Kurt wants to say "du" to Lore.   2. However, as a foreigner he doesn't know who is supposed to make the suggestion.   3. Lore says: "Let's not worry about that."   4. Young people who have known each other for months say "du" to each other.   5. Kurt wants to learn those customs that he doesn't know.   6. He wants to see everything he can.   7. There is nothing he doesn't want to see.   8. Tonight he and Lore will see a play which they have not yet seen.   9. Brecht, whose plays Kurt admires, spent several years in America.   10. The only play by Brecht which Lore has seen is the Three-Penny Opera.   11. It is the same play which she has also read.   12. It is in this same play that they sing *Mack the Knife.*   13. This is a song which was also very popular in America.   14. It is the same song which sounds funny as Mackey Messer.   15. It is a song Kurt and Lore are laughing about. 16. Whoever hears Weill's music has to get used to it slowly. 17. But you never forget his music.

Johann Wolfgang von Goethe
GERMAN INFORMATION CENTER

I. UNTERHALTUNG

VATERS EUROPAREISEN

Herr Lenz: Ich habe mich sehr über den Brief von Ihrem Vater gefreut.

Kurt: Mir hat er noch nicht geschrieben. Wann hat er denn den Brief abgeschickt?

Herr Lenz: Lassen Sie mich mal nachsehen! Am 7. März.

Kurt: Er ist am 5. abgereist. Er hat keine Zeit versäumt.

Herr Lenz: Ihr Vater hat anscheinend schon viele Europareisen gemacht.

Kurt: Ja, das Reisen ist ihm nichts Neues. Er findet es anstrengend, aber sehr interessant.

Herr Lenz: Das war schon seine dritte oder vierte Reise, nicht wahr?

Kurt: Seine fünfte. Die erste war im Jahre 1939, kurz vor dem Kriege; die zweite 1944 als Soldat.

Herr Lenz: Wie lange war er hier als Soldat?

Kurt: Anderthalb Jahre. Sie sollten Photographien aus seiner Militärzeit sehen. Er war damals sehr dünn.

Herr Lenz: Er ist heute noch nicht dick.

FATHER'S TRIPS TO EUROPE

Mr. Lenz: I was very happy to get the letter from your father.

Kurt: He hasn't written to me yet. When did he mail the letter?

Mr. Lenz: Let me check. On March 7th.

Kurt: He left on the 5th. He lost no time.

Mr. Lenz: Your father has apparently made many trips to Europe.

Kurt: Yes, traveling is nothing new for him. He finds it strenuous, but very interesting.

Mr. Lenz: This was his third or fourth trip, wasn't it?

Kurt: His fifth. The first was 1939, shortly before the war, the second in 1944 as a soldier.

Mr. Lenz: How long was he here as a soldier?

Kurt: A year and a half. You should see pictures of him while in the service. He was very thin in those days.

Mr. Lenz: He isn't very heavy even today.

LESSON 17

Kurt:	Heute wiegt er 190 Pfund, damals wog er nur 145.
Herr Lenz:	Das ist ein gewaltiger Unterschied.
Kurt:	Dann kam er geschäftlich 1949, 1955 und natürlich jetzt herüber.
Herr Lenz:	Ihr Vater spricht perfekt Deutsch, fließend und fehlerfrei.
Kurt:	Er hat es im Elternhaus gehört und auch acht Jahre in der Schule gelernt. Und dann hat er Deutsch in der Besatzungsarmee gesprochen.
Herr Lenz:	Ihr Vater hat auch Geschichte studiert, nicht wahr?
Kurt:	Wie haben Sie das erraten?
Herr Lenz:	Er hat so viele wichtige Jahreszahlen auswendig gewußt, wie z.B. die Daten im Leben der Könige, ihre Schlachten usw.
Kurt:	Mutter ärgert sich darüber, daß er oft ihren Geburtstag vergißt.
Herr Lenz:	Wie lange sind Ihre Eltern schon verheiratet?
Kurt:	Annähernd 25 Jahre. Sie feiern im Juni ihre silberne Hochzeit. Das heißt, ich muß sparen, damit ich ihnen etwas Anständiges kaufen kann.

Kurt:	Today he weighs 190 pounds; at that time he weighed only 145.
Mr. Lenz:	That's a considerable difference.
Kurt:	Then he came over on business in 1949, in 1955 and, of course, this time.
Mr. Lenz:	Your father speaks German perfectly, fluently, and without mistakes.
Kurt:	He heard it spoken in his parents' house and also studied it for eight years in school. And then he spoke German in the Army of Occupation.
Mr. Lenz:	Your father studied history, too, didn't he?
Kurt:	How did you guess?
Mr. Lenz:	He knew so many important dates by heart such as, for example, the dates in the lives of the kings, their battles, etc.
Kurt:	Mother gets angry over the fact that he often forgets her birthday.
Mr. Lenz:	How long have your parents been married?
Kurt:	Nearly 25 years. They celebrate their silver anniversary in June. That means I have to save up so that I can buy them something nice.

II. KOMBINATIONEN

Sagen Sie auf deutsch:

a. 1. I was very happy to get the letter from your father. 2. He was not very happy to get the letter from his father. 3. We were all very happy to get his letter.

b. 1. Let me check. —When did he mail the letter? 2. Let me check.—On the 7th of March. 3. Let me check. —He left on the 5th.

c. 1. He lost no time. 2. He doesn't like to lose time. 3. Why did he lose so much time?

d. 1. Your father has apparently made many trips. 2. His father has apparently traveled a lot. 3. Traveling is nothing new for him.

e. 1. He finds traveling strenuous, but interesting. 2. Do you find traveling strenuous and interesting? 3. For me traveling has always been difficult.

f. 1. You should see pictures from his service years. 2. He was very thin during his service years. 3. Is he still very thin today?

g. 1. He's come over on business three times. 2. He came over on business in 1949. 3. He came over as a soldier in 1944.

h. 1. Your father speaks German perfectly. 2. His brother also speaks it fluently. 3. Our whole family speaks without mistakes.

i. 1. He heard German spoken at home. 2. He studied German in school. 3. He spoke German in the Army of Occupation.

j. 1. Your father studied German, didn't he? 2. He studied history, too, didn't he? 3. You studied English, didn't you?

k. 1. He knew all dates by heart. 2. He knew the dates of the kings and presidents. 3. Did he also know the dates of their battles?

l. 1. Mother often gets angry that he forgets her birthday. 2. A good husband doesn't forget his wife's birthday. 3. Have you ever forgotten your mother's birthday?

m. 1. How long have your parents been married? —Some 25 years. 2. How long have you been married? —I'm not married. 3. How long has your older sister been married? —About a year.

n. 1. I have to save up so that I can buy them something nice.
2. We want to save so that we can buy her a nice watch.
3. Have you saved enough to buy your parents something expensive?

III. SAGEN UND FRAGEN

a. *Sie sind Herr Lenz. Sie sagen zu Kurt:*

1. Sie freuen sich über den Brief von seinem Vater. 2. Sie möchten mal nachsehen, wann er den Brief abgeschickt hat. 3. Sein Vater hat anscheinend viele Europareisen gemacht. 4. Sein Vater ist heute noch nicht dick. 5. Sie finden, daß zwischen 145 und 190 ein gewaltiger Unterschied besteht. 6. Sein Vater spricht perfekt Deutsch. 7. Sein Vater hat auch Geschichte studiert. 8. Sie haben gemerkt, daß er viele wichtige Jahreszahlen wußte.

b. *Sie sind Kurt und sagen zu Herrn Lenz:*

1. Ihr Vater hat Ihnen noch nicht geschrieben. 2. Das Reisen ist Ihrem Vater nichts Neues. 3. Für Ihren Vater ist das Reisen nicht anstrengend. 4. Ihr Vater war anderthalb Jahre Soldat. 5. Er (Herr Lenz) sollte Fotografien aus des Vaters Militärzeit sehen. 6. Ihr Vater hat lange Deutsch studiert und gesprochen. 7. Ihre Mutter ärgert sich darüber, daß er ihren Geburtstag vergißt. 8. Ihre Eltern feiern im Juni ihre silberne Hochzeit.

c. *Sie sind Herr Lenz und fragen Kurt:*

1. wie lange sein Vater Soldat war. 2. wo sein Vater so fließend Deutsch gelernt hat. 3. wie lange seine Eltern schon verheiratet sind. 4. wann sie ihre silberne Hochzeit feiern.

IV. AUFSATZ

WICHTIGE EREIGNISSE IN GOETHES LEBEN

In den zwanzig Jahren seines Lebens ist Kurt erst einmal in einem Fach[1] durchgefallen. Dies geschah in seinem 17. Lebensjahr. Er war damals[2] im 3. Jahr in der „High School". Das Fach

1. **das Fach,** ⸚er subject. 2. at that time.

war Geschichte. Kurt konnte einfach die Daten nicht behalten; 16.
5 oder 17. Jahrhundert war ihm gleich—sie gehörten beide derselben toten Vergangenheit an. Leider hatte sein Geschichtslehrer
ganz andere Gedanken darüber und erwies[3] dem armen Kurt recht
wenig Verständnis und Mitleid.[4]

Kurt hat wiederum ein Problem mit der Vergangenheit. Er soll
10 die folgenden wichtigen Daten im Leben Goethes auswendig
lernen. Immer wieder liest er:

28. August 1749
Goethe in Frankfurt am Main geboren.
1765–1768
15 Studium der Rechte[5] in Leipzig.
1770–1771
Abschluß[6] des Studiums in Straßburg. Entwickelt Pläne zu
„Götz" und „Faust".[7]
1775
20 Verlobung und Lösung[8] der Verlobung mit Lili Schönemann.
Einladung des Herzogs[9] Karl-August nach Weimar. Am 7.
November Ankunft in Weimar.
1776–1788
Freundschaft mit Charlotte von Stein. Viele Briefe und Ge-
25 dichte an sie.
1780
Ernennung[10] zum Minister, zwei Jahre später zum Finanzminister und Verleihung[11] des Adelstitels.[12]
1786–1788
30 Erste italienische Reise; Aufenthalt in Rom, intensive Beschäftigung mit antiker Kunst.
1790
Zweite italienische Reise.
1792–1793
35 Teilnahme[13] am Feldzug[14] in Frankreich.
1794
Beginn der Freundschaft mit Schiller.
1805–1806
Schillers Tod. „Faust, Erster Teil" beendet.

---

3. showed. 4. **das Mitleid** sympathy, pity. 5. **die Rechte** (*pl.*) law (*as a field of study*). 6. **der Abschluß** conclusion. 7. Götz von Berlichingen, **Faust** *plays by Goethe*. 8. dissolution, breakup. 9. **der Herzog** duke. 10. appointment. 11. conferment. 12. **der Adelstitel** title of nobility. 13. **die Teilnahme** participation. 14. **der Feldzug,** ⸚e campaign.

40 1808

Zusammentreffen[15] mit Napoleon.

22. März 1832

Goethes Tod.

Kurt hat nur noch eine halbe Stunde zum Lernen. Er ist ärger-
45 lich über diese Aufgabe. Wie kann ich diese Zahlen behalten,
fragt er sich, wenn ich viel Wichtigeres vergesse? Zum Beispiel
habe ich Frau Kolb die Miete von DM 9,50 noch nicht bezahlt.
Und ich schulde Karl DM 20,30. Hoffentlich schickt Vater mir
bald die erwünschte Summe von DM 200. Dann komme ich viel-
50 leicht mit meinem Geld aus. Aber jetzt zurück zur Chronologie!

Beantworten Sie die folgenden Fragen:

1. Wie oft ist Kurt schon durchgefallen? 2. Wann geschah das?
3. Im wievielten Jahr war er? 4. Wie alt war Kurt damals?
5. Was konnte Kurt einfach nicht behalten? 6. Was war ihm ganz
gleich? 7. Was bedeuteten das 16. und 17. Jahrhundert für
Kurt? 8. Was hat der Lehrer Kurt gar nicht erwiesen?
9. Welche Daten soll er heute auswendig lernen? 10. Wann ist
Goethe geboren? 11. In welchem Jahre hat er die Rechte studiert? 12. Wo hat er sein Studium beendet und wann?
13. Wann ist Goethe in Weimar angekommen? 14. Wer hat ihn
eingeladen? 15. Mit wem war er 1776–1788 eng befreundet?
16. In welchem Jahr hat man ihm den Adelstitel verliehen?
17. Wann hat er seine erste Reise gemacht? Und seine zweite?
18. Wann hat Goethe Napoleon getroffen? 19. An welchem Tag
ist Goethe gestorben? 20. Worüber ist Kurt ärgerlich? 21. Was
hat er noch nicht bezahlt? 22. Wieviel Mark soll der Vater ihm
schicken?

15. das Zusammentreffen meeting.

V. WORTSCHATZ

ab/schicken	to send off, dispatch, mail	**beenden**	to end
anderthalb	one and a half	der **Beginn**	beginning
an/gehören + *dative*	to belong to	**behalten, behielt, behalten, behält**	to retain, hold, keep
annähernd	nearly, approaching	die **Besatzungsarmee, -n**	army of occupation
anständig	proper, suitable, nice	die **Beschäftigung**	occupation
anstrengend	strenuous	die **Chronologie**	chronology

	damals	at that time, then		italienisch	Italian
das	Datum, die Daten	date	die	Jahreszahl, -en	date (*in history*)
das	Lebensdatum	date (*in a person's life*)		kompliziert	complicated
				lernen	to study, learn
	dick	fat	der	König, -e	king
	durch/fallen, fiel durch, ist durchgefallen, fällt durch	to fail (*a test*)	die	Kunst, ⁼e	art
			die	Miete, -n	rent
			die	Militärzeit	military service (*years*)
	erraten, erriet, erraten, errät	to guess		nach/sehen, sah nach, nachgesehen, sieht nach	to check
	erwünscht	desired			
	fehlerfrei	free of errors, without mistakes	das	Pfund	pound
			die	Schlacht, -en	battle
				schulden	to owe
	feiern	to celebrate		silbern	silver
	fließend	fluent		spannend	exciting, fascinating
die	Freundschaft, -en	friendship		sparen	to save
	geboren sein	to be born	die	Summe, -n	sum
der	Geburtstag, -e	birthday		tot	dead
				verheiratet	married
	geschehen, geschah, ist geschehen, geschieht	to happen	die	Verlobung, -en	betrothal, engagement
				versäumen	to miss
			das	Verständnis	understanding
	gewaltig	considerable		wiederum	again
	gleich	all the same		wiegen, wog, gewogen	weigh
die	Hochzeit, -en	wedding	die	Zahl, -en	number

VI. ERKLÄRUNGEN UND ÜBUNGEN

1. Cardinal Numbers

0	null				
1	eins	11	elf	21	einundzwanzig
2	zwei	12	zwölf	22	zweiundzwanzig
3	drei	13	dreizehn	30	dreißig
4	vier	14	vierzehn	31	einunddreißig
5	fünf	15	fünfzehn	40	vierzig
6	sechs	16	sechzehn	50	fünfzig
7	sieben	17	siebzehn	60	sechzig
8	acht	18	achtzehn	70	siebzig
9	neun	19	neunzehn	80	achtzig
10	zehn	20	zwanzig	90	neunzig
				100	hundert

101	hunderteins
102	hundertzwei
112	hundertzwölf
188	hundertachtundachtzig
200	zweihundert
651	sechshunderteinundfünfzig
1000	tausend, eintausend
1749	(ein)tausendsiebenhundertneunundvierzig, siebzehn-hundertneunundvierzig (*date*)
100 000	hunderttausend
1 000 000	eine Million

Note that in giving the numbers 21–29, 31–39, etc. the order is the reverse of English: *not twenty-one, but one and twenty,* etc.

a. Inflection

Er hat es **vier** Jahre in der Schule studiert.
He studied it in school for four years.

Ich warte nur **eine** Stunde.
I'll wait only one hour.

Es ist halb **eins.**
It is half past twelve.

Es ist **ein** Uhr.   *but*   Es ist **eine** Uhr.
It is one o'clock.   *It is a clock.*

With the exception of **eins,** cardinal numbers are rarely inflected. **Eins** is used only when it stands by itself or when it is the final element in a combination. In all other cases **ein** is used unless it modifies a noun.

b. Repeated Numerical Occurrence

einmal, zweimal, dreimal, etc.
once, twice, three times, etc.

Repeated occurrence is expressed by adding **-mal** to the cardinal number.

PRACTICE

A. *Observe the example and then perform the exercise aloud:*

Example: Wieviel ist 3 + (und) (plus) 4?
$3 + 4 =$ (ist) (gleicht) 7
Wieviel ist 10 − (weniger) (minus) 3?
$10 − 3 = 7$
Wieviel ist 5 × (mal) 4?
$5 × 4 = 20$
Wieviel ist 12 : (geteilt durch) 4?
$12 : 4 = 3$

Wieviel ist:

5 + 3 =	7 − 3 =	4 × 2 =	9 : 3 =
8 + 2 =	11 − 9 =	7 × 4 =	12 : 6 =
10 + 4 =	18 − 16 =	9 × 6 =	72 : 9 =
12 + 9 =	23 − 7 =	10 × 12 =	80 : 10 =
21 + 34 =	50 − 46 =	11 × 7 =	120 : 30 =

B. Say in German:

1. He came once. 2. He wrote three times. 3. He had spoken to me twice. 4. He made the same mistake five times.

C. Read the following sentences aloud:

1. Herr Klein war 1939 in Deutschland. 2. Er kam 1944 als Soldat zurück. 3. Er besuchte Deutschland auch im Jahre 1955. 4. Die Schlacht bei Waterloo fand 1815 statt. 5. Deutschlands Wiedervereinigung fand im Jahre 1871 statt. 6. 122 Jahre vorher, im Jahre 1749, wurde Goethe in Frankfurt geboren. 7. Er ist über 80 Jahre später, 1832, in Weimar gestorben. 8. 1788 machte er seine erste italienische Reise. 9. 1790 machte er die zweite. 10. Die ersten Pläne zum „Faust" hat er 1770 entwickelt. 11. 1808 hat Goethe Napoleons Bekanntschaft gemacht.

2. Telling Time
a. Conversational Time

Asking for time:

Wieviel Uhr ist es?
or: **Wie spät ist es?**

What time is it?

Answers:

Es ist vier (Uhr).
Es ist fünf (Minuten) nach vier.
Es ist zehn (Minuten) nach vier.
Es ist Viertel nach vier.
or: **Es ist (ein) Viertel (auf) fünf.**
Es ist zwanzig (Minuten) nach vier.
Es ist fünf (Minuten) vor halb fünf.
or: **Es ist fünfundzwanzig (Minuten) nach vier.**
Es ist halb fünf.
Es ist fünf (Minuten) nach halb fünf.
or: **Est ist fünfundzwanzig (Minuten) vor fünf.**
Es ist zwanzig (Minuten) vor fünf.
Es ist Viertel vor fünf.
or: **Es ist dreiviertel fünf.**
Es ist zehn (Minuten) vor fünf.

It's four (o'clock).
It's five (minutes) after four.
It's ten (minutes) after four.

It's (a) quarter past four.
It's twenty past four.

It's twenty-five past four.

It's half past four.

It's twenty-five to five.

It's twenty to five.

It's (a) quarter to five.

It's ten of five.

Es ist fünf (Minuten) vor fünf.	*It's five of five.*
Es ist genau fünf (Uhr).	*It's exactly five.*
or: Es ist Punkt fünf (Uhr).	
vormittags	*a.m.*
nachmittags (*after 6:00:* abends)	*p.m.*

b. Official Time

6.15 = sechs Uhr fünfzehn (*6:15 a.m.*)
6.30 = sechs Uhr dreißig (*6:30 a.m.*)
18.30 = achtzehn Uhr dreißig (*6:30 p.m.*)
18.55 = achtzehn Uhr fünfundfünfzig (*6:55 p.m.*)

Public transportation, communications media, and the like utilize the 24-hour system.

PRACTICE

A. Say in German:

6:00; 6:10; 6:15; 6:25; 6:30; 6:35; 6:45; 6:55; 7 sharp; 8:05; 8:15; 8:20; 8:35; 8:50; 9:10.
6:00 a.m.; 7:15 a.m.; 10:45 a.m.; 1:25 p.m.; 3:15 p.m.; 6:20 p.m.

B. Answer each question using the indicated expressions:

Example: Um wieviel Uhr macht Kurt seine Aufgaben? (*um 4 Uhr*)
Kurt macht seine Aufgaben um 4 Uhr.

Um wieviel Uhr...
1. ist der Vater abgereist? (um 3.20) 2. ist er in Bonn angekommen? (um 5.05) 3. hat er mit dem Leiter der Filiale gesprochen? (um 8.00) 4. hat er zu Abend gegessen? (um 9.15) 5. ist er eingeschlafen? (um 11.15) 6. ist er morgens aufgestanden? (um 7.00) 7. ist er ins Geschäft gegangen? (um 9.45) 8. hat er zu Mittag gegessen? (um 12.30)

C. Read aloud:

1. Der Zug fährt um 15.20 ab. 2. Das stimmt nicht. Er kommt schon um 15.15 Uhr an. 3. Sie haben das auch falsch gelesen. 4. Er kommt um 14.55 an. 5. Um wieviel Uhr kann man das Programm sehen? Um 23 Uhr. 6. Ein anderes gutes Programm ist um 19.15.

3. Ordinal Numbers

der, die, das erste	*the first*
zweite	*second*
dritte	*third*
vierte	*fourth*
sieb(en)te	*seventh*
achte	*eighth*

zwanzigste	*twentieth*
einundzwanzigste	*twenty-first*
zweiundzwanzigste	*twenty-second*
vierzigste	*fortieth*
hundertste	*hundredth*
hunderterste	*hundred-first*

Ordinals are formed from the corresponding cardinals by adding -t- to the cardinal up to 19, and -st- from 20 upwards, plus appropriate adjective endings. Note: **erst-**, **dritt-**, and **acht-** are irregular forms; **siebt-** is standard usage, **siebent-** is an older form.

a. Inflection

der erste Brief
the first letter

mein erster Brief
my first letter

am fünften Tag
on the fifth day

in den ersten Monaten
in the first months

Ordinals have endings like attributive adjectives.

b. Writing

der 3. (dritte) Jahrgang
am 5. (fünften) Januar
Friedrich II. (der zweite)
Wilhelm I. (der erste)

To express the ordinals in Arabic or Roman numerals, German uses a period after the numeral.

4. Days, Months, and Seasons

a. The Days of the Week

Sonntag
Montag
Dienstag
Mittwoch
Donnerstag
Freitag
Samstag, Sonnabend

All the days are masculine.

b. The Months

Januar	**Juli**
Februar	**August**
März	**September**
April	**Oktober**
Mai	**November**
Juni	**Dezember**

All the months are masculine.

255

c. The Seasons   **Frühling**
Sommer
Herbst
Winter

All the seasons are masculine.

5. Expressing   **Der wievielte ist heute?**
Dates   or: **Den wievielten haben wir heute?**
What is today's date?

a. The Day   **Heute ist der 8. September 1970.**
Today is the 8th of September, 1970.

b. On the Day: **am 28. August 1749**
(always the   *on August 28, 1749*
dative)

c. In Letters: (always   **Bonn, den 3. April 1969**
the accusative)   *Bonn, April 3, 1969*

6. Ordinal   **erstens, zweitens, drittens**
Adverbs   *in the first place, second place (secondly), third place (thirdly)*

Ordinal adverbs add **-ens** to the ordinal stem.

PRACTICE   *A.   Say in German, using masculine nominative singular:*

1st; 3rd; 8th; 12th; 16th; 20th; 25th; 33rd; 60th; 100th

B.   Say in German:

1.	the first assignment	7.	on the first day
2.	the third book	8.	the seventh day
3.	the fifth game	9.	in the eighth month
4.	his first problem	10.	in the twelfth month
5.	her first husband	11.	for his first son
6.	his fifth daughter	12.	our third assignment

C.   Complete the following with ordinals as indicated:

1. Montag ist der (2) Tag der Woche.   2. Samstag ist der (7) Tag der Woche.   3. März ist der (3) Monat.   4. Der (6) Monat heißt Juni.   5. Kennen Sie seinen (5) Sohn?   6. Ich sehe mir den Film zum (2) Mal an.

D.   Read the following dates:

1. Der 4. Februar   2. Der 7. März   3. Bonn, den 20. Juli 4. Berlin, den 21. Oktober   5. Am 30. Dezember   6. Der 27. Januar 1897

E. Say in German:

1. Today is February 1, 1970. 2. Yesterday was January 31, 1970. 3. My letter begins: Cologne, April 7, 1970. 4. My parents will celebrate their Silver Anniversary on December 22nd. 5. Mine will celebrate theirs on July 15th. 6. Why do you say this? —In the first place, it is Sunday; in the second place, I know the story.

F. Answer the following questions using the indicated expressions:

> *Example:* Wann feiern wir Washingtons Geburtstag? (*am 22. Februar*)
> Wir feiern seinen Geburtstag am 22. Februar.

1. Wann feiern wir Lincolns Geburtstag? (am 12. Februar) 2. Wann hat man Lincoln ermordet? (am 15. April 1865) 3. Wann ist Amerika in den 2. Weltkrieg eingetreten? (am 7. Dezember 1941) 4. Wann wurde Goethe geboren? (am 28. August 1749) 5. Wann wählt man den Präsidenten der Vereinigten Staaten? (gewöhnlich am ersten Dienstag im November, alle 4 Jahre)

7. Fractions

½	**ein halb**	1½	**eineinhalb, anderthalb**
⅓	**ein Drittel**	2½	**zweieinhalb**
¼	**ein Viertel**	3⅓	**drei ein Drittel**
⅕	**ein Fünftel**	¹⁄₂₀	**ein Zwanzigstel**
⅔	**zwei Drittel**	⁵⁄₁₀₀	**fünf Hundertstel**

Add **-el** to the ordinal stem to form a fraction (*except* ½). Fractions are neuter nouns.

Note: Commas are used to set off decimals: 6,7 = **sechs Komma sieben.**

PRACTICE

Read aloud:

½; ⅔; ¾; ¼; ⅖; ⅙; ¹⁄₂₄

3,5; 4,6; 8,9; 1,4; 0,1

FINAL PRACTICE

A. Read the following numbers and dates:

1.

437	568
789	842
980	1080
1002	7769

2.

$71 + 4 = 75$	$20 \times 6 = 120$
$88 + 12 = 100$	$1 \times 8 = 8$
$32 + 54 = 86$	$10 \times 4 = 40$
$100 - 30 = 70$	$180 : 3 = 60$
$6 - 2 = 4$	$50 : 2 = 25$
$176 - 62 = 114$	$100 : 20 = 5$

3. der 5. April   der 11. November
    der 27. Juni   der 31. August
    der 5. Februar   am 6. April
    am 11. November   am 27. Juni
    am 31. August   am 1. Juli

4. Paris, den 5. September   London, den 28. Januar
    Köln, den 3. Mai   New York, den 8. Juli
    Leipzig, den 1. Juni 1970   Wien, den 2. März 1969

5. Wichtige Daten:
    1066   1815
    1492   1871
    1776   1914
    1812   1941

6. $\frac{1}{4} + \frac{1}{4} = \frac{1}{2}$
    $\frac{1}{4} + \frac{1}{3} = \frac{7}{12}$
    $\frac{1}{4} + \frac{1}{2} = \frac{3}{4}$

7. DM 3,40 (DM = Deutsche Mark)
    4,80
    5,10
    7,80

8. 4,3 Meter
    25,6 Quadratmeter
    78,5 Kilometer
    76 Kilogramm

B. *Answer the following questions:*

1. Wieviel Uhr ist es jetzt? 2. Wie lang ist unser Klassenzimmer? 3. Wie groß sind Sie? 4. Wie alt sind Sie? 5. Wann sind Sie geboren? 6. Wann ist Ihr Vater geboren? 7. Wann hat Ihre Mutter Geburtstag? 8. Wann gratulieren Sie Ihrem Bruder (Ihrer Schwester) zum Geburtstag? 9. Wie alt ist Ihr Vater? 10. Wie alt sind die meisten Studenten in dieser Klasse? 11. Wie alt war Goethe bei seinem Tode? 12. Wie viele Ziffern (*numerals*) stehen auf der Uhr? 13. Wie viele Stunden hat der Tag? 14. Wie viele Tage hat das Jahr? 15. Wann sind Sie heute morgen aufgestanden? 16. Wann sind Sie gestern abend zu Bett gegangen? 17. Wann sind Sie eingeschlafen? 18. Wann fangen die nächsten Ferien an? 19. Wie schreibt man das Datum in einem Brief? Geben Sie ein Beispiel! 20. Wieviel wiegen Sie?

C. *Say first, then write in German:*

1. Kurt's father left at seven last night and arrived two and a half hours later in Bonn. 2. It had rained heavily and it had become foggy. 3. Kurt was driving the car to the station, but he almost

missed the train. 4. His father was very angry about the bad weather. He had had bad weather during the trip from New York to Cologne. 5. Kurt's father came to Europe for the first time in 1939, the last time in 1970. 6. Mr. Klein had heard German in his father's house. 7. Later on, he studied it for four years in school. 8. His main subject was history, and he knows the important dates very well. 9. The history of Europe has always made a big impression on him, and he reads many books on history. 10. But he is also interested in literature, especially in Goethe, his life, and works. 11. Last night at the Lenz's he had talked about Goethe. 12. Goethe studied law and literature, first in Leipzig, then in Frankfurt. 13. 1775 was an important date in Goethe's life: his engagement, the breakup of the engagement, and the first plans for *Faust*. 14. He was friends with several women, especially with Mrs. von Stein, and with several men, especially with Schiller. 15. He made two trips to Italy and he learned much during these trips. 16. He was also the first minister of the duke and, as minister, had a meeting with Napoleon I in 1808. 17. Goethe wrote over ten letters every day. 18. Kurt says, "My father remembers dates very well. Why can't I remember them? I owe Mrs. Kolb DM 20 and I keep forgetting to pay." 19. Everyone makes mistakes, and Kurt thinks he makes more of them than most people.

Im Jazzkeller
GERMAN INFORMATION CENTER

I. UNTERHALTUNG

KURT IST KRANK

(Karl telefoniert, um Kurt zu einer Gesellschaft einzuladen.)

Karl: Mach dich gegen sechs fertig, Junge! Heute abend wird gesungen und getanzt.

Kurt: Ich habe heute keine Lust dazu.

Karl: Wie ist denn das möglich? Du möchtest nicht tanzen gehen?

Kurt: Das ist leicht zu erklären. Ich bin im Bett mit einer schweren Grippe.

Karl: Wann hat denn das angefangen? Wir haben uns doch noch gestern gesprochen.

Kurt: Gestern war ich schon heiser und hatte Schnupfen. Dann bekam ich Husten und jetzt habe ich auch Halsweh.

Karl: Du hast gewiß auch erhöhte Temperatur.

Kurt: Der Arzt hat das Fieber gemessen. Ich hatte 38.

Karl: Wie lange sollst du im Bett bleiben?

Kurt: Mindestens zwei Tage. Dann soll ich wieder untersucht werden.

Karl: Hat der Arzt dir etwas verschrieben?

KURT IS SICK

(Karl telephones to invite Kurt to a party.)

Karl: Be ready by six, fellow! Tonight there's going to be singing and dancing.

Kurt: I'm not in the mood for it today.

Karl: How is that possible? You don't want to go dancing?

Kurt: It's easy to explain. I'm in bed with a bad case of the grippe.

Karl: When did it start? We just saw each other yesterday.

Kurt: I was hoarse even yesterday and had a head cold. Then came this cough, and now I have a sore throat.

Karl: You undoubtedly have a temperature, too.

Kurt: The doctor took my temperature. It was 38 ($38°$ C $=100.5°$F).

Karl: How long are you supposed to stay in bed?

Kurt: At least two days. Then I'm to be checked again.

Karl: Did the doctor prescribe any medicine?

Kurt: Ich habe zwei Rezepte hier. Sie müssen zur Apotheke gebracht werden. Ich warte auf Frau Kolb.

Karl: Ausgeschlossen. Ich komme sofort hinüber. Ich möchte nach dir sehen und kann dir dann auch die Arznei besorgen.

Kurt: Bitte, komm nicht! Wahrscheinlich ist es ansteckend, und ich will nicht, daß du auch krank wirst.

Nach einer Stunde.

Karl: Die Tabletten sind zweimal täglich zu nehmen, morgens und abends, und die Tropfen dreimal.

Kurt: Wieviel schulde ich dir?

Karl: Wir rechnen ein anderes Mal ab. Kann ich dir noch etwas besorgen?

Kurt: Alles andere ist schon erledigt worden. Frau Kolb hat Verschiedenes bestellt. Es wird sowieso bald geliefert werden.

Karl: Warum hältst du den rechten Arm so vorsichtig?

Kurt: Ich habe eine Spritze bekommen, und es hat sehr weh getan.

Karl: Ich kenne das. Tu mir einen Gefallen! Wenn du etwas brauchst, ruf sofort an! Die ganze Familie steht dir zur Verfügung.

Kurt: I have two prescriptions here. They have to be taken to the pharmacy. I'm waiting for Mrs. Kolb.

Karl: Out of the question. I'm coming over at once. I'd like to take a look at you and then I can also get you the medicine.

Kurt: Please don't come. It's probably contagious, and I don't want you to get sick, too.

After an hour.

Karl: The tablets are to be taken twice daily, in the morning and evening, and the drops three times.

Kurt: How much do I owe you?

Karl: We'll settle some other time. Can I get you anything else?

Kurt: Everything else has already been taken care of. Mrs. Kolb has ordered different things. They will be delivered soon anyway.

Karl: Why are you holding your right arm so carefully?

Kurt: I got a shot and it hurt a lot.

Karl: I know what you mean. Do me a favor. If you need anything, call immediately. The whole family is at your disposition.

II. KOMBINATIONEN

Sagen Sie auf deutsch:

a. 1. Be ready by six, Kurt. 2. Please be ready by seven, Mr. Klein. 3. I can't be ready so early.

b. 1. Tonight there is singing and dancing. 2. Tonight there's going to be eating and drinking. 3. Tonight there's much talking and smoking.

c. 1. I'm not in the mood for it. 2. She isn't in the mood for it. 3. Why aren't they in the mood for it?

d. 1. That's easy to explain. 2. Why is this so hard to explain? 3. It is very difficult to do.

e. 1. I'm in bed with a bad case of the grippe. 2. How long has he been in bed? 3. How long does he have to stay in bed?

f. 1. When did this start? 2. Kurt doesn't know when this started. 3. They just talked to each other yesterday.

g. 1. He was hoarse and had a head cold. 2. He was hoarse and then he got a sore throat. 3. When did the cough start?

h. 1. You probably have a temperature. 2. The doctor took his temperature. 3. He also took my temperature.

i. 1. I'm supposed to be checked again tomorrow. 2. When is he supposed to be checked again? 3. The physician didn't say when he is to be checked again.

j. 1. The prescriptions have to be taken to the pharmacy. 2. Karl wants to take the prescriptions to the pharmacy. 3. Kurt ought not to wait for Mrs. Kolb.

k. 1. I'm coming over at once. 2. Karl says he will come immediately. 3. Karl will get Kurt the medicine.

l. 1. I don't want you to get sick, too. 2. He doesn't want me to get sick. 3. Nobody wants us to get sick.

m. 1. These tablets are to be taken twice daily. 2. Are they to be taken in the morning and evening? 3. The drops are to be taken three times a day.

n. 1. We'll settle some other time. 2. They will settle some other time. 3. Karl doesn't want to settle immediately.

o. 1. Everything has been taken care of. 2. Nothing has been taken care of. 3. Has everything else been taken care of?

III. SAGEN UND FRAGEN

a. *Sie sind Kurt. Sie sagen zu Karl:*

1. Sie haben keine Lust zum Tanzen. 2. Sie sind im Bett mit einer schweren Grippe. 3. Sie waren gestern schon heiser. 4. Sie hatten auch schon Schnupfen. 5. Sie haben auch einen Husten bekommen. 6. Jetzt haben Sie auch schon Halsweh. 7. Der Arzt hat Ihnen das Fieber gemessen. 8. Sie sollen mindestens zwei Tage im Bett bleiben. 9. Sie sollen dann wieder untersucht werden. 10. Sie glauben, die Rezepte müssen sofort zur Apotheke gebracht werden. 11. Sie befürchten, Ihre Krankheit ist ansteckend. 12. Sie wollen nicht, daß er auch krank wird. 13. Frau Kolb hat Ihnen Verschiedenes bestellt. 14. Sie denken, es wird bald geliefert werden. 15. Sie haben eine Spritze bekommen.

b. *Sie sind Karl und sagen zu Kurt:*

1. Sie haben sich noch gestern gesprochen. 2. Er hat gewiß auch erhöhte Temperatur. 3. Was er sagt, ist ausgeschlossen. 4. Sie kommen sofort hinüber. 5. Sie möchten nach ihm sehen. 6. Sie wollen ihm die Arznei besorgen. 7. Er soll die Tabletten zweimal täglich nehmen. 8. Sie rechnen ein anderes Mal ab. 9. Wenn er etwas braucht, soll er sofort anrufen. 10. Ihre ganze Familie steht ihm zur Verfügung.

c. *Sie sind Karl und fragen Kurt:*

1. wie so etwas möglich ist. 2. ob er wirklich nicht tanzen gehen möchte. 3. wann diese Grippe denn angefangen hat. 4. wie lange er im Bett bleiben soll. 5. ob der Arzt ihm etwas verschrieben hat. 6. ob die Krankheit ansteckend sein soll. 7. was mit seinem rechten Arm los ist. 8. ob es weh getan hat, als er die Spritze bekam.

IV. AUFSATZ

DIE MUSIK IN DEUTSCHLAND

Nachdem Kurt sich einigermaßen[1] von seiner Grippe erholt hatte, führte er Lore Lenz zum Tanz in ein erstklassiges Hotel, wo eine berühmte Kapelle[2] spielte. Man tanzte meistens zu amerikanischen Schlagern,[3] die Lore viel besser kannte als er.

1. to some extent. 2. band. 3. **der Schlager, -** hit tune.

5 „Wie ist das zu erklären?" fragte er sie, „daß du dich so gut in unserer Tanzmusik auskennst?"

„Das ist leicht zu verstehen", lachte sie. „Ich war schließlich auch einmal 16 Jahre alt. Mit meinem erstverdienten[4] Geld wurde ein Plattenspieler gekauft und danach habe ich mir auch langsam

10 Schallplatten angeschafft.[5] Natürlich wurden mir auch manche zum Geburtstag geschenkt.[6] In dem Alter interessierte ich mich hauptsächlich für Beat-Musik. Meine Eltern waren nicht davon begeistert und haben sich immer wieder über den Lärm beklagt. Es war aber nicht der Lärm, der sie störte. Ich hatte das Gefühl,

15 daß sie, wie so viele Eltern, diese Musik als eine Gefahr betrachteten, vor der ich geschützt werden mußte. Du hast vielleicht gelesen, daß in manchen Städten die Jazz-Keller polizeilich[7] bewacht[8] und sogar kontrolliert werden. Die Jazz-Musik soll nicht gut für unsere Jugend sein. Selbstverständlich denkt die Jugend

20 anders darüber."

„Werden denn die alten Volkslieder gar nicht mehr gesungen?" fragte Kurt enttäuscht.

„Doch", antwortete Lore, „sie werden noch immer in der Schule gelehrt und man singt sie auch bei besonderen Gelegenheiten. Bei

25 den Teenagern sind sie jedoch weniger in Mode."[9]

„Und die ältere Generation?" erkundigte sich Kurt. Bei ihr wird doch ‚gute' Musik bevorzugt . . ."

„Ganz gewiß", lachte Lore, und erzählte ihm, wie sehr ihr Vater noch immer die Symphonien und Opern liebte. Herr Lenz ging

30 zum Beispiel zu fast allen Konzerten, die von dem berühmten Kölner Gürzenich Orchester aufgeführt wurden. Manchmal klagte er aber, daß man zu viele klassische und romantische Stücke spielte und dabei die zeitgenössische[10] Musik vernachlässigte.[11] Herr Lenz gehörte zu den wenigen, die sich für die neuen Tech-

35 niken[12] interessierten, mit denen man besonders in Deutschland viel experimentiert und interessante Resultate erzielt[13] hatte. Diese modernen Kompositionen konnte man eher bei den jungen Rundfunkorchestern[14] hören als bei den altberühmten philharmonischen Orchestern.

40 Auch fuhr Herr Lenz mehrere Male im Jahr zu Musikfestspielen,[15] die man in fast allen Großstädten und auch in einigen kleinen Orten veranstaltete.[16] „So fährt er zum Beispiel im-

4. first-earned.   5. (sich) an/schaffen to acquire (for oneself).   6. schenken to give (as a present).   7. by the police.   8. bewachen to watch, guard.
9. style.   10. contemporary.   11. neglected.   12. techniques.
13. obtained.   14. das Rundfunkorchester, - radio orchestra.   15. das Musikfestspiel, -e music festival.   16. veranstalten to organize, arrange.

mer nach Bonn", erzählte Lore, „wo das Beethovenfest gefeiert wird. Zwischen Mozart in Würzburg und Wagner in Bayreuth
45 wird gewöhnlich abgewechselt.[17] Wo er auch[18] hinfährt, schleppt[19] er Mutti immer mit. Aber ich glaube, sie interessiert sich mehr für die Modenschau,[20] die Eleganz des Publikums und die Schaufensterdekorationen als für die Musik. Sie hat natürlich nicht den Mut, das einzugestehen."[21]
50 „Ich würde auch ganz gerne zu einem Festspiel fahren", sagte Kurt. „Vielleicht finde ich die Zeit dazu."

Beantworten Sie die folgenden Fragen:

1. Was machte Kurt, nachdem er sich erholt hatte? 2. Wozu tanzte man meistens? 3. Was fragte Kurt Lore? 4. Was machte Lore mit ihrem erstverdienten Geld? 5. Woher bekam sie Schallplatten? 6. Für was für Musik interessierte sie sich als 16jähriges Mädchen? 7. Worüber haben sich Lores Eltern immer wieder beklagt? 8. Als was betrachteten sie diese Musik, glaubte Lore? 9. Was hat Kurt vielleicht in den Zeitungen gelesen? 10. Werden die alten Volkslieder noch immer gesungen? Wann? 11. Zu welchen Konzerten ging Herr Lenz? 12. Worüber klagte er aber manchmal? 13. Für welche Techniken interessierte sich Herr Lenz auch? 14. Wohin fuhr Herr Lenz auch mehrere Male im Jahr? 15. Wo wird das Beethovenfest gefeiert? 16. Wen schleppt Herr Lenz immer mit? 17. Wofür interessiert sich Frau Lenz am meisten? 18. Wozu findet Kurt vielleicht die Zeit?

17. ab/wechseln to alternate. **18. wo . . . auch** wherever. **19. schleppen** to drag. **20.** fashion show, dress parade. **21. ein/gestehen** to confess, admit.

V. WORTSCHATZ

ab/rechnen	to settle (*accounts*)	**eher**	sooner, rather
ansteckend	contagious	**erhöhen**	to increase, heighten
die **Apotheke, -n**	pharmacy	**erledigen**	to take care of, settle
die **Arznei, -en**	medicine		
der **Arzt, ⁓e**	physician	das **Fieber**	fever
auf/führen	to perform	**führen**	to lead, conduct, take
ausgeschlossen	out of the question	die **Gefahr**	danger
berühmt	famous	die **Gesellschaft, -en**	company, party, social gathering
besorgen	to get, take care of		
betrachten	to consider, view	die **Grippe**	grippe, flu
bevorzugen	to prefer	das **Halsweh**	sore throat

heiser	hoarse	selbstver-	of course
der Husten	cough	ständlich	
der Keller, -	cellar	sowieso	anyhow, anyway
kontrollieren	to check	die Spritze, -n	shot, injection
krank	ill	die Tablette, -n	tablet, pill
der Lärm	noise	der Tanz, ⸚e	dance
lehren	to teach	tanzen	to dance
messen, maß,	to measure	die Temperatur	temperature
gemessen,		der Tropfen, -	drop
mißt		untersuchen	to investigate,
mindestens	at least		check
der Mut	courage	die Verfügung	disposal
der Ort, -e	place, locality,	einem zur	to be at some-
	region	Verfügung	one's disposal
der Platten-	record player	stehen	
spieler, -		verschreiben,	to prescribe
das Rezept, -e	prescription;	verschrieb,	
	recipe	verschrie-	
die Schallplatte,	phonograph rec-	ben	
-n	ord	das Volkslied, -er	folksong
der Schnupfen	head cold	vorsichtig	careful, cautious
schützen	to protect		

VI. ERKLÄRUNGEN UND ÜBUNGEN

1. Passive

a. Formation

wählen *to elect*

Present:	**Er wird gewählt.**	*He is being elected.*
Past:	**Er wurde gewählt.**	*He was elected.*
Compound Past:	**Er ist gewählt worden.**[1]	*He has been elected.*
		He was elected.
Past Perfect:	**Er war gewählt worden.**	*He had been elected.*
Future:	**Er wird gewählt werden.**	*He will be elected.*
Future Perfect:	**Er wird gewählt worden sein.**	*He will have been elected.*

English expresses the passive by means of *to be* plus past participle. German uses **werden** plus past participle.

b. Changing from Active to Passive

Active: **Die Deutschen wählen einen Präsidenten.**
The Germans are electing a President.

Passive: **Ein Präsident wurde von den Deutschen gewählt.**
A President was elected by the Germans.

Active: **Die Medizin hat Kurt geheilt.**
The medicine cured Kurt.

Passive: **Kurt ist durch die Medizin geheilt worden.**
Kurt has been cured by the medicine.

1. **Worden** is used instead of **geworden** in the perfect tenses.

267

When changing a sentence from the active to the passive, the direct object of the active becomes the subject of the passive. The subject of the active ser.tence becomes the agent of the passive.

The agent by whom the action is performed is usually expressed by **von.** Occasionally, **durch** may be used to imply *by means of, through.*

Note: Verbs requiring the dative in an active context also require it in the passive, usually with impersonal **es** as subject:

Active: Man hat **ihm** nicht geholfen.
They did not help him.

Passive: Es ist **ihm** nicht geholfen worden.
He was not helped.

Active: Man erzählte **uns** vieles.
They told us many things.

Passive: Es wurde **uns** vieles erzählt.
or
Uns wurde vieles erzählt.[1]
or
Vieles wurde **uns** erzählt.[1]
We were told many things. (Many things were told us.)

c. Impersonal Passive Constructions

Es wurde viel gelacht.
There was much laughing.

Heute abend **wird gesungen und getanzt.**
This evening there will be singing and dancing.

Impersonal passive constructions are common in German. In such constructions the subject is the impersonal pronoun **es,** either expressed or implied.

PRACTICE

A. *Conjugate the following sentences in the 3rd person in the simple past, compound past, past perfect, future, and future perfect:*

1. Es wird gesungen. 2. Auch wird getanzt. 3. Es wird viel gespielt. 4. Es wird viel darüber gesprochen.

B. *Put the following active sentences into the corresponding forms of the passive:*

Example: Karl lädt Kurt zu einer Gesellschaft ein.
Kurt wird von Karl zu einer Gesellschaft eingeladen.

1. **Es** is omitted when the pronoun or an element other than **es** introduces the sentence.

268

1. Der Arzt hat das Fieber gemessen. 2. Zwei Ärzte werden Kurt untersuchen. 3. Sie schicken ihn dann nach Hause. 4. Karl besucht Kurt. 5. Der Arzt hatte Tabletten und Tropfen verschrieben. 6. Frau Kolb bringt die Rezepte zur Apotheke. 7. Frau Kolb hat auch alles andere bestellt. 8. Die Apotheke wird bald alles liefern.

C. *Express the following sentences as impersonal passive constructions in the same tense:*

Examples: Sie singen oft.
Es wird oft gesungen.
Sie lachten viel.
Es wurde viel gelacht.

1. Sie tanzen viel. 2. Sie reden viel. 3. Sie sprachen laut. 4. Sie haben bis in die Nacht gesungen. 5. Sie tranken aber nicht viel. 6. Sie spielen viel. 7. Sie rauchten auch genug. 8. Sie lachen andauernd. 9. Sie haben sehr wenig studiert. 10. Sie hatten selten gearbeitet.

2. Apparent Passive

Passive:	Das Haus **wird verkauft.** *The house is being sold.*
Apparent Passive:	Das Haus **ist verkauft.** *The house is (already) sold.*

In the first statement, the action is in the process of taking place. In the second statement, the action has already occurred, and the resulting condition is described. The apparent passive construction requires **sein** with a past participle, the latter functioning as a predicate adjective.

PRACTICE

Answer the following questions by confirming a completed action:

Example: Wird das Fieber jetzt gemessen?
Es ist schon gemessen.

1. Wird die Arznei jetzt verschrieben? 2. Werden die Tabletten bald bestellt? 3. Werden die Tropfen auch heute bestellt? 4. Wird alles andere bald erledigt? 5. Werden alle Sachen sofort geliefert? 6. Wird Kurt geheilt?

3. Review of werden, Meanings and Uses

Es wird immer **besser.**
It's getting better all the time.

Die Jugend **ist realistisch geworden.**
Youth has become realistic.

Werden is used as an independent verb meaning *to get, to become.*

Er wird morgen **kommen.**
He'll come tomorrow.

Werden is used with the infinitive to form the future.

Gute Musik **wird bevorzugt.**
Good music is (being) preferred.

Er **soll** wieder **untersucht werden.**
He's supposed to be examined again.

Werden is also the passive auxiliary.

PRACTICE

Say in German:

1. He's becoming tall. 2. He's getting fat (**dick**). 3. He has become thin. 4. They have gotten old. 5. This work has become interesting. 6. It will become even more interesting. 7. His work will be read in the future. 8. It cannot be easily understood. 9. His poems have been admired by all. 10. Two poems were read in class last week.

4. Replacing the Passive

In German the passive is used less frequently than in English. When the agent is not expressed, a passive construction is often replaced by an active one.

a. Replacing the Passive with man

Man hat Kurt sofort **untersucht.** (*Instead of:* Kurt **wurde** sofort **untersucht.**)
Kurt was examined right away.

Man spricht nie von politischen Problemen. (*Instead of:* Von politischen Problemen **wird** nie **gesprochen.**)
Political problems are never discussed.

The passive is most frequently replaced by the indefinite pronoun **man** and an active verb.

b. Replacing the Passive with sein + zu + Infinitive

Es ist wenig davon **zu sehen.**
Little of this can be seen.

Wo **ist** etwas **zu essen?**
Where is something to eat?

Das **ist** leicht **zu tun.**
This is easy to do (easily done).

In this construction the active infinitive often conceals a passive meaning.

270

c. Replacing the Passive with <u>sich</u> <u>lassen</u>

Das **läßt sich erledigen.** (*Instead of:* Das **kann erledigt werden.**)
That can be taken care of.

The construction **sich lassen** plus infinitive is used to replace **können** plus passive infinitive.

PRACTICE

A. *Replace the passive with* **man,** *retaining the original tense of the verb:*

Example: Der Präsident wird heute gewählt.
Man wählt heute den Präsidenten.

1. Der Bundestag wird nächsten Sonntag gewählt.   2. Der Kanzler ist schon gewählt worden.   3. Die politische Lage ist klar beschrieben worden.   4. Die Lehrer werden oft schlecht bezahlt. 5. Die Bücher dieses Professors sind sehr oft gelesen worden. 6. Es wird ihm nicht viel geholfen.   7. Ihr wird auch nicht geglaubt.   8. Diese Probleme sind immer viel diskutiert worden.

B. *Replace the following passive constructions with the corresponding tense of* **sein** *plus infinitive:*

Example: Das kann nicht leicht gefunden werden.
Das ist nicht leicht zu finden.

1. Dieses Buch kann nicht leicht verstanden werden.   2. Es kann kaum gelesen werden.   3. Das konnte nicht leicht behauptet werden.   4. Dieser Autor kann nicht bewundert werden. 5. Er konnte nicht gefunden werden.   6. Es konnte nichts gemacht werden.

C. *Say in German without using the passive:*

1. They were laughing a lot.   2. They worked little and played a great deal.   3. This is hard to believe.   4. It isn't easy to say this.   5. This is difficult to comprehend.   6. But it was easy to get.   7. That can be done.   8. That can't be explained quickly.

5. Participles Used as Adjectives

a. Present Participle

tanzend
dancing

singend
singing

The present participle of German verbs is formed by adding **-end** to the present stem.

ein tanzender Student
a dancing student

271

das singende Mädchen
the singing girl

The present participle in German is used mostly as an adjective and takes both weak and strong adjective endings.

Lachend antwortete er mir.
Laughing, he answered me.

The present participle is also occasionally used as an adverb.

b. Past Participle **das geteilte Land**
the divided country

eine geschlossene Tür
a closed door

The past participle in German is often used as an attributive adjective. It then takes the usual adjective endings.

PRACTICE A. *Change the verb in each sentence to a present participle modifying the noun:*

        Example: Der Sommer kommt.
                   Der kommende Sommer.

1. Der Mann spricht. 2. Die Leute lachen. 3. Viele Studenten tanzen. 4. Eine Frau trinkt. 5. Eine Studentin liest. 6. Ein Freund wartet. 7. Das Kind leidet.

    B. *Change each verb to a past participle modifying the accompanying noun:*

        Example: vernachlässigen, die Musik
                 die vernachlässigte Musik

1. verdienen, das Geld 2. bewachen, ein Keller 3. singen, Volkslieder 4. bevorzugen, die Musik 5. aufführen, Konzerte

FINAL PRACTICE *Say first, then write in German:*

1. Kurt has been invited to a party by Karl. 2. There will be much singing and dancing. 3. Why isn't Kurt in the mood for it? 4. That is easy to explain. 5. He has become ill. 6. Yesterday he had been hoarse and also had a head cold. 7. The doctor came and took his temperature. 8. He will have to stay in

bed at least two days. 9. Then he is to be examined again. 10. The prescriptions which the doctor ordered have to be taken to the pharmacy. 11. "That can very easily be taken care of," says Karl. 12. But Kurt does not want him to come over. 13. Karl will perhaps get sick, too. 14. After an hour Karl brings the tablets and drops. 15. The tablets are to be taken twice daily. 16. The drops must be taken three times a day. 17. Everything else has been taken care of. 18. Mrs. Kolb has ordered different things which will soon be delivered.

„Ich hätte wenigstens einmal nach dem Norden fahren sollen."
Bauernhaus mit Strohdach, typisch für Schleswig-Holstein
HENLE FROM MONKMEYER

I. UNTERHALTUNG

KURT DENKT AN DIE RÜCKFAHRT

Kurt: Ach, wenn ich nur noch drei Tage hätte . . .

Karl: Was würdest du dann tun?

Kurt: Erstens könnte ich mich von jedem verabschieden. Zweitens könnte ich Geschenke für meine Familie kaufen. Drittens . . .

Karl: Na, wenn es in meiner Macht wäre, gäbe ich dir ein ganzes Jahr. Ich würde auch manches anders tun.

Kurt: Zum Beispiel . . . ?

Karl: Ja, wenn ich nicht arbeiten müßte, würde ich gleich mit dir nach Amerika fahren.

Lore: Du würdest nach Amerika fahren! Du warst doch schon dort. Ich bin jetzt an der Reihe.

Kurt: Ja, Lore. Warum kommst du nicht nächsten Sommer? Es würde dir bestimmt gefallen.

Lore: Das bezweifle ich nicht. Wenn die Eltern nur nicht so streng wären, . . .

Kurt: Leider kennen wir alle das Sprichwort: „Wenn das Wörtchen *wenn* nicht wär', dann wär' mein Vater ein Millionär!"

KURT THINKS OF THE RETURN TRIP

Kurt: If only I had three more days.

Karl: What would you do in that case?

Kurt: First, I could say good-by to everyone. Secondly, I could buy presents for my family. Thirdly, . . .

Karl: Well, if it were in my power, I'd give you a whole year. I'd also do many things differently.

Kurt: For example . . . ?

Karl: Well, if I didn't have to work, I'd go with you to America in a moment.

Lore: You would go to America! You've already been there. Now it's my turn.

Kurt: Yes, Lore. Why don't you come next summer? You'd certainly like it.

Lore: I don't doubt that. If only my parents weren't so strict . . .

Kurt: Unfortunately, we all know the proverb: "If the word 'if' did not exist, then my father would be a millionaire."

Karl: Aber das Wörtchen besteht, und unser Vater ist kein Millionär.
Lore: Und so muß ich weiterhin meine Reise verschieben.
Karl: Ich soll dich an das Studienbuch erinnern. Hast du es zurückbekommen?
Kurt: Ich hätte es wahrhaftig vergessen. Und wenn ich es vergessen hätte, hätte es schlimm um mich gestanden.
Lore: Wieso? Ist es so wichtig für dich?
Kurt: Ich könnte kaum beweisen, daß ich hier studiert habe.
Karl: Ich hätte dich nicht ohne dein Studienbuch abreisen lassen.

Karl: But the word does exist, and our father is no millionaire.
Lore: And so I have to keep postponing my trip.
Karl: I am supposed to remind you of the course-record book. Did you get it back?
Kurt: I surely would have forgotten it. And if I had forgotten it, I would have been in a difficult situation.
Lore: How come? Is it that important to you?
Kurt: I could scarcely prove that I took courses here.
Karl: I wouldn't have let you leave without your record book.

II. KOMBINATIONEN

Sagen Sie auf deutsch:

a. 1. If only I had three more days. 2. If only I had another week! 3. If only he had another hour.

b. 1. What would you do in that case? 2. What would you write in that case? 3. What would you think in that case?

c. 1. First, I could say good-bye to everybody. 2. Second, I could buy presents for my family. 3. Third, I could pack my suitcase better.

d. 1. If I didn't have to work, I'd go with you to America. 2. If I didn't have to stay here, I'd accompany you. 3. If he didn't have to study, he'd have more spare time.

e. 1. You would go to America! —It's my turn now. 2. He would go to America! —It's our turn now. 3. No, it's her turn.

f. 1. I don't doubt that. 2. Nobody can doubt that. 3. Everybody doubts that.

g. 1. But the word exists, and Dad is no millionaire. 2. This word doesn't exist. 3. Which word doesn't exist?

h. 1. And so I have to keep postponing my trip. 2. Does she really have to keep postponing it? 3. Why don't we postpone our trip?

i. 1. I was supposed to remind you of the book. 2. He wasn't supposed to remind me of this job. 3. We were supposed to remind you of the present.

j. 1. I would surely have forgotten it. 2. I surely would not have written this letter. 3. Would you really have spoken to him?

k. 1. I could scarcely prove that I had been taking courses here. 2. He could not prove that he was enrolled here. 3. Why couldn't he have proved it?

l. 1. I would not have let you leave without your book. 2. Lore would not have let him leave either. 3. His father would not have let him leave without money.

III. SAGEN UND FRAGEN

a. *Sie sind Kurt und sagen zu Karl oder Lore:*

1. Ach, wenn Sie nur noch drei Tage hätten! 2. Sie könnten sich dann von jedem verabschieden. 3. Sie könnten auch Geschenke für Ihre Familie kaufen. 4. Amerika würde ihr *(Lore)* bestimmt gefallen. 5. Sie kennen alle das Sprichwort: „Wenn das Wörtchen *wenn* nicht wär' . . .“ 6. Sie hätten wahrhaftig Ihr Studienbuch vergessen. 7. Sie könnten kaum beweisen, daß Sie hier studiert haben.

b. *Sie sind Karl oder Lore und sagen zu Kurt:*

1. Wenn es in Ihrer Macht wäre, gäben Sie ihm ein ganzes Jahr. 2. Ja, Sie würden auch manches anders tun. 3. Wenn Sie nicht arbeiten müßten, würden Sie nach Amerika fahren. 4. Sie sind jetzt an der Reihe, nach Amerika zu fahren. 5. Sie müssen aber weiterhin Ihre Reise verschieben. 6. Sie sollen ihn (Kurt) an sein Studienbuch erinnern. 7. Sie hätten ihn nicht ohne sein Studienbuch abreisen lassen.

c. *Sie sind Karl oder Lore und fragen Kurt:*

1. was er tun würde, wenn er noch drei Tage hätte. 2. ob er sein Studienbuch zurückbekommen hat. 3. wieso es schlimm um ihn gestanden hätte. 4. was er nicht beweisen könnte.

IV. AUFSATZ

VERPASSTE GELEGENHEITEN

Am letzten Tage seines Aufenthaltes in der Bundesrepublik war Kurt mürrisch.[1] Die Ursache seiner schlechten Laune war weder der Gedanke an die morgige[2] Abreise noch die Trennung von Lore und anderen netten Freunden. Es war eher die Tatsache, daß
5 gewisse Ziele, die er sich für seinen Aufenthalt in Deutschland gesetzt[3] hatte, nicht erreicht waren. Auch mancher Plan, den er vor seiner Abfahrt gefaßt[4] hatte, hatte sich als unrealistisch erwiesen. Was hatte er falsch gemacht? Stünde er jetzt erneut[5] vor seinem Besuch, was würde er anders machen?
10 „Ich würde gewiß weniger bummeln", dachte er. „Ich habe mich immer großartig im Café unterhalten und zweifellos viel dabei gelernt, aber ich hätte öfter auf die Uhr schauen sollen. Was meine Reisepläne anbetrifft — sie waren nicht immer die besten. Es wäre doch klüger gewesen, wenn ich mich nicht auf
15 das Rheinland und Bayern beschränkt[6] hätte. Ich hätte wenigstens einmal nach dem Norden fahren sollen. Auch ist es schwer zu verstehen, daß ich keiner einzigen Sitzung[7] des Bundeshauses[8] beigewohnt habe, obwohl die Hauptstadt nur ein paar Kilometer entfernt ist.
20 „Außerdem bestehen noch zu viele Lücken[9] in meinem Studium der deutschen Literatur. Wenn ich mehr von den Werken jener Dichter gelesen hätte, die nicht so leicht zu verstehen sind, und wenn ich mir überhaupt mehr Zeit zum Lesen genommen hätte, so wäre ich heute abend befriedigter. Dann würde mir auch
25 meine gesamte Leistung in einem viel günstigeren[10] Lichte erscheinen."
Plötzlich fing Kurt zu lachen an. „Ich Idiot",[11] sagte er vor sich hin, „ich spreche ja, als ob ich ein Greis[12] wäre und Deutschland nie wieder besuchen würde. Gewiß, ich habe nicht immer klug
30 gehandelt und manchmal wichtige Gelegenheiten verpaßt. Aber im großen und ganzen[13] hätte ich längst nicht so viel gelernt, wenn ich zu Hause geblieben wäre. Ich habe großen Vorteil aus meinem Studium hier gezogen. Also muß ich zufrieden sein."
Mit diesem Gedanken schlief Kurt endlich ein.

1. morose, sullen. 2. **morgig** (on) the next day, tomorrow('s). 3. **sich ein Ziel setzen** to set a goal for oneself. 4. **einen Plan fassen** to make plans. 5. again. 6. **(sich) beschränken auf** to limit (oneself), confine. 7. session. 8. **das Bundeshaus** *the German Parliament.* 9. **die Lücke, -n** gap. 10. **günstig** favorable. 11. **der Idiot, -en** moron. 12. **der Greis, -e** old man. 13. **im großen (und) ganzen** on the whole.

Beantworten Sie die folgenden Fragen:

1. In welcher Stimmung war Kurt am letzten Tage in Deutschland? 2. Was war eigentlich nicht die Hauptursache seiner schlechten Laune? 3. Welche Ziele waren nicht erreicht worden? 4. Hatten sich gewisse Pläne als realistisch erwiesen? 5. Welche Frage stellt sich Kurt? 6. Würde er gerade so viel bummeln wie vorher? 7. Was hätte er öfter im Café tun sollen? 8. Auf welche Teile Deutschlands hatten sich seine Reisepläne beschränkt? 9. Wohin hätte er wenigstens einmal fahren sollen? 10. Was ist besonders schwer zu verstehen? 11. Weshalb ist Kurt nicht ganz mit seinem Studium zufrieden? 12. Die Werke welcher Dichter hat er nicht genug gelesen? 13. Was sagte Kurt vor sich hin, als er zu lachen anfing? 14. Hat Kurt immer klug gehandelt? Erklären Sie Ihre Antwort! 15. Hätte er so viel gelernt, wenn er zu Hause geblieben wäre? 16. Mit welchem Gedanken schlief Kurt ein?

V. WORTSCHATZ

die Abreise, -n	departure	schlimm	bad
an/betreffen, betraf an, anbetroffen	to concern	das Sprichwort, ⁝er	proverb
was . . . anbetrifft	as far as . . . is concerned	streng	strict
		das Studienbuch, ⁝er	course-record book
die Änderung, -en	change	die Trennung	separation
bei/wohnen + *dative*	to attend	verschieben, verschob, verschoben	to postpone
beweisen, bewies, bewiesen	to prove	vor/schlagen, schlug vor, vorgeschlagen, schlägt vor	to propose, suggest
bummeln	to loaf, waste time		
einzig	sole, only	der Vorteil, -e	advantage
entfernt	away, distant	aus etwas Vorteil ziehen	to benefit from something
erscheinen, erschien, ist erschienen	to appear	wahrhaftig	truly, certainly
		weiterhin	for the future, furthermore
sich erweisen, erwies, erwiesen	to turn out	ziehen, zog, gezogen	to draw, pull
das Geschenk, -e	present	das Ziel, -e	aim, goal, target
längst	by far	zufrieden	satisfied
der Millionär, -e	millionaire		
die Reihe, -n	row, turn		
Ich bin an der Reihe.	It's my turn.		

VI. ERKLÄRUNGEN UND ÜBUNGEN

1. Subjunctive

There are three moods in German as in English—the indicative, the imperative, and the subjunctive. The indicative states facts or describes situations or events; the imperative expresses commands. The subjunctive expresses doubtful or unreal situations, wishes, and desires.

a. Tenses

The indicative has six tenses, but the subjunctive makes only four time distinctions: present, past, future, and future perfect.[1]

b. Types

These four tenses are formed from the stems of the present and the simple past indicative. There are, therefore, two types of subjunctive, each with four tenses:

Subjunctive I (*based on the present*)
Subjunctive II (*based on the simple past*)

2. Subjunctive I
a. Present

sagen (sag-)	haben (hab-)	tragen (trag-)
ich sage	ich habe	ich trage
du sagest	du habest	du tragest
er sage	er habe	er trage
wir sagen	wir haben	wir tragen
ihr saget	ihr habet	ihr traget
sie sagen	sie haben	sie tragen
Sie sagen	Sie haben	Sie tragen

gehen (geh-)	können (könn-)	werden (werd-)
ich gehe	ich könne	ich werde
du gehest	du könnest	du werdest
er gehe	er könne	er werde
wir gehen	wir können	wir werden
ihr gehet	ihr könnet	ihr werdet
sie gehen	sie können	sie werden
Sie gehen	Sie können	Sie werden

Note sein: ich sei   wir seien
             du seiest   ihr seiet
             er sei   sie seien
                          Sie seien

All German verbs except **sein** form their present Subjunctive I by means of the present stem plus the endings **-e, -est, -e; -en, -et, -en.** For all verbs except the modals and **sein** there are no distinctive Subjunctive I forms for the 1st person singular and plural, 3rd person plural, or the conventional form of address. These forms are identical with the indicative forms.

1. The future perfect is even less frequently used in the subjunctive than in the indicative.

b. Past

ich **habe gesagt**	ich **sei gefahren**
du **habest gesagt**	du **seiest gefahren**
er **habe gesagt**	er **sei gefahren**
wir **haben gesagt**	wir **seien gefahren**
ihr **habet gesagt**	ihr **seiet gefahren**
sie **haben gesagt**	sie **seien gefahren**
Sie **haben gesagt**	Sie **seien gefahren**

The past Subjunctive I consists of the present Subjunctive I of **haben** or **sein** plus past participle.

c. Future

ich **werde sagen**	wir **werden sagen**
du **werdest sagen**	ihr **werdet sagen**
er **werde sagen**	sie **werden sagen**
	Sie **werden sagen**

The future Subjunctive I consists of the present Subjunctive I of **werden** plus infinitive.[1]

PRACTICE

Conjugate each of the following verbs in present and past Subjunctive I:

studieren, tragen, sein, kommen, bringen, haben, werden, müssen, machen, kennen, sterben, sehen, reisen.

3. Subjunctive II   Regular Weak Verbs:

a. Present

sagen: Past Stem **sagt-**

ich **sagte**	wir **sagten**
du **sagtest**	ihr **sagtet**
er **sagte**	sie **sagten**
	Sie **sagten**

Note that the present Subjunctive II of regular weak verbs is identical with their past indicative.

Strong and Very Irregular Verbs:

tragen (trüg-)	**gehen (ging-)**	**haben (hätt-)**	**sein (wär-)**
ich **trüge**	ich **ginge**	ich **hätte**	ich **wäre**
du **trügest**	du **gingest**	du **hättest**	du **wärest**
er **trüge**	er **ginge**	er **hätte**	er **wäre**
wir **trügen**	wir **gingen**	wir **hätten**	wir **wären**
ihr **trüget**	ihr **ginget**	ihr **hättet**	ihr **wäret**
sie **trügen**	sie **gingen**	sie **hätten**	sie **wären**
Sie **trügen**	Sie **gingen**	Sie **hätten**	Sie **wären**

1. The future perfect consists of the present Subjunctive I of **werden** plus perfect infinitive:

er werde gesagt haben etc.   **er werde gefahren sein** etc.

281

bringen (brächt-)	**wissen (wüßt-)**
ich **brächte**	ich **wüßte**
du **brächtest**	du **wüßtest**
er **brächte**	er **wüßte**
wir **brächten**	wir **wüßten**
ihr **brächtet**	ihr **wüßtet**
sie **brächten**	sie **wüßten**
Sie **brächten**	Sie **wüßten**

Strong and very irregular verbs form their present Subjunctive II by means of the past stem plus umlaut, if possible, and the personal endings **-e, -est, -e; -en, -et, -en**.[1]

The mixed verbs **brennen, kennen, nennen, rennen** (*to run*), **senden, wenden** (*to turn*) form their present Subjunctive II as if they were regular weak verbs. For example:

kennen (kennt-)

ich **kennte**	wir **kennten**
du **kenntest**	ihr **kenntet**
er **kennte**	sie **kennten**
	Sie **kennten**

Modals:

müssen (müßt-)   **sollen (sollt-)**

ich **müßte**	wir **müßten**	ich **sollte**	wir **sollten**
du **müßtest**	ihr **müßtet**	du **solltest**	ihr **solltet**
er **müßte**	sie **müßten**	er **sollte**	sie **sollten**
	Sie **müßten**		Sie **sollten**

The present Subjunctive II of the modals is formed in the same way as that of the strong and very irregular verbs except that **sollen** and **wollen** do not add umlaut.

b. Past

ich **hätte gesagt**	ich **wäre gegangen**
du **hättest gesagt**	du **wärest gegangen**
er **hätte gesagt**	er **wäre gegangen**
wir **hätten gesagt**	wir **wären gegangen**
ihr **hättet gesagt**	ihr **wäret gegangen**
sie **hätten gesagt**	sie **wären gegangen**
Sie **hätten gesagt**	Sie **wären gegangen**

The past Subjunctive II consists of the present Subjunctive II of **haben** or **sein** plus past participle.

1. The following strong verbs usually have irregular Subjunctive II forms: **helfen (hülf-), sterben (stürb-), werfen (würf-), stehen (stünd-).**

c. Future

ich **würde sagen**   wir **würden sagen**
du **würdest sagen**   ihr **würdet sagen**
er **würde sagen**   sie **würden sagen**
                     Sie **würden sagen**

The future of Subjunctive II (also known as present conditional) consists of the present Subjunctive II of **werden** plus present infinitive.[1]

PRACTICE

Conjugate each of the following verbs in the present and past Subjunctive II:

machen, fahren, denken, sein, spielen, können, haben, geben, brennen, singen, senden, sein, kommen, verstehen, einladen.

4. Conditional Sentences
a. Simple Conditions

Wenn es morgen regnet, gehen wir nicht.
If it rains tomorrow, we won't go.

Wenn Sie schnell fahren, können Sie bis Abend ankommen.
If you drive fast, you can arrive by evening.

Esse ich zu viel, so werde ich krank.
If I eat too much, (then) I'll get sick.

The examples above state a realizable condition upon which some action or result depends and will follow. The indicative expresses such real conditions.

Remember that **wenn** may be omitted in the if-clause, but the verb stands first and the main clause usually begins with **so** or **dann.**

b. Contrary-to-Fact Conditions

Wenn ich das Geld **hätte, ginge ich.**
If I had the money, I'd go.
(The fact is that I don't have the money, but if I did . . .)

In an unreal condition, the likelihood of fulfillment is more remote or does not exist at all, and the subjunctive is required. Other examples:

Wenn ich noch drei Tage **hätte, verabschiedete ich mich** von jedem.
If I had three more days, I'd say good-by to everybody.

Wenn ich noch drei Tage **gehabt hätte, hätte ich mich** von jedem **verabschiedet.**
If I had had three more days, I'd have said good-bye to everybody.

Where English requires a past tense or a subjunctive form in the

---

1. The future perfect of Subjunctive II (also known as the perfect conditional) consists of the present Subjunctive II of **werden** plus perfect infinitive:
   ich würde gesagt haben etc.   **ich würde gegangen sein** etc.

if-clause and the conditional mood in the main clause, German usually has Subjunctive II in both clauses.

Wenn ich noch drei Tage **hätte, würde ich mich** von jedem ver-abschieden.
If I had three more days, I'd say good-by to everybody.

The future Subjunctive II may be used in the main clause instead of the present Subjunctive II.[1] The future perfect Subjunctive II is generally avoided in the spoken language.

PRACTICE

A. *Combine the following sentence parts:*

Example: Wenn ich Zeit hätte, (*ins Kino gehen*).
Wenn ich Zeit hätte, ginge ich ins Kino.

Wenn ich Zeit hätte,

1. (mit ihm sprechen). 2. (sich verabschieden). 3. (Geschenke kaufen). 4. (dir den Gefallen tun). 5. (dich nach Amerika begleiten). 6. (auch manches anders tun). 7. (alles niederschreiben).

B. *Combine the sentence parts in A above:*

Example: Wenn ich Zeit gehabt hätte, (*ins Kino gehen*).
Wenn ich Zeit gehabt hätte, wäre ich ins Kino gegangen.

C. *Combine the sentence pairs in A and B above, omitting* **wenn:**

Example: Hätte ich Zeit, so ginge ich ins Kino.
Hätte ich Zeit gehabt, so wäre ich ins Kino gegangen.

D. *Form unreal conditional sentences from the following sentence pairs:*

Example: Ich muß nicht arbeiten. Ich kann mit dir fahren.
Wenn ich nicht arbeiten müßte, könnte ich mit dir fahren.

1. Ich habe noch drei Tage. Ich kann mich von allen verabschieden. 2. Ich habe mehr Zeit. Ich kann Geschenke kaufen. 3. Es ist in seiner Macht. Er gibt Kurt ein ganzes Jahr. 4. Lore kann nächsten Sommer nach Amerika kommen. Kurt freut sich. 5. Die Eltern sind nicht so streng. Lore darf Kurt in Amerika besuchen. 6. Das Wörtchen *wenn* besteht nicht. Mein Vater ist ein Millionär. 7. Ich vergesse mein Studienbuch. Ich habe Schwierigkeiten.

1. For auxiliaries and modals, the present Subjunctive II is preferred in conversation to **würde** plus infinitive in the conclusion.

E. Combine the sentence pairs in D above, omitting **wenn:**

Example: Ich muß nicht arbeiten. Ich kann mit dir fahren.
Müßte ich nicht arbeiten, so könnte ich mit dir fahren.

F. Say in German:

1. If Kurt had one more day, he'd say good-by to Mrs. Lenz. 2. He would also buy a present for his mother if he had more time. 3. Karl would do many things differently if Kurt would stay longer. 4. Lore would go to America if her parents were less strict. 5. If she were to go, it would certainly please Kurt. 6. If Kurt forgot his course book, it would be bad.

FINAL PRACTICE *Say first, then write in German:*

1. If it weren't so late, Kurt would be able to say good-by to his German friends. 2. He would also buy presents for his family in America. 3. Karl wants Kurt to stay another year. 4. If he didn't have to work, he would go with Kurt. 5. But Karl has already been to America. 6. Lore wants to go next summer. 7. If her father and mother were not so strict, she could visit Kurt. 8. She doesn't doubt that it would please him. 9. But the fact is that she will have to put off her trip. 10. Wasn't Karl supposed to remind Kurt of his course book? 11. Kurt got it back, but he truly would have forgotten it. 12. If he had forgotten it, it would have gone badly with him. 13. After all, the course book was very important to Kurt. 14. Without it he would not have been able to prove that he had studied in Cologne. 15. Karl would have called Kurt later if he hadn't met him. 16. He wouldn't have gone off without his book.

Abflug mit der Lufthansa
BOEING PHOTO

I. UNTERHALTUNG

DER LETZTE ABEND: EINE ÜBERRASCHUNG

Lore: Und warst du wirklich überrascht?
Kurt: Ihr habt es glänzend fertiggebracht. Dein Bruder lügt wie gedruckt.
Lore: Was hat er dir denn vorgemacht?
Kurt: Er sagte, ich solle zu euch kommen— ihr hättet ein paar Freunde eingeladen.
Karl: Und wir hätten Gesellschaft und der Abend wäre ziemlich formell.
Lore: Warum hast du denn das gesagt?
Karl: Damit er sich passend anziehen würde.
Kurt: Man muß sich vor Karl in acht nehmen. Er ist ein erfahrener Lügner.
Lore: Ich sollte mich eigentlich über ihn schämen.
Karl: Hast du auch gar nichts geahnt, als wir das Haus verließen?
Kurt: Er behauptete, die Gäste kämen erst um 10 Uhr. In der Zwischenzeit könnten wir einen Spaziergang machen.
Lore: Wir sind doch mit dem Wagen gefahren.
Kurt: Er meinte plötzlich, es wäre zu kalt für dich, Lore.

THE LAST NIGHT: A SURPRISE

Lore: And were you really surprised?
Kurt: You pulled it off splendidly. Your brother lies like a professional.
Lore: What ruse did he use anyhow?
Kurt: He said that I should come to your house—that you had invited a few friends.
Karl: And that we had a party and that the evening was pretty formal.
Lore: Why did you say that?
Karl: So that he would dress appropriately.
Kurt: You have to watch out for Karl. He's an experienced liar.
Lore: I should really be ashamed of him.
Karl: Didn't you suspect anything at all when we left the house?
Kurt: He claimed the guests weren't coming till 10. In the meantime, we could take a walk.
Lore: But we went by car.
Kurt: All of a sudden he thought it was too cold for you, Lore.

287

LESSON 20

Lore: Da liegt ihm gewöhnlich nichts dran.

Karl: Du mußt zugeben, es war eine schöne Ausrede.

Lore: Was hat dir denn am besten im Kabarett gefallen?

Kurt: Der politische Humor — wie man Zeitkritik treibt und alles lächerlich macht.

Karl: Vater sagt immer, der Mensch müsse über seine Schwächen lachen, sonst könne er das Leben nicht aushalten.

Kurt: Ich glaube, daß er recht hat. Auf jeden Fall bin ich sehr dankbar. Ich werde diesen Abend nie vergessen.

Lore: He usually doesn't care anything about that.

Karl: You have to admit it was a beautiful excuse.

Lore: Tell me, what did you like best in the cabaret?

Kurt: The political humor. How they poke fun at the times and make everything seem ludicrous.

Karl: Dad always says that man has to laugh at his weaknesses or else he couldn't stand life.

Kurt: I think he's right. In any case, I'm very grateful. I'll never forget this evening.

II. KOMBINATIONEN

Sagen Sie auf deutsch:

a. 1. You pulled it off splendidly. 2. We pulled it off very well. 3. How did you pull it off so well?

b. 1. He said I should come to your house. 2. He said I should be there at eight. 3. He said I should arrive on time.

c. 1. He said you had invited a few friends. 2. He said you were having a party. 3. He said the evening was pretty formal.

d. 1. I said it so that he would dress appropriately. 2. I said it so that he would not come late. 3. I said it so that he would be surprised.

e. 1. You have to watch out for Karl. 2. I have to be on my guard with your brother. 3. One has to be on his guard with an experienced liar.

f. 1. I really should be ashamed of him. 2. Lore should be ashamed of her brother. 3. We should be ashamed of a liar.

g. 1. Didn't you suspect anything when we left the house? 2. Didn't you suspect anything when he invited friends? 3. Didn't they suspect anything when he had a party?

h. 1. He said the guests weren't coming till 10. 2. He said that in the meantime we could take a walk. 3. He said in the meantime we could drink a cup of coffee.

i. 1. He doesn't usually care about that. 2. She doesn't usually care about that. 3. We don't usually care about that.

j. 1. You have to admit it was a beautiful excuse. 2. We have to admit he is a professional liar. 3. Don't you want to admit that it was a beautiful excuse?

k. 1. What did you like best about the cabaret? 2. What did he like best about the play? 3. What did he like least in the movie?

l. 1. Dad says man has to laugh at his weaknesses. 2. He also says man couldn't stand life otherwise. 3. I think that he is right as always.

m. 1. In any case, I'm very grateful. 2. In any case, we're all grateful. 3. In any case, you pulled it off very well.

III. SAGEN UND FRAGEN

a. *Sie sind Kurt und sagen zu Karl oder Lore:*

1. Sie haben alles glänzend fertiggebracht. 2. Karl lügt wie gedruckt. 3. Karl sagte, sie hätten Gesellschaft. 4. Sie müssen sich vor Karl in acht nehmen. 5. Sie wissen jetzt, daß er ein erfahrener Lügner ist. 6. Er sagte, in der Zwischenzeit könnten Sie spazierengehen. 7. Ihnen hat gefallen, wie man Zeitkritik treibt. 8. Sie fanden es amüsant, wie man alles lächerlich macht. 9. Sie glauben, Herr Lenz hat recht. 10. Sie sind auf jeden Fall sehr dankbar.

b. *Sie sind Lore und fragen Kurt oder Karl:*

1. was er ihm denn vorgemacht hat. 2. warum er so was gesagt hat. 3. was ihm am besten im Kabarett gefallen hat. 4. ob ihm auch der politische Humor gefallen hat. 5. ob der Mensch wirklich über seine Schwächen lachen kann.

IV. AUFSATZ

KURT FLIEGT NACH LONDON

„Guten Tag", sagte die Stewardeß im Lautsprecher des Flug-
zeuges. „Dies ist Lufthansa Flug Nr. 87 nach London. Bitte sofort anschnallen.[1] Und vergessen Sie nicht, daß das Rauchen
während des Starts[2] verboten ist."

5   Kurt hörte kaum auf die Stimme der Stewardeß. Er war so ans
Fliegen gewöhnt, daß diese mechanischen Ansagen[3] keinen Eindruck mehr auf ihn machten. Auch war er in Gedanken vertieft.
Er dachte an den rührenden Abschied von Frau Kolb, deren
kleine Aufmerksamkeiten[4] er nie vergessen würde. Später hatte er
10 nochmal mit Herrn und Frau Lenz telefoniert, um sich für die
vielen Gefälligkeiten[5] zu bedanken. Dann hatten Karl und Lore
ihn abgeholt und zum Flughafen gefahren. Karl entschuldigte
sich bald, da er noch etwas erledigen müsse. Es war ganz klar,
daß er Kurt und Lore Gelegenheit geben wollte, noch einmal pri-
15 vat miteinander zu sprechen. Als Kurt jetzt im Flugzeug saß,
machte er auch Pläne für seinen fünftägigen[6] Aufenthalt in London, wo er sich mit mehreren Verwandten und Freunden treffen
sollte. Aber seine Gedanken kamen immer wieder auf dasselbe
Thema zurück — auf den Brief, den er heute morgen noch bei
20 Frau Kolb erhalten hatte. Er enthielt die Antwort seiner Eltern auf
seine Ankündigung,[7] daß er sich noch vor seiner Abfahrt mit Lore
Lenz verloben würde.

    Der Vater schrieb, Kurt wisse bestimmt, wie hoch er Lore
schätze. Jedoch sei er besorgt. Habe Kurt sich alles gründlich
25 überlegt? Sei er sicher, daß er eine gute Wahl getroffen habe?
Könne er fest behaupten, schrieb seine Mutter, daß er sich nicht
zu schnell in ein schönes Mädchen verliebt habe? Vor allen Dingen[8] — sei Kurt fähig, sich an eine nichtamerikanische Familie
zu gewöhnen? Sich zu verständigen sei ja kein Problem für ihn,
30 aber könne er sich auch gut mit ihnen verstehen?

    Kurt lächelte im Stillen. Sofort nach seiner Ankunft in London
würde er sich hinsetzen und einen Brief an die Eltern schreiben,
um sie zu beruhigen. Lore und er hatten sich sowieso entschlos-

---

1. **anschnallen** to fasten (your seatbelts). 2. **der Start** *here:* take-off.
3. **die Ansage, -n** announcement. 4. **die Aufmerksamkeit, -en** attention.
5. **die Gefälligkeit, -en** favor. 6. **five-day.** 7. announcement. 8. **vor
allen Dingen** above all.

35 sen, ihre Verlobungspläne[9] aufzuschieben. In Gedanken verfaßte
er seinen Brief:[10]

Liebe Eltern!

Bitte macht Euch keinerlei Sorgen um mich! Ich kann
Euch die feste Versicherung geben, daß sowohl Lore als auch
ich uns jeden Schritt genau überlegt haben. Obwohl wir
40 unsere Pläne geändert haben, lieben wir uns immer noch und
verstehen uns bestens. Mit ihren Eltern haben wir uns auch
verständigt. Ich habe oft das Gefühl, daß wir uns viel länger
kennen als ein Jahr. Gestern sagte Lore, daß fast kein Unterschied in unserer Lebensanschauung[11] bestehe.

45 Auch braucht Ihr Euch keine Sorgen darüber zu machen,
daß sie Deutsche ist und ich Amerikaner bin. Seit 1945
hatten Deutsche und Amerikaner viel Gelegenheit, einander
kennenzulernen und zu schätzen. Meine Professoren sind
auch der Meinung, daß viele der alten Vorurteile[12] am Ver-
50 schwinden seien.[13] Man hört immer weniger von Deutschen,
daß Amerikaner materialistisch seien; auch behaupten heute
wenige Amerikaner, daß Deutsche nur Sinn für Militär und
Krieg haben. Natürlich weiß man, daß kulturelle Unterschiede weiterhin bestehen werden, aber es sind Unterschiede,
55 die das Leben bereichern[14] und daher zu begrüßen sind.

Also, liebe Eltern, beruhigt Euch und glaubt mir, daß wir
vernünftig sind und ohne Hast handeln.[15] In acht Tagen hoffe
ich, Euch persönlich alles zu erklären. Bis dahin herzliche
Grüße und Küsse,

60 Euer Sohn
Kurt

Kurt dachte, daß er noch heute den Brief abschicken könnte,
und daß die Eltern ihn schon übermorgen erhalten würden. Sie
werden glücklicher sein, sagte er vor sich hin, wenn sie bald von
65 mir hören. Den Rest kann ich ihnen ja später sagen.

Schon hörte er wieder die Stimme der Stewardeß: ,,Bitte anschnallen! In fünf Minuten landen wir in London. Wir hoffen,
daß Sie einen angenehmen Flug hatten und daß wir Sie bald
wiedersehen werden.''

9. engagement plans. 10. **einen Brief verfassen** to compose a letter.
11. conception of life. 12. **das Vorurteil, -e** prejudice. 13. **am Verschwinden sein** to be in the process of disappearing. 14. **bereichern** to
enrich. 15. **ohne Hast handeln** to act without haste.

Beantworten Sie die folgenden Fragen:

1. Was sagte die Stewardeß? 2. Weshalb machte die Ansage keinen Eindruck auf Kurt? 3. Woran dachte er? 4. Wer hat ihn an den Flughafen gebracht? 5. Warum hat sich Karl bald entschuldigt? 6. Wird Kurt direkt nach Amerika fliegen? 7. Worauf kamen Kurts Gedanken immer wieder zurück? 8. Wen schätzt der Vater sehr hoch? 9. Worüber war er besorgt? 10. Was fragt die Mutter? 11. Kann Kurt sich mit einer nichtamerikanischen Familie verstehen? 12. Wie will Kurt die Eltern beruhigen? 13. Worüber sollen sich die Eltern keinerlei Sorgen machen? 14. Haben Kurt und Lore viel über diesen Schritt nachgedacht? 15. Welches Gefühl hat Kurt oft? 16. Welche Gelegenheit haben Deutsche und Amerikaner seit 1945? 17. Welche Vorurteile sind am Verschwinden? 18. Was schreibt Kurt über die kulturellen Unterschiede, die weiterhin bestehen werden? 19. Wann wird Kurt den Eltern die Lage persönlich erklären? 20. Wann werden die Eltern den Brief erhalten? 21. Welche Wirkung (*effect*) soll der Brief haben?

V. WORTSCHATZ

der **Abschied**	parting, farewell	**fertig/**	to pull off, man-
ahnen	to suspect, have a presentiment of	**bringen,** **brachte fer-** **tig, fertig-**	age
amüsant	amusing	**gebracht**	
auf/schieben,	to postpone	**fest**	firm
schob auf,		der **Flug, ⸚e**	flight
aufgescho-		der **Flughafen, ⸚**	airport
ben		das **Flugzeug, -e**	airplane
aus/halten,	to stand, endure	**formell**	formal
hielt aus,		der **Gruß, ⸚e**	greeting
ausgehal-		**gründlich**	thorough
ten, hält		**herzlich**	cordial
aus		sich **hin/setzen**	to sit down
die **Ausrede, -n**	excuse	das **Kabarett, -e**	cabaret
sich **bedanken**	to thank, return thanks	**keinerlei**	no . . . at all
		der **Kuß, Küsse**	kiss
begrüßen	to greet, welcome	der **Lautspre-**	loudspeaker
beruhigen	to reassure, pac- ify, calm (down)	**cher, -**	
		liegen	to matter
		dran liegen	
besorgt	worried, con- cerned	**lügen**	to lie
		der **Lügner, -**	liar
bestens	very well	**nehmen**	to take
dankbar	grateful	**in acht**	to watch out for,
erfahren	experienced	**nehmen**	be on one's
fähig	capable		guard

passend	suitable	**sich verlieben in**	to fall in love
schätzen	to esteem, appreciate	*+ accusative*	
der Schritt, -e	step	**vernünftig**	reasonable
die Schwäche, -n	weakness	**die Versicherung**	assurance, insurance
der Sinn, -e	mind, intellect, sense	**sich verständigen**	to communicate
sowohl ...	... as well as	**sich verstehen mit**	to get along with
als auch		**der Verwandte,**	relative
der Spaziergang,	walk	**-n, -n**	
⁝e		**vor/machen:**	to put something
einen Spaziergang machen	to take a walk	**einem etwas vor/ machen**	over on somebody, take someone in
der Tag	day	**die Wahl**	choice
in acht Tagen	in a week	**eine Wahl treffen**	to make a choice
verbieten, verbot, verboten	to forbid, prohibit	**treiben:**	
		Zeitkritik treiben	to poke fun at the times

VI. ERKLÄRUNGEN UND ÜBUNGEN

1. Indirect Discourse

a. Present

Direct Statement: „Ich sehe den Mann."

"I see the man."

Indirect Statement: Er sagte, { er sehe den Mann.
                                { er sähe den Mann.

He said he saw (sees) the man.

Direct Question: „Ist der Mann da?"

"Is the man there?"

Indirect Question: Er fragte, { ob der Mann da sei.
                               { ob der Mann da wäre.

He asked whether the man was there.

b. Past

Direct Statement: „Ich habe den Mann gesehen."

"I saw the man."

Indirect Statement: Er sagte, { er habe den Mann gesehen.
                               { er hätte den Mann gesehen.

He said he had seen (saw) the man.

c. Future

Direct Statement: „Ich werde den Mann sehen."

"I shall see the man."

Indirect Statement: Er sagte, { er werde den Mann sehen.
                               { er würde den Mann sehen.

He said he would see the man.

A statement or a question which is not quoted directly but is reported or paraphrased by another person is called indirect discourse.

Indirect discourse occurs in dependent clauses after verbs of thinking, hoping, believing, saying, writing, asserting, asking, etc. English uses a "sequence of tenses" in indirect discourse. German uses subjunctive forms to indicate that the reported information is uncertain.

2. Tense and Mood Sequence
a. Indirect Statement

Er sagte, sie kämen erst um 10 Uhr.
Derived from direct statement: „Sie kommen erst um 10 Uhr."

Note that the indirect statement uses the same tense—in this instance, the present tense of Subjunctive II—as the direct statement. In the absence of a distinctive Subjunctive I form, a Subjunctive II form is preferred.

Er sagte, er habe (hätte) den Mann gesehen.
Derived from: „Ich habe den Mann gesehen."

Where both subjunctive forms are distinctive, either may be used, though Subjunctive II forms are more prevalent in speech.[1]

b. Introductory Statement

Use the indicative rather than the subjunctive in indirect discourse if:

a) the introductory verb is in the first person:

Ich sagte, daß Kurt noch zu jung ist.
I said that Kurt is still too young.

b) the introductory verb expresses certainty:

Er wußte, daß der Mann da war.[2]
He knew that the man was there.

Note: When the introductory verb is in the present tense, there is a tendency for the indirect statement to be in the indicative:

Er sagt, er sieht den Mann.
He says he sees the man.

1. To a large extent, the use of Subjunctive I or II is a regional matter. To a speaker from southern Germany, there exists a subtle difference in meaning.
2. In indirect discourse using the indicative, a daß-clause is usually preferred.

PRACTICE

A. *Change from direct to indirect discourse by introducing each sentence with* **Er sagte,** *using Subjunctive I:*

Example: „Ich fahre nach Hause."
Er sagte, er fahre nach Hause.

1. „Ich habe es glänzend fertiggebracht." 2. „Karl lügt wie gedruckt." 3. „Man muß sich vor Karl in acht nehmen." 4. „Karl ist ein erfahrener Lügner." 5. „Der politische Humor hat mir am besten gefallen." 6. „Ich bin sehr dankbar." 7. „Ich werde diesen Abend nie vergessen." 8. „Ich habe kein Geld mehr." 9. „Es ist ein Glück, daß ich heimfahre." 10. „Das Wetter wird morgen bestimmt schön sein."

B. *Change the sentences in A above from direct to indirect discourse by introducing each sentence with* **Er sagte,** *using Subjunctive II:*

Example: „Ich fahre nach Hause."
Er sagte, er führe nach Hause.

C. *Change the sentences in A above, introducing the indirect statement with* **daß:**

Example: Er sagte, daß er nach Hause fahre.

D. *Change from direct to indirect discourse by introducing each sentence with* **Der Vater schrieb,** *using Subjunctive I:*

Example: „Ich schätze Lore sehr."
Der Vater schrieb, er schätze Lore sehr.

1. „Du weißt bestimmt, wie hoch ich Lore Lenz schätze." 2. „Ich bin aber etwas besorgt." 3. „Ich hoffe, Du hast Dir alles gründlich überlegt." 4. „Ich hoffe auch, daß Du eine gute Wahl getroffen hast." 5. „Mutter wird auch mal schreiben." 6. „Ich freue mich auf Deine Heimkehr." 7. „Ich kann kaum warten." 8. „Die ganze Familie kommt zum Flughafen."

E. *Change the sentences in D above from direct to indirect discourse by introducing each sentence with* **Der Vater schrieb,** *using Subjunctive II:*

Example: „Ich schätze Lore sehr."
Der Vater schrieb, er schätzte Lore sehr.

F. *Change to indirect questions by preceding each sentence with* **Die Mutter hat gefragt,** *using Subjunctive I:*

Example: „Kannst Du das wirklich behaupten, Kurt?"
Die Mutter hat gefragt, ob Kurt das wirklich behaupten könne.

1. „Hast Du Dich nicht zu schnell in das Mädchen verliebt?" 2. „Bist Du sicher, daß Du keinen Fehler machst?" 3. „Kannst Du Dich mit einer deutschen Familie verstehen?" 4. „Schreibst Du bald, Kurt?" 5. „Machst Du Dir keinerlei Sorgen?" 6. „Haben Deutsche und Amerikaner jetzt wirklich mehr Gelegenheit, einander kennenzulernen?" 7. „Gibt es noch viele kulturelle Unterschiede?"

G. *Change the sentences in F above to indirect questions by preceding each sentence with* **Die Mutter hat gefragt,** *using Subjunctive II:*

Example: „Kannst Du das wirklich behaupten, Kurt?"
Die Mutter hat gefragt, ob Kurt das wirklich behaupten könnte.

H. *Say in German:*

1. Kurt said he had received a letter yesterday. 2. He said it was from his parents. 3. They hoped he had thoroughly considered everything. 4. He answered that he had forgotten nothing. 5. He had told me he wanted to reassure his parents right away. 6. He wrote them that he'd come to an understanding with Lore's family.

3. Indirect Commands

Direct Command: **Karl sagte zu Kurt: „Komme zu uns!"**
Karl said to Kurt: "Come to our house."

Indirect Command: **Karl sagte zu Kurt,** $\left\{ \begin{array}{l} \textbf{er solle zu ihnen kommen.} \\ \textbf{er sollte zu ihnen kommen.} \end{array} \right.$

Karl told Kurt to come to their house.

Use present Subjunctive I or II of **sollen** to express an indirect command.

PRACTICE

A. *Change the following sentences to indirect commands, using Subjunctive I:*

Example: Sie sagte zu mir: „Machen Sie einen Spaziergang!"
Sie sagte mir, ich solle einen Spaziergang machen.

1. Er sagte zu mir: „Besuche uns doch heute abend!" 2. Ich sagte zu ihm: „Komme heute abend zu mir!" 3. Kurt sagte zu ihr: „Nimm dich in acht vor Karl!" 4. Lore sagte zu Kurt: „Komme bald zurück!" 5. Karl sagte zu ihm: „Bleibe nicht zu lange weg!" 6. Beide sagten zu Kurt: „Schreibe oft und bald!"

B. *Change the sentences in A above to indirect commands, using Subjunctive II:*

Example: Sie sagte: ,,Machen Sie einen Spaziergang!"
Sie sagte, ich sollte einen Spaziergang machen.

C. *Change the sentences in A above, introducing the indirect statement with* **daß:**

Example: Sie sagte mir, daß ich einen Spaziergang machen solle.

4. als ob; als wenn; als

Er spricht, als ob er viel Zeit hätte.
He talks as if he had a lot of time.

Er handelt, als wenn er nichts gewußt hätte.
He acts as if he hadn't known anything.

Er sprach, als wäre er ein alter Mann.
He spoke as if he were an old man.

Er handelte, als ob er nicht fort gewesen wäre.
He acted as though he hadn't been away.

Following **als ob** and **als wenn** either Subjunctive I or II must be used. Subjunctive II is much more frequent. If **ob** or **wenn** is omitted, the finite verb follows **als** directly.

PRACTICE

A. *Combine the following sentences with* **als ob:**

Example: Er sieht aus. Er ist krank.
Er sieht aus, als ob er krank wäre.

1. Er sieht aus. Er ist froh.   2. Er spricht. Er hat große Sorgen. 3. Er spricht. Er hat viel gesehen.   4. Er handelt. Er hat viel gelitten.   5. Er spricht. Er hat sich verliebt.

B. *Combine the sentences in A above with* **als:**

Example: Er sieht aus. Er ist krank.
Er sieht aus, als wäre er krank.

C. *Say in German:*

1. He talks as though he were rich.   2. He acts as though he had never heard of this.   3. He looks as though he had passed his exam.   4. He speaks as if he'd been to Berlin.   5. She looked as though she wanted to go.

5. Other Uses of the Subjunctive

a. Wishes

Gott segne uns alle!
May God bless us all!

Es lebe der Präsident!
Long live the President!

Wenn Lore nur hier gewesen wäre!
If Lore had only been here!

If the wish is likely to be fulfilled, then Subjunctive I is used, otherwise Subjunctive II.

b. Polite Phrases

Dürfte ich um Auskunft bitten?
Could I ask for some information?

Ich hätte noch eine Bitte an Sie.
I have one more favor to ask of you.

Würden Sie (bitte) **so gut sein** und mir die Adresse geben?
Would you (please) be good enough to give me the address?

Könnten Sie mir sagen, we er wohnt?
Could you (would you be able to) tell me where he lives?

Ich möchte noch einen Moment mit ihm **sprechen.**
I would like to talk to him for one moment longer.

The subjunctive is used in some common idiomatic phrases of politeness.

c. Expressions of Possibility

Das wäre möglich.
That might be possible.

Das hätte passieren können.
That might have happened.

Das dürfte nicht der Fall **sein.**
That should not be the case.

Subjunctive II forms are often used to express possibility.

PRACTICE

A. *Say in German:*

1. If only he were here! 2. If only he had been here! 3. If only she believed this! 4. If only she had believed this! 5. If only I had gotten up earlier! 6. If only I were less tired! 7. If only this were easier! 8. God bless you! 9. If only you were right! 10. If only she had gone home!

B. *Form polite phrases from the following imperative sentences, using* **würden** *plus infinitive:*

Example: Zeigen Sie mir bitte den Weg!
Würden Sie mir bitte den Weg zeigen?

1. Gehen Sie bitte mit ihr!   2. Nein, bleiben Sie bei ihr!
3. Schicken Sie bitte Frau Lenz ein Geschenk!   4. Senden Sie bitte dieses Paket nach Amerika!   5. Erzählen Sie bitte dem Vater alles!   6. Überlegen Sie sich das bitte noch einmal!

C. *Form polite phrases from the sentences in B above, using* **wären** *plus infinitive phrase:*

Example: Zeigen Sie mir bitte den Weg!
Wären Sie so gut, mir den Weg zu zeigen?

D. *Form additional polite phrases from the sentences below, using* **dürfte** *plus infinitive:*

Example: Ich bitte um ein Glas Milch.
Dürfte ich um ein Glas Milch bitten?

Ich bitte um
1. eine Tasse Kaffee.   2. ein Päckchen Zigaretten.   3. eine Briefmarke.   4. ein Stück Schreibpapier.   5. einen Bleistift.

E. *Form polite phrases from the sentences in D above, using* **hätten** *plus* **vielleicht:**

Example: Haben Sie ein Glas Milch?
Hätten Sie vielleicht ein Glas Milch?

F. *Say in German:*

1. Would you please be good enough to ask him when he is coming back?   2. I would like to chat with him for a few minutes.
3. Yes, that might be possible.   4. I have one more favor to ask of you.   5. Could you tell me where he lives?

FINAL PRACTICE   *Say first, then write in German:*

1. Lore asked if the surprise had succeeded.   2. Kurt answered that they had brought it off brilliantly.   3. He added that Lore's brother lied like a professional.   4. Lore wanted to know what Karl had put over on Kurt.   5. Karl had told Kurt he should come

over to their house.   6. They had invited a few friends.   7. Karl also said the evening would be rather formal.   8. Lore asked why he had said that.   9. Karl said he had told Kurt to dress suitably. 10. Kurt thinks you have to watch out for Karl.   11. Kurt maintained he suspected nothing when they left the house.   12. Karl suggested that they take a walk.   13. "But we went in the car," said Lore.   14. Karl said it would be too cold for Lore.   15. "If he only worried about me like that always," thought Lore.   16. They all went to a cabaret.   17. Kurt said he enjoyed the political humor best of all.   18. Mr. Lenz says people have to laugh at their weaknesses.   19. Kurt thought he was right.   20. He said he'd never forget this evening.

1. ORAL PRACTICE

A. LEARN THIS DIALOGUE:

Kurt: Hättest du Lust, dir die Dreigroschenoper anzusehen?
Lore: Ich habe das Stück schon einmal gesehen.
Kurt: Hat es dir damals gefallen?
Lore: So gut, daß ich es gerne wieder sehen würde.
Kurt: Es wird morgen abend im Odeon gespielt. Ich bestelle Karten.
Lore: Übrigens, was hältst du von der Musik?
Kurt: Zuerst klingt sie fremd. Man muß sich langsam daran gewöhnen.
Lore: Danach vergißt man sie aber nie.
Kurt: Ich werde das Lied am Anfang nie vergessen.
Lore: Du meinst wohl Mackey Messer.
Kurt: Bei uns wird es „Mack the Knife" genannt.
Lore: Kommt dir das nicht komisch vor?
Kurt: Was komisch ist, ist Ansichtssache (*matter of opinion*).
Lore: Ja, da hast du wohl recht.

B. COMPLETE THE SENTENCES:

Herr Lenz: Ich habe mich sehr über den Brief von Ihrem Vater
_____ .

Kurt: Mir hat er noch nicht _____ . Wann hat er den Brief _____ ?

Herr Lenz: Lassen Sie mich mal _____ ! Am 7. März. Er hat keine Zeit _____ . Übrigens, wie viele Reisen hat Ihr Vater schon _____ ?

Kurt: Das Reisen ist ihm nichts _____ . Er findet es _____ aber interessant.

Herr Lenz: Wie lange war Ihr Vater hier _____ Soldat?

Kurt: Zweieinhalb Jahre. Sie sollten _____ aus seiner _____ sehen. Er war damals sehr dünn.

Herr Lenz: Er ist heute noch nicht _____ .

Kurt: Er _____ heute aber 210 Pfund.

Herr Lenz: Für seine Größe ist das nicht zu _____ . Wissen Sie, Ihr Vater spricht perfekt Deutsch, _____ und _____ .

Kurt: Er hat es als Kind im _____ gehört und
auch in der _____ gesprochen.

Herr Lenz: Wie lange sind Ihre Eltern schon _____?

Kurt: Annähernd 25 Jahre. Sie _____ im Juni ihre
_____ Hochzeit. Das heißt, ich muß _____,
damit ich ihnen etwas _____ kaufen kann.

C. *COMPLETE APPROPRIATE RESPONSES BY KURT:*

Karl: Wann hast du denn diese Grippe bekommen?

Kurt: Gestern _____. Dann _____.

Karl: Hast du auch erhöhte Temperatur?

Kurt: Der Arzt _____. Ich hatte _____.

Karl: Wie lange mußt du im Bett bleiben?

Kurt: _____. Dann soll ich _____.

Karl: Was hat der Arzt dir verschrieben?

Kurt: Ich habe _____. Sie müssen _____
_____ werden.

Karl: Ich komme sofort hinüber. Ich möchte nach dir sehen.

Kurt: Bitte _____! Wahrscheinlich _____.

Karl: Vergiß nicht, die ganze Familie steht dir zur Verfügung!

D. *EXPRESS THE FOLLOWING IDEAS IN GERMAN:*

Kurt: It's a shame. If only I had more time.

Karl: And what would you do if you had more time?

Kurt: I'd be able to say good-by to my friends. I could buy presents for my parents and sister.

Karl: If it were in my power, I'd give you a whole year. You need time, and I need money.

Kurt: How would you spend it if you had it?

Lore: He'd go to America again. He always talks about it. I wouldn't let him go. Now it's my turn!

Karl: You're lucky that your sister is so much younger than you. I'm sure you don't quarrel as much!

2. STRUCTURAL PRACTICE

A. *CONNECT THE FOLLOWING SENTENCES BY AN*
   APPROPRIATE RELATIVE PRONOUN:

1. Es war ein schöner Tag. Kurt wird ihn nie vergessen.
2. Das ist ein Thema. Keiner will es anschneiden.
3. Die Lorelei ist ein Lied. Jeder war davon begeistert.
4. Ich muß jetzt etwas sagen. Keiner will es hören.
5. Hier ist das Mädchen. Karl liebt es.
6. Mackey war ein Verbrecher. Man fürchtete sich vor ihm.
7. Er hat alles gestohlen. Er wollte es.
8. Er erklärte etwas. Niemand verstand es.
9. Es ist schöne Musik. Man muß sich daran gewöhnen.
10. Kennen Sie das Gedicht? Er spricht viel darüber.

B. *FILL IN THE BLANKS WITH APPROPRIATE RELATIVE*
   PRONOUNS:

1. Das Dorf, aus _____ Frau Kolb kommt, liegt in Norddeutsch-
land. 2. Da gibt es mehrere Leute, _____ selten das Dorf verlassen haben. 3. Herr Klein, _____ Bekanntschaft Sie gemacht
haben, ist noch jung. 4. Die Firma, für _____ er arbeitet, ist
sehr bekannt. 5. Sie haben auch eine Bonner Filiale, in _____
Herr Klein einige Tage verbracht hat. 6. Ich weiß alles, _____
mit seiner Arbeit zu tun hat. 7. _____das nicht glaubt, soll sich
schämen. 8. _____ sie sagt, stimmt nicht.

C. *RESTATE THE FOLLOWING SENTENCES IN THE PASSIVE:*

1. Man holt meinen Freund bald ab. 2. Man bringt ihn gleich
zu uns. 3. Wir empfangen ihn sofort. 4. Mein Vater lädt ihn
zu einem Musikfestspiel ein. 5. Wissen Sie, was man spielt?
6. Voriges Jahr hat man moderne Stücke aufgeführt. 7. Man
soll heute abend das Programm ansagen. 8. Es ist ihm nicht
wohl. Der Arzt wird ihn untersuchen. 9. Man muß zwei Rezepte
zur Apotheke bringen. 10. Frau Kolb hat die Arznei besorgt.

D. *RESTATE THE FOLLOWING SENTENCES AVOIDING THE PASSIVE:*

1. Die Prüfung ist vor mehreren Tagen angesagt worden. 2. Was geprüft werden wird, ist nicht gesagt worden. 3. Kurt ist von seiner Freundin kritisiert worden. 4. Die Arbeit muß bis sechs Uhr fertiggemacht werden. 5. Das kann nicht so schnell getan werden. 6. Er ist nicht mehr nervös; er ist durch die Arznei beruhigt worden. 7. Heute abend soll er vom Arzt untersucht werden. 8. Das Fieber wurde sofort gemessen.

E. *FORM CONTRARY-TO-FACT CONDITIONS FROM THE FOLLOWING SENTENCE PAIRS:*

1. Ich weiß es. Ich sage es dir.
2. Er ist hier. Er hilft mir.
3. Er ist sicher. Er macht den Vorschlag.
4. Es gibt diesen Unterschied nicht. Ich bin froh.
5. Es ist nicht schwer. Ich kann mich daran gewöhnen.
6. Wir bleiben bis morgen. Wir können uns den Film ansehen.
7. Ich habe mit ihm gesprochen. Ich habe alles verstanden.
8. Er hat mir die Wahrheit gesagt. Das ist nicht passiert.
9. Ich habe ihn eine Zeitlang gekannt. Wir haben uns geduzt.
10. Er hat es nicht richtig verstanden. Er hat nicht gelacht.
11. Sie lesen diesen Roman. Er gefällt Ihnen bestimmt.
12. Er hat uns nicht gefallen. Ich habe es Ihnen gesagt.

F. *CHANGE TO INDIRECT DISCOURSE:*

1. Er sagte: „Das Wetter ist sehr schön". 2. Er meinte: „Es ist gestern schlecht gewesen". 3. Er sagte: „Ich habe Lust, einen Spaziergang zu machen". 4. Er sagte auch: „Ich muß an meine Eltern schreiben". 5. Er schrieb: „Ich habe mich über Euren Brief gefreut". 6. Er schrieb weiter: „Ich habe mir ein schönes Bühnenstück angesehen". 7. Er berichtete: „Meine Freunde haben mich überrascht". 8. Er schrieb: „Mein Freund Karl lügt wie gedruckt". 9. Er meinte: „Man kann ihm nicht mehr trauen". 10. Er schrieb: „Ich muß mich morgen von der Familie Lenz verabschieden". 11. Er sagte auch: „Es wird mir leid tun". 12. Er fügte hinzu: „Ich habe nie so eine nette Familie gekannt".

G. *WRITE IN GERMAN:*

1. Karl, who wanted to surprise Kurt, said that he had invited a few friends. 2. He said it so that Kurt would be appropriately dressed for the cabaret. 3. He also told him he should come between 9:15 and 9:30 and that the guests would arrive half an hour later. 4. If only Kurt noticed nothing! 5. Karl acted as though they had a lot of time and could take a walk. 6. All of a sudden, he thought it was too cold for Lore. 7. He felt they should take a cab. 8. It would only cost DM 5.50, which was not very expensive. 9. Kurt suspected nothing when they left in the cab. 10. Kurt enjoyed the political humor, which was new to him. 11. Everything was criticized; everybody laughed; no one was insulted. 12. There was much smoking and drinking, and the band played several American hits. 13. If Kurt hadn't had to get up so early, they could have stayed longer. 14. It was an evening he would never forget. 15. He would always be grateful to this family, which had been so kind to him.

APPENDIX 1

1. Punctuation   *The salient features of German punctuation include:*

The use of the comma:

a. to set off all dependent clauses:

Ich weiß, **daß sie kommen wird.**
Das Mädchen, **das an der Ecke steht,** heißt Lore Lenz.
Er sagte, **er kenne sie nicht.**

b. to set off independent clauses introduced by **denn, aber,** and **sondern:**

Er kannte mich, **aber ich kannte ihn nicht.**

c. to set off infinitive phrases:

Er versuchte, **seinen Eltern einen langen Brief zu schreiben.**
Es ist schwer, **ihn zu verstehen.**

d. to denote decimals where English uses a period:

3,75 (read: *drei Komma fünfundsiebzig*)

The omission of the comma:

a. after parenthetical elements, such as adverbs or adverbial phrases:

Selbstverständlich kann er nicht gehen.
Of course, he can't go.

Er wollte natürlich gehen.
Naturally, he wanted to go.

Vor allen Dingen wollte er nach Deutschland fahren.
Above all, he wanted to go to Germany.

b. before **und** or **oder** in a series:

Er studiert **Philosophie, Deutsch und Geographie.**
He's studying philosophy, German, and geography.

Soll ich **Karl, Lore oder Kurt einladen?**
Shall I invite Karl, Lore, or Kurt?

The use of the exclamation point:

after imperatives: **Nehmen Sie Platz! Gehen wir!**

The use of the period:

to designate an ordinal numeral: der 2. Juli (*der zweite Juli*)

2. Capitalization

Like English, the first word of each sentence and all proper names are capitalized. In addition, all nouns and all forms of the pronoun **Sie** are capitalized. In letters, the familiar forms of the second person (**Du**) are also capitalized.

3. Syllabification

When a word is divided into syllables:

a. a single consonant between vowels belongs to the vowel that follows it:
re-den, kau-fen, kei-ner, Bru-der

b. only the second of two consonants is carried over:
Her-ren, klin-gen, sit-zen, gefal-len

c. ck is divided as **k-k**:
Rücken, Rük-ken

d. ch, ph, sch, st, ß behave as single consonants:
lä-cheln, Philoso-phie, Fi-sche, Mu-ster, Stra-ße

4. Summary of Verb Endings

	Singular	Plural
1.	**-e**, no ending	**-en**
2.	**-(e)st**	**-(e)t**
3.	**-(e)t, -e**, no ending	**-en**
		-en (**Sie** form)

The above endings are used on present and past stems to form all tenses and moods of all German verbs except **haben, sein, werden.**

5. Conjugation of haben

Principal Parts: **haben, hatte, gehabt, hat**

Indicative	*Subjunctive I*	*Subjunctive II*
	Present	
ich habe	ich habe	ich hätte
du hast	du habest	du hättest
er hat	er habe	er hätte
wir haben	wir haben	wir hätten
ihr habt	ihr habet	ihr hättet
sie haben	sie haben	sie hätten

Simple Past

ich hatte
du hattest
er hatte
wir hatten
ihr hattet
sie hatten

Compound Past

ich habe gehabt	ich habe gehabt	ich hätte gehabt
du hast gehabt	du habest gehabt	du hättest gehabt
er hat gehabt	er habe gehabt	er hätte gehabt
wir haben gehabt	wir haben gehabt	wir hätten gehabt
ihr habt gehabt	ihr habet gehabt	ihr hättet gehabt
sie haben gehabt	sie haben gehabt	sie hätten gehabt

Past Perfect

ich hatte gehabt
du hattest gehabt
er hatte gehabt
wir hatten gehabt
ihr hattet gehabt
sie hatten gehabt

Future

ich werde haben	ich werde haben	ich würde haben
du wirst haben	du werdest haben	du würdest haben
er wird haben	er werde haben	er würde haben
wir werden haben	wir werden haben	wir würden haben
ihr werdet haben	ihr werdet haben	ihr würdet haben
sie werden haben	sie werden haben	sie würden haben

Future Perfect

ich werde gehabt haben	ich werde gehabt haben	ich würde gehabt haben
du wirst gehabt haben etc.	du werdest gehabt haben etc.	du würdest ge-habt haben etc.

Imperative

Conventional:	haben Sie!
First Person Pl.:	haben wir!
Familiar Sing.:	hab(e)!
Familiar Pl.:	habt!

6. Conjugation of <u>sein</u>

Principal Parts: **sein, war, ist gewesen, ist**

Indicative	*Subjunctive I*	*Subjunctive II*

Present

ich bin	ich sei	ich wäre
du bist	du sei(e)st	du wärest
er ist	er sei	er wäre
wir sind	wir seien	wir wären
ihr seid	ihr seiet	ihr wäret
sie sind	sie seien	sie wären

Simple Past

ich war
du warst
er war
wir waren
ihr wart
sie waren

Compound Past

ich bin gewesen	ich sei gewesen	ich wäre gewesen
du bist gewesen	du sei(e)st gewesen	du wärest gewesen
er ist gewesen	er sei gewesen	er wäre gewesen
wir sind gewesen	wir seien gewesen	wir wären gewesen
ihr seid gewesen	ihr seiet gewesen	ihr wäret gewesen
sie sind gewesen	sie seien gewesen	sie wären gewesen

Past Perfect

ich war gewesen
du warst gewesen
er war gewesen
wir waren gewesen
ihr wart gewesen
sie waren gewesen

Future

ich werde sein	ich werde sein	ich würde sein
du wirst sein	du werdest sein	du würdest sein
er wird sein	er werde sein	er würde sein
wir werden sein	wir werden sein	wir würden sein
ihr werdet sein	ihr werdet sein	ihr würdet sein
sie werden sein	sie werden sein	sie würden sein

Future Perfect

ich werde gewesen sein	ich werde gewesen sein	ich würde ge- wesen sein
du wirst gewesen sein etc.	du werdest ge- wesen sein etc.	du würdest ge- wesen sein etc.

Imperative

Conventional:	seien Sie!
First Person Pl.:	seien wir!
Familiar Sing.:	sei!
Familiar Pl.:	seid!

7. Conjugation of <u>werden</u>

Principal Parts: **werden, wurde, ist geworden, wird**

Indicative	*Subjunctive I*	*Subjunctive II*
	Present	
ich werde	ich werde	ich würde
du wirst	du werdest	du würdest
er wird	er werde	er würde
wir werden	wir werden	wir würden
ihr werdet	ihr werdet	ihr würdet
sie werden	sie werden	sie würden

	Simple Past	
ich wurde		
du wurdest		
er wurde		
wir wurden		
ihr wurdet		
sie wurden		

	Compound Past	
ich bin geworden	ich sei geworden	ich wäre geworden
du bist geworden	du sei(e)st geworden	du wärest geworden
er ist geworden	er sei geworden	er wäre geworden
wir sind geworden	wir seien geworden	wir wären geworden
ihr seid geworden	ihr seiet geworden	ihr wäret geworden
sie sind geworden	sie seien geworden	sie wären geworden

	Past Perfect	
ich war geworden		
du warst geworden		
er war geworden		
wir waren geworden		
ihr wart geworden		
sie waren geworden		

	Future	
ich werde werden	ich werde werden	ich würde werden
du wirst werden	du werdest werden	du würdest werden
er wird werden	er werde werden	er würde werden
wir werden werden	wir werden werden	wir würden werden
ihr werdet werden	ihr werdet werden	ihr würdet werden
sie werden werden	sie werden werden	sie würden werden

	Future Perfect	
ich werde ge- worden sein	ich werde ge- worden sein	ich würde ge- worden sein
du wirst ge- worden sein	du werdest ge- worden sein	du würdest ge- worden sein
etc.	etc.	etc.

Imperative

Conventional:	werden Sie!
First Person Pl.:	werden wir!
Familiar Sing.:	werde!
Familiar Pl.:	werdet!

8. Conjugation of a Weak Verb: fragen

Principal Parts: **fragen, fragte, gefragt**

Indicative	*Subjunctive I*	*Subjunctive II*
	Present	
ich frage	ich frage	ich fragte
du fragst	du fragest	du fragtest
er fragt	er frage	er fragte
wir fragen	wir fragen	wir fragten
ihr fragt	ihr fraget	ihr fragtet
sie fragen	sie fragen	sie fragten

	Simple Past	
ich fragte		
du fragtest		
er fragte		
wir fragten		
ihr fragtet		
sie fragten		

	Compound Past	
ich habe gefragt	ich habe gefragt	ich hätte gefragt
du hast gefragt	du habest gefragt	du hättest gefragt
er hat gefragt	er habe gefragt	er hätte gefragt
wir haben gefragt	wir haben gefragt	wir hätten gefragt
ihr habt gefragt	ihr habet gefragt	ihr hättet gefragt
sie haben gefragt	sie haben gefragt	sie hätten gefragt

	Past Perfect	
ich hatte gefragt		
du hattest gefragt		
er hatte gefragt		
wir hatten gefragt		
ihr hattet gefragt		
sie hatten gefragt		

	Future	
ich werde fragen	ich werde fragen	ich würde fragen
du wirst fragen	du werdest fragen	du würdest fragen
er wird fragen	er werde fragen	er würde fragen
wir werden fragen	wir werden fragen	wir würden fragen
ihr werdet fragen	ihr werdet fragen	ihr würdet fragen
sie werden fragen	sie werden fragen	sie würden fragen

311

Future Perfect

ich werde gefragt haben	ich werde gefragt haben	ich würde gefragt haben
du wirst gefragt haben etc.	du werdest ge- fragt haben etc.	du würdest ge- fragt haben etc.

Imperative

Conventional:	fragen Sie!
First Person Pl.:	fragen wir!
Familiar Sing.:	frag(e)!
Familiar Pl.:	fragt!

9. Conjugation of a Strong Verb: tragen

Principal Parts: **tragen, trug, getragen, trägt**

Indicative	*Subjunctive I*	*Subjunctive II*
Present		
ich trage	ich trage	ich trüge
du trägst	du tragest	du trügest
er trägt	er trage	er trüge
wir tragen	wir tragen	wir trügen
ihr tragt	ihr traget	ihr trüget
sie tragen	sie tragen	sie trügen

Indicative
Simple Past
ich trug
du trugst
er trug
wir trugen
ihr trugt
sie trugen

Indicative	*Subjunctive I*	*Subjunctive II*
Compound Past		
ich habe getragen	ich habe getragen	ich hätte getragen
du hast getragen	du habest getragen	du hättest getragen
er hat getragen	er habe getragen	er hätte getragen
wir haben getragen	wir haben getragen	wir hätten getragen
ihr habt getragen	ihr habet getragen	ihr hättet getragen
sie haben getragen	sie haben getragen	sie hätten getragen

Indicative
Past Perfect
ich hatte getragen
du hattest getragen
er hatte getragen
wir hatten getragen
ihr hattet getragen
sie hatten getragen

Future

ich werde tragen	ich werde tragen	ich würde tragen
du wirst tragen	du werdest tragen	du würdest tragen
er wird tragen	er werde tragen	er würde tragen
wir werden tragen	wir werden tragen	wir würden tragen
ihr werdet tragen	ihr werdet tragen	ihr würdet tragen
sie werden tragen	sie werden tragen	sie würden tragen

Future Perfect

ich werde getragen haben	ich werde ge- tragen haben	ich würde ge- tragen haben
du wirst getragen haben etc.	du werdest ge- tragen haben etc.	du würdest ge- tragen haben etc.

Imperative

Conventional: tragen Sie!
First Person Pl.:   tragen wir!
Familiar Sing.:   trag(e)!
Familiar Pl.:   tragt!

10. Conjugation of a Verb with Separable Prefix: abfahren

Principal Parts: **abfahren, fuhr ab, ist abgefahren, fährt ab**

Indicative	Subjunctive I	Subjunctive II
	Present	
ich fahre ab	ich fahre ab	ich führe ab
du fährst ab	du fahrest ab	du führest ab
er fährt ab	er fahre ab	er führe ab
wir fahren ab	wir fahren ab	wir führen ab
ihr fahrt ab	ihr fahret ab	ihr führet ab
sie fahren ab	sie fahren ab	sie führen ab

Simple Past

ich fuhr ab
du fuhrst ab
er fuhr ab
wir fuhren ab
ihr fuhrt ab
sie fuhren ab

Compound Past

ich bin abgefahren	ich sei abgefahren	ich wäre abgefahren
du bist abgefahren	du sei(e)st abgefahren	du wärest abgefahren
er ist abgefahren	er sei abgefahren	er wäre abgefahren
wir sind abgefahren	wir seien abgefahren	wir wären abgefahren
ihr seid abgefahren	ihr seiet abgefahren	ihr wäret abgefahren
sie sind abgefahren	sie seien abgefahren	sie wären abgefahren

313

Past Perfect

ich war abgefahren
du warst abgefahren
er war abgefahren
wir waren abgefahren
ihr wart abgefahren
sie waren abgefahren

Future

ich werde abfahren	ich werde abfahren	ich würde abfahren
du wirst abfahren	du werdest abfahren	du würdest abfahren
er wird abfahren	er werde abfahren	er würde abfahren
wir werden abfahren	wir werden abfahren	wir würden abfahren
ihr werdet abfahren	ihr werdet abfahren	ihr würdet abfahren
sie werden abfahren	sie werden abfahren	sie würden abfahren

Future Perfect

ich werde abge- fahren sein	ich werde abge- fahren sein	ich würde abge- fahren sein
du wirst abge- fahren sein	du werdest abge- fahren sein	du würdest abge- fahren sein
etc.	etc.	etc.

Imperative

Conventional:	fahren Sie ab!
First Person Pl.:	fahren wir ab!
Familiar Sing.:	fahr(e) ab!
Familiar Pl.:	fahrt ab!

**11. Modal
Auxiliaries**

Principal Parts:

dürfen	**durfte**	**gedurft (dürfen)**	**darf**
können	**konnte**	**gekonnt (können)**	**kann**
mögen	**mochte**	**gemocht (mögen)**	**mag**
müssen	**mußte**	**gemußt (müssen)**	**muß**
sollen	**sollte**	**gesollt (sollen)**	**soll**
wollen	**wollte**	**gewollt (wollen)**	**will**

Sample Conjugation: Present Tense

Indicative	*Subjunctive I*	*Subjunctive II*
ich kann	ich könne	ich könnte
du kannst	du könnest	du könntest
er kann	er könne	er könnte
wir können	wir können	wir könnten
ihr könnt	ihr könnet	ihr könntet
sie können	sie können	sie könnten

12. Conjugation of a Verb in the Passive Voice: <u>gelobt werden</u>

Indicative	*Subjunctive I*	*Subjunctive II*
	Present	
ich werde gelobt	ich werde gelobt	ich würde gelobt
du wirst gelobt	du werdest gelobt	du würdest gelobt
er wird gelobt	er werde gelobt	er würde gelobt
wir werden gelobt	wir werden gelobt	wir würden gelobt
ihr werdet gelobt	ihr werdet gelobt	ihr würdet gelobt
sie werden gelobt	sie werden gelobt	sie würden gelobt

Simple Past

ich wurde gelobt
du wurdest gelobt
er wurde gelobt
wir wurden gelobt
ihr wurdet gelobt
sie wurden gelobt

Compound Past

ich bin gelobt worden	ich sei gelobt worden	ich wäre gelobt worden
du bist gelobt worden	du sei(e)st gelobt worden	du wärest gelobt worden
er ist gelobt worden	er sei gelobt worden	er wäre gelobt worden
wir sind gelobt worden	wir seien gelobt worden	wir wären gelobt worden
ihr seid gelobt worden	ihr seiet gelobt worden	ihr wäret gelobt worden
sie sind gelobt worden	sie seien gelobt worden	sie wären gelobt worden

Past Perfect

ich war gelobt worden
du warst gelobt worden
er war gelobt worden
wir waren gelobt worden
ihr wart gelobt worden
sie waren gelobt worden

Future

ich werde gelobt werden	ich werde gelobt werden	ich würde gelobt werden
du wirst gelobt werden	du werdest gelobt werden	du würdest gelobt werden
er wird gelobt werden	er werde gelobt werden	er würde gelobt werden
wir werden gelobt werden	wir werden gelobt werden	wir würden gelobt werden

ihr werdet gelobt werden	ihr werdet gelobt werden	ihr würdet gelobt werden
sie werden gelobt werden	sie werden gelobt werden	sie würden gelobt werden

Future Perfect

ich werde gelobt worden sein	ich werde gelobt worden sein	ich würde gelobt worden sein
du wirst gelobt worden sein	du werdest gelobt worden sein	du würdest gelobt worden sein
etc.	etc.	etc.

13. Selective List of Strong and Irregular Verbs

Verbs with prefixes are not included if the simple verb appears in the list. For modal auxiliaries, see 11, above.

Infinitive	Past	Past Participle	3rd Sing. Pres. (*if irregular*)
an/fangen (*to begin*)	fing an	angefangen	fängt an
beginnen (*to begin*)	begann	begonnen	
bieten (*to offer*)	bot	geboten	
bitten (*to ask, request*)	bat	gebeten	
bleiben (*to stay*)	blieb	ist geblieben	
brechen (*to break*)	brach	(ist) gebrochen	bricht
brennen (*to burn*)	brannte	gebrannt	
bringen (*to bring*)	brachte	gebracht	
denken (*to think*)	dachte	gedacht	
ein/laden (*to invite*)	lud ein	eingeladen	lädt ein
empfehlen (*to recommend*)	empfahl	empfohlen	empfiehlt
erschrecken (*to be frightened*)	erschrak	ist erschrocken	erschrickt
essen (*to eat*)	aß	gegessen	ißt
fahren (*to drive, go*)	fuhr	(ist) gefahren	fährt
fallen (*to fall*)	fiel	ist gefallen	fällt
finden (*to find*)	fand	gefunden	
fliegen (*to fly*)	flog	(ist) geflogen	
geben (*to give*)	gab	gegeben	gibt
gehen (*to go*)	ging	ist gegangen	
gelingen (*to succeed*)	gelang	ist gelungen	
geschehen (*to happen*)	geschah	ist geschehen	geschieht
gewinnen (*to win*)	gewann	gewonnen	
haben (*to have*)	hatte	gehabt	hat
halten (*to hold*)	hielt	gehalten	hält
heißen (*to be called*)	hieß	geheißen	
helfen (*to help*)	half	geholfen	hilft
kennen (*to know*)	kannte	gekannt	
kommen (*to come*)	kam	ist gekommen	
lassen (*to let, leave*)	ließ	gelassen	läßt
laufen (*to run*)	lief	ist gelaufen	läuft
leiden (*to suffer*)	litt	gelitten	
lesen (*to read*)	las	gelesen	liest
liegen (*to lie, recline*)	lag	gelegen	
nehmen (*to take*)	nahm	genommen	nimmt
nennen (*to name*)	nannte	genannt	

raten (*to advise*)	riet	geraten	rät
rufen (*to call*)	rief	gerufen	
scheinen (*to seem; to shine*)	schien	geschienen	
schlafen (*to sleep*)	schlief	geschlafen	schläft
schließen (*to close*)	schloß	geschlossen	
schneiden (*to cut*)	schnitt	geschnitten	
schreiben (*to write*)	schrieb	geschrieben	
schwimmen (*to swim*)	schwamm	(ist) geschwommen	
sehen (*to see*)	sah	gesehen	sieht
sein (*to be*)	war	ist gewesen	ist
senden (*to send*)	sandte	gesandt	
singen (*to sing*)	sang	gesungen	
sitzen (*to sit*)	saß	gesessen	
sprechen (*to speak*)	sprach	gesprochen	spricht
stehen (*to stand*)	stand	gestanden	
steigen (*to climb*)	stieg	ist gestiegen	
sterben (*to die*)	starb	ist gestorben	stirbt
tragen (*to carry, wear*)	trug	getragen	trägt
treffen (*to hit, meet*)	traf	getroffen	trifft
treiben (*to drive*)	trieb	getrieben	
treten (*to step; to kick*)	trat	(ist) getreten	tritt
trinken (*to drink*)	trank	getrunken	
tun (*to do*)	tat	getan	
vergessen (*to forget*)	vergaß	vergessen	vergißt
vergleichen (*to compare*)	verglich	verglichen	
verlieren (*to lose*)	verlor	verloren	
verschwinden (*to disappear*)	verschwand	ist verschwunden	
wachsen (*to grow*)	wuchs	ist gewachsen	wächst
waschen (*to wash*)	wusch	gewaschen	wäscht
werden (*to become*)	wurde	ist geworden	wird
werfen (*to throw*)	warf	geworfen	wirft
wissen (*to know*)	wußte	gewußt	weiß
ziehen (*to pull; to move*)	zog	(ist) gezogen	

14. Der-Words

Singular		Plural	
dieser, diese, dieses	*this, the latter*	diese	*these, the latter*
jener, jene, jenes	*that, the former*	jene	*those, the former*
jeder, jede, jedes	*each, every*	alle	*all*
mancher, manche, manches	*many a*	manche	*some*
solcher, solche, solches	*such a*	solche	*such*
welcher, welche, welches	*which, what*	welche	*which, what*

15. Ein-Words

kein, keine, kein	*no, not any*
mein, meine, mein	*my*
dein, deine, dein	*your* (familiar sing.)
sein, seine, sein	*his, its* (referring to a masc. or neut. possessor)

ihr, ihre, ihr	*her, its* (referring to a feminine possessor)
unser, uns(e)re, unser	*our*
euer, eu(e)re, euer	*your* (familiar plural)
ihr, ihre, ihr	*their*
Ihr, Ihre, Ihr	*your* (conventional)

16. Sample Noun Declensions with the Definite Article

Singular

	Masculine	Feminine	Neuter
Nom.	der Bruder	die Schwester	das Buch
Gen.	des Bruders	der Schwester	des Buches
Dat.	dem Bruder	der Schwester	dem Buch(e)
Acc.	den Bruder	die Schwester	das Buch

Plural

Nom.	die Brüder	die Schwestern	die Bücher
Gen.	der Brüder	der Schwestern	der Bücher
Dat.	den Brüdern	den Schwestern	den Büchern
Acc.	die Brüder	die Schwestern	die Bücher

17. Sample Noun Declensions with the Indefinite Article

Singular

	Masculine	Feminine	Neuter
Nom.	ein Wagen	eine Reise	ein Haus
Gen.	eines Wagens	einer Reise	eines Hauses
Dat.	einem Wagen	einer Reise	einem Haus(e)
Acc.	einen Wagen	eine Reise	ein Haus

(*No plural*)

18. Summary of Key Sounds

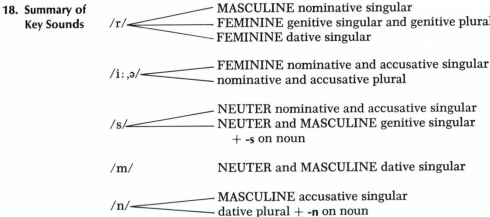

/r/ ———— MASCULINE nominative singular
———— FEMININE genitive singular and genitive plural
———— FEMININE dative singular

/iː,ə/ ———— FEMININE nominative and accusative singular
———— nominative and accusative plural

/s/ ———— NEUTER nominative and accusative singular
———— NEUTER and MASCULINE genitive singular + -s on noun

/m/ ———— NEUTER and MASCULINE dative singular

/n/ ———— MASCULINE accusative singular
———— dative plural + -n on noun

19. Declension of   **a.**   After a Definite Article or Other **Der**-Word
Adjectives

Singular

Masculine	Feminine	Neuter
Nom. **der** gute Mann	**diese** nette Frau	**welches** alte Schiff
Gen. **des** guten Mannes	**dieser** netten Frau	**welches** alten Schiffes
Dat. **dem** guten Mann(e)	**dieser** netten Frau	**welchem** alten Schiff(e)
Acc. **den** guten Mann	**diese** nette Frau	**welches** alte Schiff

Plural (*all genders*)

Nom. **die** guten Männer (Frauen, Schiffe)
Gen. **der** guten Männer (Frauen, Schiffe)
Dat. **den** guten Männern (Frauen, Schiffen)
Acc. **die** guten Männer (Frauen, Schiffe)

b.   After an Indefinite Article or Other **Ein**-Word

Singular

Masculine	Feminine	Neuter
Nom. **ein** guter Mann	**meine** gute Frau	**unser** altes Schiff
Gen. **eines** guten Mannes	**meiner** guten Frau	**uns(e)res** alten Schiffes
Dat. **einem** guten Mann(e)	**meiner** guten Frau	**uns(e)rem** alten Schiff(e)
Acc. **einen** guten Mann	**meine** gute Frau	**unser** altes Schiff

Plural (*all genders*)

Nom. **keine** guten Männer (Frauen, Schiffe)
Gen. **keiner** guten Männer (Frauen, Schiffe)
Dat. **keinen** guten Männern (Frauen, Schiffen)
Acc. **keine** guten Männer (Frauen, Schiffe)

c.   Unpreceded

Singular

Masculine	Feminine	Neuter
Nom. guter Wein	gute Milch	gutes Wasser
Gen. guten Weines	guter Milch	guten Wassers
Dat. gutem Wein(e)	guter Milch	gutem Wasser
Acc. guten Wein	gute Milch	gutes Wasser

Plural (*all genders*)

Nom. gute Kinder
Gen. guter Kinder
Dat. guten Kindern
Acc. gute Kinder

20. Noun Classes   a.   Class I Nouns (*Strong*)[1]

No ending in plural; umlaut: masculines sometimes, feminines always, neuters never.

	Singular		Plural
-	**der Vater**	(÷)-	**die Väter**
-s	des Vaters	(÷)-	der Väter
-	dem Vater	(÷)n	den Vätern
-	den Vater	(÷)-	die Väter

To Class I belong:
a.   masculine and neuter nouns ending in **-el, -en, -er**;
b.   nouns with the suffixes **-chen** and **-lein** (*always neuter*);
c.   neuter nouns with the prefix **Ge-** and the ending **-e (das Gebirge)**;
d.   the two feminines **die Mutter, die Tochter.**

b.   Class II Nouns (*Strong*)[1]

Plural in **-e**; umlaut: masculines often, feminines always, neuters never.

	Singular		Plural
-	**der Satz**	(÷)e	**die Sätze**
-(e)s	des Satzes	(÷)e	der Sätze
-(e)	dem Satz(e)	(÷)en	den Sätzen
-	den Satz	(÷)e	die Sätze

To Class II belong:
a.   most masculine, feminine, and some neuter monosyllabic nouns;
b.   masculine nouns ending in **-ich, -ig, -ling**;
c.   feminine and neuter nouns ending in **-nis** and **-sal**;
d.   neuter nouns of more than one syllable with the prefix **Ge- (das Geschenk)** and some neuter nouns of non-German origin with the word accent on the last syllable **(das Paket).**

c.   Class III Nouns (*Strong*)

Plural in **-er**; umlaut: wherever possible.

	Singular		Plural
-	**das Buch**	÷er	**die Bücher**
-(e)s	des Buches	÷er	der Bücher
-(e)	dem Buch(e)	÷ern	den Büchern
-	das Buch	÷er	die Bücher

1. Feminine nouns have no inflectional endings in the singular.

To Class III belong:

a. a few monosyllabic masculine nouns;
b. most monosyllabic neuter nouns;
c. nouns ending in **-tum**;
d. no feminine nouns.

d. Class IV Nouns (*Weak*)[1]

Singular and plural in -(e)n; umlaut: never.

	Singular		Plural
-	**der Deutsche**	-(e)n	**die Deutschen**
-(e)n	des Deutschen	-(e)n	der Deutschen
-(e)n	dem Deutschen	-(e)n	den Deutschen
-(e)n	den Deutschen	-(e)n	die Deutschen

To Class IV belong:

a. masculine nouns ending in **-e** and denoting male beings;
b. masculine nouns of non-German origin with the accent on the last syllable;
c. a few monosyllabic nouns (**der Mensch, der Fürst, der Herr** [**-n** in the singular, **-en** in the plural], and others);
d. feminine nouns of more than one syllable (*except:* **die Mutter, die Tochter**);
e. a few monosyllabic feminines not in Class II (**die Frau, die Tür, die Uhr, die Zeit**, and others);
f. no neuter nouns.

A few masculine and neuter nouns have strong forms in the singular and weak forms in the plural; they never have umlaut:

	Singular		Plural
-	**der Staat**	-en	**die Staaten**
-(e)s	des Staates	-en	der Staaten
-(e)	dem Staat(e)	-en	den Staaten
-	den Staat	-en	die Staaten

The following nouns belong to Class I but occur without a final **-n** in the nominative singular: **der Friede, der Funke, der Gedanke, der Glaube, der Name, der Wille**:

Singular	Plural
der Name	**die Namen**
des Namens	der Namen
dem Namen	den Namen
den Namen	die Namen

1. Feminine nouns have no inflectional endings in the singular.

Herz is declined as follows:

Singular	Plural
das Herz	**die Herzen**
des Herzens	**der Herzen**
dem Herzen	**den Herzen**
das Herz	**die Herzen**

21. Personal Pronouns

Singular

Nom.	ich	du	er	sie	es
Gen.	meiner	deiner	seiner	ihrer	seiner
Dat.	mir	dir	ihm	ihr	ihm
Acc.	mich	dich	ihn	sie	es

	Plural			Conventional Address Singular and Plural
Nom.	wir	ihr	sie	Sie
Gen.	unser	euer	ihrer	Ihrer
Dat.	uns	euch	ihnen	Ihnen
Acc.	uns	euch	sie	Sie

22. Relative and Demonstrative Pronoun der, die, das

	Singular			Plural
	Masculine	Feminine	Neuter	(*all genders*)
Nom.	der	die	das	die
Gen.	dessen	deren	dessen	deren
Dat.	dem	der	dem	denen
Acc.	den	die	das	die

23. Prepositions

a. With the Accusative

durch	*through, by (means of)*	ohne	*without*
für	*for*	um	*around, about, at (time)*
gegen	*against, toward*		

b. With the Dative

aus	*out of, from*	nach	*after, according to, to*
außer	*except, besides*	seit	*since*
bei	*near, beside, with, at the house of*	von	*of, by, from*
		zu	*to*
mit	*with*		

c. With the Accusative or Dative

an	*at, to, on(to)*	über	*over, above, about*
auf	*on(to)*	unter	*under, among*
hinter	*behind*	vor	*before, in front of, ago*
in	*in(to), to*	zwischen	*between*
neben	*beside, near*		

d. Common Prepositions with the Genitive

anstatt (statt)	*instead of*	während	*during*
trotz	*in spite of*	wegen	*because of*

24. Numerals

	Cardinals	Ordinals
0	null	
1	eins	der, die, das erste
2	zwei	zweite
3	drei	dritte
4	vier	vierte
5	fünf	fünfte
6	sechs	sechste
7	sieben	sieb(en)te
8	acht	achte
9	neun	neunte
10	zehn	zehnte
11	elf	elfte
12	zwölf	zwölfte
13	dreizehn	dreizehnte
14	vierzehn	vierzehnte
15	fünfzehn	fünfzehnte
16	sechzehn	sechzehnte
17	siebzehn	siebzehnte
18	achtzehn	achtzehnte
19	neunzehn	neunzehnte
20	zwanzig	zwanzigste
21	einundzwanzig	einundzwanzigste
22	zweiundzwanzig	zweiundzwanzigste
30	dreißig	dreißigste
40	vierzig	vierzigste
50	fünfzig	fünfzigste
60	sechzig	sechzigste
70	siebzig	siebzigste
80	achtzig	achtzigste
90	neunzig	neunzigste
100	hundert	hundertste
101	hunderteins	hunderterste
121	hunderteinundzwanzig	hunderteinundzwanzigste
200	zweihundert	zweihundertste
1000	tausend	tausendste

eine Million	*one million*
zwei Millionen	*two million*
eine Milliarde	*one billion*
eine Billion	*1000 billions*

APPENDIX 2

AUFSÄTZE IN GERMAN TYPE

1.   Der Student Kurt Klein

Der Student Kurt Klein wohnt in der Stadt Milwaukee. Die Stadt Milwaukee liegt im Staate Wisconsin. Kurts Vater wohnt schon viele Jahre in Milwaukee. Die Mutter kommt aus New York. Sie wohnt erst zwanzig (20) Jahre in Wisconsin. Kurt ist neunzehn (19) Jahre alt. Er ist groß und stark für sein Alter.

Kurt stammt aus einer deutschen Familie. Er spricht Deutsch, aber er möchte es besser lernen. „Darf ich in Deutschland studieren?“ fragt er seine Eltern. „Selbstverständlich“, antwortet Herr Klein.

Kurt kauft eine Fahrkarte nach Deutschland. Er reist nach New York; von da fährt er mit dem Dampfer nach Hamburg. In Hamburg nimmt er den Zug nach Köln. Er bleibt nur ein Jahr in Köln. Das Studium ist sehr teuer.

Kurt ist jetzt in Köln. Er sucht ein Taxi und gibt dem Chauffeur eine Adresse. „Bitte fahren Sie mich zu dieser Adresse“, sagt Kurt. Das Haus gehört Frau Kolb. Frau Kolb öffnet die Tür. Kurt trägt seinen Koffer ins Haus.

Frau Kolb ist nett und freundlich. Sie zeigt Kurt das Zimmer. Es ist sauber und schön. Die Miete ist billig. „Bis später“, sagt er. „Auf Wiedersehen“, antwortet Frau Kolb.

2.   Köln

Kurt ist erst einen Tag in Köln. Heute macht er eine Stadtrund=fahrt. Aber zuerst stellt er viele Fragen an Frau Kolb. Sie beantwortet sie alle. Dann gibt sie Kurt einen Stadtplan. Kurt braucht ihn sehr. Leider ist er nicht neu.

Kurt geht an die Ecke. Hier wartet er auf den Bus. Aber er kommt nicht. Plötzlich sieht Kurt einen Touristenbus. Er steigt in den Bus. Er bezahlt sechs (6) Mark für die Fahrt.

Zuerst besuchen sie den Dom. Kurt erkennt sofort den Baustil. Er ist gotisch. Kurt bewundert den Dom. Der Reiseführer erzählt eine Geschichte über den Dom. Er erzählt sie auf französisch. Kurt versteht kein Wort. Er erzählt dieselbe Geschichte auf englisch. Natürlich versteht Kurt jetzt alles. Kurt kennt die Geschichte nicht. Sie interessiert ihn sehr. Der Reiseführer erzählt sie noch einmal, diesmal auf deutsch. Er spricht klar und deutlich. Kurt versteht ihn perfekt.

Gerade erklärt der Reiseführer: „Auf deutsch heißt die Stadt Köln. In England und Frankreich heißt sie ‚Cologne‘. Die Römer nannten sie ‚colonia‘, auf deutsch ‚Kolonie‘."

Jetzt verläßt die Reisegruppe den Dom. Sie fahren alle zusammen an den Rhein. Sie bewundern die Brücke. Kurt mag die schöne Aussicht. Er findet die Landschaft märchenhaft und romantisch.

Danach fahren sie in die Neustadt. Zuerst besuchen sie ein Museum, eine Kirche, eine Volksschule und ein Gymnasium. Dann sagt der Reiseführer: „Meine Damen und Herren, Sie sind alle müde. Ich zeige Ihnen nur noch das Theater. Wie das Opernhaus ist es nur ein paar Jahre alt. Dieser Stadtteil ist ganz neu."

Kurt ist sehr müde. Plötzlich hat er auch Hunger. Er sieht auf die Uhr. Es ist schon Mittag. Ein Franzose und ein Engländer sammeln Geld für den Reiseführer und den Chauffeur. Sie sagen: „Vielen Dank für das Trinkgeld."

Kurt denkt: „Ich bin froh, ich bin hier in Köln. Die Stadt ist schön und modern. Ich mag sie sehr."

3. Über die Universität in Deutschland

Kurt besucht schon einen Monat die Universität Köln. Jeden Morgen spaziert er gemütlich zur Universität. Manchmal trifft er einen Freund unterwegs. Dann gehen sie zusammen in den Hörsaal. Sie setzen sich nebeneinander auf die Bank und warten geduldig auf den Professor. Kurt weiß leider nicht viel über die Universität in Deutschland. Er will ein Buch über das Universitätsleben lesen.

Er liest zum Beispiel: Für die Universität in Deutschland ist die Forschung oft wichtiger als die Erziehung. Man hat viel Interesse an der Theorie, weniger an der Praxis. Die Universität in Deutschland ist hauptsächlich bekannt für das Studium der Philosophie, Geschichte und Sprachwissenschaft. Heute besteht auch Interesse für Chemie, Physik und Technologie. Die Universität muß modern sein.

Kurt liest weiter. Alle Universitäten haben eine Tradition und erhalten die Erinnerung an einen großen Lehrer aufrecht, wie z.B. Kant in Königsberg oder Hegel in Berlin. Der Professor in Deutschland ist Staatsbeamter, aber er denkt und darf schreiben, was er will.

Kurt versteht jetzt viel. Er weiß aber, er muß noch mehr lernen.

4. Die Geographie Deutschlands

Es ist kurz vor sieben (7:00). In einer Stunde ißt Kurt bei seinem Freund Karl zu Abend. Er denkt an Karls Einladung. „Wir erwarten Sie gegen acht (8:00). Die Familie ist zu Hause, der Vater, die Mutter, und meine Schwester. Sie ist achtzehn (18) Jahre alt und sehr hübsch."

Aber zuerst schreibt Kurt einen Aufsatz für die Deutschstunde. Das Thema ist die Geographie Deutschlands. Er findet die Aufgabe leicht. Er beschreibt einfach das Klima und die Landschaft.

„Deutschland liegt in Mitteleuropa. Das Klima ist mild und im allgemeinen angenehm. Im Sommer ist es nicht zu heiß und im Winter nicht zu kalt. Das Wetter ist sehr veränderlich. Es regnet zu jeder Jahreszeit. Es ist warm im Sommer, kalt im Winter. Es schneit oft im Winter, besonders im Januar und Februar.

„Die Landschaften in Deutschland sind sehr verschieden. Im Norden ist das Land flach; im Süden jedoch ist es gebirgig. Die Alpen in Bayern sind bis zu dreitausend (3 000) Meter hoch. Wir nennen sie Hochgebirge.

„Köln, wo ich wohne, liegt am Rhein. Die Hafenstadt Hamburg liegt an der Elbe. Bremen ist ebenfalls eine Hafenstadt und liegt an der Weser. Der Rhein, die Weser und die Elbe fließen von Süden nach Norden und münden in die Nordsee. Die Donau kommt aus dem Schwarzwald und fließt nach Osten."

Kurt sieht auf die Uhr. Es ist höchste Zeit. Er läuft schnell die Treppe hinunter. Unten begegnet er Frau Kolb. „Gehen Sie am Postamt vorbei?" fragt sie ihn. „Ja? Dann darf ich Ihnen diesen Brief geben. Werfen Sie ihn bitte in den Briefkasten!" Kurt tut ihr gerne diesen Gefallen.

5. Auf dem Dampfer

Kurt und Karl stehen an der Reling des Rheindampfers. Genau wie Herr Lenz sind sie von der Schönheit der Landschaft begeistert. Nie möchten sie diese Reise vergessen. Aus diesem Grunde photographieren sie fleißig. Bei jeder Biegung des Rheins wird das Bild anders. Jedoch bleibt es immer gleich schön.

Auf beiden Seiten des Flusses stehen Ziffern. Kurt versteht die Bedeutung der Ziffern nicht. Karl erklärt sie ihm: „Schau auf die Rheinkarte! Hier steht die Nummer 550 (fünfhundertfünfzig). Daneben steht der Name der Stadt. Wir sind eben in Bonn, in der Hauptstadt der Bundesrepublik. Siehst du? Ein bißchen weiter ist Mehlem. Hier ist die Botschaft der Vereinigten Staaten, ganz in der Nähe von Bonn. Bonn, eine Universitätsstadt, ist auch die Geburtsstadt Beethovens."

Während der nächsten halben Stunde frühstücken Kurt und Karl unten im Speisesaal des Dampfers. Sie trinken eine Tasse Kaffee und essen Brot mit Butter und etwas Marmelade darauf. Dann gehen sie wieder nach oben auf das Deck zurück.

Seit dem ersten Teil des 19. (neunzehnten) Jahrhunderts ist der Rhein der Lieblingsfluß der deutschen Dichtung. Er ist auch seit derselben Epoche die große Straße für Touristen. Der Rhein, so sagt man oft, ist das Prunkstück der deutschen Geographie.

„Was für ein Mensch ist der Rheinländer?" fragt Kurt.

„Er ist besonders wegen seiner Lebensfreude bekannt", antwortet Karl. „Wie du siehst, ist er auch sehr gastfreundlich. Die Gastfreundschaft des Rheinländers drückt sich in der Gemütlichkeit des Menschen aus."

Kurt ist mit der Auskunft zufrieden. „Ich lerne wirklich viel", denkt er. „Aber warum ist Lore nicht bei uns?"

6. Die Sehenswürdigkeiten

Kurt und Karl amüsieren sich großartig. Tagsüber besuchen sie dieses oder jenes Schloß, manchmal auch eine Kirche oder gar ein Museum. Immer wieder sagt Karl: „Der Reiseführer gibt hier eine Ruine an. Wir müssen uns die Ruine ansehen." Am nächsten Tag heißt es: „Diese Kirche ist weltberühmt. Die sollten wir uns auch ansehen." Oder Karl sagt: „Das Museum in dem Städtchen ist sehenswert. Ich möchte es dir zeigen."

Kurt interessiert sich natürlich für alles. Heute ist er jedoch müde. Er möchte sich einfach ausruhen, in einem Café sitzen und die schöne Natur genießen.

Kurt schlägt das Reisebuch auf. „Jeder Teil Deutschlands kann dem Reisenden etwas bieten. Welchen Teil des Landes wollen Sie besuchen? Das kommt ganz auf Sie an. Sind Sie Bergsteiger oder Schifahrer? Dann fahren Sie nach Bayern oder Österreich. Schwimmen Sie gerne und ziehen Sie das Meer vor? Dann begeben Sie sich an den Strand der Nord= oder Ostsee! Sind Sie erschöpft und müssen sich erholen? Jede Gegend in Deutschland hat einen Kurort oder ein Heilbad."

Der junge Student liest das Kapitel genau durch. Dann überlegt er sich: Wohin soll er während der Weihnachtsferien fahren? Im Stillen entschließt er sich: die Weihnachtsferien verbringt er in Bayern. Er wird Wintersport treiben und sich dabei — wie immer — erkälten.

7. Film und Bühne

Während seines Aufenthalts in Deutschland hat sich Kurt hauptsäch= lich mit kulturellen bzw. literarischen Dingen beschäftigt. In der Archi= tektur, wie auch auf anderen Gebieten, hat das Land große Fortschritte gemacht. Im Gegensatz dazu haben nur wenige Filme Kurt beeindruckt. Sehr viele sind romantisch und sentimental, sogar ein bißchen kitschig. Sie haben das Leben und die Liebe verschönert und romantisiert. Nur ein paar haben sich mit wichtigen Themen befaßt. Kurt hatte sich von den Filmen des Auslands eine bessere Meinung gebildet. Die Regisseure Frankreichs, Italiens und Japans z.B. haben vorzügliche Filme ge= dreht.

Das Theater hat in der Geschichte Deutschlands immer eine große Rolle gespielt. Es hat aber seine frühere Höhe noch nicht wieder erreicht. Man hat zwar die Jahre über viele Theater gebaut, sogar während der Nachkriegszeit; aber Gebäude ersetzen keine Dichter.

Was hat man also in den letzten Jahren aufgeführt? Man bevorzugt die Dramatiker der Vergangenheit, wie Lessing, Goethe, Schiller und Hauptmann. Auch die Meisterwerke des Auslands hat man inszeniert, wie z.B. Stücke von Tennessee Williams und Jean Anouilh. Die deutschen Dramatiker der Nachkriegszeit dagegen haben nicht sehr viel geleistet. Gewiß haben sie der Bühne neue Schauspiele geliefert, aber diese Werke haben keinen besonderen Wert. Weder im Film noch im Theater kommt man den Leistungen der Vorkriegsjahre nahe.

8. Schule und Laufbahn

Kurt plaudert gern. Vor einer Woche hat er neben einem Herrn im Café gesessen. Dieser stellte sich vor: Dr. Hans Greiber, Gymnasiallehrer. „Ich unterhalte mich immer gerne mit Amerikanern", sagte Dr. Greiber. „Ich bin ein Jahr in Amerika gewesen und es hat mir gut dort gefallen."

„Warum sind Sie nicht länger geblieben?" erkundigte sich Kurt.

„Unser Kultusministerium hatte mich nach Amerika geschickt", erklärte Dr. Greiber. „Ich sollte dort das Erziehungswesen studieren. Dafür hat man mich auf ein Jahr beurlaubt."

„Ich bin schon fünf (5) Wochen hier, verstehe aber das Schulsystem und die Ausbildungsmöglichkeiten noch nicht."

„Es kommt auf die Wahl des Berufes an", erklärte Dr. Greiber. „Nehmen wir an, Sie sind Bäcker. Sie sind im Alter von sechs (6) Jahren in die Volksschule eingetreten. Sie sind acht (8) Jahre dort geblieben. Mit vierzehn (14) Jahren haben Sie die Volksschule verlassen. Dann sind Sie Bäckerlehrling geworden. Als Lehrling besuchten Sie drei (3) Jahre lang mehrere Male in der Woche eine Berufsschule. Nach dem dritten Jahr mußten Sie eine Gesellenprüfung machen. Nach einigen weiteren Jahren im Beruf haben Sie Ihre Meisterprüfung gemacht. Heute haben Sie Ihre eigene Bäckerei."

„Und Sie?" lachte Kurt. „Sie sind ja nicht Handwerker, sondern Akademiker."

„Ich bin auch mit sechs Jahren in die Volksschule gegangen. Mit zehn (10) bin ich ins Gymnasium gekommen. Mit neunzehn (19) Jahren habe ich das Abitur gemacht, das heißt die Schlußprüfung in einem Gymnasium. Danach habe ich mein Studium an der Universität begonnen. Ich habe in Heidelberg und Tübingen Philosophie studiert und meine Examen in Heidelberg abgelegt. Ich habe gut abgeschnitten und kurz danach meine Doktorarbeit geschrieben. Die Behörden haben mich zum Studienassessor ernannt. Ich bin jetzt in Köln angestellt."

Dr. Greiber und Kurt sind zusammen an die Haltestelle gegangen. Zuerst aber haben sie ihre Adressen und Telefonnummern ausgetauscht.

9. Deutsche Cafés und Wirtschaften

Kurt und Lore saßen gemütlich auf der Terrasse des Cafés Continental, tranken langsam eine Tasse Kaffee, hörten Musik und blickten auf den Rhein hinaus. Nebenan unterhielten sich zwei Damen auffallend laut über Schönheitsmittel und die neuesten Moden. „Diese Damen scheinen schon mehrere Stunden hier zu sitzen", bemerkte Kurt endlich. „Seit unserer Ankunft haben sie kaum etwas verzehrt. Der Kaffeeklatsch mag angenehm für die Damen sein, aber er bedeutet schlechtes Geschäft für den Besitzer. Wird sie denn niemand hinaus= werfen?"

„Nein, sie haben einen Kaffee bestellt, und das genügt", erklärte Lore. „Das verleiht ihnen das Recht, die schöne Landschaft zu genießen und weiter zu plaudern. Einige Herren und Damen kommen fast jeden Tag in dieses Lokal, bestellen eine Tasse Kaffee oder Tee und unterhalten sich stundenlang mit ihren Kollegen oder Freundinnen. Natürlich kommen manche Leute allein und verlangen dann noch Zeitungen oder Zeit= schriften, um sich zu beschäftigen. Insgesamt zahlen sie recht wenig für einen angenehmen Nachmittag."

„Gibt es solche Cafés auch auf dem Land?"

„Viel weniger", erwiderte Lore. „In den Dörfern bleiben die Frauen meistens zu Hause bei den Kindern. Die Männer machen sich das Leben leicht. Sie gehen abends aus, in ein Gasthaus oder in eine Wirtschaft. Sie besuchen dasselbe Wirtshaus jahraus, jahrein und werden Stamm= gäste des Lokals. Man reserviert ihnen also einen Stammtisch, denn sie wollen immer mit ihren Freunden zusammensitzen."

„Ich kann mir das ganz gut vorstellen", sagte Kurt. „Gerade wie die Damen neben uns, haben auch diese Herren ihre Lieblingsthemen. Sie diskutieren politische Fragen, beschweren sich über die Steuern und ihre Familien und spielen Karten. Dabei serviert man ihnen eine Maß Bier oder ein Glas Wein."

„Ja, auf dem Land und in der Kleinstadt ist das die Regel", sagte Lore. „Bei einer Flasche Wein und einer Zigarre vergeht die Zeit sehr schnell für die Väter. Die Mütter und Töchter hingegen sitzen zu Hause . . ."

„. . . und amüsieren sich auf ihre Art", lachte Kurt. „Vielleicht fahre ich dieses Wochenende mal aufs Land und sehe mir so eine Gaststätte an. Man soll da gut und billig zu essen bekommen. Das ist das richtige für mich."

Plötzlich sah Kurt auf seine Uhr. Beide erschraken, weil es schon spät geworden war. Sie hatten um 5 Uhr Verabredungen. Kurt rief den Kellner. „Herr Ober, zahlen, bitte", sagte er. Der Kellner schrieb die Rechnung. Kurt legte einen Zehnmarkschein auf den Tisch, und der Kellner gab ihm auf zehn Mark heraus. Dann standen sie auf und verließen das Café.

10. Das Familienleben

Kurt und sein Freund Karl sind am Bahnhof. Sie haben den Tag in Aachen verbracht und fahren jetzt wieder nach Hause. Sie lösen ihre Fahrkarten, kaufen sich ein paar Zeitschriften und steigen zusammen in den Zug. Sie hören wiederholt den Lautsprecher: „Achtung! Achtung! Der Personenzug in Richtung Köln fährt sogleich ab. Bitte einsteigen und die Türen schließen!"

Karl möchte ruhig seine Illustrierte lesen, aber Kurt unterbricht ihn immer wieder. Er stellt seinem Freund allerlei Fragen über das Familienleben in Deutschland. Zuerst spricht Karl von seinem Vater und seiner Mutter, dann von seinen Großeltern; zu guter Letzt erwähnt er auch seine Schwester Lore.

Karl erklärt seinem Freund: „Unser Familienleben in Deutschland ist sehr eng und die Familie als Gemeinschaft ist sehr wichtig. In vielen Familien herrscht immer noch die Autorität des Vaters. Auf der andern Seite hat sich vieles geändert, und die Jugend trifft jetzt oft ihre eigenen Entscheidungen. In meiner Familie bestimmt der Vater über ziemlich alles: über Lores und meine Erziehung, unsere Berufsausbildung, unsere Geldausgaben. Unsere Mutter kümmert sich nicht viel um diese Fragen. Natürlich ist auch mein Vater, wie die meisten deutschen Väter, der Ernährer seiner Familie. Unsere Frauen sind noch nicht so frei wie eure Frauen in Amerika. Meine Mutter steht dem Haushalt vor; sie macht die Hausarbeit, kocht und widmet sich den Kindern.

„Der deutsche Vater ist das Familienoberhaupt. Er spielt gewöhnlich nicht mit seinen Kindern. Er ist sozusagen nicht der Kamerad seiner Kinder, sondern ihr Vorgesetzter. Er verlangt Respekt und Gehorsam."

Der Schaffner ruft aus: „Nächste Station Köln." Karl sagt: „Genug geredet. Es ist Zeit auszusteigen."

11. Bei der Familie Lenz

„Das war ein ausgezeichnetes Essen, Frau Lenz", sagte Herr Klein. Dann wandte er sich an Herrn Lenz. „Ihre Frau ist eine hervorragende Köchin. Die deutsche Küche hat mir immer vorzüglich geschmeckt, aber die Mahlzeit heute abend war besonders gut."

„Sie haben ja unseren kleinen Nachtisch noch nicht versucht", sagte Frau Lenz bescheiden. „Vielleicht werden Sie dann Ihre Meinung ändern."

„Das bezweifle ich", lächelte Herr Klein. „Den leckeren Sauerbraten werde ich so schnell nicht vergessen. Und auch die Bratkartoffeln waren erstklassig."

„Und jetzt zum Nachtisch bekommen Sie frische Erdbeeren."

Nach dem Essen setzten sich die Herren gemütlich ins Wohnzimmer. (Währenddessen spülten die armen Frauen das Geschirr in der Küche ab.) Bald waren sie in ein interessantes Gespräch vertieft.

Herr Lenz bemerkte: „Ihr Kurt hat prima Deutsch gelernt. Er macht ab und zu noch einen grammatischen Fehler, besonders mit den Endungen der Adjektive, aber er hat seinen amerikanischen Akzent fast ganz verloren. Unser Karl spricht rheinländisches Deutsch. Kurt wird reines Hochdeutsch sprechen."

„Hochdeutsch?" fragte Kurt.

„Ja", erwiderte Herr Lenz. „Dieser Begriff ist für den Ausländer oft verwirrend. Er bezeichnet die Sprache von Ober- und Mitteldeutsch im Gegensatz zu Nieder- oder Plattdeutsch. Aber er bezeichnet auch die deutsche Schriftsprache im Gegensatz zu den Mundarten und der Umgangssprache."

„Deutsch", fuhr Herr Lenz fort, „zeigt viel Verwandtschaft mit anderen modernen westlichen Sprachen. Deutsch hat aber mehr Formen als Französisch, Spanisch oder Italienisch, denn man dekliniert alle Substantive, Adjektive und Pronomen. Die Verben hingegen sind leicht — Deutsch teilt sie nicht in Konjugationen ein wie die romanischen Sprachen. Die Verben zeigen oft eine enge Verwandtschaft mit dem Englischen."

In diesem Augenblick kamen die Damen aus der Küche. „Will jemand mehr Kaffee oder vielleicht ein Gläschen Wein?" erkundigte sich Frau Lenz.

Alle lehnten mit Dank ab. „Möchtet ihr euch jetzt nicht zu uns setzen?" fragte Herr Lenz seine Gattin und Tochter.

„Gerne", antwortete Lore sofort.

12. **Persönliche Anzeigen**

Nach mehreren Stunden kehrte Kurt ins Hotel zurück. Sein Vater saß bequem in einem Ledersessel und war wach und munter. Auf dem Tisch neben ihm lagen einige Zeitungen und auch etliche Illustrierte.

„Eines kann ich immer noch nicht verstehen", bemerkte Herr Klein. „Sieh dir dieses Blatt an! Die deutschen Zeitungsausgaben sind im

allgemeinen viel dünner als unsere und doch bringen sie so viele Nach=
richten über Außen= und Innenpolitik, Wirtschaftsprobleme und
Lokalangelegenheiten wie bei uns. Und sieh dir auch diese Spalten an mit
persönlichen Anzeigen . . ."

Kurt lachte. „Du meinst gewiß die vielen Geburts=, Verlobungs=,
Vermählungs= und Todesanzeigen. Wie zum Beispiel hier: ,Die Geburt
unseres ersten Sohnes Heinz zeigen wir hocherfreut an'. Oder diese
andere: ,Statt Karten. Wir vermählen uns am . . .' Oder: ,Gestern
abend verschied nach langem Leiden unser lieber Großvater, Friedrich
Müller'. Ich finde das alles ganz nett und sehr geschmackvoll."

„Und das hältst du hiervon?" fragte der Vater und fing zu lesen an.
„ ,Hübsche kultivierte Witwe, heitere Natur, zuverlässiger Charakter,
attraktive Erscheinung, sucht neues Eheglück mit gebildetem, gut aus=
sehendem Herrn im Alter bis 58 Jahre. Vertraulich . . .' "

Kurt hatte viele solche Anzeigen gesehen. Zuerst fand er sie lächerlich,
sogar grotesk. „Das verstößt doch gegen den guten Geschmack!" hatte er
sich öfter gesagt. Dann dachte er: „Andere Länder, andere Sitten."

Der Vater hatte unterdessen eine andere Anzeige entdeckt: „Wie ge=
fällt dir diese Anzeige? ,Ich danke der Feuerwehr und allen Nachbarn,
die so tapfer mitgeholfen haben, den großen Brand bei mir zu löschen'.
Und dann steht der Name und die Adresse des Bauern."

„Warum nicht?" fragte Kurt. „Auf diese Art und Weise sprechen die
Deutschen oft ihren Dank aus oder teilen ihren Bekannten ihre Fa=
milienereignisse mit. Natürlich haben manche Leute besseren Geschmack
als andere. Und das ist überall so."

13.   Haben die Amerikaner es besser?

Die Unterhaltung hatte sich gestern abend lange um Unterschiede
zwischen dem Leben in Deutschland und Amerika gedreht. Im Laufe des
Abends hatte Herr Lenz oft mit dem Kopf genickt. „Ja, Goethe hatte
recht", hat er immer wiederholt. „Er hatte zweifellos recht." Kurts
Vater hatte entweder nicht richtig achtgegeben oder die Bemerkung nicht
verstanden, denn er hatte gar nicht darauf reagiert.

Auch Kurt hatte sie nicht richtig verstanden. Goethe war Deutschlands
größter und bekanntester Dichter, und Kurt hatte seine besten Gedichte
und berühmtesten Stücke gelesen. Diese Bemerkung konnte er sich aber
nicht erklären, solange er auch darüber nachdachte. Womit hatte Goethe

recht? Endlich konnte er sich nicht mehr bezähmen und gab seine Verlegen=
heit zu.

Karl lachte: „Goethe schrieb einmal ein Gedicht, ‚Amerika, du hast es
besser‘. Als mein Vater deinem Vater zuhörte, dachte er besonders an
Goethes Worte. Er kennt ja Goethe in= und auswendig, und sogar ich
kann mich an die erste Strophe erinnern“:

> Amerika, du hast es besser
>
> Als unser Kontinent, der alte.
>
> Hast keine verfallenen Schlösser
>
> Und keine Basalte.

„Verstehe ich ihn richtig?“ fragte Kurt. „Amerikaner sind weniger an
die Tradition gebunden.“

„Sie haben dadurch weniger Vorurteile als die Europäer“, fügte Karl
hinzu. „Unsere politischen Einrichtungen z.B. sind vielleicht veraltet,
und wir sind deshalb nicht in der Lage, so rasche Fortschritte zu machen.“

„Aber haben wir es heute wirklich besser?“ fragte Kurt.

„Vielen Deutschen kommt das so vor“, sagte Karl. „Für sie ist
Amerika immer noch das Land der reichen Leute und der unbegrenzten
Möglichkeiten. Amerika hat schon über hundert Jahre keinen Krieg auf
eigenem Boden geführt. Sie wissen, wie stark die Schwerindustrie ist
und wie sie das Leben des einzelnen Menschen beeinflußt hat. Aber viel
mehr noch bewundern und beneiden sie die schönen, modernen Wohnungen
in den amerikanischen Filmen: Wohnungen mit den neuesten Einrichtun=
gen und Geräten. Alle Amerikaner scheinen wenigstens ein Auto zu
besitzen und viele Leute aus dem Mittelstand sogar zwei. Das Leben der
amerikanischen Hausfrau scheint viel leichter zu sein als das unserer
Frauen. Siehst du, Kurt, meinen Eltern geht es prima für deutsche
Verhältnisse, viel besser als den meisten Deutschen. Aber im Vergleich
zum amerikanischen Leben...“

„Ihr habt doch seit dem Kriege viele Amerikaner kennengelernt. Sind
sie glücklicher oder zufriedener als ihr? Ich wiederhole: geht es uns
wirklich besser?“

Karl mußte lachen, denn Kurt verlangte anscheinend eine direkte
Antwort. „Die Unterschiede zwischen den Ländern werden kleiner und
unwichtiger“, sagte er, „aber eines wird immer schwieriger, mein
Freund.“

„Und was ist das?“

„Der Unterschied zwischen Mythus und Wirklichkeit. Und dies ist
vielleicht unser Hauptproblem.“

14. Eine Reise nach Bonn

„Ein Ferngespräch", rief Frau Kolb am Spätnachmittag. Ihre Stimme klang etwas erregt. In ihrem ganzen Leben hatte sie nur drei Ferngespräche bekommen und alle drei hatten mit traurigen Nachrichten zu tun.

Kurts Vater, Herr Klein, war am Apparat. Es war ihm gelungen, den geschäftlichen Teil seiner Reise früher als erwartet abzuschließen. Könnte Kurt nach Bonn kommen? Sie würden zusammen eine Stadtrundfahrt machen und am Abend vielleicht nach Bad Godesberg fahren. Herr Klein war mit einem Sekretär der amerikanischen Botschaft befreundet, und dieser Herr mit einem so verantwortungsvollen Posten hatte sie zum Abendessen eingeladen. Kurt war noch immer mißgestimmt wegen der Prüfung und wollte sich zerstreuen.

Also hielt er kurz nach vier vor dem Büro der amerikanischen Firma. Der Vater hatte längere Zeit auf ihn gewartet und war unruhig geworden, denn der Verkehr auf der Autobahn war äußerst stark. Jetzt stellte er Kurt stolz seinen Kollegen vor. Dann verabschiedeten sie sich, um ihre Stadtrundfahrt zu machen.

Sie fuhren zusammen durch die Hauptstadt. Sie fanden sie hübsch, friedlich und ruhig, aber waren doch ein bißchen enttäuscht. Sie fragten sich, ob so ein kleines, anscheinend unbedeutendes Städtchen wirklich die Hauptstadt eines großen Landes sein könnte. Herr Klein hatte Berlin früher sehr gut gekannt und zog immer wieder Vergleiche.

Nein, Bonn war doch so verschieden von Berlin! Hier gab es keine historischen Denkmäler wie das Brandenburger Tor, keine herrlichen Straßen wie den Kurfürstendamm, verhältnismäßig wenige Kinos, keine Untergrundbahnen und auch weniger Tageszeitungen, Konzertsäle und Kaufhäuser als in vielen anderen deutschen Städten. Außerdem ist Berlin heute noch eine der größten deutschen Industriestädte mit großer wirtschaftlicher Bedeutung. Mit der Entstehung des vereinigten deutschen Reiches im Jahre 1871 ist es auch weltpolitisch immer wichtiger geworden. Zur gleichen Zeit hat sich die preußische Hauptstadt zu einem kulturellen Zentrum entwickeln können. Aber Berlin ist heute von der Bundesrepublik geographisch getrennt und selbst in zwei Teile gespalten. Es eignet sich also nicht mehr zur Hauptstadt der Bundesrepublik.

„Ja, warum gerade Bonn?" fragte der Vater. „Gab es keine anderen Städte? Warum hat sich Frankfurt oder Köln nicht dazu geeignet?"

Karl hatte Kurt seine Ansichten über diese Frage dargelegt. Man hatte Bonn vornehmlich aus praktischen Gründen gewählt. Größere Städte waren zerstört. Man hatte Sorgen genug damit, Wohnungen zu bauen und konnte die Städte nicht mit solchen Problemen belasten. In Bonn war auch manches zerstört, aber es gab noch reichlich Platz zur Errichtung von neuen Regierungsgebäuden. Auch hatte es den Politikern und Diplomaten sehr gut gefallen, daß man von Bonn aus herrliche Fahrten unternehmen konnte und eine schöne Aussicht auf den Rhein und das Siebengebirge hatte.

„Weißt du, Vater, vor dem Krieg wohnten hier weniger als 20 000 Leute, meistens Beamte, Universitätsprofessoren und Studenten. Jetzt ist die Einwohnerzahl auf 141 000 gestiegen."

Vater und Sohn hatten die Hauptstraßen besichtigt, auch das Beethovenhaus und das Rathaus. Das Bundeshaus war schon geschlossen. Herr Klein telefonierte mit der amerikanischen Botschaft. Man erwartete sie gegen acht Uhr, sagte der Sekretär, und Kurt und Herr Klein machten sich sofort auf den Weg.

15. Eine Einladung nach Bayern

Es war schon nach neun Uhr abends, als es bei Kolbs klingelte. Zuerst achtete Kurt nicht darauf, weil Herr Kolb oft spät Gäste zum Kartenspiel empfing. Aber dann hörte Kurt Schritte auf der Treppe, und er wußte, daß er jetzt Besuch bekommen würde. Ganz verlegen fuhr er sich schnell mit dem Kamm durch das Haar, öffnete die Tür und war überrascht, als er die Geschwister Lenz erblickte.

„Was wollt ihr denn so spät?" fragte er, ohne zu merken, wie unhöflich das klang.

„So heißt du uns willkommen?" Karl schien fast beleidigt zu sein. „Nun, dann brauchen wir dir auch nichts von der Einladung zu sagen."

„Einladung? Davon höre ich immer gern."

Albert Lorreng, ein alter Freund von Karl Lenz, hatte vor einer halben Stunde angerufen und Karl und Lore eingeladen, mit ihm zum Schilaufen in die Bayrischen Alpen zu fahren. Er hatte noch Platz in seinem großen Wagen und Kurt konnte selbstverständlich mitkommen.

Kurt hatte immer dem Wunsch gehabt, einmal Bayern zu besuchen. Eigentlich wußte er nicht warum, denn er interessierte sich recht wenig für Schilaufen. Seitdem er vor langer Zeit in Colorado gestürzt war und sich das Bein gebrochen hatte, hatte er fast alles Interesse für diesen Sport verloren. Jetzt dachte er, daß er vielleicht ein zu starkes Vorurteil gegen einen Sport hatte, der jetzt bei der Jugend so beliebt war. Er sollte ihn doch wieder probieren, da er ja inzwischen älter und reifer geworden war.

Nachdem die Freunde ihn wieder verlassen hatten, nahm Kurt ein Reisebuch über Bayern von seinem Bücherregal. „Obwohl es heute Fabriken in den Städten gibt", las er leise vor sich hin, „bleibt Bayern doch ein Agrarland, ein Land mit Höfen und Feldern, Weiden und Wäldern." Kurt blätterte weiter. „Der Bayer ist kein Träumer; er ist Realist und liebt deshalb nur das Echte." Kurt dachte: „Wie komisch, daß diese Reisebücher immer alles verallgemeinern."

Dann kam er zu dem Kapitel „Wintersport". Er las weiter: „Wenn Sie nach Garmisch-Partenkirchen kommen, dem bekanntesten Winter-sportplatz Bayerns, dann bewundern Sie nicht nur seine Lage am Fuße der Alpen. Nein, Sie werden staunen, daß Garmisch trotz seiner Be-rühmtheit seinen ländlichen Charakter bewahren konnte. Ideal für Sportler sind die Schilifte, Bergbahnen, und das große Eisstadion. Neben dem Schilaufen können Sie Ausflüge machen in die vielen kleinen, idyllisch gelegenen Dörfer, die Sie überall in den Bayrischen und Österreichischen Alpen finden."

Ein anderes Kapitel handelte von der Geschichte Bayerns und betonte, daß Bayern immer ein Grenzland war, daß seine Macht durch den Dreißigjährigen Krieg größer wurde, daß seine Hauptstädte — wie München und Nürnberg — viel im Zweiten Weltkrieg gelitten hatten und daß es seitdem einen starken Zustrom von Flüchtlingen gab. Kurt wollte noch die Kapitel über München und Nürnberg lesen, merkte jedoch, wie er immer müder wurde. Endlich legte er das Buch nieder. Als er am Einschlafen war, dachte er: „Komisch, ich habe nicht mal ge-fragt, wann wir abfahren. Nun, ich hoffe nur, daß wir fahren . . . ."

16. Franz Kafka

Kurt war die Brechtarbeit satt, an der er schon so lange arbeitete. Er mußte eine Zeitlang damit aussetzen, um mehr Abstand von der Sache zu gewinnen. In der Zwischenzeit wollte er aber nicht faulenzen. Hier war die Gelegenheit, nach der er sich so lange gesehnt hatte, nämlich einige Werke von Franz Kafka zu lesen. Dieser Schriftsteller, der ihm bisher nur durch ein paar kurze Erzählungen bekannt war, hatte schnell sein Interesse geweckt. Vor allen Dingen hatte „Die Verwandlung" einen sehr großen Eindruck auf ihn gemacht. Eine unglaubliche Geschichte: Ein Geschäftsreisender, der immer seine Pflicht getan hatte, findet sich eines Morgens in ein Insekt verwandelt! Kurt hatte keinerlei Probleme gehabt, diese Erzählung zu interpretieren.

Als er nun zweihundert Seiten von Kaffas „Der Prozeß" gelesen hatte, sah er plötzlich ein, daß er daraus nicht klug werden konnte. Dieser Roman, dessen Stil er bewunderte, dessen Handlung er jedoch nicht zu deuten wußte, schien ihm ein Rätsel zu sein.

Bei anderen Schriftstellern hatte ihm der Lebenslauf manchmal einige Anhaltspunkte gegeben. Jetzt las er: „Kaffa, Franz. In Prag geboren, studierte Jura in Prag und München. Begann früh mit schriftstellerischen Arbeiten. Danach Angestellter an einer Versicherungsanstalt in Prag. Unternahm verschiedene Auslandsreisen. Zog 1923 nach Berlin; im folgenden Jahr in Wien im Alter von 41 Jahren gestorben."

„Das hilft nicht viel", dachte Kurt. „Ich muß wohl eine ganze Biographie lesen." Und dann stellten sich mehrere interessante Tatsachen heraus.

Denn hier fand er endlich Kaffas großes Problem: sein Verhältnis zu seinem Vater. Der junge Schriftsteller sah in seinem Vater all das verkörpert, was er selbst werden wollte, aber was er nie sein konnte. Er fühlte sich von ihm unterdrückt und mißverstanden. Kaffa, der an einem furchtbaren Minderwertigkeitsgefühl litt, fand es unmöglich, mit seinem Vater zu brechen. So unsicher fühlte er sich, daß er sich zweimal verlobte, aber es nie wagte, zu heiraten. Dieser schöpferische Schriftsteller, dessen Werk in alle Kultursprachen übersetzt ist und Gegenstand akademischer Studien bleibt, hatte in seinem Nachlaß verfügt, daß man nach seinem Tode alle Manuskripte verbrennen sollte. Kaffas Freund, der Schriftsteller Max Brod, weigerte sich, im Sinne Kaffas zu handeln, und ließ seine Manuskripte veröffentlichen.

Angst vor aller Autorität — Vater, Polizei, Gericht, Staat; Selbstbefreiung von Schuldgefühl; der modellhafte Mensch, der sich nicht behaupten kann — hier waren Themen in Kaffas Leben, die auch im Roman vorhanden waren. Jetzt konnte Kurt zu seiner Lektüre zurückkehren. Diesmal las er den Roman fertig und hatte das Gefühl, ihn viel besser zu verstehen.

17. Wichtige Ereignisse in Goethes Leben

In den zwanzig Jahren seines Lebens ist Kurt erst einmal in einem Fach durchgefallen. Dies geschah in seinem 17. Lebensjahr. Er war damals im 3. Jahr in der „High School". Das Fach war Geschichte.

Kurt konnte einfach die Daten nicht behalten; 16. oder 17. Jahrhundert war ihm gleich — sie gehörten beide derselben toten Vergangenheit an. Leider hatte sein Geschichtslehrer ganz andere Gedanken darüber und erwies dem armen Kurt recht wenig Verständnis und Mitleid.

Kurt hat wiederum ein Problem mit der Vergangenheit. Er soll die folgenden wichtigen Daten im Leben Goethes auswendig lernen. Immer wieder liest er:

28. August 1749
Goethe in Frankfurt am Main geboren.

1765–1768
Studium der Rechte in Leipzig.

1770–1771
Abschluß des Studiums in Straßburg. Entwickelt Pläne zu „Götz" und „Faust".

1775
Verlobung und Lösung der Verlobung mit Lili Schönemann. Einladung des Herzogs Karl=August nach Weimar. Am 7. November Ankunft in Weimar.

1776–1788
Freundschaft mit Charlotte von Stein. Viele Briefe und Gedichte an sie.

1780
Ernennung zum Minister, zwei Jahre später zum Finanzminister und Verleihung des Adelstitels.

1786–1788
Erste italienische Reise; Aufenthalt in Rom, intensive Beschäfti= gung mit antiker Kunst.

1790
Zweite italienische Reise.

1792–1793
Teilnahme am Feldzug in Frankreich.

1794
Beginn der Freundschaft mit Schiller.

1805–1806
Schillers Tod. „Faust, Erster Teil" beendet.

1808
Zusammentreffen mit Napoleon.

22. März 1832
Goethes Tod.

Kurt hat nur noch eine halbe Stunde zum Lernen. Er ist ärgerlich über diese Aufgabe. Wie kann ich diese Zahlen behalten, fragt er sich, wenn ich viel Wichtigeres vergesse? Zum Beispiel habe ich Frau Kolb die Miete von DM 9,50 noch nicht bezahlt. Und ich schulde Karl DM 20,30. Hoffentlich schickt Vater mir bald die erwünschte Summe von DM 200. Dann komme ich vielleicht mit meinem Geld aus. Aber jetzt zurück zur Chronologie!

18. Die Musik in Deutschland

Nachdem Kurt sich einigermaßen von seiner Grippe erholt hatte, führte er Lore Lenz zum Tanz in ein erstklassiges Hotel, wo eine berühmte Kapelle spielte. Man tanzte meistens zu amerikanischen Schlagern, die Lore viel besser kannte als er.

„Wie ist das zu erkären"? fragte er sie, „daß du dich so gut in unserer Tanzmusik auskennst"?

„Das ist leicht zu verstehen", lachte sie. „Ich war schließlich auch einmal 16 Jahre alt. Mit meinem erstverdienten Geld wurde ein Plattenspieler gekauft und danach habe ich mir auch langsam Schallplatten angeschafft. Natürlich wurden mir auch manche zum Geburtstag geschenkt. In dem Alter interessierte ich mich hauptsächlich für Beat=Musik. Meine Eltern waren nicht davon begeistert und haben sich immer wieder über den Lärm beklagt. Es war aber nicht der Lärm, der sie störte. Ich hatte das Gefühl, daß sie, wie so viele Eltern, diese Müsik als eine Gefahr betrachteten, vor der ich geschützt werden mußte. Du hast vielleicht gelesen, daß in manchen Städten die Jazz=Keller polizeilich bewacht und sogar kontrolliert werden. Die Jazz=Musik soll nicht gut für unsere Jugend sein. Selbstverständlich denkt die Jugend anders darüber."

„Werden denn die alten Volkslieder gar nicht mehr gesungen"? fragte Kurt enttäuscht.

„Doch", antwortete Lore, „sie werden noch immer in der Schule gelehrt und man singt sie auch bei besonderen Gelegenheiten. Bei den Teenagern sind sie jedoch weniger in Mode."

„Und die ältere Generation?" erkundigte sich Kurt. „Bei ihr wird doch ‚gute' Musik bevorzugt . . ."

„Ganz gewiß", lachte Lore, und erzählte ihm, wie sehr ihr Vater noch immer die Symphonien und Opern liebte. Herr Lenz ging zum Beispiel zu fast allen Konzerten, die von dem berühmten Kölner Gürzenich Orchester aufgeführt wurden. Manchmal klagte er aber, daß man zu viele klassische und romantische Stücke spielte und dabei die zeitgenössische Musik vernachlässigte. Herr Lenz gehörte zu den wenigen, die sich für die neuen Techniken interessierten, mit denen man besonders in Deutschland viel experimentiert und interessante Resultate erzielt hatte. Diese modernen Kompositionen konnte man eher bei den jungen Rundfunkorchestern hören als bei den altberühmten philharmonischen Orchestern.

Auch fuhr Herr Lenz mehrere Male im Jahr zu Musikfestspielen, die man in fast allen Großstädten und auch in einigen kleinen Orten veranstaltete. „So fährt er zum Beispiel immer nach Bonn", erzählte Lore, „wo das Beethovenfest gefeiert wird. Zwischen Mozart in Würzburg und Wagner in Bayreuth wird gewöhnlich abgewechselt. Wo er auch hinfährt, schleppt er Mutti immer mit. Aber ich glaube, sie interessiert sich mehr für die Modenschau, die Eleganz des Publikums und die Schaufensterdekorationen als für die Musik. Sie hat natürlich nicht den Mut, das einzugestehen".

„Ich würde auch ganz gerne zu einem Festspiel fahren", sagte Kurt. „Vielleicht finde ich die Zeit dazu."

19. Verpaßte Gelegenheiten

Am letzten Tage seines Aufenthaltes in der Bundesrepublik war Kurt mürrisch. Die Ursache seiner schlechten Laune war weder der Gedanke an die morgige Abreise noch die Trennung von Lore und anderen netten Freunden. Es war eher die Tatsache, daß gewisse Ziele, die er sich für seinen Aufenthalt in Deutschland gesetzt hatte, nicht erreicht waren. Auch mancher Plan, den er vor seiner Abfahrt gefaßt hatte, hatte sich als unrealistisch erwiesen. Was hatte er falsch gemacht? Stünde er jetzt erneut vor seinem Besuch, was würde er anders machen?

„Ich würde gewiß weniger bummeln", dachte er. „Ich habe mich immer großartig im Café unterhalten und zweifellos viel dabei gelernt, aber ich hätte öfter auf die Uhr schauen sollen. Was meine Reisepläne anbetrifft — sie waren nicht immer die besten. Es wäre doch klüger gewesen, wenn ich mich nicht auf das Rheinland und Bayern beschränkt hätte. Ich hätte wenigstens einmal nach dem Norden fahren sollen. Auch ist es schwer zu verstehen, daß ich nicht einer einzigen Sitzung des Bundeshauses beigewohnt habe, obwohl die Hauptstadt nur ein paar Kilometer entfernt ist.

„Außerdem bestehen noch zu viele Lücken in meinem Studium der deutschen Literatur. Wenn ich mehr von den Werken jener Dichter

gelesen hätte, die nicht so leicht zu verstehen sind, und wenn ich mir über=
haupt mehr Zeit zum Lesen genommen hätte, so wäre ich heute abend
befriedigter. Dann würde mir auch meine gesamte Leistung in einem viel
günstigeren Lichte erscheinen."

Plötzlich fing Kurt zu lachen an. „Ich Idiot", sagte er vor sich hin,
„ich spreche ja, als ob ich ein Greis wäre und Deutschland nie wieder
besuchen würde. Gewiß, ich habe nicht immer klug gehandelt und manch=
mal wichtige Gelegenheiten verpaßt. Aber im großen und ganzen hätte
ich längst nicht so viel gelernt, wenn ich zu Hause geblieben wäre. Ich
habe großen Vorteil aus meinem Studium hier gezogen. Also muß ich
zufrieden sein."

Mit diesem Gedanken schlief Kurt endlich ein.

VOCABULARIES

Numbers after German items indicate the lesson in which the expression first occurs. (I) stands for Introduction.

The plural of nouns is indicated as follows: der **Mann, ⁻er.** The genitive ending is given only for masculine and neuter nouns forming the genitive in -(e)n or -(e)ns: der **Präsident, -en, -en;** das **Herz, -ens, -en.**

Principal parts are listed for strong and irregular verbs. A separable prefix is indicated by a slash: **ab/holen.**

Words not stressed on the first syllable are marked as follows: a dot to indicate a stressed short vowel **(entfernt)**, a dash to indicate a stressed long vowel or diphthong **(gewöhnt, verkaufen).**

Most words of low frequency in the pronunciation exercises are omitted from the end vocabulary.

ab (5) off, away from, from; **auf und ab** (4) up and down **ab und zu** (11) now and then

der **Abend, -e** (I) evening; **abends** (18) in the evening; **guten Abend** (I) good evening; **heute Abend** (I) tonight, this evening; **zu Abend essen** (I) to eat dinner

das **Abendessen, -** (14) supper, dinner
  aber (I) but, however
  ab/fahren, fuhr ab, ist abgefahren, fährt ab (6) to leave, depart *(by vehicle)*

die **Abfahrt, -en** (19) departure

der **Abflug, ⁓e** (20) departure by air
  abgemacht (12) settled, agreed
  abgetragen (15) worn out, threadbare
  ab/holen (14) to meet, pick up, call for *(somebody or something)*

das **Abitur** (8) *a comprehensive final examination at certain secondary schools (see: Gymnasium);* **das Abitur machen** (8) to take the (Abitur) examination
  ab/kommen, kam ab, ist abgekommen; vom Thema ab/kommen (13) to get off the subject
  ab/legen: ein Examen ab/legen (8) to take an examination
  ab/lehnen (11) to refuse, decline
  ab/nehmen, nahm ab, abgenommen, nimmt ab (8) to take off, remove
  ab/rechnen (18) to settle accounts

die **Abreise, -n** (19) departure
  ab/reisen (14) to depart, leave
  ab/schicken (17) to send off, dispatch

der **Abschied, -e** (20) farewell, good-by
  ab/schließen, schloß ab, abgeschlossen (14) to conclude, bring to a close

der **Abschluß, ⁓sse** (17) conclusion
  ab/schneiden, schnitt ab, abgeschnitten (8) to make out *(on an examination)*
  ab/spülen (11) to wash *(dishes)*

der **Abstand, ⁓e** (16) distance, perspective, interval

die **Abteilung, -en** (9) department
  ab/tragen, trug ab, abgetragen, trägt ab (15) to wear out *(clothes)*
  ab/wechseln (18) to alternate
  ach (I) oh
  acht (2) eight
  acht: sich in acht nehmen (20) to watch out, be on one's guard
  achten (10) to respect
  achten auf *(with acc.)* (15) to pay attention to

acht/geben auf *(with acc.),* **gab acht, acht-gegeben, gibt acht** (13) to pay attention to, take care of

die **Achtung** (10) attention; respect
  achtzehn (4) eighteen

der **Adelstitel** (17) title of nobility

das **Adjektiv, -e** (11) adjective

die **Adresse, -n** (1) address

das **Agrarland, ⁓er** (15) agrarian region
  ahnen (20) to suspect, have a presentiment

die **Ahnung, -en** (7) idea, inkling; **ich habe keine Ahnung** I haven't the slightest idea

der **Akademiker, -** (8) academician
  akademisch (16) academic

der **Akzent, -e** (4) accent
  all- (I) all
  allein (4) alone
  allerlei (10) all sorts of
  alles (2) everything
  allgemein (4) general(ly); **im allgemeinen** (4) in general

die **Alpen** (4) the Alps
  als (11) as, than
  also (2) thus, so
  alt (1) old
  altberühmt (18) long-famous

das **Alter, -** (1) age
  altmodisch (16) old-fashioned

(das) **Amerika** (1) America

das **Amt, ⁓er** (I) office
  amüsieren (13) to amuse; **sich amüsieren** (6) to have a good time
  an *(with acc. or dat.)* (1) to, at, on
  an/betreffen, betraf an, anbetroffen, betrifft an (19) to concern; **was . . . anbetrifft** as far as . . . is concerned
  andauernd (18) constantly, continuously, continually

(sich) **ändern** (10) to change; **die Meinung ändern** (11) to change one's opinion
  anders (5) different(ly)
  anderthalb (17) one and a half

die **Änderung, -en** (19) change

der **Anfang, ⁓e** (5) beginning
  an/fangen, fing an, angefangen, fängt an (18) to begin

der **Anhaltspunkt, -e** (16) point of reference, foothold
  an/geben, gab an, angegeben, gibt an (6) to indicate, specify
  an/gehören (17) to belong to

angenehm (I) pleasant; **sehr angenehm** pleased to meet you

der **Angestellte, -n, -n** (16) employee

die **Angst, ⁻e** (16) fear, anxiety
Angst haben (**vor,** with dat.) (9) to be afraid (of)

an/kommen, kam an, ist angekommen (6) to arrive
an/kommen auf (with acc.), **kam an, ist angekommen** (6) to depend on

die **Ankündigung, -en** (20) announcement

die **Ankunft, ⁻e** (1) arrival
annähernd (17) approaching, close to
an/nehmen, nahm an, angenommen, nimmt an (8) to assume, accept

der **Anruf, -e** (8) (telephone) call
an/rufen, rief an, angerufen (8) to call (up)

die **Ansage, -n** (20) announcement
an/sagen (14) to announce

(**sich**) (dat.) **an/schaffen** (18) to acquire, get, procure (for oneself)
anscheinend (13) apparently
an/schnallen (20) to fasten (seat belts), buckle up
an/schneiden, schnitt an, angeschnitten (16) to start (a conversation, etc.); **ein Thema an/schneiden** to tackle a subject

(**sich**) (dat.) **an/sehen, sah an, angesehen, sieht an** (5) to look at, take a look at

die **Ansicht, -en** (14) opinion

die **Ansichtskarte, -n** (8) picture postcard

die **Ansichtssache, -n** (20) matter of opinion
anständig (17) nice, decent
anstatt (5) (with gen.) instead of
ansteckend (18) contagious
an/stellen (8) to employ; **angestellt** (8) employed, working
anstrengend (17) strenuous
antik (17) antique, ancient

die **Antwort, -en** (20) answer
antworten (1) to answer

die **Anweisung, -en** (11) instruction, order, direction

die **Anzeige, -n** (12) ad, announcement

sich an/ziehen, zog an, angezogen (6) to get dressed

der **Anzug, ⁻e** (15) suit

der **Apfel, ⁻** (3) apple

die **Apotheke, -n** (18) pharmacy

der **Apparat, -e** (14) telephone, apparatus, utensil

(der) **April** (17) April

die **Arbeit, -en** (15) work, job
arbeiten (I) to work

der **Architekt, -en, -en** (2) architect

die **Architektur** (7) architecture
ärgerlich (6) angry

sich ärgern über (with acc.) (6) to be angry, annoyed (at, about); **es ärgert mich** it makes me angry

arm (11) poor

die **Art, -en** (9) kind, type; **auf ihre Art** (9) in their way; **auf diese Art und Weise** (12) in this way

die **Arznei, -en** (18) medicine

der **Arzt, ⁻e** (18) physician

der **Assistent, -en, -en** (12) assistant

der **Atlantik** (4) Atlantic Ocean
atmen (I) to breathe
attraktiv (12) attractive
auch (I) also
auf (with acc. or dat.) (I) on, onto; **auf und ab** (4) up and down
auf Wiedersehen (I) good-by

der **Aufenthalt, -e** (7) stop, stay, sojourn
auffallend (9) conspicuous(ly), striking
auf/führen (7) to perform

die **Aufgabe, -n** (I) lesson
auf/hören (15) to cease, stop
aufmerksam (12) attentive, helpful

die **Aufmerksamkeit, -en** (20) kindness, kind attention

die **Aufnahme, -n** (7) snapshot
aufrecht/erhalten, erhielt aufrecht, aufrechterhalten, erhält aufrecht (3) to preserve, maintain

sich auf/richten (6) to sit upright

der **Aufsatz, ⁻e** (I) composition, essay
auf/schieben, schob auf, aufgeschoben (20) to postpone
auf/schlagen, schlug auf, aufgeschlagen, schlägt auf (I) to open (a book)
auf/stehen, stand auf, ist aufgestanden (I) to get up
auf/wachen, ist aufgewacht (6) to wake up

das **Auge, -n** (6) eye

der **Augenblick, -e** (11) moment

(der) **August** (17) August
aus (with dat.) (I) from, out of

die **Ausbildungsmöglichkeit, -en** (8) educational possibility

(**sich**) **aus/drücken** (5) to express

die **Ausgabe, -n** (15) expenditure
aus/geben, gab aus, ausgegeben, gibt aus (12) to spend (money)
aus/gehen, ging aus, ist ausgegangen (9) to go out
ausgeschlossen (18) out of the question
ausgezeichnet (11) excellent
aus/halten, hielt aus, ausgehalten, hält aus (20) to stand, endure

sich aus/kennen, kannte aus, ausgekannt (8) to know one's way around

aus/kommen mit, kam aus, ist ausgekommen (17)   to get along on, make do with
die **Auskunft, ⁼e** (I)   information
das **Ausland** (7)   foreign countries, abroad
die **Auslandsreise, -n** (16)   trip abroad
die **Ausrede, -n** (20)   excuse
aus/rufen, rief aus, ausgerufen (10)   to proclaim, exclaim
sich **aus/ruhen** (6)   to take a rest
aus/sehen, sah aus, ausgesehen, sieht aus (8)   to look, appear
die **Außenpolitik** (12)   foreign policy
außer *(with dat.)* (4)   except, besides
außerdem (14)   besides, moreover
außerordentlich (11)   extraordinary
äußerst (14)   extreme(ly)
aus/setzen (16)   to pause, take a break
die **Aussicht, -en** (2)   view, prospect
die **Aussprache** (4)   pronunciation
aus/sprechen, sprach aus, ausgesprochen, spricht aus (12)   to express, pronounce
aus/steigen, stieg aus, ist ausgestiegen (6)   to get off
aus/tauschen (8)   to exchange
der **Ausverkauf, ⁼e** (15)   clearance sale
ausverkauft (12)   sold out
auswendig (5)   by heart; **auswendig können** (5)   to know by heart, memorize
sich **aus/ziehen, zog aus, ausgezogen** (6)   to undress
das **Auto, -s** (4)   automobile
die **Autobahn, -en** (13)   super highway
die **Autorität** (10)   authority
die **Autostraße, -n** (13)   highway

der **Bach, ⁼e** (2)   brook, stream
backen, backte (buk), gebacken, bäckt (I)   to bake
der **Bäcker, -** (8)   baker
die **Bäckerei, -en** (8)   bakery
der **Bäckerlehrling, -e** (8)   baker's apprentice
das **Bad, ⁼er** (6)   bath, bathroom
die **Bahn, -en** (I)   path, road, railroad
der **Bahnhof, ⁼e** (10)   railroad station
bald (I)   soon
der **Band, ⁼e** (5)   volume
die **Bank, ⁼e** (3)   bench
der **Basalt, -e** (13)   basalt
bauen (7)   to build
der **Bauer, -n** (12)   farmer, peasant
das **Bauernhaus, ⁼er**   farmhouse
der **Baum, ⁼e** (I)   tree
der **Baustil** (2)   style of architecture
der **Bayer, -n, -n** (7)   Bavarian
(das) **Bayern** (I)   Bavaria
der **Beamte, -n, -n** (14)   official
beantworten (1)   to answer *(a question)*

sich **bedanken (für)** (20)   to thank (for)
bedeuten (I)   to mean
bedeutend (14)   important
die **Bedeutung, -en** (5)   meaning, significance
sich **beeilen** (6)   to hurry
beeindrucken (7)   to make an impression
beeinflussen (13)   to influence
beenden (17)   to end
das **Beethovenfest, -e** (18)   Beethoven Festival
sich **befassen** (7)   to be concerned with, treat
befreunden (14)   to befriend
befriedigt (19)   satisfied, gratified
sich **begeben, begab, begeben, begibt** (6)   to betake oneself
begegnen, ist begegnet *(with dat.)* (4)   to meet, come upon *(by chance)*
begeistert sein von (5)   to be enthusiastic about
der **Beginn** (17)   beginning
beginnen, begann, begonnen (8)   to begin
begleiten (12)   to accompany
der **Begriff, -e** (11)   concept, idea
begrüßen (20)   to greet
behalten, behielt, behalten, behält (8)   to keep, hold; to retain
behaupten (16)   to claim, maintain
behilflich (10)   helpful
die **Behörde, -n** (8)   official
bei *(with dat.)* (2)   near, beside, at the house of
beide (5)   both, the two; **beides** (7)   both things
beinahe (8)   almost, nearly
das **Beispiel, -e** (I)   example; **z.B. = zum Beispiel** (I)   for example
bei/wohnen *(with dat.)* (19)   to attend
bekannt (I)   well-known
der **Bekannte, -n, -n** (12)   acquaintance
bekannt/machen (11)   to introduce
die **Bekanntschaft, -en** (11)   acquaintance, acquaintanceship
sich **beklagen über** *(with acc.)* (18)   to complain about
bekommen, bekam, bekommen (8)   to get, receive; **gut zu essen bekommen** (9)   to get good food; **es scheint dir zu bekommen** (11)   it seems to agree with you
belasten (14)   to burden
beliebt (15)   popular
bellen (3)   to bark
bemerken (11)   to observe, remark
beneiden (13)   to envy
beobachten (16)   to observe
bequem (4)   comfortable
bereichern (20)   to enrich
die **Bergbahn, -en** (15)   alpine railway
der **Bergsteiger, -** (6)   mountain climber

berichten (7) to report
der **Beruf, -e** (8) profession, occupation
die **Berufsausbildung, -en** (10) occupational training
die **Berufsschule, -n** (8) trade school
beruhigen (20) to calm, pacify
berühmt (6) famous; **weltberühmt** (6) world-famous
die **Berühmtheit** (15) fame
die **Besatzungsarmee -n** (17) army of occupation
sich beschäftigen (7) to be busy, be occupied
beschäftigt (5) busy, occupied
die **Beschäftigung, -en** (17) occupation, concern
bescheiden (11) modest
(sich) beschränken auf *(with acc.)* (19) to confine (oneself), to limit (oneself) to
beschreiben, beschrieb, beschrieben (4) to describe
sich beschweren (9) to complain
der **Besen, -** (I) broom
besichtigen (14) to take a look at, inspect, visit
sich besinnen, besann, besonnen (6) to remember
besitzen, besaß, besessen (4) to own, possess
der **Besitzer, -** (9) owner
besonder- (18) special
besonders (4) particularly, especially
besorgen (18) to get; to take care of
die **Besorgung, -en** (9) *(act of)* taking care of, errand
besorgt (20) worried
besser (I) better; **es besser haben** (13) to be better off
bessern (10) to improve
bestehen, bestand, bestanden (3) to exist, pass *(an examination)*; **bestehen aus** to consist of
bestellen (6) to order
bestens (20) very well
Bestes: **ich würde mein Bestes tun** (10) I would do my best
bestimmen (10) to decide, determine; **bestimmen über** (10) to have a say about
bestimmt (4) surely
der **Besuch, -e** (11) visit, attendance
besuchen (I) to visit, attend
betonen (15) to emphasize, stress
das **Bett, -en** (I) bed
betrachten (18) to consider, look at
beurlauben (8) to grant a leave
bevor *(conj.)* (15) before
bevorzugen (7) to favor, prefer
bewachen (18) to watch, guard

bewahren (15) to keep, preserve
der **Beweis, -e** (13) proof
beweisen, bewies, bewiesen (19) to prove
bewundern (2) to admire
bezahlen (2) to pay (for)
bezähmen (13) to tame; **sich bezähmen** (13) to control oneself
bezeichnen (11) to designate
bezweifeln (11) to doubt
die **Bibliothek, -en** (I) library
die **Biegung, -en** (5) bend, curve
das **Bier, -e** (9) beer
bieten, bot, geboten (I) to offer
das **Bild, -er** (5) picture
bilden (7) to form
billig (1) cheap, inexpensive
binden, band, gebunden (13) to bind
die **Biographie, -n** (16) biography
bis (1) until; (up) to *(with acc. or plus zu with dat.);* **bis später** (1) until later; **bis dahin** (20) until then
bisher (10) up to now
der **Biß, -sse** (I) bit, bite
bißchen: **ein bißchen** (I) a little (bit)
bitte (I) please; you're welcome; **wie bitte?** (1) how's that? **bitte schön** (1) please; you're welcome
bitten, bat, gebeten **(um)** (I) to ask, beg (for)
das **Blatt, ⸚er** (12) leaf; sheet; newspaper
blättern (15) to leaf through
bleiben, blieb, ist geblieben (1) to stay, remain
der **Bleistift, -e** (20) pencil
der **Blick, -e** (15) look, glance; view; **Blick auf München** view of Munich
der **Blitz, -e** (3) (flash of) lightning
blitzen (13) to lighten; **es blitzt** (13) it's lightening
die **Blume, -n** (3) flower
der **Boden, ⸚** (I) ground, soil
(das) **Böhmen** (1) Bohemia
die **Bohne, -n** (I) bean
böse (16) angry, mean, evil
die **Botschaft, -en** (5) embassy
der **Brand, ⸚e** (12) fire, conflagration
die **Bratkartoffeln** *(pl.)* (11) fried potatoes
brauchen (I) to need
braun (I) brown
brav (5) honest, upright
brechen, brach, gebrochen, bricht (16) to break, break off
die **Brechtarbeit, -en** (16) Brecht paper, assignment *(on Brecht)*
brennen, brannte, gebrannt (I) to burn
der **Brief, -e** (1) letter
der **Briefkasten, -** (4) mailbox

die **Briefmarke, -n** (2)   postage stamp
die **Brille, -n** (3)   (pair of) spectacles
   bringen, brachte, gebracht (I)   to bring; to take
das **Brot, -e** (5)   bread, loaf of bread
der **Bruch, ⁻e** (2)   fracture
die **Brücke, -n** (2)   bridge
der **Bruder, ⁻** (I)   brother
der **Bub, -en, -en** (I)   boy, lad
das **Buch, ⁻er** (I)   book
   buchen (I)   to book
das **Bücherregal, -e** (15)   bookshelves
die **Bucht, -en** (I)   inlet, bay
die **Bühne, -n** (7)   stage
das **Bühnenstück, -e** (16)   stage performance, play
   bummeln (19)   to loaf, waste time
das **Bundeshaus** (14)   Parliament Building
die **Bundesrepublik** (5)   Federal Republic
der **Bundestag** (18)   Parliament *(membership)*
das **Büro, -s** (3)   office
der **Bus, -se** (I)   bus
die **Butter** (5)   butter
   bzw. = **beziehungsweise** (7)   respectively, or

das **Café, -s** (I)   café
der **Charakter, Charaktere** (12)   character
der **Chauffeur, -e** (1)   chauffeur, driver
die **Chemie** (3)   chemistry
das **Chemieexamen, -** (9)   chemistry examination
(das) **China** (2)   China
der **Chor, ⁻e** (I)   choir, chorus
der **Christ, -en, -en** (12)   Christian
die **Chronologie** (17)   chronology

   da (1)   here, there; then; since, because
   (15)   **da drüben** (1)   over there
   dabei (6)   at the same time, in the process
   dagegen (7)   on the other hand
   daher (20)   therefore
   damals (17)   at that time
die **Dame, -n** (I)   lady
   damit (15)   so that
der **Dampfer, -** (I)   steamer
   danach (2)   afterwards
der **Dank** (1)   thanks, gratitude
   dankbar (20)   grateful
   danke (schön) (I)   thank you
   dann (2)   then
   dar/legen (14)   to state, set forth
   das (I)   that
   daß (15)   that *(subord. conj.)*
das **Datum, Daten** (17)   date
   dauern (10)   to last
   dazu (5)   of it, for that purpose
das **Deck, -e** (5)   deck

der **Dekan, -e** (3)   dean
   deklinieren (11)   to decline
die **Dekoration, -en** (18)   decoration
   denken, dachte, gedacht (2)   to think; **denken an** *(with acc.)* to think of
das **Denkmal, ⁻er** (14)   monument
   denn (1)   *idiomatic particle used to strengthen a question; (conj.)* (15)   for
   der, die, das (I)   the
   derjenige, diejenige, dasjenige (16)   the one, that one
   derselbe, dieselbe, dasselbe (2)   the same
   deshalb (15)   therefore, that is why
   deswegen (5)   on that account, for that reason
   deuten (16)   to interpret
   deutlich (2)   distinct(ly)
   deutsch (1)   German; **auf deutsch** in German
(das) **Deutsch** (1)   German *(language)*
der **Deutsche, -n, -n** (1)   German
(das) **Deutschland** (1)   Germany
die **Deutschstunde, -n** (4)   German class
(der) **Dezember** (17)   December
der **Dichter, -** (2)   poet
die **Dichtung** (5)   poetry
   dick (17)   fat
   dienen (I)   to serve
(der) **Dienstag** (17)   Tuesday
   dieser, diese, dieses (I)   this, the latter
   diesmal (2)   this time
das **Ding, -e** (I)   thing; **vor allen Dingen** (20)   above all (things)
der **Diplomat, -en, -en** (14)   diplomat
   direkt (I)   direct(ly)
   diskutieren (9)   to discuss
   doch (1)   yet; *emphatic particle*
der **Doktor, Doktoren** (I)   doctor
die **Doktorarbeit, -en** (8)   doctoral dissertation
der **Dom, -e** (I)   cathedral
die **Donau** (4)   Danube
   donnern (13)   to thunder; **es donnert** it's thundering
(der) **Donnerstag** (17)   Thursday
das **Dorf, ⁻er** (9)   village, small town
   dort (1)   there, over there
der **Dramatiker, -** (7)   dramatist
   dran (daran) (20):   **da liegt ihm nichts dran** he doesn't care about that
   drehen (7)   to turn (out)
   drüben (1):   **da drüben** over there
   drucken (5)   to print; **lügen wie gedruckt** (20)   to lie like a professional
die **Druckschrift, -en** (5)   print
   dunkel (8)   dark
   dünn (12)   thin
   durch *(with acc.)* (3)   through

durch/fallen, fiel durch, ist durchgefallen, fällt durch (17) to fail *(a test, etc.)*

durch/lesen, las durch, durchgelesen, liest durch (6) to read through

dürfen, durfte, gedurft *(or* **dürfen), darf** (1) to be permitted to, may

duzen (15) to say **"du"** *(use the familiar way of addressing a person)*

eben (5) just, now; **das ist es eben** (16) that's just it

ebenfalls (3) likewise

echt (15) genuine

die **Ecke, -n** (I) corner

ehe *(conj.)* (15) before

das **Eheglück** (12) conjugal bliss

eher (18) sooner, rather

der **Eid, -e** (I) oath

der **Eiermarkt, ⸚e** (15) egg market

eigen (8) own

eigentlich (10) actually

sich **eignen** (14) to be suited for

die **Eile** (15) hurry

eilen (8) to hurry

ein, eine, ein (I) a, one

einander (6) each other, one another

ein/biegen, bog ein, ist eingebogen (9) to turn (in)

der **Eindruck, ⸚e** (16) impression

einfach (I) simple, simply; easy

der **Eingang, ⸚e** (9) entrance

ein/gestehen, gestand ein, eingestanden (18) to confess, admit

einige (8) some, a few

einigermaßen (18) to some extent, somewhat

ein/laden, lud ein, eingeladen, lädt ein (14) to invite

die **Einladung, -en** (4) invitation

einmal (I) once; **noch einmal** (I) again, once again, once more

die **Einrichtung, -en** (13) arrangement, facility, institution

einsam (13) lonely

ein/schlafen, schlief ein, ist eingeschlafen, schläft ein (14) to fall asleep

ein/sehen, sah ein, eingesehen, sieht ein (16) to perceive, comprehend

ein/steigen (in, *with acc.)*, **stieg ein, ist eingestiegen** (9) to board, get on *(a train, etc.)*

ein/teilen (11) to divide, classify

ein/treten (in, *with acc.)*, **trat ein, ist eingetreten, tritt ein** (8) to enter

die **Eintrittskarte, -n** (16) (admission) ticket

die **Einwohnerzahl, -en** (14) (total) population

einzeln (13) single, individual

einzig (19) single, only

das **Eisstadion, -stadien** (15) ice stadium

die **Elbe** (4) Elbe *(German river)*

die **Eleganz** (18) elegance

elektronisch (12) electronic

die **Eltern** *(pl. only)* (1) parents

das **Elternhaus** (17) house of one's parents

empfangen, empfing, empfangen, empfängt (4) to receive

empfehlen, empfahl, empfohlen, empfiehlt (15) to recommend

das **Ende, -n** (5) end

endlich (9) finally

die **Endung, -en** (11) ending

eng (10) narrow; **eng befreundet mit** (17) close friends with

der **Engländer, -** (2) Englishman

englisch (I) English; **auf englisch** (I) in English

entdecken (12) to discover

entfernt (19) away, distant

enthalten, enthielt, enthalten, enthält (20) to contain

die **Entscheidung, -en** (10) decision: **eine Entscheidung treffen** to make a decision

sich **entschließen, entschloß, entschlossen** (6) to decide

entschuldigen (I) to excuse; **sich entschuldigen** to excuse oneself, apologize

die **Entschuldigung, -en** (9) excuse, apology

sich **entspannen** (9) to relax

entstehen, entstand, ist entstanden (4) to originate

die **Entstehung, -en** (14) origin

enttäuscht (14) disappointed

entweder . . . oder (13) either . . . or

(sich) **entwickeln** (14) to develop

entzückt (5) delighted, enchanted

die **Epoche, -n** (5) epoch

erblicken (14) to catch sight of

die **Erdbeere, -n** (11) strawberry

das **Ereignis, -se** (12) event

erfahren (20) *(adj.)* experienced

erfrischt (12) refreshed

erhalten, erhielt, erhalten, erhält (11) to receive

erhöhen (18) to elevate, increase; **erhöhte Temperatur haben** (18) to run a temperature

sich **erholen** (6) to recover

erinnern an (19) to remind of

sich **erinnern an** *(with acc.)* (6) to remember

die **Erinnerung, -en** (3) reminder, memory

sich **erkälten** (6) to catch cold

die **Erkältung, -en** (4) cold

erkennen, erkannte, erkannt (2) to recognize

erklären (2) to explain; **sich** *(dat.)* **etwas erklären** (13) to account for something (to oneself)

sich erkundigen (6) to inquire

das **Erlebnis, -se** (5) experience

erledigen (18) to take care of, settle

ermorden (17) to murder

der **Ernährer, -** (10) breadwinner

ernennen, ernannte, ernannt (8) to name, appoint

die **Ernennung, -en** (17) appointment

erneut (19) again

erraten, erriet, erraten, errät (17) to guess

erregt (14) excited

erreichen (7) to reach

die **Errichtung, -en** (14) erection

erscheinen, erschien, ist erschienen (19) to appear

die **Erscheinung, -en** (12) appearance

erschöpft (6) exhausted

erschrecken, erschrak, ist erschrocken, erschrickt (9) to be frightened

ersetzen (7) to replace

erst (1) only *(with expressions of time)*

erstklassig (2) first-class

erstverdient (19) first-earned

erwähnen (10) to mention

erwarten (4) to expect, await

erweisen, erwies, erwiesen (17) to show

erwidern (9) to reply

erwünscht (17) desired

erzählen (2) to tell *(a story)*

die **Erzählung, -en** (16) story, tale

die **Erziehung** (3) education

das **Erziehungswesen** (8) educational system

erzielen (18) to obtain

es (1) it

essen, aß, gegessen, ißt (I) to eat

das **Essen** (I) food, meal

der **Essig** (I) vinegar

etliche (12) some

etwas (I) *(used only in the singular)* something; some

(das) **Europa** (I) Europe

die **Europareise, -n** (17) trip to Europe

das **Examen, -** (5) examination; **vor einem Examen stehen** to have an examination ahead of one

experimentieren (18) to experiment

fabelhaft (1) fabulous

die **Fabrik, -en** (15) factory

das **Fach, ⁓er** (3) subject (of instruction)

fähig (20) capable

fahren, fuhr, ist gefahren, fährt (1) to drive; to ride; to go *(by vehicle)*

die **Fahrkarte, -n** (1) ticket

die **Fahrt, -en** (5) trip

der **Fall, ⁓e** (20) case; **auf jeden Fall** in any case

falsch (3) wrong

die **Familie, -n** (1) family

das **Familienereignis, -se** (12) family event, family experience

das **Familienleben** (10) family life

das **Familienoberhaupt, ⁓er** (10) head of the family

fassen: einen Plan fassen (19) to make plans

fast (7) almost

faulenzen (15) to loaf, be lazy

(der) **Februar** (4) February

fegen (I) to sweep

der **Fehler, -** (10) error, mistake

fehlerfrei (17) faultless, free of errors

feiern (17) to celebrate

das **Feld, -er** (10) field

der **Feldzug, ⁓e** (17) campaign

das **Ferngespräch, -e** (14) long-distance call

fertig (6) ready

fertig/bringen, brachte fertig, fertiggebracht (20) to bring off, pull, manage

fertig/lesen, las fertig, fertiggelesen, liest fertig (16) to read (through) to the end

fest (I) firm(ly)

das **Feuer, -** (I) fire

die **Feuerwehr** (12) fire department

das **Fieber** (18) fever; **das Fieber messen** (18) to take (one's) temperature

die **Filiale, -n** (11) branch, affiliate

der **Film, -e** (7) film, movie

der **Finanzminister, -** (17) minister of finance

finden, fand, gefunden (I) to find

der **Finger, -** (I) finger

die **Firma, Firmen** (14) firm, concern

flach (2) flat

die **Flasche, -n** (9) bottle

fleißig (3) industrious

fliegen, flog, ist geflogen (4) to fly

fließen, floß, ist geflossen (I) to flow

fließend (17) fluent

der **Fluch, ⁓e** (2) curse

fluchen (I) to curse

die **Flucht, -en** (I) flight, escape

der **Flüchtling, -e** (15) refugee

der **Flug, ⁓e** (20) flight

der **Flughafen, ⁓** (20) airport

das **Flugzeug, -e** (13) airplane

der **Fluß, ⁓sse** (5) river

folgen, ist gefolgt (16) to follow; **folgend** following

die **Form, -en** (11) form

formell (20) formal

die **Forschung, -en** (3) research

fort (8) away
fort/fahren, fuhr fort, ist fortgefahren, fährt fort (11) to drive away, go away
der **Fortschritt, -e** (7) progress
die **Frage, -n** (I) question
fragen (1) to ask
(das) **Frankreich** (2) France
der **Franzose, -n, -n** (2) Frenchman
französisch (2) French
die **Frau, -en** (I) woman, Mrs., wife
das **Fräulein, -** (I) Miss, young lady
frei (10) free
das **Freie** (9) out-of-doors
(der) **Freitag** (17) Friday
fremd (4) strange, foreign
die **Fremdsprache, -n** (4) foreign language
die **Freude, -n** (I) pleasure, joy
sich **freuen (auf,** with acc.) (6) to look forward to; sich **freuen (über,** with acc.) (6) to be happy (about); **es freut mich** (13) I'm glad
der **Freund, -e** (3) friend (male)
die **Freundin, -nen** (3) friend (female)
freundlich (1) friendly
die **Freundschaft, -en** (17) friendship
friedlich (14) peaceful
frieren (13) to freeze; **es friert mich** I'm cold
frisch (11) fresh
froh (2) happy
die **Frucht, ⸚e** (2) fruit, product
früh (I) early; **früher** (5) formerly
die **Frühe** (13) early morning; **in aller Frühe** (13) bright and early
der **Frühling** (17) spring
frühstücken (5) to have breakfast
das **Frühstück, -e** (5) breakfast
fühlen (1) to feel
führen (13) to lead, carry (merchandise); **Krieg führen** (13) to wage war
füllen (1) to fill
fünftägig (20) five-day
für (with acc.) (1) for; **was für (ein)** (3) what kind of (a)
furchtbar (14) terrible
sich **fürchten (vor,** with dat.) (13) to be afraid (of)
der **Fuß, ⸚e** (I) foot; **zu Fuß gehen** (2) to go on foot, walk
der **Fußgänger, -** (2) pedestrian

ganz (2) quite, very, entirely
gar (adv. and part.) (I) quite, entirely; **gar nicht** (I) not at all
die **Garage, -n** (3) garage
der **Gast, ⸚e** (5) guest

gastfreundlich (5) hospitable
die **Gastfreundschaft** (5) hospitality, hospitableness
das **Gasthaus, ⸚er** (9) inn
die **Gaststätte, -n** (9) inn
die **Gattin, -nen** (11) wife
das **Gebäude, -** (7) building
geben, gab, gegeben, gibt (1) to give; **es gibt** there is, are
das **Gebet, -e** (I) prayer
das **Gebiet, -e** (7) area, region
gebildet (12) educated, cultured
gebirgig (4) mountainous
geboren (1) born
gebrauchen (2) to use
gebräunt (8) tanned
die **Geburtsanzeige, -n** (12) birth announcement
die **Geburtsstadt, ⸚e** (5) birthplace
der **Geburtstag, -e** (17) birthday
der **Gedanke, -ns, -n** (12) thought, idea
das **Gedicht, -e** (5) poem
geduldig (3) patient
die **Gefahr, -en** (18) danger
gefährlich (13) dangerous
gefallen, gefiel, gefallen, gefällt (with dat.) (4) to appeal to, be pleasing to; **es gefällt mir, dir,** etc. I, you, etc. like it; **was gefällt Ihnen an** + dat.? what do you like about . . .?
der **Gefallen, -** (4) favor
die **Gefälligkeit, -en** (20) favor, service
das **Gefühl, -e** (16) feeling
gegen (with acc.) (3) against, toward, about
die **Gegend, -en** (6) area
das **Gegenteil: im Gegenteil** (8) on the contrary
der **Gegenstand, ⸚e** (16) subject, object
gegenüber (with dat.) (I) opposite, across from
gehen, ging, ist gegangen (I) to go (usually: to walk); **wie geht es Ihnen?** (I) how are you?
gehören (with dat.) (1) to belong
der **Gehorsam** (10) obedience
das **Geld, -er** (2) money
die **Geldausgabe, -n** (10) expenditure
gelegen (15) situated
die **Gelegenheit, -en** (20) opportunity
gelingen, gelang, ist gelungen (with dat. and inf.) (13) to succeed; **es gelingt (mir) . . . zu tun** (I) succeed in doing
die **Gemeinschaft, -en** (10) community
gemütlich (3) cozy, comfortable, homelike; leisurely, easygoing

die **Gemütlichkeit** (5) comfortableness; pleasantly unhurried manner
genau (5) exact, precise
die **Generation, -en** (12) generation
genießen, genoß, genossen (6) to enjoy
genug (I) enough
genügen (9) to be enough, suffice
die **Geographie** (4) geography
gerade (2) just; **gerade wie** (8) just as
das **Gerät, -e** (13) utensil
das **Gericht, -e** (16) court
gern(e) (4) gladly
gesamt (19) total, whole
das **Geschäft, -e** (9) business, store
geschäftlich (11) related to business, commercial
der **Geschäftsreisende, -n, -n** (16) traveling salesman
die **Geschäftsstraße, -n** (2) business street
geschehen, geschah, ist geschehen, geschieht (17) to happen
das **Geschenk, -e** (19) present
die **Geschichte, -n** (2) story, history
der **Geschichtslehrer, -** (17) history teacher
das **Geschirr** (11) dishes
der **Geschmack, ⸚e** (12) taste
geschmackvoll (12) tasteful
die **Geschwister** (pl. only) (I) brothers and sisters
die **Gesellenprüfung, -en** (8) journeyman's test
die **Gesellschaft, -en** (18) company, party, social gathering
das **Gespräch, -e** (11) conversation, talk
gesprächig (7) talkative, sociable
gestehen, gestand, gestanden (4) to confess, admit
gestern (8) yesterday
gesundheitlich (6) from the standpoint of health
gewaltig (17) powerful
gewinnen, gewann, gewonnen (16) to win, gain
gewiß (I) certain
das **Gewitter, -** (13) thunderstorm
sich **gewöhnen an** (with acc.) (16) to get used to something
gewöhnlich (10) usual(ly)
der **Gipfel, -** (3) summit, peak
glänzend (11) brilliant
das **Glas, ⸚er** (9) glass
glauben (4) to believe, think
gleich (I) right away; immediately; same (14)
gleichen (17) to equal
gleichzeitig (13) at the same time
das **Glied, -er** (I) limb
das **Glück** (1) happiness, good luck; **zum**

Glück (14) luckily; **Glück haben** (6) to be lucky
glücklich (20) happy
die **Gnade, -n** (4) grace, mercy
gotisch (2) Gothic
grammatisch (11) grammatical
gratulieren (17) to congratulate
der **Greis, -e** (19) old man
das **Grenzland, ⸚er** (15) border country
die **Grippe** (18) grippe, flu
grob (13) coarse; rude
groß (1) big; **im großen (und) ganzen** (19) on the whole
großartig (6) grand(ly), magnificent(ly)
die **Größe, -n** (1) size
die **Großeltern** (pl. only) (10) grandparents
die **Großstadt, ⸚e** (18) metropolis
grotesk (12) grotesque
grün (I) green
der **Grund, ⸚e** (I) reason, basis; **es besteht Grund zu** (4) there is reason for; **aus diesem Grund** (5) for this reason
gründlich (20) thorough(ly)
günstig (19) favorable
gut (I) good
der **Gymnasiallehrer, -** (18) teacher in a Gymnasium
das **Gymnasium, Gymnasien** (2) *secondary school roughly equivalent to American high school plus junior college*

haben, hatte, gehabt, hat (I) to have; **gern haben** to like, love
die **Hafenstadt, ⸚e** (4) port city
die **Hafenszene, -n** (1) harbor scene
halb (5) half
das **Halsweh** (18) sore throat
halten, hielt, gehalten, hält to hold, stop (14): **halten von** (12) to consider, think of
die **Haltestelle, -n** (8) *(bus or streetcar)* stop
die **Hand, ⸚e** (I) hand
handeln to act; **handeln von** (15) to deal with, treat of
die **Handlung, -en** (16) plot
der **Handwerker, -** (8) artisan, workman
hart (I) hard
die **Hast** (20) haste, hurry
hauptsächlich (3) main(ly)
das **Hauptproblem, -e** (13) main problem
die **Hauptstadt, ⸚e** (5) capital
die **Hauptstraße, -n** (14) main street
die **Hauptursache, -n** (19) main cause
das **Haus, ⸚er** (1) house; **zu Hause** at home; **nach Hause** *(indicates direction toward)* home; **von zu Hause** (10) from home
die **Hausarbeit, -en** (10) housework

das **Häuschen, -** (4)   little house
die **Hausfrau, -en** (13)   housewife
der **Haushalt** (10)   household
die **Haut, ̈e** (I)   skin, hide
das **Heft, -e** (I)   notebook
das **Heilbad, ̈er** (6)   mineral bath
 heilen (18)   to cure
die **Heimkehr** (20)   homecoming, return home
 heiraten (16)   to marry
 heiser (18)   hoarse
 heiß (4)   hot
 heißen, hieß, geheißen (I)   to be called;
  d.h. = das heißt that is to say; **es heißt**
  (6)   they say; it's a question of
der **Held, -en, -en** (5)   hero
 helfen, half, geholfen, hilft (2)   to help
 hell (3)   bright
 **her<u>au</u>s/geben, gab heraus, herausgegeben,
  gibt heraus** (9)   to give change
sich **her<u>au</u>s/stellen** (16)   to come out, be revealed
 **her<u>ei</u>n/kommen, kam herein, ist hereinge-
  kommen** (14)   to come in
der **Herbst** (17)   fall, autumn
 her/kommen, kam her, ist hergekommen
  (I)   to come from, come here (toward
  speaker)
der **Herr, -n, -en** (I)   Mr., gentleman
 herrlich (5)   splendid
 herrschen (10)   to rule, prevail
 her<u>ü</u>ber (17)   over (toward speaker)
 her<u>u</u>nter (6)   down(stairs) (toward speaker)
der **Herzog, ̈e** (17)   duke
 heute (I)   today; **heute abend** (I)   tonight,
  this evening; **heute morgen** this morning
 heutig (18)   of today, today's
 hervorragend (11)   prominent, distinguished
 hie und da (10)   here and there
 hier (1)   here; **hiervon** (12)   of this
die **Hilfe** (3)   help
 hin<u>au</u>s/blicken auf (with acc.) (9)   to look
  out upon
 **hin<u>au</u>s/werfen, warf hinaus, hinausgeworfen,
  wirft hinaus** (9)   to throw out
 **hin/fahren, fuhr hin, ist hingefahren, fährt
  hin** (9)   to drive there
die **Hinfahrt, -en** (8)   trip (there, to that place)
 hingegen (9)   on the other hand
 hin/gehen, ging hin, ist hingegangen (9)   to
  go there
sich **hin/legen** (6)   to lie down
sich **hin/setzen** (20)   to sit down
 hinter (with acc. or dat.) (3)   behind
 hin<u>ü</u>ber (18)   over there (away from
  speaker)

 hin<u>u</u>nter (4)   down(stairs) (away from
  speaker)
 hinzu/fügen (13)   to add
die **Hitze** (3)   heat
 hoch (13)   high; **höchst** (4)   very, ex-
  tremely
das **Hochdeutsch** (11)   High German
 hocherfreut (12)   highly pleased
das **Hochgebirge, -** (4)   high mountain chain
die **Hochzeit, -en** (17)   wedding
der **Hof, ̈e** (15)   court, courtyard, farm
 hoffentlich (3)   I hope, let's hope, it is to
  be hoped
 höflich (5)   polite
die **Höhe, -n** (7)   height
 hören (I)   to hear, listen
der **Hörsaal, -säle** (3)   lecture hall
das **Hotel, -s** (6)   hotel
 hübsch (4)   pretty
der **Humor** (20)   (sense of) humor
der **Hund, -e** (5)   dog
der **Hunger** (2)   hunger; **Hunger haben** (2)   to
  be hungry
der **Husten** (18)   cough
der **Hut, ̈e** (I)   hat

der **Idiot, -en, -en** (19)   blockhead, moron;
  ich Idiot what a moron I am
 idyllisch (15)   idyllic
 ihr, ihre, ihr (I)   her, their
 Ihr, Ihre, Ihr (I)   your
die **Illustrierte, -n** (10)   picture magazine
 immer (3)   always; **immer wieder** (6)
  again and again
 in (with acc. or dat.) (1)   in, into, to
die **Industriestadt, ̈e** (14)   industrial city
 informieren (15)   to inform
die **Innenpolitik** (12)   domestic policy
das **Insekt, -en** (16)   insect
 insgesamt (19)   altogether
 inszenieren (7)   to stage, put on (a play)
 interessant (1)   interesting
das **Interesse, -n** (3)   interest
 interessieren (2)   to interest; **Interesse haben an** (3), **sich interessieren für** (6)   to
  be interested in
 interpretieren (16)   to interpret
 inwendig (13)   interior, inside, inward
 inwiefern (10)   in what respect
 irgendwie (10)   somehow, anyhow
 irgendwo (15)   somewhere, anywhere
sich **irren** (6)   to be wrong, be mistaken
(das) **Italien** (7)   Italy
der **Italiener, -** (11)   Italian
 italienisch (11)   Italian

 ja (I)   yes; indeed

das **Jahr, -e** (1) year; **jahraus, jahrein** (9) year in, year out
der **Jahrgang, ⁓e** (17) (school) year of graduation
die **Jahreszahl, -en** (17) date *(in history)*
die **Jahreszeit, -en** (4) season
das **Jahrhundert, -e** (17) century
(der) **Januar** (4) January
(das) **Japan** (7) Japan
der **Jazzkeller, -** (18) jazz basement
jeder, jede, jedes (3) each, every
jedermann (10) everybody
jedoch (4) however
jemand (10) somebody
jener, jene, jenes (6) that, the former
jetzt (I) now
der **Journalist, -en, -en** (I) journalist
die **Jugend** (10) youth, early years
die **Jugendherberge, -n** (8) youth hostel
jung (18) young
(der) **Juli** (17) July
der **Junge, -n, -n** (12) boy
(der) **Juni** (17) June
Jura (16) law, jurisprudence *(as a field of study)*

das **Kabarett, -s** *or* **-e** (20) cabaret, night club
der **Kaffee** (I) coffee
der **Kaffeeklatsch** (9) coffee (and cake) party
kalt (4) cold
die **Kälte** (5) cold
der **Kamerad, -en, -en** (10) comrade, buddy
der **Kamm, ⁓e** (I) comb
sich **kämmen** (6) to comb one's hair
der **Kanzler, -** (18) chancellor
die **Kapelle, -n** (18) band
das **Kapitel, -** (6) chapter
kaputt *(colloquial)* (I) broken, torn, unusable
die **Karte, -n** (9) card, ticket; **Karten spielen** (9) to play cards
die **Kartoffel, -n** (I) potato
die **Katze, -n** (I) cat
kaufen (1) to buy
das **Kaufhaus, ⁓er** (14) department store
kaum (8) hardly, scarcely
kein, keine, kein (2) no, not any
keinerlei *(indeclinable adj.)* (16) of no sort
der **Keller, -** (18) cellar
der **Kellner, -** (9) waiter
kennen, kannte, gekannt (I) to know *(a person or object)*
kennen/lernen, lernte kennen, kennengelernt (13) to get to know, become acquainted with
der **Kilometer, -** (4) kilometer

das **Kind, -er** (1) child
die **Kindheit** (4) childhood
das **Kino, -s** (2) movie theater
die **Kirche, -n** (2) church
kitschig (7) trashy, cheap
klagen (14) to complain
klar (2) clear
klassisch (18) classic
das **Kleid, -er** (15) dress
die **Kleider** *(pl.)* (15) clothes
das **Kleidungsstück, -e** (15) piece of clothing
die **Kleinstadt, ⁓e** (9) small town
das **Klima** (4) climate
klingeln (15) to ring
klingen, klang, geklungen (I) to sound
klopfen (3) to knock
klug (13) intelligent; **klug werden aus** (16) to make sense of
knapp (an) (6) short (of)
das **Knipsen** (7) shooting pictures
der **Koch, ⁓e** (2) cook *(male)*
kochen (I) to cook
die **Köchin, -nen** (11) cook *(female)*
der **Koffer, -** (1) suitcase, trunk
der **Kollege, -n, -n** (9) colleague
komisch (15) comical, funny
kommen, kam, ist gekommen (I) to come
kompliziert (16) complicated
der **Komponist, -en, -en** (12) composer
die **Komposition, -en** (18) composition
die **Konfektion** (15) (ready-to-wear) clothing
das **Konfektionsgeschäft, -e** (15) clothing store
die **Konjugation, -en** (11) conjugation
können, konnte, gekonnt (*or* **können**), **kann** (I) to be able to; to know *(a language)*
kontrollieren (18) to check
das **Konzert, -e** (18) concert
der **Konzertsaal, -säle** (14) concert hall
der **Kopf, ⁓e** (3) head; **es geht mir durch den Kopf** (14) it runs through my mind
korrigieren (10) to correct
kosten (I) to cost
krank (13) ill, sick
der **Krieg, -e** (10) war; **der Dreißigjährige Krieg** (15) the Thirty Years' War
kritisieren (7) to criticize
die **Krone, -n** (6) crown
die **Küche, -n** (11) kitchen; cuisine
kühl (1) cool
kultiviert (12) cultivated
die **Kultur** (I) culture
kulturell (14) cultural
die **Kultursprache, -n** (16) language of a (civilized) society
das **Kultusministerium** (8) *an authority similar to a state department of education*
sich **kümmern um** (10) to care (about)

die **Kunst, ⸚e** (17) art
der **Kurfürstendamm** (14) *main shopping street in West Berlin*
der **Kurort, -e** (6) health resort
 kurz (4) short

 lächeln (2) to smile
 lachen (8) to laugh
 lächerlich (20) absurd, ridiculous
 laden, lud, geladen, lädt (I) to load
die **Lage, -n** (13) situation; **in der Lage sein** to be in a position
 lahm (I) lame
das **Land, ⸚er** (1) land, country, state; **auf dem Land** in the country; **auf das Land** to the country
 landen (6) to land
 ländlich (15) rural
die **Landschaft, -en** (2) landscape
 lange (1) long, a long time
 langsam (I) slow(ly)
 längst: längst nicht (19) not nearly
der **Lärm** (18) noise
 lassen, ließ, gelassen, läßt (I) to leave; to let, have (*something*) done
die **Laufbahn, -en** (8) career
der **Lauf** course; **im Laufe** (13) in the course of
 laufen, lief, ist gelaufen, läuft (2) to run
die **Laune, -n** (10) mood
 laut (I) loud
der **Laut, -e** (I) sound
der **Lautsprecher, -** (10) loudspeaker
 leben (7) to live; to reside
die **Lebensanschauung** (20) conception of life
die **Lebensfreude** (5) enjoyment of life
das **Lebensjahr, -e** (17) year (*of one's life*)
der **Lebenslauf** (16) career; biography
 lecker (11) delicious, dainty
der **Ledersessel, -** (12) leather (easy) chair
 ledig (I) single
die **Legende, -n** (5) legend
 lehren (18) to teach
der **Lehrer, -** (I) teacher (*male*)
die **Lehrerin, -nen** (9) teacher (*female*)
der **Lehrling, -e** (8) apprentice
 leicht (9) easy; light; **es sich leicht machen** (9) to take it easy
 leid: es tut mir leid (13) I'm sorry
das **Leiden** (12) suffering, pain
 leiden, litt, gelitten (8) to suffer
 leider (I) unfortunately
 leihen, lieh, geliehen (6) to lend
 leise (3) low, soft
 leisten (7) to achieve; **sich** (*dat.*) **etwas leisten** (6) to afford something
die **Leistung, -en** (7) achievement

die **Leitung, -en** (11) line, wire; management
die **Lektüre, -n** (16) reading
 lernen (1) to study, learn
 lesen, las, gelesen, liest (I) to read
 letzt- (7); **zu guter Letzt** (10) finally, as a fitting conclusion
die **Leute** (*pl. only*) (I) people
das **Licht, -er** (19) light; **in einem günstigen Licht erscheinen** (19) to appear in a favorable light
 lieb (I) dear
die **Liebe** (7) love
 lieben (18) to love
der **Lieblingsfluß, ⸚sse** (5) favorite river
das **Lieblingsthema, -themen** (9) favorite theme
 liefern (7) to deliver, furnish
 liegen, lag, gelegen (I) to lie, be situated; **da liegt ihm nichts dran** (20) he doesn't care about that
 links (1) left
 literarisch (7) literary
die **Literatur, -en** (3) literature
 sich lohnen (9) to pay, be worth it; **es lohnt sich nicht** (20) it doesn't pay
das **Lokal, -e** (9) locality, place
die **Lokalangelegenheit, -en** (12) local affair
die **Lorelei** (5) *a siren in German Rhine legends*
der **Loreleifelsen** Lorelei reef
 los (I) loose; **was ist los?** (6) what's wrong?, what's the matter?
 löschen (12) to extinguish
 lösen: eine Fahrkarte lösen (10) to buy a ticket
die **Lösung, -en** (17) solution, dissolution
die **Lücke, -n** (9) gap
 lügen (20) to lie, tell a falsehood; **lügen wie gedruckt** (20) to lie like a professional
der **Lügner, -** (20) liar
 Lust haben (**auf** *with acc. or* **zu** *with dat.*) (9) to feel like, be in the mood (for)
 lustig (15) funny, gay

 machen (I) to make, do; **sich auf den Weg machen** (14) to set out, be on one's way
die **Macht, ⸚e** (15) power
das **Mädchen, -** (4) girl
 mager (I) thin
die **Mahlzeit, -en** (3) meal
(der) **Mai** (I) May
das **Mal, -e** (8) time (*in sequence*); **mal** (*short for* **einmal**) once (*unemphatic flavoring particle*), (17) times (*in multiplication*)
der **Maler, -** (7) painter
 man (3) one, you, people
 mancher, manche, manches (9) many a;

manche *(pl.)* some; **manches** *(used only in the singular)* (19) some things
manchmal (3) sometimes
der **Mann, ̈er** (5) man; husband
das **Manuskript, -e** (16) manuscript
märchenhaft (2) as in a fairy-tale, fabulous
die **Mark** (I) mark *(monetary unit)*
die **Marke, -n** (9) brand
die **Marmelade, -n** (5) jam
(der) **März** (17) March
die **Maß** (9) quart *(of beer, Bavarian dialect)*
materialistisch (20) materialistic
mechanisch (20) mechanical
das **Meer, -e** (I) ocean, sea
mehr (3) more; **nicht mehr** (6) no longer, no more
mehrere (7) several
mein, meine, mein (I) my
meinen (20) to mean, think
die **Meinung, -en** (7) opinion; **der Meinung sein** (20) to be of the opinion, believe
meist- (8) most; **meistens** mostly, usually
die **Meisterprüfung, -en** (8) (trade) master's examination
das **Meisterwerk, -e** (7) masterwork, masterpiece
die **Mensa, -en** (3) university cafeteria
der **Mensch, -en, -en** (5) person, human being
merken (4) to note, observe
messen, maß, gemessen, mißt (18) to measure
der **Meter, -** (4) meter
das **Messer, -** (16) knife
die **Miete, -n** (1) rent
die **Milch** (13) milk
mild (I) mild
die **Militärzeit** (17) (period of) military service
der **Millionär, -e** (19) millionaire
das **Minderwertigkeitsgefühl, -e** (16) inferiority complex
mindestens (18) at least
die **Minute, -n** (I) minute
mißgestimmt (14) in a bad mood, out of sorts
mißverstehen, mißverstand, mißverstanden (16) to misunderstand
mit *(with dat.)* (I) with
mit/bringen, brachte mit, mitgebracht (9) to bring along, take along
mit/helfen, half mit, mitgeholfen, hilft mit (12) to assist, cooperate
mit/kommen, kam mit, ist mitgekommen (11) to come along
das **Mitleid** (17) pity, sympathy
mit/nehmen, nahm mit, mitgenommen, nimmt mit (8) to take along
mit/schleppen (18) to drag along

der **Mittag, -e** (2) midday, noon; **zu Mittag essen** to eat dinner; to eat lunch
das **Mittagessen, -** (2) dinner; lunch
die **Mitte** (4) middle
mit/teilen (12) to inform
das **Mitteldeutsch** (11) Middle German
(das) **Mitteleuropa** (4) central Europe
der **Mittelstand** (13) middle class(es)
(das) **Mittenwald** *town in the Bavarian Alps*
(der) **Mittwoch** (17) Wednesday
die **Mode, -n** (9) style, fashion; **in Mode** (18) in style
modellhaft (16) model *(adj.)*
die **Modenschau** (18) fashion show, dress parade
modern (2) modern
modisch (15) in style
mögen, mochte, gemocht *(or* **mögen)**, **mag** (I) to like
möglich (11) possible
die **Möglichkeit, -en** (5) possibility, chance
der **Moment, -e** (4) moment
der **Monat, -e** (3) month
(der) **Montag, -e** (17) Monday
der **Mörder, -** (1) murderer
der **Morgen, -** (I) morning; **guten Morgen** (I) good morning
morgen (I) tomorrow
morgens (5) in the morning, mornings; **von morgens bis abends** (5) from morning to night
morgig (19) of tomorrow, tomorrow's
das **Motiv, -e** (5) motive, motif
müde (2) tired
die **Mundart, -en** (11) dialect
münden (4) to empty into
munter (12) gay
mürrisch (19) morose, peevish
das **Museum, Museen** (2) museum
die **Musik** (9) music
der **Musiker, -** (1) musician
das **Musikfestspiel, -e** (18) music festival
müssen, mußte, gemußt *(or* **müssen)**, **muß** (I) to have to, must
der **Mut** (18) courage
die **Mutter, ̈** (1) mother; **Mutti** (11) Mom, Mommy
der **Mythus, Mythen** (13) myth

na (19) well
nach *(with dat.)* (I) after, to, according to
der **Nachbar, -n** (12) neighbor
nachdem *(conj.)* (15) after
der **Nachlaß, ̈sse** (16) legacy, literary remains
die **Nachkriegsjahre** (7) post-war years
die **Nachkriegszeit** (7) post-war years

nachmittags (5)   in the afternoon, afternoons
die **Nachricht, -en** (10)   news, report
nach/schlagen, schlug nach, nachgeschlagen, schlägt nach (10)   to look up *(in a book)*
nach/sehen, sah nach, nachgesehen, sieht nach (17)   to check
nächst- (3)   next
der **Nachtisch, -e** (11)   dessert
nahe (I)   near
die **Nähe** (5)   vicinity
nahe/kommen, kam nahe, ist nahegekommen (7)   to approach, come close to
der **Name, -ns, -n** (I)   name
nämlich (16)
die **Nation, -en** (3)   nation
die **Natur, -en** (6)   nature
natürlich (I)   naturally, of course
neben *(with dat. or acc.)* (3)   beside, near
nebenan (5)   next door
nebeneinander (3)   next to one another
neblig (14)   foggy
nein (I)   no
nehmen, nahm, genommen, nimmt (1)   to take; **sich in acht nehmen** (20)   to watch out for, be on one's guard
nennen, nannte, genannt (2)   to name, call
nett (1)   nice
neu (2)   new
neugierig (7)   curious
die **Neustadt, ⁼e** (2)   the new part of the city
nicht (I)   not; **nicht nur . . . sondern auch** (8)   not only . . . but (also); **nicht wahr?** (I)   *changes a statement into a question to which an affirmative reply is expected:* don't you?, won't we?, isn't she?   etc.; **gar nicht**   not at all
nichtamerikanisch (20)   non-American
nichts (I)   nothing
nicken (13)   to nod
nie (I)   never
das **Niederdeutsch** (11)   Low German
nieder/legen (15)   to put down
nieder/schreiben, schrieb nieder, niedergeschrieben (19)   to write down
niemand (9)   nobody
noch (I)   still, yet; **noch ein**   another, an additional; **noch einmal** (I), **noch mal** (20)   once more, again; **noch nicht**   not yet
der **Norden** (4)   North
die **Nordsee** (4)   North Sea
die **Not, ⁼e** (9)   need, necessity, emergency
(der) **November** (I)   November
null (17)   zero
die **Nummer, -n** (2)   number
nun (5)   well, well then; now
nur (I)   only

nützen (1)   to be of use

ob (1)   whether
oben (1)   upstairs
der **Ober, -** (9)   waiter
das **Oberdeutsch** (11)   Upper German
obgleich (15)   although
obwohl (15)   although
der **Ochs, -en, -en** (I)   ox
oder (I)   or
der **Ofen, ⁼** (I)   oven
offen (I)   open; (16)   frankly
öffnen (I)   to open
ohne *(with acc.)* (3)   without
(der) **Oktober** (17)   October
das **Öl, -e** (I)   oil
die **Oper, -n** (12)   opera
die **Operette, -n** (16)   operetta
das **Opernhaus, ⁼er** (2)   opera house
das **Orchester, -** (18)   orchestra
die **Ordnung, -en** (14)   order
der **Ort, -e** (18)   place, spot
der **Osten** (4)   East
(das) **Österreich** (6)   Austria
die **Ostsee** (6)   Baltic Sea

paar: ein paar (2)   a few
der **Pack, -e** (*or* **Päcke**) (I)   pack, packet
die **Packung, -en** (I)   package
der **Park, -s** (4)   park
parken (9)   to park
der **Parkplatz, ⁼e** (9)   parking place
der **Paß, ⁼sse** (3)   passport
passen (I)   to suit, fit
passend (13)   suitable, suitably
passieren, ist passiert (14)   to happen
perfekt (2)   perfect
der **Personenzug, ⁼e** (10)   local train
persönlich (20)   personal(ly)
pessimistisch (10)   pessimistic
pflanzen (4)   to plant
die **Pflicht, -en** (4)   duty
das **Pfund, -e** (3)   pound
philharmonisch (18)   philharmonic
der **Philosoph, -en, -en** (I)   philosopher
die **Philosophie, -n** (3)   philosophy
die **Photographie, -n** (17)   photograph
photographieren (7)   to photograph
die **Physik** (3)   physics
der **Plan, ⁼e** (I)   plan
das **Plattdeutsch** (11)   Low German
der **Plattenspieler, -** (18)   record player
der **Platz, ⁼e** (9)   place; **Platz nehmen** (11)   to take a seat
plaudern (7)   to chat
plötzlich (2)   suddenly
der **Politiker, -** (14)   politician

politisch (9) political
die **Polizei** (16) police
polizeilich (18) police *(adj.)*, by the police
die **Post** (1) post office, mail
das **Postamt, ⁻er** (4) post office
der **Posten, -** (14) post
praktisch (14) practical
die **Praxis** (3) practice
die **Preislage, -n** (9) price range
preiswert (15) worth the price
preußisch (14) Prussian
prima (11) first-rate, excellent
der **Prinz, -en, -en** (12) prince
privat (3) private(ly)
die **Probe, -n** (I) rehearsal
probieren (12) to try
das **Problem, -e** (2) problem
der **Professor, Professoren** (3) professor
das **Pronomen, -** (11) pronoun
der **Prozeß, -sse** (16) process, trial
die **Prüfung, -en** (5) test
das **Prunkstück, -e** (5) showpiece
der **Psalm, -en** (4) psalm
das **Publikum** (18) the (general) public; audience
der **Pullover, -** (6) sweater
der **Punkt, -e** (13) point, period; **(um) Punkt sieben** (at) exactly seven
pünktlich (16) punctual, precise

das **Quadrat, -e** (17) square
die **Qualität, -en** (4) quality
die **Quelle, -n** (4) source, spring
die **Quittung, -en** (4) receipt

rasch (13) speedy, swift, rapid
sich rasieren (6) to shave
der **Rat** (3) advice, piece of advice
das **Rathaus, ⁻er** (2) town hall
das **Rätsel, -** (16) riddle
rauchen (7) to smoke
reagieren (13) to react
der **Realist, -en, -en** (15) realist
realistisch (18) realistic
rechnen (2) to reckon, calculate
die **Rechnung, -en** (9) bill, check, tab; **die Rechnung schreiben** (9) to make out the bill
das **Recht, -e** (9) right; law
recht (2) right; rather, quite, very; **recht vielen Dank** (2) thanks very much
recht haben (7) to be right; **es ist mir recht** (9) it's all right with me
rechts (2) right, to the right
rechtzeitig (14) punctual, on time
reden (10) to talk
die **Regel, -n** (9) rule

regelmäßig (3) regular
der **Regen** (13) rain
das **Regierungsgebäude, -** (14) government building
der **Regisseur, -e** (7) stage manager, film director
regnen (4) to rain
(sich) reiben, rieb, gerieben (6) to rub
das **Reich, -e** (14) empire, kingdom
reich (13) rich
reichen (2) to reach, hand
reichlich (14) abundant
reif (15) mature
die **Reihe, -n** (I) row; turn; **ich bin an der Reihe** (19) it's my turn
die **Reise, -n** (19) trip
das **Reisebuch, ⁻er** (6) travel book
das **Reisebüro, -s** (5) travel bureau
der **Reiseführer, -** (2) guide
die **Reisegruppe, -n** (2) travel group
reisen (1) to travel
der **Reisende, -n, -n** (6) traveler
die **Reisepläne** *(pl.)* (19) travel plans; itinerary
reißen, riß, gerissen (2) to tear
der **Reiz, -e** (5) charm
die **Reling, -e** *or* **-s** (5) railing
reservieren (9) to reserve
der **Respekt** (10) respect
der **Rest, -e** (20) rest, remainder
das **Restaurant, -s** (5) restaurant
das **Resultat, -e** (9) result
das **Rezept, -e** (18) prescription, receipt
der **Rhein** (2) Rhine
die **Rheinfahrt, -en** (5) boat trip on the Rhine, Rhine journey
der **Rheinländer, -** (5) Rhinelander
rheinländisch (11) Rhinelandish
das **Rheinlied, -er** (8) Rhine song
die **Rheinreise, -n** (5) Rhine journey
die **Rheinsage, -n** (5) Rhine legend
der.**Rheinwein, -e** (8) Rhine wine
richtig (9) correct(ly)
die **Richtung, -en** (10) direction
der **Rinderbraten, -** (5) pot roast (of beef)
die **Rolle, -n** (7) rôle, part; **eine Rolle spielen** (7) to play a part
der **Roman, -e** (16) novel
romanisch (11) Romance
romantisch (2) romantic
romantisieren (7) romanticize
rot (2) red
die **Rückfahrt, -en** (8) return trip
rufen, rief, gerufen (9) to call
ruhig (10) calm
der **Ruhm** (I) fame
rührend (20) touching
die **Ruine, -n** (5) ruin

das **Rundfunkorchester, -** (18)   radio orchestra
runter (6)   down(stairs) *(colloquially used for both* **herunter** *and* **hinunter)**
der **Russe, -n, -n** (12)   Russian

der **Saal, Säle** (I)   hall
die **Sache, -n** (9)   thing, matter
sagen (I)   to say; **vor sich hin sagen** (19)   to mumble to oneself
der **Salat, -e** (I)   salad
sammeln (2)   to gather, collect
(der) **Samstag** (17)   Saturday
satt (I)   satiated; **etwas satt sein** *or* **haben** (16)   to have enough of, be sick of something
der **Satz, ̈e** (3)   sentence
sauber (1)   clean
der **Sauerbraten** (11)   marinated beef or pork
die **Schachtel, -n** (I)   small box
schade: es ist schade (5)   it's a pity, it's too bad
der **Schaffner, -** (10)   (train) conductor
die **Schallplatte, -n** (18)   phonograph record
sich schämen (7)   to be ashamed
schätzen (20)   to esteem, appreciate
schauen (5)   to see
das **Schaufenster, -** (18)   store window
das **Schauspiel, -e** (7)   play
der **Scheck, -s** (6)   check
scheinen, schien, geschienen (9)   to shine; to seem
schenken (18)   to give, present, bestow
schicken (8)   to send
der **Schifahrer, -** (6)   skier
das **Schiff, -e** (10)   ship
Schi laufen (5)   to ski
der **Schilift, -e** (15)   ski lift
die **Schlacht, -en** (17)   battle
schläfrig (5)   sleepy
schlagen, schlug, geschlagen, schlägt (I)   to beat
der **Schlager, -** (18)   hit tune
schlecht (I)   bad
schleppen (18)   to drag
schließen, schloß, geschlossen (10)   to close
schließlich (14)   after all, in the final analysis
schlimm (19)   bad(ly); **es hätte schlimm um mich gestanden** (19)   things would have gone badly for me
das **Schloß, ̈sser** (6)   castle
der **Schluß, ̈sse** (7)   end, conclusion; **am Schluß** (7)   finally
die **Schlußprüfung, -en** (8)   final test
schmecken (11)   to taste good
der **Schnee** (13)   snow

schneien (4)   to snow; **es schneit** it's snowing
schnell (I)   fast, quick
der **Schnupfen, -** (18)   head cold
schon (1)   already; **das schon** (16)   that's true
schön (I)   pretty; beautiful; **bitte schön** (I)   please; you're welcome
die **Schönheit, -en** (5)   beauty
das **Schönheitsmittel, -** (9)   cosmetic
schöpferisch (16)   creative
schreiben, schrieb, geschrieben (I)   to write
die **Schriftsprache, -n** (11)   written language
der **Schriftsteller, -** (16)   writer
schriftstellerisch (16)   literary
der **Schritt, -e** (15)   step
die **Schuld** (14)   fault; guilt; **es ist Ihre Schuld** (14)   it's your fault
schulden (18)   to owe
das **Schuldgefühl, -e** (16)   guilt feeling
die **Schule, -n** (2)   school
der **Schüler, -** (1)   pupil
das **Schulsystem, -e** (8)   school system
schützen (18)   to protect
die **Schwäche, -n** (20)   weakness
schwarz (4)   black
der **Schwarzwald** (4)   Black Forest
schweigen, schwieg, geschwiegen (4)   to be silent
schwer (4)   hard, difficult; heavy
schwer/fallen   to be difficult, cause struggle, effort
die **Schwerindustrie, -n** (13)   heavy industry
die **Schwester, -n** (I)   sister
das **Schwesterchen, -** (4)   little sister
schwierig (13)   difficult
die **Schwierigkeit, -en** (16)   difficulty
schwimmen, schwamm, ist geschwommen (6)   to swim
schwören (1)   to swear
segnen (20)   to bless
sehen, sah, gesehen, sieht (1)   to see; **sehen auf** (2)   to look at
sehenswert (6)   worth seeing
die **Sehenswürdigkeit, -en** (6)   object of interest; *plural:* sights *(in a town)*
sich sehnen (16)   to long for
sehr (I)   very
sein, war, ist gewesen, ist (I)   to be
sein, seine, sein (1)   his, its
seit *(with dat.)* (4)   since
seitdem *(conj.)*   since *(time)*
die **Seite, -n** (I)   side, page
die **Sekretärin, -nen** (3)   secretary
selbst (7)   itself, himself, etc. *(following nouns or pronouns)*

die **Selbstbefreiung** (16) self-liberation
selbstverständlich (1) of course, it is understood
das **Semester, -** (3) semester
die **Semesterarbeit, -en** (9) term paper
die **Semestergebühren** *(pl.)* (3) tuition
das **Seminar, -e** (10) seminar
senden, sandte, gesandt (8) to send
sentimental (7) sentimental
(der) **September** (17) September
servieren (9) to serve
der **Sessel, -** (12) easy chair
sich **setzen** (I) to sit down; **sich zu jemandem setzen** (11) to sit down next to someone
sich (I) oneself, himself, herself, itself, yourself, yourselves, themselves
sicher (13) certain, sure
das **Siebengebirge** (14) the Seven Hills *(on the right bank of the Rhine near Bonn)*
siezen (16) to say "Sie" *(use the conventional way of addressing a person)*
silbern: die silberne Hochzeit (17) silver wedding anniversary
singen, sang, gesungen (5) to sing
der **Sinn, -e** (5) sense; mind; **Sinn haben für** (20) to care for, have an understanding for
die **Sitte, -n** (12) custom
sitzen, saß, gesessen (3) to sit
die **Sitzung, -en** (19) meeting, session
die **Skizze, -n** (7) sketch
so (1) so
sobald (4) as soon as; **sobald wie möglich** (5) as soon as possible
sofort (2) immediately
sogar (4) even
sogleich (10) right away
der **Sohn, ⸚e** (1) son
solcher, solche, solches (9) such
der **Soldat, -en, -en** (12) soldier
sollen, sollte, gesollt (or **sollen**), **soll** (I) to be (supposed) to, be said to
der **Sommer, -** (4) summer
sondern (8) but *(rather, on the contrary)*
(der) **Sonnabend, -e** (15) Saturday
(der) **Sonntag, -e** (17) Sunday
sonst (I) otherwise, else
die **Sorge, -n** (4) care, worry; **sich** *(dat.)* **Sorgen machen über** (6) to worry about
sich **sorgen** (9) to worry
soviel (12) so much, as much
sowieso (18) anyhow
sowohl . . . als auch . . . (20) . . . as well as . . .
sozusagen (10) so-to-speak
die **Spalte, -n** (12) column *(in a newspaper)*
spalten (14) to split

spanisch (11) Spanish
spannend (16) exciting
sparen (17) to save
spät (1) late
spätestens (13) at the latest
der **Spätnachmittag** (14) late afternoon
spazieren (gehen) (3) to walk, take a walk
der **Spaziergang, ⸚e** (20) walk; **einen Spaziergang machen** (20) to take a walk
der **Speisesaal, -säle** (5) dining hall
der **Spiegel, -** (6) mirror
spielen (7) to play
der **Sport** (15) sport(s)
der **Sportler, -** (15) sportsman
die **Sprache, -n** (4) language
die **Sprachkenntnisse** *(pl.)* (3) language ability
die **Sprachwissenschaft** (3) philology, linguistics
sprechen, sprach, gesprochen, spricht, (I) to speak
das **Sprichwort, ⸚er** (19) proverb
springen (4) to jump
der **Sprit** (4) *(colloq.)* gasoline
die **Spritze, -n** (18) shot, injection
der **Staat, -en** (I) state, country
der **Staatsbeamte, -n, -n** (3) government official
die **Stadt, ⸚e** (I) city
das **Städtchen, -** (4) small town
der **Stadtplan, ⸚e** (2) city map
die **Stadtrundfahrt, -en** (12) sightseeing tour
der **Stadtteil, -e** (2) section of a city
das **Stadtviertel, -** (12) quarter, section of a city
der **Stahl, -e** *or* **⸚e** (I) steel
stammen aus, ist gestammt (1) to come from, be descended from
der **Stammgast, ⸚e** (9) regular guest
der **Stammtisch, -e** (9) table reserved for regular guests
stark (1) strong; **starker Verkehr** (13) heavy traffic
der **Start, -e** *or* **-s** (20) take-off
statt *(with gen.)* (I) instead of
staunen (15) to be surprised
stehen, stand, gestanden (I) to stand
stehlen, stahl, gestohlen, stiehlt (I) to steal
steigen, stieg, ist gestiegen (2) to climb; **steigen in** (2) to get in
die **Stelle, -n** (10) passage, position, job
stellen (I) to place, put; **Fragen stellen** (2) to ask questions; **sich ein Ziel setzen** (19) to set a goal for oneself
sterben, starb, ist gestorben, stirbt (16) to die
die **Stewardeß, -ssen** (20) stewardess
die **Steuer, -n** (9) tax
der **Stil, -e** (I) style

still (I)   quiet; **im Stillen** (6)   to oneself
die **Stimme, -n** (14)   voice
stimmen (3)   to be correct; **das stimmt** (3) that's true
die **Stimmung, -en** (10)   mood
stolz (14)   proud
stören (7)   to disturb
der **Strand, -e** (6)   strand, beach
die **Straße, -n** (5)   street, road
die **Strecke, -n** (4)   stretch, distance
sich **strecken** (6)   to stretch
der **Streich, -e** (4)   trick
das **Streichholz, ‑‑er** (I)   match
der **Streit, -e** *or* **-igkeiten** (15)   quarrel
streng (19)   strict
das **Strohdach, ‑‑er** (19)   thatched roof
die **Strophe, -n** (13)   strophe, stanza
das **Stück, -e** (7)   piece, play
der **Student, -en, -en** (1)   student *(male)*
das **Studentenheim, -e** (3)   students' home, dorm in town
die **Studentin, -nen** (11)   student *(female)*
das **Studienbuch, ‑‑er** (19)   student class record book
studieren (1)   to study
das **Studium, -ien** (1)   study, studies
der **Studienassessor, -en** (8)   *academic rank in a Gymnasium*
der **Stuhl, ‑‑e** (I)   chair
die **Stunde, -n** (4)   hour
stundenlang (9)   for hours
stürmisch (11)   stormy
stürzen, ist gestürzt (15)   to (take a) plunge, fall
das **Substantiv, -e** (11)   noun, substantive
suchen (1)   to seek, search, look for
der **Süden** (4)   South
die **Symphonie, -n** (18)   symphony
die **Szene, -n** (4)   scene
die **Szenerie, -n** (4)   scenery
das **Szepter, -** (4)   scepter

die **Tablette, -n** (18)   tablet, pill
die **Tafel, -n** (I)   blackboard
der **Tag, -e** (I)   day; **eines Tages** (5)   one day, some day; **guten Tag** (I)   hello, good day; **jeden Tag** (3)   every day; **in acht Tagen** (20)   in a week
täglich (4)   daily
tagsüber (6)   during the day
der **Takt, -e** (I)   time, measure
der **Tanz, ‑‑e** (18)   dance
tanzen (17)   to dance
tapfer (12)   brave
die **Tasse, -n** (5)   cup
die **Tat, -en** (I)   deed, action
die **Tatsache, -n** (6)   fact

täuschen (I)   to deceive
das **Taxi, -s** (1)   taxi
die **Technik** (18)   technique
die **Technologie** (3)   technology
der **Tee** (9)   tea
der **Teenager,** (18)   teenager, adolescent
der **Teil, -e** (6)   part
teilen (11)   to divide; **geteilt durch** (17) divided by
die **Teilnahme** (17)   participation; sympathy
das **Telefon, -e** (I)   telephone
telefonieren (14)   to telephone
die **Telefonnummer, -n** (8)   telephone number
das **Telegramm -e** (11)   telegram
die **Temperatur, -en** (18)   temperature
die **Terrasse, -n** (9)   terrace
teuer (1)   expensive
das **Theater, -** (2)   theater
das **Thema, -men** (4)   theme, subject
die **Theorie, -n** (3)   theory
ticken (I)   to tick
tief (I)   deep
der **Tisch, -e** (I)   table
die **Tochter, ‑‑** (9)   daughter
der **Tod, -e** *or* **Todesfälle** (I)   death
die **Todesanzeige, -n** (12)   death notice
der **Ton, ‑‑e** (I)   sound, tone; note
das **Tor, -e** (14)   gate
tot (17)   dead
töten (1)   to kill
der **Tourist, -en, -en** (5)   tourist
der **Touristenbus, -se** (2)   tourist bus
die **Tradition, -en** (3)   tradition
tragen, trug, getragen, trägt (1)   to carry; to wear
der **Träumer, -** (15)   dreamer
traurig (10)   sad
(sich) **treffen, traf, getroffen, trifft** (2)   to meet; **Entscheidungen treffen** (10)   to make decisions; **eine Wahl treffen** (20)   to make a choice
treiben, trieb, getrieben (6)   to engage in
trennen (14)   to separate
die **Trennung, -en** (19)   separation
die **Treppe, -n** (4)   steps, stairs, staircase
treten, trat, (ist) getreten, tritt (I)   to step; to kick
trinken, trank, getrunken (I)   to drink
das **Trinkgeld, -er** (2)   tip
der **Tropfen, -** (18)   drop
trotz *(with gen.)* (5)   in spite of
trotzdem (7)   nevertheless, all the same
trüb (7)   sad, melancholy, gloomy
tun, tat, getan (I)   to do
die **Tür, -en** (1)   door
typisch (7)   typical

übel (13)   bad, evil; **es ist mir übel** (13)   I don't feel well
das **Übel, -** (1)   evil, malady
über *(with acc. or dat.)* (I)   over, across; about
überall (15)   everywhere
die **Überfahrt, -en** (11)   crossing, trip across *(the ocean)*
überhaupt (19)   generally, altogether
sich *(dat.)* **etwas überlegen** (6)   to consider, think about something
übermorgen (11)   day after tomorrow
übernachten (8)   to stay overnight
übernehmen, übernahm, übernommen, übernimmt (11)   to take over
überqueren (2)   to cross *(a street)*
überrascht (15)   surprised
die **Überraschung, -en** (11)   surprise
übersetzen (I)   to translate
übrigens (I)   by the way
die **Übung, -en** (I)   exercise
die **Uhr, -en** (2)   clock, watch; **wieviel Uhr ist es?** what time is it?; **es ist . . . Uhr** (17) it is . . . o'clock; **um . . . Uhr** (17) at . . . o'clock
um *(with acc.)* (I)   around, about, at; **um . . . zu** (13)   in order to
die **Umgangssprache, -n** (11)   colloquial language
der **Umschlag, ⁼e** (8)   envelope
unbedeutend (14)   insignificant
unbedingt (3)   absolute(ly)
unbegrenzt (13)   unlimited
und (I)   and
unerwartet (14)   unexpected
der **Unfall, ⁼e** (13)   accident
unglaublich (16)   unbelievable
unhöflich (15)   impolite
die **Universität, -en** (3)   university
das **Universitätsleben** (3)   university life
der **Universitätsprofessor, -en** (14)   university professor
die **Universitätsstadt, ⁼e** (5)   university town
unmöglich (16)   impossible
unruhig (4)   restless
unsicher (16)   insecure
unten (1)   downstairs
unter *(with acc. or dat.)* (3)   under; among
unterbrechen, unterbrach, unterbrochen, unterbricht (10)   to interrupt
unterdessen (12)   meanwhile
unterdrücken (16)   to repress, restrain
die **Untergrundbahn, -en** (14)   subway
sich **unterhalten, unterhielt, unterhalten, unterhält** (6)   to converse, chat; to have a good time
die **Unterhaltung, -en** (1)   conversation

unternehmen, unternahm, unternommen, unternimmt (16)   to undertake
der **Unterricht** (3)   instruction
der **Unterschied, -e** (16)   difference
untersuchen (18)   to examine, investigate
unterwegs (3)   on the way
unzufrieden (9)   dissatisfied
die **Ursache, -n** (8)   cause

der **Vater, ⁼** (1)   father
die **Verabredung, -en** (9)   appointment
sich **verabschieden** (14)   to say good-bye
verallgemeinern (15)   to generalize
veraltet (13)   outmoded, passé, obsolete
veränderlich (4)   changeable
veranstalten (18)   to arrange, organize
verantwortungsvoll (14)   responsible
das **Verb, -en** (11)   verb
verbessern (3)   to improve, correct
verbieten, verbot, verboten (20)   to forbid, prohibit
der **Verbrecher, -** (16)   criminal
verbrennen, verbrannte, verbrannt (16)   to burn
verbringen, verbrachte, verbracht (6)   to spend *(time)*
verdienen (18)   to earn
vereinigen (I)   to unite; **die Vereinigten Staaten** (I)   the United States
verfallen (13)   *(adj.)* delapidated
verfassen (20)   to compose
verfügen (16)   to order, decree
die **Verfügung, -en** (18)   disposal; **einem zur Verfügung stehen** (18)   to be at someone's disposal
die **Vergangenheit** (7)   past
vergehen, verging, ist vergangen (9)   to pass, slip away
vergessen, vergaß, vergessen, vergißt (16)   to forget
der **Vergleich, -e** (13)   comparison; **Vergleiche ziehen** (14)   to make comparisons
das **Vergnügen, -** (7)   pleasure
das **Verhältnis, -se** (13)   relation; condition
verhältnismäßig (14)   relative(ly), proportional
sich **verheiraten** (I)   to get married
verkaufen (18)   to sell
der **Verkehr** (13)   traffic
verkörpern (16)   to embody
verlangen (9)   to insist upon, demand
verlassen, verließ, verlassen, verläßt *(trans.)* (2)   to leave
verlegen (15)   *(adj.)* embarrassed
die **Verlegenheit** (13)   embarrassment
verleihen, verlieh, verliehen (9)   to lend; to confer, bestow

die **Verleihung** (17) conferring *(of a title)*
sich **verlieben (in),** *(with acc.)* (16) to fall in love (with)
verlieren, verlor, verloren (11) to lose
sich **verloben** (16) to become engaged
die **Verlobung, -en** (17) engagement
die **Verlobungsanzeige, -n** (12) engagement announcement
die **Verlobungspläne** *(pl.)* (20) engagement plans
sich **vermählen** (12) to marry, get married
die **Vermählungsanzeige, -n** (12) marriage announcement
vernachlässigen (18) to neglect
vernünftig (20) reasonable
veröffentlichen (16) to publish
verpassen (14) to miss
versäumen (17) to miss
verscheiden, verschied, ist verschieden (12) to die, expire
sich **verschlafen, verschlief, verschlafen, verschläft** (14) to oversleep
verschönern (7) to beautify
verschreiben, verschrieb, verschrieben (18) to prescribe
verschwinden, verschwand, ist verschwunden to disappear: **am Verschwinden sein** (20) to be on the way out
die **Versicherung, -en** (20) insurance; assurance
die **Versicherungsanstalt, -en** (16) insurance establishment
sich **verspäten** (6) to be late
die **Verspätung, -en** (14) delay; **Verspätung haben** (14) to be late *(planes, trains, etc.)*
sich **verständigen** (20) to make oneself understood; to communicate
sich **verständigen mit** (20) to come to an understanding with
das **Verständnis** (17) understanding
verstehen, verstand, verstanden (I) to understand; **sich mit jemandem verstehen** (20) to get along with someone, understand someone
verstoßen, verstieß, verstoßen, verstößt (12) to go against
versuchen (5) to try
vertieft (11) engrossed
vertraulich (12) confidential
verträumt (5) dreamy
verwandeln (16) to transform, change
die **Verwandlung, -en** (16) transformation, metamorphosis
der **Verwandte, -n, -n** (20) relative
die **Verwandtschaft, -en** (11) relationship
verwirrend (11) confusing
verzehren (9) to consume

die **Verzeihung** (I) pardon, forgiveness; **Ach, Verzeihung!** Oh, I beg your pardon!
viel (I) much; **viele** (1) many; **vieles** *(used only in the singular)* many things
vielleicht (3) perhaps
vielmal(s) (4) often, frequently
das **Volk, ⁓er** (1) nation, people
das **Volkslied, -er** (18) folk song
die **Volksschule, -n** (2) elementary school
von *(with dat.)* (I) of, by; **von (hier) aus** (14) from (here)
vor *(with acc. or dat.)* (1) before; in front of; ago
vorbei (4) past
(sich) vor/bereiten (auf, *with acc.)* (14) to prepare (for)
der **Vordergrund, ⁓e** (15) foreground
der **Vorgesetzte, -n, -n** (10) superior
vorhanden (16) at hand, on hand, present
vorig- (14) past
vor/kommen, kam vor, ist vorgekommen (8) to happen; (14) to impress: **vielen Leuten kommt das so vor** (13) this is how it impresses (strikes) many people
die **Vorkriegsjahre** *(pl.)* (7) pre-war years
vor/machen: einem etwas vor/machen (20) to put something over on somebody; pretend
vornehmlich (14) particularly, above all
der **Vorschlag, ⁓e** (16) suggestion
vor/schlagen, schlug vor, vorgeschlagen, schlägt vor (16) to suggest
vorsichtig (18) careful
die **Vorstadt, ⁓e** (4) suburb
vor/stehen, stand vor, vorgestanden *(with dative)* (10) to preside over, manage; **dem Haushalt vorstehen** to run the house
(sich) vor/stellen (8) to introduce (oneself); **sich** *(dat.)* **etwas vor/stellen** to imagine
die **Vorstellung, -en** (12) introduction; performance
der **Vorteil, -e** (19) advantage; **einen Vorteil aus etwas ziehen** to benefit from something
das **Vorurteil, -e** (13) prejudice
vor/ziehen, zog vor, vorgezogen (6) to prefer
vorzüglich (7) excellent

wach (12) awake
wachsen, wuchs, ist gewachsen, wächst (I) to grow
wagen (16) to dare
der **Wagen, -** (9) car
die **Wahl, -en** (8) choice; election; **eine Wahl treffen** (20) to make a choice

wählen (14) to choose; elect
wahr (I) true; nicht wahr (I) isn't it, won't she, didn't he, etc.
die Wahrheit, -en (12) truth
während *(with gen.)* (5) during; *(conj.)* (15) while
währenddessen (11) meanwhile
wahrhaftig (19) truly, really
wahrscheinlich (9) probable, probably
der Wald, ⸚er (15) forest
die Wand, ⸚e (10) wall
wann (I) when
das Warenhaus, ⸚er (9) department store
warten (2) to wait; warten auf *(with acc.)* (2) to wait for
warum (1) why
was (I) what
was für (ein) (3) what kind of (a)
(sich) waschen, wusch, gewaschen, wäscht (6) to wash (oneself)
das Wasser, - (I) water
wecken (16) to wake
weder . . . noch (7) neither . . . nor
der Weg, -e (14) way, road; sich auf den Weg machen (14) to set out, be on one's way
weg/gehen, ging weg, ist weggegangen (5) to go away
wegen *(with gen.)* (5) because of, on account of
weh: es tut mir weh (13) it hurts me
die Weide, -n (15) meadow
sich weigern (16) to refuse
(das) Weihnachten (6) Christmas
die Weihnachtsferien *(pl. only)* (6) Christmas holidays
weil (15) because
der Wein (I) wine
der Weinberg, -e (5) vineyard
die Weise, -n (12) manner; auf diese Art und Weise (12) in this way
weiß (8) white
weit (2) far
weiter (3) further; farther
weiterhin (19) for the future, furthermore
weiter/lesen, las weiter, weitergelesen, liest weiter (3) to read on, continue to read
welcher, welche, welches (I) which, what
die Welt, -en (19) world; weltberühmt (6) world-famous; weltpolitisch (14) from the standpoint of world politics
sich wenden an *(with acc.)*, wandte, gewandt (11) to turn to
wenig (3) little; ein wenig (8) a little
wenige (6) few, a few
weniger (17) less, minus
wenigstens (2) at least

wenn (I) if; when; wenn nur if only
wer (I) who
werden, wurde, ist geworden, wird (7) to become
werfen, warf, geworfen, wirft (4) to throw
das Werk, -e (16) work
der Wert, -e (7) value, worth
die Weser (4) Weser *(German river)*
weshalb (20) why
der Westen (4) West; der Wilde Westen (4) the Wild West
westlich (11) western, westerly
das Wetter (4) weather
wichtig (3) important
(sich) widmen (10) to devote, dedicate (oneself)
wie (I) how, as, like; such as; wieviel how much; wie viele how many
wieder (1) again
wiederholen (I) to repeat
wiederholt (10) repeatedly
wieder/sehen, sah wieder, wiedergesehen (20) to see again, meet again; auf Wiedersehen (I) good-bye
wiederum (17) again
wiegen, wog, gewogen (17) to weigh
wieso (9) "how come"; why
wieviel how much: der wievielte ist heute? (17) what's today's date?
wild (4) wild; der Wilde Westen (4) the Wild West
willkommen: willkommen heißen (15) to welcome
der Winter, - (4) winter
der Wintersport (6) winter sports
der Wintersportplatz, ⸚e (15) winter sports area
wirklich (2) really
die Wirklichkeit, -en (13) reality
die Wirkung, -en (20) effect
das Wirtshaus, ⸚er (9) inn
die Wirtschaft, -en (9) economy; inn
das Wirtschaftsproblem, -e (12) economic problem
wissen, wußte, gewußt, weiß (3) to know
die Witwe, -n (12) widow
der Witz, -e (I) joke
wo (I) where; wo . . . auch (18) wherever . . .
die Woche, -n (3) week
das Wochenende, -n (9) week end
woher (8) from where
wohin (2) where (to)
wohl (I) probably; well
wohnen (1) to reside, live
die Wohnung, -en (13) apartment
das Wohnzimmer, - (11) living room

das **Wort, ⁼er** or **-e** (2)   word
das **Wörtchen, -** (19)   little word
das **Wörterbuch, ⁼er** (10)   dictionary
der **Wortschatz, ⁼e** (1)   vocabulary
   wunderbar (4)   wonderful
der **Wunsch, ⁼e** (15)   wish
   wünschen (I)   to wish

die **Zahl, -en** (3)   number, figure
   zahlen (3)   to pay
die **Zahnpasta** (9)   toothpaste
der **Zehnmarkschein, -e** (9)   ten-mark bill
   zeigen (5)   to show
die **Zeit, -en** (2)   time; **zur Zeit** (17)   at the
   (present) time; **höchste Zeit** (4)   high
   time
   zeitgenössisch (18)   current, contemporary
die **Zeitkritik: Zeitkritik treiben** (20)   to poke
   fun at the times
die **Zeitlang** (15)   while
die **Zeitschrift, -en** (9)   magazine
die **Zeitung, -en** (3)   newspaper
die **Zelle, -n** (I)   cell
das **Zentrum, Zentren** (14)   center
   zerreißen, zerriß, zerrissen (4)   to tear up,
   tear to pieces
   zerstören (14)   to destroy
sich **zerstreuen** (14)   to amuse oneself
   ziehen, zog, (ist) gezogen (14)   to draw,
   pull; move
das **Ziel, -e** (19)   goal
   ziemlich (2)   somewhat, rather
die **Ziffer, -n** (5)   figure, numeral
die **Zigarette, -n** (I)   cigarette
die **Zigarre, -n** (7)   cigar
das **Zimmer, -** (1)   room
   zögern (1)   to hesitate

zu (with dat.) (I)   to; too
zuerst (2)   at first
zufällig (8)   by chance, accidentally
zufrieden (5)   satisfied, content
der **Zug, ⁼e** (1)   train
zu/geben, gab zu, zugegeben, gibt zu (6)
   to admit
zu/hören (I)   to listen
zurück (2)   back; **wir sollten ins Hotel
   zurück (gehen)**   we ought to go back to
   the hotel
**zurück/bekommen, bekam zurück, zurück-
   bekommen** (19)   to get back
**zurück/fahren, fuhr zurück, ist zurückge-
   fahren, fährt zurück** (6)   to drive back,
   go back
**zurück/gehen, ging zurück, ist zurückge-
   gangen** (5)   to go back
zurück/kehren, ist zurückgekehrt (12)   to
   return
**zurück/kommen, kam zurück, ist zurückge-
   kommen** (20)   to come back
zurück/reisen, ist zurückgereist (7)   to
   travel back
zusammen (I)   together
**zusammen/sitzen, saß zusammen, zusam-
   mengesessen** (9)   to sit together
das **Zusammentreffen, -** (17)   meeting
der **Zustrom, ⁼e** (15)   influx
zuverlässig (12)   reliable
zwar (7)   to be sure, indeed
zweifellos (19)   doubtless, without a doubt
zweimal (16)   twice
zwischen (with acc. or dat.) (3)   between;
   among
die **Zwischenzeit** (20)   meantime

This vocabulary contains all words used in the English-to-German exercises.

able: be able können, konnte, gekonnt, kann
about von *(dat.)*; über *(acc.)*
accept an/nehmen, nahm an, angenommen, nimmt an
accident der Unfall, ⸚e
accustomed: be accustomed to sich gewöhnen an *(acc.)*
across über *(acc.)*
act tun, tat, getan
add hinzu/fügen
address die Adresse, -n
admire bewundern
afraid: be afraid (of) Angst haben (vor + *dat.)*; sich fürchten vor
after *(prep.)* nach *(dat.)*; *(conj.)* nachdem
after all schließlich
afternoon der Nachmittag, -e
afterwards danach
again wieder
against gegen *(acc.)*
age das Alter, -; **at the age of 14** im Alter von 14 Jahren, mit 14 Jahren
agree with einem (gut) bekommen
all all-
allowed: be allowed dürfen, durfte, gedurft, darf
almost fast
along mit
already schon
also auch
although obgleich, obwohl
always immer
America (das) Amerika
American *(adj.)* amerikanisch; *(noun)* der Amerikaner, -; die Amerikanerin, -nen
and und
angry zornig; **be angry** sich ärgern
announce an/sagen
another noch ein; **one another** einander
answer *(verb)* antworten *(dat.)*; *(noun)* die Antwort, -en; **answer a question** eine Frage beantworten
any jeder, jede, jedes; etwas, einige
anything: not anything nichts
appeal (to) gefallen, gefiel, gefallen, gefällt *(dat.)*
appointment die Verabredung, -en
April der April
architecture die Architektur
around um *(acc.)*

arrive an/kommen, kam an, ist angekommen
as wie; **as . . . as** so . . . wie; **not as . . .** nicht so; **as if** als ob
ask fragen; **ask a question** eine Frage stellen; **ask for** bitten um
assignment die Aufgabe, -n
assume an/nehmen, nahm an, angenommen, nimmt an
at an, auf *(dat.)*; **at the house of** bei
away weg

back zurück
bad schlimm; schlecht; **be (go) bad(ly) with** schlimm stehen um
band die Kapelle, -n
bank (of a river) das Ufer, -
Bavarian der Bayer, -n, -n
be sein, war, ist gewesen, ist; **there is, there are** es gibt; **How is he?** Wie geht es ihm?
beautiful schön
beauty die Schönheit, -en
because weil; **because of** wegen *(gen.)*
become werden, wurde, ist geworden, wird
beer das Bier, -e
bed das Bett, -en
before *(prep.)* vor *(dat.)*; *(conj.)* ehe; bevor
begin beginnen, begann, begonnen; an/fangen, fing an, angefangen, fängt an
beginning der Anfang, ⸚e
believe glauben
beside neben *(dat. or acc.)*
beside(s) außer *(with dat.)*
between zwischen *(dat. or acc.)*
big groß
bill die Rechnung, -en
bless segnen
book das Buch, ⸚er
both beide
boy der Junge, -n, -n
branch die Filiale, -n
bread das Brot, -e
breakfast das Frühstück, -e
breakup die Lösung, -en
bridge die Brücke, -n
bright and early in aller Frühe
brilliant glänzend
bring bringen, brachte, gebracht; **bring off** fertig/bringen
broken kaputt
brother der Bruder, ⸚
bus der Bus, -se
business *(noun)* das Geschäft, -e; *(adj.)* geschäftlich

busy beschäftigt
but aber; *(on the contrary)* sondern
buy kaufen
by von *(dat.)*
by the way übrigens

cab das Taxi, -s
cabaret das Kabarett, -s *or* -e
café das Café, -s
call rufen, rief, gerufen; *(name)* nennen, nannte, genannt; **be called** heißen, hieß, geheißen
can *(be able)* können, konnte, gekonnt, kann
car das Auto, -s; der Wagen, -
card die Karte, -n
care: take care of besorgen; **care for** gern haben, mögen *(see:* **like***)*
carry tragen, trug, getragen, trägt
cathedral der Dom, -e
celebrate feiern
center die Mitte, -n
certain sicher
charm der Reiz, -e
chat plaudern; sich unterhalten, unterhielt, unterhalten, unterhält
check der Scheck, -s; die Rechnung, -en
chemistry die Chemie
child das Kind, -er
church die Kirche, -n
cigar die Zigarre, -n
city die Stadt, ÷e
city map der Stadtplan, ÷e
class die Klasse, -n
class (record) book das Studienbuch, ÷er
clean sauber
clock die Uhr, -en
clothes die Kleider
coffee der Kaffee
cold kalt
cold der Schnupfen, -
Cologne Köln
comb der Kamm, ÷e
come kommen, kam, ist gekommen
comfortable gemütlich; bequem
complain sich beschweren; klagen
composition der Aufsatz, ÷e
consider (sich) *(dat.)* überlegen
corner die Ecke, -n
correct *(verb)* korrigieren; verbessern; *(adj.)* richtig
cosmetic das Schönheitsmittel, -
cost kosten
country das Land, ÷er; **in the country** auf dem Lande; **to the country** auf das Land
criticize kritisieren
cross überqueren
crossing Überfahrt, -en

cup die Tasse, -n
custom die Sitte, -n

daily täglich
dangerous gefährlich
date das Datum, -ten
daughter die Tochter, ÷
day der Tag, -e; **every day** jeden Tag; **good day** guten Tag; **one day** eines Tages
dean der Dekan, -e
deck das Deck, -e
December der Dezember
delighted entzückt
deliver liefern
department store das Kaufhaus, ÷er; das Warenhaus, ÷er
depend (on) ab/hängen, hing ab, abgehangen (von); an/kommen, kam an, ist angekommen (auf) *(acc.)*
dictionary das Wörterbuch, ÷er
different ander-; verschieden
dining hall die Mensa, -sen; der Speisesaal, -säle
directly direkt
discuss besprechen, besprach, besprochen, bespricht
disturb stören
do tun, tat, getan; machen
doctor der Doktor, -en; der Arzt, ÷e
door die Tür, -en
dormitory das Studentenheim, -e
downstairs unten
downtown in die Stadt *(motion)*; in der Stadt *(rest)*
doubt bezweifeln
dressed: get dressed sich an/ziehen, zog an, angezogen
drink trinken, trank, getrunken
drive fahren, fuhr, ist gefahren, fährt
driver der Autofahrer, -; der Chauffeur, -e
drop der Tropfen, -
duke der Herzog, ÷e
during während *(gen.)*

early früh
East der Osten
easy leicht
eat essen, aß, gegessen, ißt
electronic elektronisch
end das Ende, -n
engagement die Verlobung, -en
English (das) Englisch
enjoy genießen, genoß, genossen
envelope der Umschlag, ÷e
errand: run errands Besorgungen machen
error der Fehler, -
especially besonders

Europe (das) Europa
even sogar, selbst
evening der Abend, -e; **this evening** heute abend
every jeder, jede, jedes
everyone jeder, jedermann
everything alles
everywhere überall
examination das Examen, -; die Prüfung, -en
examine untersuchen
excellent ausgezeichnet
exhausted erschöpft
expect erwarten
expenditure die Ausgabe, -n
expense die Ausgabe, -n
expensive teuer
explain erklären

face das Gesicht, -er
fact die Tatsache, -n
fail *(a test)* durch/fallen, fiel durch, ist durchgefallen, fällt durch
family die Familie, -n; **family life** das Familienleben, -
far weit
fast schnell
fat dick
father der Vater, ⸚
fault die Schuld, -en
favor der Gefallen, -; die Bitte, -n
February der Februar
feel sich fühlen
few: a few einige, ein paar
find finden, fand, gefunden
first zuerst; erst-
foggy neblig
for *(prep.)* für *(acc.)*; *(conj.)* denn
foreigner der Ausländer, -
forget vergessen, vergaß, vergessen, vergißt
formal formell
French (das) Französisch
Frenchman der Franzose, -n, -n
fresh frisch
Friday (der) Freitag
friend der Freund, -e; die Freundin, -nen
friendly freundlich
friends: be friends with befreundet sein mit
from von *(dat.)*
front: in front of vor *(dat. or acc.)*
fun das Vergnügen, -
future die Zukunft

game das Spiel, -e
generation die Generation, -en
gentleman der Herr, -n, -en
geography die Geographie
German der Deutsche, -n, -n; die Deutsche, -n, -n; *(language)* (das) Deutsch; **in German** auf deutsch; **German class** die Deutschstunde, -n; **German teacher** der Deutschlehrer, -
Germany (das) Deutschland
get bekommen, bekam, bekommen; *(become)* werden, wurde, ist geworden, wird; **to get dressed** sich an/ziehen, zog an, angezogen; **to get out, off** aus/steigen, stieg aus, ist ausgestiegen; **to get up** auf/stehen, stand auf, ist aufgestanden; **to get used to** sich gewöhnen an *(acc.)*
girl das Mädchen, -
give geben, gab, gegeben, gibt
glad froh
gladly gern(e)
go *(walk)* gehen, ging, ist gegangen
go *(by vehicle)* fahren, fuhr, ist gefahren, fährt
good gut, besser, best-
good-by auf Wiedersehen; **to say good-by** sich verabschieden
Gothic gotisch
grade die Note, -n; die Zensur, -en
grateful dankbar
guest der Gast, ⸚e
guide der Reiseführer, -

hair das Haar, -e
half halb; die Hälfte
hand die Hand, ⸚e
hand: on the other hand dagegen
happen geschehen, geschah, ist geschehen, geschieht; passieren, ist passiert
happy froh; **to be happy about** sich freuen über *(acc.)*
hard schwer; fleißig
have haben, hatte, gehabt, hat; **to have to** müssen, mußte, gemußt, muß; *(causative)* lassen, ließ, gelassen, läßt
head der Kopf, ⸚e
head (of family) das Familienoberhaupt, ⸚er
headway: to make headway Fortschritte machen
hear hören
heart das Herz, -ens, -en
heavy schwer; stark
help helfen, half, geholfen, hilft
helpful behilflich
her *(adj.)* ihr
here hier
high hoch, höher, höchst-
highway die Autostraße, -n; die Autobahn, -en
his sein, seine, sein
history die Geschichte, -n
hit (tune) der Schlager, -
hoarse heiser

home nach Hause; **(at) home** zu Hause
hope hoffen; **I hope** hoffentlich
hot heiß
hotel das Hotel, -s
hour die Stunde, -n
house das Haus, ⸚er
how wie; **how much** wieviel; **how many** wie viele; **how long** wie lange
however aber
humor der Humor
hungry: to be hungry Hunger haben
hurry *(verb)* sich beeilen; *(noun)* die Eile
husband der Mann, ⸚er

if wenn; *(whether)* ob
immediately sofort, sogleich
important wichtig
impress beeindrucken
impression der Eindruck, ⸚e
improve sich bessern
in in *(dat. or acc.)*
information die Auskunft, ⸚e
instead (of) anstatt, statt *(gen.)*
instruction die Anweisung, -en
insult die Beleidigung, -en
interest *(verb)* interessieren; *(noun)* das Interesse, -n; **to be interested in** sich interessieren für
interesting interessant
into in *(acc.)*
invitation die Einladung, -en
invite ein/laden, lud ein, eingeladen, lädt ein

January der Januar
July der Juli
just gerade; nur

kind gütig, freundlich
know kennen, kannte, gekannt; *(a fact)* wissen, wußte, gewußt, weiß; *(a language)* können, konnte, gekonnt, kann; *(one's way around)* sich aus/kennen, kannte aus, ausgekannt
knowledge die Kenntnis, -se

lady die Dame, -n
landscape die Landschaft, -en
large groß
last *(verb)* dauern; *(adj.)* letzt-
late spät; **at the latest** spätestens; **to be late** *(trains, etc.)* Verspätung haben
laugh lachen
law das Gesetz, -e
learn lernen
least: at least wenigstens
leave *(trans.)* lassen, ließ, gelassen, läßt; ver-

lassen; *(intrans.)* ab/fahren, fuhr ab, ist abgefahren, fährt ab
lecture hall der Hörsaal, -säle
left, to the left links
legend die Legende, -n; die Sage, -n
lend leihen, lieh, geliehen
less weniger
lesson die Aufgabe, -n
let lassen, ließ, gelassen, läßt
letter der Brief, -e
library die Bibliothek, -en
lie lügen; **lie like a professional** lügen wie gedruckt
life das Leben
lighten blitzen
like gern haben; mögen, mochte, gemocht, mag; gefallen, gefiel, gefallen, gefällt; **I like it** es gefällt mir
literature die Literatur, -en
little klein
live leben; *(dwell)* wohnen
long lang; **(for) a long time** lange; **no longer** nicht mehr
look sehen, sah, gesehen, sieht; *(appear)* aus/sehen; **to look at** an/sehen; **to look for** suchen; **to look forward to** sich freuen auf *(acc.)*; **to take a look at** sich *(dat.)* an/sehen; **to look up** *(in a book)* nach/schlagen, schlug nach, nachgeschlagen, schlägt nach
luckily zum Glück, glücklicherweise
lucky: to be lucky Glück haben

magazine die Zeitschrift, -en
mail die Post
mainly hauptsächlich
maintain behaupten
make machen
man der Mann, ⸚er
management die Leitung
many viele
map die Landkarte, -n; die Karte, -n
mark die Mark *(same in pl.)*
marmalade die Marmelade, -n
marvelous herrlich, fabelhaft, ausgezeichnet
may dürfen, durfte, gedurft, darf
maybe vielleicht
meal die Mahlzeit, -en; das Essen, -
mean bedeuten; meinen
meet treffen, traf, getroffen, trifft; begegnen, ist begegnet *(with dat.)*
meeting das Zusammentreffen, -
mention erwähnen
minister der Minister, -
minute die Minute, -n
miss *(a train, etc.)* verpassen; versäumen
Miss Fräulein *(term of address)*
mistake der Fehler, -

modern modern
money das Geld, -er
month der Monat, -e
mood die Laune, -n; die Stimmung, -en
more mehr; **not any more** nicht mehr; **no more** kein- . . . mehr; **once more** noch einmal
morning der Morgen, -; **good morning** guten Morgen; **in the morning** morgens, am Morgen
mother die Mutter, ⸚
movies das Kino; **at the movies** im Kino; **to the movies** ins Kino
Mr. Herr *(term of address)*
Mrs. Frau *(term of address)*
much viel
Munich München
museum das Museum, Museen
music die Musik
must müssen, mußte, gemußt, muß
my mein, meine, mein

name der Name, -ns, -n
naturally natürlich
near nahe, in der Nähe
need brauchen
neighbor der Nachbar, -n, -n
nervous nervös
never nie; **never yet** noch nie
new neu; **news** die Nachricht, -en
newspaper die Zeitung, -en
next nächst-
nice nett
night die Nacht, ⸚e; **last night** gestern abend
night club das Kabarett, -e
no nein
not nicht; **not at all** gar nicht; **not yet** noch nicht
nothing nichts
notice merken, bemerken
now jetzt; nun
numeral die Zahl, -en; die Ziffer, -n

occupied: to be occupied sich beschäftigen
of von *(dat.)*
of course natürlich, selbstverständlich
often oft
okay in Ordnung
old alt
on auf *(dat. or acc.)*; an *(dat. or acc.)*
one man; ein, eine, ein
only nur; erst; *(adj.)* einzig
open öffnen
opera die Oper, -n
opera house das Opernhaus, ⸚er
operetta die Operette, -n
or oder

order bestellen; **in order to** um . . . zu
other ander-
our unser, unsere, unser
out (of) aus *(dat.)*
outside draußen
over über *(dat. or acc.)*; **over there** da drüben
overcast trüb
oversleep sich verschlafen, verschlief, verschlafen, verschläft
owe schulden

painter der Maler, -
parents die Eltern *(pl. only)*
part der Teil, -e
particular besonder-
particularly besonders
party die Gesellschaft, -en
pass *(a test)* bestehen, bestand, bestanden
passage die Stelle
passport der Paß, Pässe
pay bezahlen
people die Leute
perfect(ly) perfekt
performance die Vorstellung, -en, die Aufführung, -en
perhaps vielleicht
pharmacy die Apotheke, -n
physician der Arzt, ⸚e
pick up ab/holen
picture das Bild, -er; das Photo, -s; die Photographie, -n; die Aufnahme, -n
pill die Tablette, -n
pity schade
plan der Plan, ⸚e
play *(verb)* spielen; *(noun)* das Schauspiel, -e; das Stück, -e
pleasant angenehm
please bitte
please gefallen, gefiel, gefallen, gefällt
pleasure das Vergnügen
poem das Gedicht, -e
political politisch
poor arm
poorly schlecht
popular beliebt
possible möglich
postpone auf/schieben, schob auf, aufgeschoben; verschieben, verschob, verschoben
powerful gewaltig, mächtig
practice die Ubung, -en
prepare vor/bereiten
prescribe verschreiben, verschrieb, verschrieben
prescription das Rezept, -e
present das Geschenk, -e
pretty hübsch
price der Preis, -e; **at a good price** preiswert

probably wahrscheinlich
problem das Problem, -e
professor der Professor, -en
pronunciation die Aussprache, -n
prove beweisen, bewies, bewiesen
pull off *(a joke)* fertig/bringen, brachte fertig, fertiggebracht
put (something) over on somebody einem (etwas) vor/machen

question die Frage, -n; **to ask questions** Fragen stellen
quick schnell
quiet still

railing die Reling, -e
railroad station der Bahnhof, ⸚e
rain regnen
rather ziemlich
read lesen, las, gelesen, liest
really wirklich
reassure beruhigen
receive erhalten, erhielt, erhalten, erhält
recognize erkennen, erkannte, erkannt
recommend empfehlen, empfahl, empfohlen, empfiehlt
remember sich erinnern an *(acc.)*
remind erinnern
reserve reservieren
respect der Respekt
restaurant das Restaurant, -s
Rhine der Rhein
rich reich
right: to be right recht haben
right, to the right rechts
right away gleich, sofort
river der Fluß, ⸚sse
road die Straße, -n; der Weg, -e
room das Zimmer, -

sad traurig
safe sicher
sale der Verkauf, ⸚e; der Ausverkauf, ⸚e
same: the same derselbe, dieselbe, dasselbe; **all (just) the same** trotzdem
satisfied zufrieden; satt
say sagen; **say "du" to** duzen
school die Schule, -n; **elementary school** die Volksschule
season die Jahreszeit, -en
seat der Platz, ⸚e; der Sitz, -e
see sehen, sah, gesehen, sieht
seem scheinen, schien, geschienen
sell verkaufen; **sold out** ausverkauft
semester das Semester, -
September der September
settled abgemacht; erledigt

several mehrere
shave sich rasieren
ship das Schiff, -e
shop das Geschäft, -e
short kurz
show zeigen
sick krank
significance die Bedeutung, -en
silver: silver wedding anniversary silberne Hochzeit
simple einfach
since da
sing singen, sang, gesungen
sister die Schwester, -n
sit sitzen, saß, gesessen
sleep schlafen, schlief, geschlafen, schläft
slow langsam
small klein
smoke rauchen
snapshot die Aufnahme, -n
snapshots: to take snapshots knipsen
snow schneien
so so; also
soldier der Soldat, -en, -en
some etwas; einige
someone jemand
something etwas
son der Sohn, ⸚e
song das Lied, -er
soon bald
sorry: I am sorry es tut mir leid
sort: all sorts of allerlei
sound klingen, klang, geklungen
speak sprechen, sprach, gesprochen, spricht
spend *(time)* verbringen, verbrachte, verbracht; *(money)* aus/geben, gab aus, ausgegeben, gibt aus
spite: in spite of trotz *(gen.)*
splendid herrlich
stand stehen, stand, gestanden
state der Staat, -en
stay bleiben, blieb, ist geblieben
steamer der Dampfer, -
still noch
stormy stürmisch
story die Geschichte, -n; die Erzählung, -en
strawberry die Erdbeere, -n
street die Straße, -n
stretch die Strecke, -n
strict streng
strong stark
student der Student, -en, -en; die Studentin, -nen
study studieren; lernen
style: in style, stylish modisch
subject das Fach, ⸚er; **main subject** das Hauptfach, ⸚er

succeed gelingen, gelang, ist gelungen; **I succeed in doing . . .** es gelingt mir . . . zu tun
such solcher, solche, solches; **such a** so ein, so eine, so ein
suddenly plötzlich
suggest vor/schlagen, schlug vor, vorgeschlagen, schlägt vor
suggestion der Vorschlag, ⁻e
suit der Anzug, ⁻e
suitable passend
suitcase der Koffer, -
summer der Sommer, -
Sunday (der) Sonntag
suppose an/nehmen, nahm an, angenommen, nimmt an
supposed: to be supposed to sollen, sollte, gesollt, soll
sure(ly) sicher; **for sure** sicherlich; **to be sure** zwar
surprise *(verb)* überraschen; *(noun)* die Überraschung, -en
suspect ahnen
sweater der Pullover, -

tablet die Tablette, -n
take nehmen, nahm, genommen, nimmt; *(last)* dauern; **to take a trip** eine Reise machen; **to take over** übernehmen, übernahm, übernommen, übernimmt
talk sich unterhalten, unterhielt, unterhalten, unterhält; reden; sprechen, sprach, gesprochen, spricht
talkative gesprächig
tall · groß
tanned gebräunt
tax die Steuer, -n
taxi das Taxi, -s
tea der Tee
teacher der Lehrer, -; die Lehrerin, -nen
telegram das Telegramm, -e
telephone telefonieren
tell sagen; erzählen; merken
temperature die Temperatur, -en; **take the temperature** das Fieber messen
term paper die Semesterarbeit, -en
terrace die Terrasse, -n
terrific glänzend
test die Klassenarbeit, -en; die Prüfung, -en
than als
thank danken
thanks danke, vielen Dank, danke schön
that das; daß; was
theater das Theater, -
their ihr
then dann
theory die Theorie, -n

there dort; da
therefore deshalb; darum; daher
thin dünn; mager
thing die Sache, -n
think glauben; denken, dachte, gedacht; **think of** denken an *(acc.)*
this dieser, diese, dieses
thorough gründlich
through durch *(acc.)*
thunder donnern
ticket die Fahrkarte, -n
time die Zeit, -en; das Mal, -e; **this time** diesmal; **at that time** damals; **on time** pünktlich; **to have a good time** sich amüsieren
tip das Trinkgeld, -er
tired müde
to zu *(dat.)*; nach *(dat.)*; an *(acc.)*; in *(acc.)*
today heute
together zusammen
tomorrow morgen
tonight heute abend
too auch; zu
toothpaste die Zahnpasta
town die Stadt, ⁻e
tradition die Tradition, -en
traffic der Verkehr
train der Zug, ⁻e
travel reisen
trip die Reise, -n; **trip there** die Hinfahrt, -en; **return trip** die Rückfahrt, -en; **to take a trip** eine Reise machen
true wahr; **to be true** stimmen
try versuchen; probieren
tuition fees die Semestergebühren

under unter *(dat. or acc.)*
understand verstehen, verstand, verstanden
understanding: come to an understanding with sich verständigen mit
unfortunately leider
United States die Vereinigten Staaten
university die Universität, -en
until bis; **not until** erst, nicht bevor
upstairs oben
up to bis (zu)
used: to get used to sich gewöhnen an *(acc.)*
usual(ly) gewöhnlich

very sehr
view die Ansicht, -en; die Aussicht, -en
visit *(verb)* besuchen; *(noun)* der Besuch, -e

wait warten; **wait for** warten auf *(acc.)*
waiter der Ober, -
wake up auf/wachen

walk *(noun)* der Spaziergang, ⸚e; *(verb)* gehen, ging, ist gegangen; **to take a walk** einen
Spaziergang machen
want wollen, wollte, gewollt, will
warm warm
wash (sich) waschen, wusch, gewaschen,
wäscht
watch out for sich in acht nehmen vor *(dat.)*
weakness die Schwäche, -n
weather das Wetter
week die Woche, -n
well gut
well-known bekannt
West der Westen
what was; welcher, welche, welches
what kind of (a) was für (ein)
when als; wann; wenn
where wo; wohin
whether ob
which welcher, welche, welches; der, die, das
who wer; der, die, das
why warum; weshalb; **that's why** darum;
deshalb
wife die Frau, -en

wine der Wein, -e
winter der Winter, -
with mit *(dat.)*; bei *(dat.)*
without ohne *(acc.)*
woman die Frau, -en
wonder sich fragen
word das Wort, ⸚er *or* -e
work *(verb)* arbeiten; *(noun)* die Arbeit, -en;
das Werk, -e
worn out kaputt
worry sich *(dat.)* Sorgen machen; sich sorgen
über *(acc.)*; sich kümmern um
write schreiben, schrieb, geschrieben

year das Jahr, -e
yes ja
yesterday gestern; **day before yesterday** vor-
gestern
yet noch; **not yet** noch nicht; **never yet**
noch nie
young jung
your Ihr, Ihre, Ihr; dein, deine, dein; euer,
eure, euer
youth hostel die Jugendherberge, -n

INDEX

Numbers refer to pages.

GLOSSARY

Accusative: That case of a noun, adjective, or pronoun which indicates the (direct) object of certain verbs and prepositions and which is used in expressions of definite time.

Adverb: A word that modifies a verb, an adjective, or another adverb.

Antecedent: The word, phrase, or clause to which a later word refers.

Attributive Adjective: A word with certain inflectional endings that qualifies or limits a noun.

Auxiliary Verb: A verb which helps form tense, mood, or voice of another verb (**haben, sein, werden**).

Cardinal Number: A numeral which answers the question "How many?"

Case: The form of a noun, pronoun, or adjective which indicates its relationship to other words (nominative, genitive, dative, accusative).

Clause: A group of words containing a subject and predicate. A main (independent) clause can stand alone; a subordinate (dependent) clause can function only as part of another clause.

Comparison: The change in the form of an adjective or adverb showing degrees of quality: positive (*old*—**alt**), comparative (*older*—**älter**), superlative (*oldest*—**ältest**).

Conjugation: The inflections or changes of form in verbs showing number, person, tense, mood, voice.

Conjunction: A word used to connect words, phrases, or clauses. Coordinating and correlative conjunctions connect expressions of equal value. Subordinating conjunctions connect a dependent clause with a main clause.

Dative: That case of a noun, adjective, or pronoun which indicates the (indirect) object of certain verbs and certain prepositions.

Declension: The change of form in nouns, pronouns, or adjectives indicating gender, number, and case.

Definite Article: **der, die, das** *(the)*.

Der-Words: Words declined like the definite article.

Ein-Words: Words declined like the indefinite article.

Finite Verb: The inflected (conjugated) verb form (other than infinitive and participles) limited as to person, number, tense.

Gender: The grammatical distinction of nouns and pronouns (masculine, feminine, neuter).

Genitive: That case of a noun or adjective which denotes possession or a close relationship between two nouns. The genitive also indicates the object of a few verbs and prepositions and is used in expressions of indefinite time.

Imperative: The mood of the verb expressing a command or directive.

Indefinite Article: **ein, eine, ein** *(a, an)*.

Indicative Mood: The mood which states a fact or asks a question.

Infinitive: The form of the verb that expresses the general meaning of the verb without regard to person or number.

Interrogative: Asking a question; also a word used for that purpose.

Intransitive Verb: A verb expressing an action or state that does not require an object.

Inversion: A reversal of the normal sequence of subject-verb.

Key Sound: That essential inflectional sound associated with and denoting the gender and/or case and number of a given noun phrase.

Modal Auxiliaries: Verbs which express the attitude of the speaker: ability, permission, compulsion, obligation, desire.

Mood: The form of the verb showing the speaker's attitude toward what he says. Mood is shown by inflection (indicative, subjunctive, imperative) as well as by modal auxiliaries.

Nominative: The case of the subject and predicate noun or pronoun.

Object of Verb: The word or phrase at which the action of the verb is directed.

Ordinal Number: A numeral expressing the order of a number in a series.

Participle: A verbal form (present participle or past participle) usually used as part of a compound tense or as an adjective.

Personal Pronoun: A pronoun used to indicate or refer to the speaker (first person), the person spoken to (second person), or the person spoken of (third person).

Phoneme: A minimally significant sound unit, carrying no meaning but distinguishing one morpheme (the smallest meaningful linguistic unit) from another, as, for example, Haus from Maus.

Predicate: That part of a sentence or clause consisting of the verb and any elements describing the action or state expressed by the verb.

Predicate Adjective: An adjective that follows a noun as part of the predicate, usually after sein or werden, and carries no inflectional ending.

Prefix: A syllable or word added to the beginning of another word to form a compound; a verb prefix may be separable (aus/sprechen) or inseparable (besprechen).

Preposition: A word that relates a noun or pronoun to some other element in the sentence.

Principal Parts: The forms of the verb (infinitive, simple past, auxiliary, past participle, and 3rd person singular present indicative) from which the six tenses are formed.

Pronoun: A word used in place of a noun.

Reflexive: Indicating that the object of the action is identical with the subject.

Subject: The word or word group performing the action expressed by the verb (active voice) or on whom the action is performed (passive voice).

Subjunctive: The mood which expresses conditions contrary to fact, wishes, doubts, what is possible rather than certain, or what is reported rather than quoted directly.

Tense: The form of the verb showing the time of the action or state of being.

Transitive Verb: A verb that takes an object.

Umlaut: The modification of a vowel sound indicated by two dots over the vowel (ä, ö, ü).

Verb: That part of speech that expresses an action or state of being. German verbs are often classified as weak (regular), strong (irregular), and very irregular.

Voice: The form of the verb indicating whether the subject acts (active) or is acted upon (passive).